PUBLICATIONS OF THE

ARMY RECORDS SOCIETY

VOL. 31

CRIMEAN CAVALRY LETTERS

CRIMEAN CAVALRY LETTERS

Edited by
GLENN FISHER

Published by

THE HISTORY PRESS
for the
ARMY RECORDS SOCIETY
2011

First published in the United Kingdom in 2011 by
The History Press · The Mill · Brimscombe Port · Stroud ·
Gloucestershire · GL5 2QG

British Library Cataloguing in Publication Data
A catalogue record for this book is available from the British Library.

ISBN 978-0-7524-6530-2

Typeset in Ehrhardt.
Typesetting and origination by
The History Press.
Printed and bound in England.

The Army Records Society was founded in 1984 in order to publish original records describing the development, organisation, administration and activities of the British Army from early times.

Any person wishing to become a Member of the Society should consult our website for details of the procedure. Members receive at least one volume per annum and are entitled to purchase back volumes at reduced prices.

The Council of the Army Records Society wish it to be clearly understood that they are not answerable for opinions or observations that may appear in the Society's publications. For these the responsibility rests entirely with the Editors of the several works.

The Society's website can be found at
www.armyrecordssociety.org.uk

Contents

Introduction

In the spring and summer of 1854 four cavalry subalterns, together with their respective regiments, prepared to embark for war with the forces of the Russian Empire. They were respectively Captain Thomas Hutton and Cornet Fiennes Wykeham Martin, both of the 4th Light Dragoons; Cornet Edward Phillips of the 8th (The King's Royal Irish) Regiment of Light Dragoons (Hussars); and Captain Edward Rowe Fisher-Rowe of the 4th (Royal Irish) Dragoon Guards. They sailed at different times on different vessels from different ports in the British Isles and wrote home to their families to inform, reassure, complain and speculate about their experiences as part of 'The Army of the East'. The country that they left cheered them off in full confidence that they would succeed. This confidence was born of the fact and feeling that Imperial Britain was chief among the nations of the world. It had the most colonies, the best navy, the biggest merchant fleet, the most dominant commerce and the most wealth.

In contrast to the conscript armies of continental Europe, Britain's army was a volunteer force of professional soldiers. As far as any army is a microcosm of the society that produces it, the British Army was officered by the aristocracy and gentry, and its rank and file came from a growing industrial and declining rural working class. Within the army's officers there was a growing number of those who came from the 'new money' of commercial and entrepreneurial wealth as well as those whose wealth was hereditary. In his study, *The Army in Victorian Society*, Gwyn Harries-Jenkins quotes the Adjutant-General, Sir John MacDonald, in 1840:

It is the proud characteristic of the British Army that its officers are gentlemen by education, manners and habits; that some are men of the first families in the country, and some of large property, but the rules and regulations of the service require strictly that they should conduct themselves as ought gentlemen in every situation in which they may be placed.[1]

Patronage, land and wealth were the prerequisites for admission into the service for most gentlemen. The purchase system ensured that entry into the infantry and cavalry was mostly restricted to a narrow socio-economic elite. In this respect the four subalterns who were the authors of the letters home fit easily into the general pattern of background, manners and education of 'officers and gentlemen'. Within their socio-economic group there was, of course, variety and differences of ability and wealth, but the latter prevailed over the former. The military theorist, Colonel John Mitchell, who advocated the abolition of the purchase system throughout the 1830s, wrote that the system 'promotes the wealthy dunces of the honourable profession ... over the heads of all the bravest and the best who cannot purchase'.[2] While the army did undergo some reforms in the 1830s and 1840s, reactionary and conservative values ensured that the impetus was slow compared to the dynamism in other parts of Victorian industrial society.

The 'long peace' after 1815 had brought pressures to reduce the size of the British Army. Already, the army's strength in 1817 was down by 220,000 on that of 1814, a figure including 80,000 militiamen.[3] Some cavalry regiments were disbanded and the establishment of the remaining regiments reduced, some infantry regiments lost their second battalions, and the Royal Waggon Train was disbanded in 1833. In the year Queen Victoria acceded to the throne, the establishment stood at just 111,000, of which 10,656 were cavalry.[4] The peacetime routine of the army at home involved postings to garrison towns and barracks all over the British Isles. There were drills, parades, reviews and inspections and calls, mostly for the cavalry, to 'aid the civil power'. There were campaigning opportunities overseas, however, in Canada, India and South Africa, and through the 1840s and the 1850s a growing fear of possible French invasion of Britain itself. To one young officer in the Grenadier Guards, later General Sir George Higginson,

---

1   G. Harries-Jenkins, *The Army in Victorian Society* (London: Routledge and Kegan Paul, 1977), p. 16.

2   Hew Strachan, *Wellington's Legacy: The Reform of the British Army 1830–1854* (Manchester: Manchester University Press, 1984), p. 117.

3   Sir John Fortescue, *A History of the British Army* 13 vols (London: Macmillan, 1923), vol. 11, p. 52.

4   The Marquess of Anglesey, *A History of the British Cavalry* 8 vols (Barnsley: Leo Cooper, 1975), vol. 2, p. 73.

A feeling that all was not right in our army began to find expression about this time, and the comforting assurance which invariably followed any proposal of reform in its administration – that 'no man could be so foolish as to think we should ever again see active service' – was ceasing to be the conviction of thoughtful people.[5]

Similarly, the contemporary historian of the Crimean War, Alexander Kinglake, wrote:

An army is but the limb of a nation, and it is no more given to a people to combine the possession of military strength with an unmeasured devotion to the arts of peace, than it is for a man to be feeble and helpless in the general condition of his body, and yet have at his command a strong right arm for the convenience of self-defence. The strength of the right arm is the strength of the man: the prowess of an army is as the valour and warlike spirit of the nation which gives it her flesh and blood. England, having suffered herself to grow forgetful of this truth, seemed, in the eyes of foreigners, to be declining.[6]

Following the death of the Duke of Wellington in 1852, however, his successor as Commander-in-Chief at the Horse Guards, Lord Hardinge, speeded reform, with a new rifled musket for the infantry, the establishment of the School of Musketry at Hythe, and the establishment of a permanent camp at Aldershot following the first camp of exercise at Chobham. The latter was innovative, enabling brigades and divisions to manoeuvre together. Chobham was widely reported in *The Times*, which observed, on 28 June 1853, 'Among the noblemen and gentlemen present we remarked the Earl of Cardigan, who is a constant attendant at the camp'.[7] Whether lessons were truly learned by the military exercises, however, was more questionable. Sweetman, for example, has described the manoeuvres as the 'greatest single opiate for the complacent', while Strachan also suggests that success was limited

5   General Sir George Higginson, *Seventy One Years of a Guardsman's Life*, (London: Smith Elder & Sons, 1916), pp. 55–6.

6   Alexander Kinglake, *The Invasion of the Crimea* 8 vols (Edinburgh: William Blackwood & Sons, 1876), vol. 1, pp. 83–4.

7   *The Times*, 28 June 1853, p. 8, col. A.

in preparing commanders and staffs for war.[8] Reviewing the experience of the Crimea, Lieutenant Colonel (later General Sir) John Adye, concluded in 1860:

> The late war, at its commencement, found England unprepared, and its people, as a general rule, ignorant of the requirements and previous preparation which war entails. The available army was small, and all the various departments which contribute to its efficiency, and are of vital importance in taking the field, either did not exist at all, or were incomplete, reduced, and consequently inefficient.[9]

The war with Russia had its origins in the conflict of interests between imperial powers. The weakness and continuing decline of the Ottoman Empire throughout the first half of the nineteenth century created opportunities for Russian expansion. From a Russian perspective their aims and interests were perfectly reasonable. If Russia controlled the straits into the Black Sea they could extend their influence into the eastern Mediterranean. From a British perspective this development was not in her interests, especially with routes across the isthmus of Suez to India as a consideration. Successful expansion would embolden the Russians and would make future conflict with British interests more likely. Superficially the quarrel that led to war was over the keys to the Christian 'holy places' in Jerusalem. Orthodox Christians looked for Russia to protect their interests. The Latin Church looked to France. The Ottomans accepted Anglo-French help when faced with Russian aggression, manifested when Russian forces crossed the Pruth River in July 1853, and advanced into the Danubian principalities of Wallachia and Moldavia.[10] The Ottoman Empire declared war on Russia on 5 October 1853. Initially, there were Russian reverses on the Danube. However, in November, Russian warships annihilated the Ottoman Black Sea squadron at Sinope on the north coast of Asia Minor. The reaction in Britain was hysterical and made the prospect of war with Russia more likely. Added to this was the autocratic, unbending character of Tsar Nicholas I, who believed that Britain would not go so far as war over the

---

8   John Sweetman, *War and Administration: The Significance of the Crimean War for the British Army* (Edinburgh: Scottish Academic Press, 1984), p. 34; Strachan, *Wellington's Legacy*, pp. 166–74.

9   John Adye, *A Review of the Crimean War* (Wakefield: E. P. Publishing, reprint edn, 1973), p. 1.

10   The Pruth River runs between what was the south-west Russian Empire and the Turkish principalities of Moldavia and Wallachia, forming the border.

question of the straits. Diplomatic efforts faltered and failed. When the ultimatums of Britain and France received no reply from the Tsar, Britain and France declared war on 28 March 1854. In fact, the British Army was already in the process of gathering for service in the east. On 23 February 1854 three battalions of foot guards left London for Malta, and became the vanguard of what became known as the 'Army of the East'.[11]

The Army of the East was to be transported to Constantinople via Gibraltar and Malta. Eventually it was decided to go on from Constantinople to Varna on the Black Sea. The British force was to number 27,000 and consist of five infantry divisions; a cavalry division; seven batteries of field artillery; six companies of sappers and miners; and, later, when Sebastopol was selected to be reduced, the battering train of siege artillery. The transports of both steam and sail were hired by the government and left from ports all over the British Isles at different times. Each infantry division was composed of two brigades, and three battalions made up each brigade. From the outset there was difficulty in finding infantry battalions that were up to strength and the same problem was also experienced in the cavalry. Not only was there a shortage of men but also of horses. When regiments were bound for India they would sail without their horses, having left their mounts to the homecoming regiment. For the Army of the East, however, the transporting of cavalry regiments with their horses was a new experience. The transports had to be adapted to accommodate the horses by the installation of stalls, but rough seas or very hot weather, or both, would inevitably mean losses.

Thomas Hutton's and Fiennes Wykeham Martin's regiment, the 4th Light Dragoons, had taken part in the Chobham camp exercises and had been brigaded there with the Royal Horse Guards, the 2nd Dragoons and the 8th Hussars. Without going into detail, the regimental history states that 'the exercises proved to be of great value on active service the next year'.[12] The order came to prepare for service in Turkey on 2 July 1854 when the regiment was in Dorchester. The letters of Wykeham Martin reveal a level of excitement in anticipating the departure of the transport, *Simla*, and the strenuous efforts to get matters settled before sailing and to make sure that the officers' equipment and chargers were accounted for. On 12 July the regiment assembled at Exeter and marched to Plymouth. Amid great excitement and cheering they embarked on 19 July 1854 with 21 officers and 297 NCOs and

---

11 For the general background, see Winfried Baumgart, *The Crimean War, 1853–56* (London: Arnold, 1999), pp. 1–33.

12 D. Scott Daniell, *4th Hussar: The Story of a British Cavalry Regiment* (Aldershot: Gale and Polden, 1959), p. 161.

other ranks.[13] Wykeham Martin uses the word 'cruelty' when describing conditions for the horses on the *Simla* and is critical of the government's preparations [8]. Captain Robert Portal, who was also on board, wrote that they had 391 men and officers and 317 horses aboard. The rolling of the ship caused havoc, officers and men were sick, and the horses snorted and tumbled about to such an extent that he fully expected to land at Varna without a single horse. As it turned out they only lost two horses who broke their legs from plunging so violently they had to be destroyed. Other horses died as they voyaged into the Mediterranean due to being positioned too close to the boiler and going mad with the heat. Lord George Paget blamed

> bad construction of the 'fittings', the things being improperly made, and the divisions between the stalls being open for two feet at the bottom, whereby the horses, when they have struggled themselves down, get across the adjoining box, and kick their neighbours, which in turn kick and struggle till they also fall.[14]

Phillips's 8th Hussars were also short of men and, to find the 295 men and 250 horses required, they were compelled to break up the band and put the musicians into the ranks. They also exchanged 25 young horses with more seasoned mounts from the 3rd Light Dragoons.[15] The regiment sailed for the east in five different sailing ships on different days at the end of April 1854. Phillips was on board a sailing ship, *Shooting Star*, in company with Captain Henry Duberly, the regiment's paymaster, and his wife, Fanny, departing on 25 April.[16] The 4th Dragoon Guards received their marching orders on 14 March, Edward Hodge of the regiment noting in his diary, 'We are to take 250 horses. Where I shall get these I do not know. Also 250 men.'[17] The regiment left in a similar fashion to the 8th Hussars on board six vessels, Fisher-Rowe sailing on the *Palmyra*.[18]

---

13   The National Archives (hereafter TNA), WO12/659, Muster Roll, 4th Light Dragoons, 1854–5.

14   Robert Portal, *Letters from the Crimea, 1854–55* (Winchester: Warren and Son, 1900), p. 5; Lord George Paget, *The Light Cavalry Brigade in the Crimea* (London: Murray, 1881; reprint edn, 1975), p. 2.

15   R. H. Murray, *A History of the VIII King's Royal Irish Hussars*. 2 vols (Cambridge: W. Heffer and Sons, 1928), vol. 2, p. 407.

16   Fanny Duberly became well known after the war through the publication of her journal. Her image, with her husband, was taken in the Crimea by Roger Fenton in 1855. See Christine Kelly, ed. *Mrs Duberly's War: Journal and Letters from the Crimea* (Oxford: Oxford University Press, 2007). The portrayal of Mrs Duberly by the actress Jill Bennett in the film *The Charge of the Light Brigade* is a fiction.

17   The Marquess of Anglesey, *Little Hodge* (London: Leo Cooper, 1971), p. 3.

18   House of Commons Parliamentary Papers (hereafter HCPP) 1854–5 (283), Transports: Return to an Order of the House of Commons, 29 January 1855, printed 5 June 1855; TNA, WO12/270, 1854 Muster List, 4th Dragoon Guards.

As is well known, the officer selected by Hardinge to command the army was the Master General of the Ordnance, Lord Raglan, Wellington's former Military Secretary. Those in the subordinate commands were a mixture of veteran and less experienced officers. Strachan, indeed, has argued that the choices made were generally logical and those appointed generally the best available.[19] In terms of the Cavalry Division, however, choices were constrained by the cavalry's lack of overseas service opportunities compared to those of the infantry. Its commander, the irascible Lieutenant General George Bingham, 3rd Earl of Lucan, had served as a volunteer in the Russian army in 1828–9. Lucan had commanded a cavalry division under the walls of Adrianople in the short Russo-Turkish War of that year, showing an indifference to discomfort and gaining a useful knowledge of both the Turks and Russians.[20] Brigadier General Sir James Scarlett commanded the Heavy Cavalry Brigade, however, and had no active service experience. Command of the Light Brigade went to Lucan's brother-in-law, Major General James Brudenell, 7th Earl of Cardigan. Immensely wealthy, Cardigan also had no active service experience and was already a controversial figure in British society. He had been dismissed as unfit to command the 15th Hussars in January 1832 and, in the years that followed, was involved in a number of scandals in the army to the exasperation of the Duke of Wellington and others at Horse Guards. Significantly Lucan and Cardigan loathed each other and were barely on speaking terms.[21] The responsibility for the absurdity of having two senior officers whose relationship was strained in the same division lay with Hardinge. He had supported Cardigan's rehabilitation in 1836 and was sympathetic to Cardigan's zeal in attaining efficiency and correctness in the regiment under his command.

None of the regimental lieutenant colonels in the cavalry brigades had any active service experience. In 1854 Lord George Paget of the 4th Light Dragoons, the 35-year-old son of the 1st Marquess of Anglesey, had just married and was greatly distressed at parting from his new bride.[22] The middle-aged commander of the 8th Hussars, Frederick Shewell, a deeply religious man, had followed the usual practice of purchasing his advancement but without ever coming into

---

19 Strachan, *Wellington's Legacy*, pp. 172–4.

20 Ibid., p. 173.

21 Saul David, *The Homicidal Earl* (London: Little Brown & Co, 1997), pp. 232–3. See also Donald Thomas, *Cardigan, Hero of Balaclava*, 2nd edn (London: Weidenfeld & Nicolson, 2002).

22 Portal, *Letters from the Crimea*, p. 3.

contact with an enemy. Lieutenant Colonel John Douglas of the 11th Hussars was a friend of Cardigan, and had assumed command when Cardigan became commander of the Light Brigade. Charles Edmund Doherty had served in the 14th Light Dragoons prior to exchanging to the 13th Light Dragoons in 1840, and purchased his way to command the regiment in October 1852.[23] Brevet Colonel John Lawrenson of the 17th Lancers had been a cavalry officer since 1818 but his health deteriorated as the Crimean campaign started and he was granted leave of absence to recover his health on 23 October 1854.[24] Major Augustus Willett then died, either of cholera or exposure, just before the battle of Balaklava, and command of the regiment passed to one of the few cavalry officers who had both ability and experience, Captain William Morris. A Devonian, Morris had seen active service in India in the Sikh Wars with the 16th Lancers. Known as the 'Pocket Hercules' from his small stature, Morris took his fitness very seriously and, perhaps ahead of his time, took exercise to keep his physical condition in a state of excellence. Apart from the Honorary Colonel of the regiment, Major General Thomas William Taylor, a Waterloo veteran, Morris was the only officer of the 17th Lancers who had had any military experience of war.[25]

As *Hart's Army List* demonstrates, throughout the Light Brigade there was a smattering of experience. In the 11th Hussars Lieutenant William Ennis had served with the regiment at the siege and capture of Bhurtpore in 1825. Paymaster Joseph Hely had served as a captain in the 1st Lancers in the Anglo-Spanish Legion in the Carlist War in Spain in 1835–6. In the 4th Light Dragoons, Quartermaster John Hill had served as Deputy Provost Marshal to the Bombay column of the Army of the Indus from December 1838 to February 1840, and was present at the storming and capture of Ghuznee. Lieutenant the Hon. Charles James Keith had served for three years as a midshipman in the Royal Navy and had been wounded in the boat action of HMS *President* and HMS *Eurydice* against Arab pirates in the River Augozha on the east coast of Africa in November 1847.

The same lack of experience was to be found in the ranks of officers of the Heavy Brigade. In the 1st Royal Dragoons not a single officer below the rank of lieutenant colonel had seen action. In the 2nd (Royal North British) Dragoons, Lieutenant Herbert Edwards had served in

---

23   *Hart's New Army List, 1853* (London: John Murray, 1853), p. 69.
24   TNA, WO12/1339, Muster Roll, 17th Lancers.
25   *Hart's New Army List 1853*, p. 143.

the Punjab campaign with the 14th Light Dragoons but was the only experienced officer with them. Lieutenant Edmund D'Arcy Hunt of the 6th Inniskillings was the only officer with experience, having served with the 9th Lancers in the Punjab campaign. Fisher-Rowe's regiment, the 4th Dragoon Guards, had two officers who had seen active service: Captain Charles Henry Douglas Donovan had served in the 9th Lancers in the Sutlej campaign in 1846 while Surgeon Chilley Pine had served in China and New Zealand. The 5th Dragoon Guards had Lieutenant Alexander Elliot, who had served five years in India, including service with the 8th Bengal Cavalry at the battle of Punniar, in the Sutlej campaign, and at the battle of Ferozeshah. In the Crimea he was to act as ADC to Scarlett.[26]

The army began to concentrate at Varna on the western shores of the Black Sea with a view to assisting the Turks in their campaign against Russian forces on the Danube. The Turks were under siege at Silistra and the allies could offer strong support to Omar Pasha's right flank from Varna. Prior to the move to Varna there was an uncomfortable pause in Constantinople. The French had arrived before the British and consequently occupied the best quarters. The vermin-ridden barracks, the dirt and the heat disgusted the British Army and most were glad to leave the place for the superficially healthier environment of Varna. Wykeham Martin described Constantinople as 'a magnificent city to look at from the harbour, but when you get on shore it is the filthiest hole' [9].

Attitudes to the new French and Turkish allies were almost universally negative. To Wykeham Martin the Turks were 'a most disgusting race of people and not worth fighting for … I would almost sooner fight for a Russian if it was not treason to say so' [9]. Similarly, for Phillips the Turks 'certainly are a very dirty people, and not worthy of such a beautiful situation for a city as this' [170]. Reactions to the French were more ambivalent. Fisher-Rowe found some French troops mutinous because of the losses they were enduring from cholera: 'The officers have no control over them, and indeed it was better as it was, for in many instances they were much worse than the men' [81]. Much later in the campaign, however, Wykeham Martin observed. 'The French beat us in taking care of their troops; their men, officers, and horses, all being covered in long ago, consequently they have few sick' [27]. Indeed, the French appeared to be more organised and professional in their practices. In similar vein to Wykeham Martin, Fisher-Rowe

---

26   TNA, WO100/24, Medal Roll. Staff, p. 27.

had written earlier, 'The French have everything comfortable, we have nothing. The British spend five times as much on their soldiers; their soldiers are five times worse cared for' [100].

Turkish resistance at Silistra surprised the Russians, and they were unable to carry the town. The Turks carried out successful diversionary attacks on the Russian forces and these, together with hostile moves from Austria, forced the Russians to raise the siege and retreat towards Bucharest, quitting the Danubian principalities. By the end of June 1854, it appeared that the hostilities were over. Cardigan had made a reconnaissance to ascertain the location of Russian forces and found none in the Dobrudsha south of the Danube. When fit men and healthy horses were precious, Cardigan's relentless excesses seemed, to many, an expensive and unnecessary waste but Cardigan's reconnaissance confirmed that the Russians had retreated. However, the Russophobic clamour at home to 'do something' prevailed over any consideration for diplomacy to recommence after the retreat of the Russians from the Danube. In any case, there was pressure within the government to neutralise the potent Russian naval facility of Sebastopol.[27] Little was known of the geography and topography of the Crimea and less known of the populace and agriculture. There was no appreciation of the strength of the Russian army in the Crimea. There were no maps and a landing-place was only decided upon after Lord Raglan's reconnaissance on 10 September in the *Caradoc*. The decision to attack Sebastopol was a political one and its execution left to the military and naval commanders. Neither service was enthusiastic about the prospect. The attack, though, would not be a surprise to the Russians. Throughout July *The Times* speculated on where the allies might strike the Russians and Sebastopol was identified as the heart of Russian power in the Black Sea.

It was while they were at Varna that cholera ravaged both the French and British armies. Tens of thousands of men camped together in the heat and stillness of the Black Sea shore delivered perfect insanitary conditions for the pestilence to thrive. Cholera was indifferent to rank and took officers and men from all regiments. The 4th and 13th Light Dragoons and the 17th Lancers got off lightly and did not lose a single officer. The 8th Hussars, however, lost Captain Charles Longmore to the disease while the 11th Hussars were more severely afflicted, losing Captain

---

27   See Andrew Lambert, *The Crimean War: British Grand Strategy against Russia, 1853–56* (Manchester: Manchester University Press, 1994), pp. 111–29; Hew Strachan, 'Soldiers, Strategy and Sebastopol', *Historical Journal*, vol. 21, 1978, pp. 303–25; Hugh Small, *The Crimean War* (Stroud: Tempus Publishing, 2007), pp. 32–42.

William Cresswell, Lieutenant the Hon. Robert Annesley and Lieutenant Arthur Saltmarshe. The Heavy Brigade also suffered losses. The 5th Dragoon Guards had lost three officers by the end of August: Captain Duckworth, Surgeon Pitcairn and Veterinary Surgeon George Fisher all succumbed. The 4th and 5th Dragoon Guards were so weakened by losses there was a grim joke about combining them to form 'the 9th'.[28] A fire at Varna deprived the army of supplies of barley and, consequently, rations for the horses were reduced even further. There were days when some regiments' horses received nothing, and The Royals also discovered an outbreak of glanders and 25 of their horses had to be destroyed.[29]

Inactivity and growing supply problems began to tell on the morale of the army. It was also obvious that the army lacked sufficient means to move and young officers, including Phillips, were sent out into the country to purchase horses to alleviate the problem. The Turks had earlier passed through the country and had left very little in their wake. Hutton described the deteriorating condition of the horses because of the poor forage while Fisher-Rowe mentioned the deterioration in the behaviour of some of the 4th Dragoon Guards who were getting drunk seemingly with impunity [82, 195]. When the General Order for the Invasion of the Crimea was issued on 31 August, it must have come as a relief. To transport 27,000 British, 30,000 French and 7,000 Turkish troops, with all their horses and artillery, created considerable demands on the available shipping resources. When the armada of transports and warships eventually sailed, the British Army was carried by 82 transports (27 steam and 55 sail). Of the four correspondents, only Hutton and Wykeham Martin went with the main invading force; the latter described the scene as 'the most magnificent sight you ever saw, 32 sail of the line, English besides French and Turkish' [11].

Only after much discussion and meetings, and Raglan's reconnaissance on 10 September, was Kalamita Bay, north of Sebastopol, chosen as a landing-ground. Resolute opposition, especially with artillery, could have driven the allies away with heavy losses. The landings started on the morning of 14 September and continued over the next three days. Phillips's letter of 21st September expressed the astonishment and relief that the landings were unopposed and sought to rationalise this by suggesting that

---

28 TNA, WO12/659, Muster Roll, 4th Light Dragoons; WO12/118, Muster Roll, 13th Light Dragoons; WO12/844, Muster Roll, 8th Hussars; WO12/1012, Muster Roll, 11th Hussars; WO12/1339, Muster Roll, 17th Lancers; WO12/324, Muster Roll, 5th Dragoon Guards; Anglesey, *History of British Cavalry*, vol. 2, p. 41.

29 Charles de Ainslie, *Historical Record of the First or Royal Regiment of Dragoons* (London: Chapman & Hall, 1887), pp. 182–4.

the Russians were not expecting the allies. Wykeham Martin believed that the allies had 'dodged the Russian camp that was waiting for us' [11, 181]. The Russians were waiting, however, in prepared positions on the heights overlooking the River Alma, confident that they would defeat the allies there. On 19 September Russian cavalry was encountered at the River Bulganak. The Russians tried to lure the British into a trap by making them attack, having concealed their infantry behind a ridge. Cardigan and Lucan could not see this mass of enemy waiting for them. Raglan, from his position, could and, accordingly, ordered his cavalry to withdraw. To the jeers of the Russians, and also some of the British infantry, the cavalry performed a textbook retirement. The 'Affair at the Bulganak' was significant because it created resentment within the cavalry that they had been wrongly held back, and that Lucan was to blame.

The following day the battle of the River Alma was fought. Hutton and Wykeham Martin were present but Phillips was still recovering from fever at Varna and Fisher-Rowe was still waiting to be taken from Varna to the Crimea with his regiment. In any case, the cavalry were spectators and not actively engaged. Consequently, Wykeham Martin referred his stepmother to *The Times* for a description [12]. When the Russians began to retreat away from the Alma, the British cavalry were forbidden by Raglan to harass them and turn the retreat into a rout. This restraint added to the frustration felt within the cavalry though Raglan's caution was prudent for he had only a small mounted force at his disposal and it would have been rash to allow it to face destruction from a larger enemy force.

The dead were buried in pits and the wounded taken back to the shore where they were put on board ships to be taken back to Constantinople and the barracks at Scutari. The ships that transported the wounded were not specifically designed for the task, being simply ordinary transports that were empty when they had discharged their primary function. When the transfer of wounded and sick ran smoothly, as it sometimes did, there was little cause for complaint. But, often, it did not and the suffering of the invalid men involved was increased. Thus, Fisher-Rowe wrote:

> The accounts we have heard of women coming out to wait upon the wounded does not give half the pleasure it appears to have given in England. The Doctors say that women nurses give an immense amount of trouble in all hospitals, and that when they become used to the wounds and horrors of a Military Hospital they become more hardened than the men and less tender to the sick. [100]

Following the Alma, the remainder of the army moved to the Crimea. The transfer of the rest of the Heavy Brigade, which was completed only on 6 October, was disastrous, Phillips gives a unique detailed description of what happened aboard the *Rip Van Winkle* transport and the other ships in the convoy after embarking on 24 September [182]. A violent storm hit the convoy and hundreds of horses were killed or crippled. This loss further weakened the heavy cavalry, the 1st Royal Dragoons being reduced to a single squadron. Indeed, the 6th Inniskilling Dragoons had already lost 57 horses, much equipment and several men, including Lieutenant Colonel Moore, in a fire on board the *Europa* some 200 miles out of Plymouth back in May.[30]

In the time between the battle of the Alma and the arrival of the British forces at the sheltered harbour of Balaklava, a number of significant events occurred. The Russians blocked the entrance to the harbour in Sebastopol by sinking a number of ships. The Russian commander, Menshikov, decided not to retreat into Sebastopol. Instead, he withdrew into the centre of the Crimea, towards Bakchi Serai and Simpheropol. From this position he would be able to threaten the flank of the allied armies as they manoeuvred around the city. Sebastopol was divided roughly east/west by the waters of the harbour and the Dockyard Creek, which came off the south side of the harbour. The city could be overlooked by higher ground to the north-east and Raglan's chief engineer, Sir John Burgoyne, suggested a 'flank march' to the east of the city with a view to attacking it from the south where it was believed the defences were weaker. By marching round Sebastopol they would also gain control of the sheltered harbour of Balaklava and also Kamiesh. After consultation between Raglan and the French general, Canrobert, who had taken over from the dying Marshal St Arnaud, it was decided that the British should occupy Balaklava as their main supply port. The French would occupy Kamiesh and Kazach. This decision meant that the British were to be responsible for the defence of the right flank of the attack, and the French the left. The two French supply ports were nearer to their forces and superior to Balaklava. When the weather deteriorated in the autumn and winter, the distance and the nature of the ground from Balaklava to the British camp on the heights before Sebastopol proved to be significant factors in the suffering endured by the British. Wykeham Martin revealed his awareness of the military situation the allies found themselves in, writing, 'We are now in rather a ticklish position, having Sevastopol before us, and a large army behind us' [12].

---

30 Anglesey, *Little Hodge*, p. 29; E. S. Jackson *The Records of the Inniskilling Dragoons* (London: Arthur L. Humphreys, 1909), pp. 157–60.

The siege of Sebastopol was not a total investment. The allies were only strong enough to attack the southern half of the city and the Russians were able to supply and reinforce their defenders from the northern side. With their field army at large, the Russians were also able to pose a threat to the allied supply ports, especially Balaklava, the loss of which would compel the allies to abandon the siege. The British cavalry therefore provided pickets and videttes to warn of any advance towards the defences of Balaklava by the Russian field army. Every morning before dawn the cavalry were prepared to go into action to repulse offensive moves by the Russians [13, 90, 183]. It was challenging work and by the eve of the battle of Balaklava, the cavalry had been significantly reduced, though figures vary.[31]

The Russian attack that came on 25 October has become one of the most celebrated engagements in British military history.[32] All four correspondents wrote about the battle of Balaklava in the days that followed it, as much to reassure their families as to describe their participation in it [13, 92, 186, 197]. The battle started at daybreak with an attack in force by the Russians on the outer ring of defences, a line of redoubts on the top of the Causeway Heights. The redoubts were overwhelmed and the Turks who manned the guns in them were either killed or put to flight. A strong force of Russian cavalry then advanced down the shallow valley between the Fedioukine Hills and the Causeway Heights, known as the North Valley, and over the gentle slopes of the Causeway Heights into what was called the South Valley. Unknown to them was the presence of a composite force made up of companies of the 93rd Highlanders and detachments of other forces scraped together by Sir Colin Campbell. As the Russians approached, the Highlanders drove them off with some steady fire. As the main body of Russian cavalry advanced behind the squadrons of hussars repulsed by the 93rd Highlanders, they almost halted when they were hit by the squadrons of the Heavy Brigade and driven back before disintegrating as an organised body. As they retreated in disorder they exposed their flank to the Light Brigade who were at the foot of the Sapouné Ridge 500 yards to the west. Morris of the 17th Lancers begged Cardigan to attack the disorganised Russians but was refused.

Subsequently, after the Russians were observed from the top of the Sapouné Ridge to be removing the guns from the captured redoubts,

---

31 See, for example, Mark Adkin, *The Charge: The Real Reason Why the Light Brigade Was Lost* (Barnsley: Leo Cooper, 1996), p. 254, where he estimates the strength of the Light Brigade at 668 officers and men.

32 For detailed analysis of the Light Brigade action, see ibid., pp. 67–214; and, for the Heavy Brigade, see Anglesey, *History of British Cavalry*, vol. 2, pp. 67–79.

there was set in train the sequence of events that led to the charge of the Light Brigade down the North Valley, the fateful order carried to Lucan by Captain Louis Nolan of the 15th Hussars, who was ADC to Raglan's Deputy Quartermaster-General, Richard Airey. Wykeham Martin, Hutton and Phillips all charged with their regiments. The Light Brigade carried the battery at the end of the valley but the men were unable to spike the guns. They continued to advance beyond the battery until they came upon a large mass of Russian cavalry. Realising they were outnumbered the survivors began to retreat. As they did so, other Russian cavalry tried to cut them off. They were brushed aside in the desperate mêlée as the remains of the Light Brigade fought their way back up the valley, now littered with dead and wounded men and horses. The losses in officers and men amounted to some 113 killed and 247 badly wounded out of 673; 475 horses had been killed and 42 injured. Hutton was among those wounded and was evacuated from the Crimea.

Wykeham Martin attempted to rationalise the seemingly absurd action of advancing into a cross-fire, writing

> now to understand why we did this rash and stupid act, you must know that lately there has been some stupid chaff about the Cavalry being afraid of the Cossacks, and Nolan had made some remarks about it to Lord Lucan, he is *rather suspected*, as he was the man sent to make the reconnaissance before we attacked, of having misrepresented to Lord Raglan the nature of the ground and the position of the enemy. [13]

This rationale, of course, is mistaken. So far as Fisher-Rowe of the Heavy Brigade was concerned, 'Very little is known of the melancholy affair; it appears that Lord Raglan sent a written order to Lord Lucan to charge' [92]. Phillips, on the other hand, wrote

> it was a mistake. A poor fellow who is dead, brought a wrong report; in consequence of this we went a mile and a half if not two, to take guns we could never have brought away under such an awful fire. [186]

Hutton was quite definite in his appreciation: 'We have had a most disastrous affair at Balaclava, the Light Brigade of Cavalry have been almost cut to pieces, through the wilful obstinacy, or wickedness I may say of a General, whose name I will not give.' He added: 'a child might have seen the trap that was laid for us, as every private dragoon did' [197]. Whether he meant Lucan or Cardigan was to blame is unclear.

Following the battle of Balaklava, the Light Cavalry Brigade ceased to function as an effective fighting force. Again, there is still a debate regarding the precise figure. About 245 officers and men were killed, wounded, missing or made prisoner and 362 horses killed. The losses in horses alone cancelled the brigade's ability adequately to fulfil its role. The Heavy Brigade had suffered less in their successful engagement, sustaining just 10 killed and 98 wounded by the end of the day. Half of the wounded had been hit as they rode to support the Light Brigade at the beginning of the charge.[33] Until replacement men and horses were sent out from England and fresh regiments sent out to the Crimea from India, the work of the Cavalry Division was carried out by a below-strength brigade and the remains of the Light Brigade [16, 17, 94, 188]. The Russian army had not been defeated at Balaklava and still held the redoubts taken from the Turks and, therefore, the eastern end of the Causeway Heights. They had failed, however, to capture Balaklava and interdict the supplies that came through it. Eleven days after the battle of Balaklava, therefore, the Russians made another serious attempt to drive the British from their positions before Sebastopol. Just before dawn on 5 November they attacked the British camp which had its right flank near Inkerman. The battle was a brutal slogging match between two determined forces of infantry and artillery. Finally the Russians withdrew back into the town after appalling casualties had been sustained. With them went any chance of the siege ending sooner rather than later. The allies were too weak to carry the siege, and the Russians too weak to drive them away. Trench warfare ensued accompanied by an ever-present background of artillery exchanges. With the weather worsening, a hurricane – the 'great storm' – on 14 November did serious damage to the allied camp and, out at sea, many transport ships were lost including the *Prince* laden with winter clothes and medical supplies for the army.

After Inkerman, the tone and content of the correspondence changes. Optimism begins to pale and the three remaining correspondents – Wykeham Martin, Fisher-Rowe and Phillips – become concerned with surviving the worsening conditions and increasingly preoccupied with how this might be achieved. Because of their backgrounds, they were able to request comforts and sustenance to be sent from home via the post. The rank and file did not enjoy this relief. Lack of confidence in

---

33   Anglesey, *History of British Cavalry*, vol. 2, p. 76.

both the government at home and the leadership of the Army of the East increased, and a number of officers began to find their way home [100, 189, 191]. In the increasingly inclement weather, officers and men were exposed to the worst of the elements. The distance from Balaklava further exacerbated the difficulties of supply for the Light Brigade and the horses started to deteriorate rapidly and even drop dead in the lines [22]. The Heavy Brigade was more fortunate as it was moved nearer to Balaklava.[34] But even that location did not spare them from withering decline, as the Commissariat was unable to supply the needs of the army [101].

If the end of 1854 had been one of stalemate, abject misery and suffering in the Crimea, the beginning of 1855 saw attempts to rectify the causes of such distress. For the editor of *Colburn's United Service Magazine*,

> What we have at stake before Sevastopol is, not merely the honour, but the integrity of the empire, and we are fighting in the Crimea for our ascendancy on the ocean, our dominions in India, and our very existence as a European power.[35]

The quantity of scandalous news from the Crimea published by *The Times* had stirred public opinion. Early in February, Lord Aberdeen resigned as Prime Minister to be replaced by Lord Palmerston and, at the War Office, the Duke of Newcastle gave way to Lord Panmure. Panmure brought energy and intelligence to address the multitude of ills afflicting the army before Sebastopol. The office of Chief of Staff was created in an attempt to take some of the pressure off Raglan and Lieutenant General Sir James Simpson was appointed to the position. The Byzantine tangle of independent departments that presided over the army was simplified and to some extent rationalised and made more effective. Commissioners Sir John McNeill and A. M. Tulloch arrived to start an inquiry into the supply of the army. In April a Land Transport Corps was established to alleviate some of the problems that had crippled the army the previous year. A decision to build a railway from Balaklava and the siege lines had also been taken in December 1854 and had made rapid progress by February.[36] In June 1855 a new Medical Staff Corps was established to provide hospital services for the sick and wounded.

Cardigan had departed the Crimea in December and, in the new year, Lucan was recalled. He would not be placated or mollified over the

34 Ibid., pp. 112–14.
35 *Colburn's United Service Magazine*, January 1855, Part 1, p. 107.
36 See Brian Cooke, *The Grand Crimean Railway* (Knutsford: Cavalier House, 1997).

question of culpability for the loss of the Light Brigade. His character and temperament exacerbated his predicament. For all his faults he took the duty of care for the division seriously. From him came a stream of memos and notes written in a poor, jagged, furious hand, complaining about deficiencies of supply for the horses and claiming for an increase. He submerged himself in the minute detail better suited for the work of subalterns than generals of division.[37] Command of the cavalry passed to the more affable Scarlett.

The siege continued with artillery exchanges and raids by both sides. On 22 March, at night, the Russians made an attack in force against the French trenches, driving them out so that they fled towards the British trenches. After hand-to-hand fighting the Russians were driven back by the British [37, 126]. By May, however, the French had eight strong divisions in the Crimea and were the dominant military partner, taking over the right flank.

The fortunes of the cavalry and the condition of both men and horses began to improve. George Loy Smith of the 11th Hussars recorded that on 4 April each cavalry regiment sent 38 men to Constantinople to bring up fresh horses that had been purchased in Spain, England and other parts. Nine days later, the first cavalry reinforcements arrived with the disembarkation of part of the 10th Hussars from India. Also on their way from India were the 12th Lancers. The two new regiments were on 'Indian Establishment', which meant they were numerically larger than the 'Home Establishment'. Incredibly on 10 May, an order was given to reduce the two newly arrived regiments to the Home Establishment. The sense of this order eluded most of the cavalry officers in the field. Detachments for four out of the five Light Cavalry regiments arrived in the middle of May and the first units of the 12th Lancers also disembarked. At the end of May transport ships delivered 108 fresh horses at Balaklava. In the first two weeks of August the 1st and 6th Dragoon Guards also arrived from England.[38] The whole of the cavalry was reorganised into three brigades (Heavy, Light and Hussar) in July. By then, they bore little similarity to the half-starved scarecrows on sickly, dying mounts that they had presented in the depths of winter. A new Light Brigade had been formed. It was composed of the 6th Dragoon Guards, Carabiniers, 4th Light Dragoons, 12th Lancers and 13th Light Dragoons. The 8th

---

37 TNA, WO28/161, Records of Military Head Quarters, Crimea, Reports and Papers, Misc. notes and Memoranda, Cavalry Division.

38 George Loy Smith, *A Victorian RSM: From India to the Crimea* (Tunbridge Wells: Costello, 1987), pp. 183–5; Anglesey, *History of British Cavalry*, vol. 2, p. 123; TNA, WO28/161, Records of Military Head Quarters, Crimea, Reports and Papers, Cavalry Returns, 1855.

Hussars were part of a new Hussar Brigade, along with the 10th Hussars, 11th Hussars and 17th Lancers. The quality of this new strength though was questionable. Many of the new drafts that had arrived during the spring and summer were barely trained and intensive work by some of the old sweats was essential to bring the new boys and their mounts up to standard.[39]

The British and French made their first assault on Sebastopol on 7 June 1855, the British attacking the quarries before the Redan and the French the Mamelon. The French attack on the Mamelon was essential for the success of the British attack on the quarries because the Mamelon enfiladed the quarries. Both allied assaults were successful, though with heavy losses, and Russian counter-attacks were driven off [47, 138]. Following further bombardment, the infantry of the French and British armies attacked the Russian defences on 18 June. Poorly coordinated and executed, the attacks failed, with heavy losses, and a few weeks later Raglan succumbed to disease along with a number of senior officers: Simpson succeeded Raglan. The failure of the attack depressed the allied camps but, on 16 August, the French and Sardinians repulsed a Russian attack across the Chernaya River, with heavy losses. Sardinia had joined the alliance in January 1855.

Another attempt was made against Sebastopol on 8 September and this time the French succeeded against the Malakoff. The British attack on the Redan was repulsed amid dreadful scenes of carnage and panic.[40] The Russians, realising that their position in Sebastopol was now untenable, evacuated the town across a pontoon bridge to the northern shore and so ended the siege. The allies took control of a ruined and battered city and set about destroying the dockyard facilities a few months later [58]. Concurrent with the activities of the Army of the East was the campaign in the Baltic Sea and also in Asia Minor. Indeed, it is arguable that the increasing naval threat to St Petersburg, coupled with signs that both Austria and Sweden might enter the war on the allied side, was what brought the Russians to the negotiating table.[41] Negotiations opened in Paris in February 1856 and the peace treaty was signed on 30 March 1856.

---

39   Loy Smith, *Victorian RSM*, p. 189.
40   William Howard Russell, *The British Expedition to the Crimea* (London: Routledge, 1877), pp. 341–59.
41   Baumgart, *Crimean War*, pp. 193–9.

The Correspondents and Their Correspondence

The four correspondents were junior officers and therefore not privy to higher-level involvement in strategy, and all four related camp rumours and 'reports' in their letters home. With the exception of Hutton, there was a diligence and regularity of correspondence home. The letters were written to family and friends and this has an influence on the content of the text since young sons would not wish to alarm their mothers and siblings. They were more explicit and frank with letters to their fathers, brothers and male friends. Much of the correspondence is transactional, with lists of what they want or expect. The unreliability, through incompetence or corruption or both, of the carrier personnel at Constantinople was a view shared by three of the four subalterns. These young officers were not controversial figures but they experienced at first hand the results of controversial decisions. They expressed their reactions to decisions that made events and circumstances worse rather than better. Their morale, resourcefulness and determination to survive in the Crimean winter, reward comparison and reflection. As the winter progressed their morale declined and their dissatisfaction with the senior commanders of the army increased. They expressed these sentiments privately and in a number of instances requested that their views remain confidential.

The original letters of Fisher-Rowe and Phillips must be presumed lost for their descendants have no idea of their present location, if they exist at all. A typed manuscript of Phillips's letters, bound and in a presentation box, came on the market some years ago. The manuscript is on very thin paper and the font style suggests the copy was made at the beginning of the twentieth century. Descendants of Edward Phillips have confirmed that this is how the bound typescript was disseminated to family members. As well as the bound manuscript, there are two letters in the box. One from W. Baring Pemberton, the author of *Battles of the Crimean War*,[42] is dated 16 June 1960 and requests access to the letters and getting them 'out of the safe deposit box'. An acknowledgement to the letters appears in his bibliography. There is also a small portrait photograph of Edward Phillips as an old man. A volume of the manuscript's contents was published for the family but has never appeared to be available for sale through antiquarian booksellers or at auction. It is likely that the text of the Phillips letters is unedited for he was alive when the originals were transcribed. Copies of the text were reprinted and bound in Hong Kong

---

42   W. Baring Pemberton, *Battles of the Crimean War* (London: Batsford, 1962).

by another member of the Phillips family in the 1960s, but on a very limited scale and exclusively for the family. The Marquess of Anglesey used the manuscript letters of Edward Phillips when writing *The History of the British Cavalry* and attributed their availability to Hugh E. Sutton Esq., Phillips's grandson, who, at that time, was the owner.[43]

A descendant of Fisher-Rowe humorously remarked that the original letters were at the bottom of the lake at Thorncombe, the family seat in Surrey. The letters were transcribed and published in August 1907, under the title 'Extracts from Letters of E. R. Fisher-Rowe (late Captain 4th Dragoon Guards) During the Crimean War, 1854–55' for private circulation, by Edward's son, Major L. R. Fisher-Rowe, Grenadier Guards. In the introduction, Major Fisher-Rowe states that he read the letters in the winter of 1906 and thought 'it would be interesting to the family if extracts were printed'. The disappearance of the originals means that the editorial process must remain a mystery. There is a tantalising statement from Major Fisher-Rowe for the letter of 11 October 1855: 'A long letter describing a number of photographs which he sent home.' What these images were and who took them is at the moment unknown. What is known, though, is that the famous photographer Roger Fenton took two images of Fisher-Rowe in the spring of 1855, with other officers and soldiers as well as Mrs Rogers. A card-bound photocopy of the 1907 edition was produced by Pallas Armata in 2002, otherwise copies of this collection of letters are rarely seen. Some of the text of Fisher-Rowe's letters appeared in a paper entitled 'Some Adventures of a Cornet of Horse in the Crimean War' by Kenneth Macrae Moir in 1938, but fewer than 200 copies of this paper were published.

The original letters of Fiennes Wykeham Martin are at present in the archives of the Centre for Kentish Studies.[44] The letters were published in 1868; the process of collecting and editing the collection was done by his stepmother, Matilda Wykeham Martin. She wrote in the introduction that 'I have been induced to have the greater part of them printed for private circulation, thinking some portions may be interesting to the surviving relatives and a few friends'. It has been possible to compare the original letters with the edited text and it appears that the collection has been 'refined'. Opinions and comments that might have upset those still living or related to the persons criticised were omitted. Most of the letters to Philip Wykeham Martin have been omitted and also a letter to Ralph Pelham Nevill was left out. This correspondence is in its nature

43   Anglesey, *History of British Cavalry*, vol. 2, p. 466.
44   Centre for Kentish Studies, Maidstone, CK5-U24 C6.

more masculine and forthright. Clearly Fiennes Wykeham Martin felt less inhibited and more able to express his views and complaints to these correspondents. In this respect the inclusion of the rejected letters and edited passages combine to provide a truer account of writer. Bound copies of the 'Letters Written from the Crimea to Several Members of His Family' occasionally appear in the catalogues of antiquarian and second-hand booksellers but they are usually described as 'scarce'.

The originals of the Hutton letters are to be found in the Victoria and Albert Museum[45] together with the papers and swords of Alfred Hutton, Thomas Hutton's brother, who was a celebrated swordsman. Mrs Helen Earle, a descendant, transcribed the letters. The text of the correspondence related to Hutton's experiences at Balaklava was published in the regimental journal of the 4th Hussars in October 1954 on the centenary of the battle.

The collection of letters in this volume will expand the stock of knowledge related to experiences in the Crimea and will complement existing publications in general, and those on the cavalry of the British Army in particular. They fill a gap in the readily available sources that cover the Crimean War from the point of view of young cavalry officers and reveal that the decline in morale amongst cavalry officers was comprehensive as the campaign unfolded in 1854, but recovered as the weather and conditions improved in 1855. They also indicate that a scandal was quietly and effectively averted when most of those who wanted to sell out were unsuccessful. Britain had gone to war in the east with an unprepared, under-strength and under-equipped army. After Turkish success on the Danube, the British with their French allies had gone to the Crimea in ignorance of the nature and character of the land and the enemy. Mistakes and poor decisions led to the 'half siege' of Sebastopol and a catalogue of maladministration, incompetence and neglect caused great suffering. The rationalisation of the administration of the army, though undramatic, was perhaps the most profound benefit to the service.

---

45 Victoria and Albert Museum, London, Hutton Bequest.

Note on editorial method

The letters here are given without their salutations and signatures. The heading indicates to whom the letter was addressed. Many of Fisher-Rowe's letters, as originally published, did not include a salutation, so these letters have no heading.

Where original letters have underlining for emphasis this has been put into italics for the reader's ease. Editorial interpolations or conjecture where the originals are difficult to decipher are given in square brackets.

Acknowledgements

For assistance with the letters of Edward Rowe Fisher-Rowe, I am indebted to Francis Greenacre, Mrs G. Paleologo, Tim Capon, Julian Delmar-Morgan and Rod Robinson, CWRS.

For assistance with the letters of Thomas Hutton I am indebted to Mrs Helen Earle, Ms Carol Haselwood, Tom Drury, and Sally Williams of the Library of the Victoria and Albert Museum.

For assistance with the letters of Edward Phillips I am indebted to Mr Michael Phillips, Mr Tim Phillips, Mr Jeremy Phillips and Ms S. Bezencenet.

For assistance with the letters of Fiennes Wykeham Martin I would like to thank Lord Cornwallis, The Centre for Kentish Studies, Leeds Castle and Dr Douglas Austin, CWRS.

My grateful thanks to Bridget Geoghegan, a descendant of John Reilly, 4th Light Dragoons and 8th Hussars, for genealogical details, and to Mr C. Astley Sparke, for manuscript copies of letters related to the death of Lieutenant Henry Astley Sparke.

I would also like to acknowledge the invaluable assistance of the staff of the National Archives at Kew, especially Ms Julie Ash.

For assistance and advice with the manuscript I would like to thank Ian Beckett, James Beach and Annie Jackson.

Major Fiennes Wykeham Martin, c. 1860. Credit: The Army Museums Ogilby Trust.

Fiennes Wykeham Martin

Charles Wykeham Martin, Esq. of Leeds Castle, Kent, and Chacombe Priory, Northants, married Jemima Isabella, daughter of the Fifth Earl Cornwallis, on 12 April 1828. Their first child, Philip, was born in January 1829. Their second child, Fiennes, the author of the letters from the Crimea, was born on 1 November 1831, the third son, Cornwallis, was born in June 1833, and a daughter, Maria, was born in 1836. Jemima died in December 1836. Charles Wykeham Martin was married again on 18 June 1838 to Matilda, the second daughter of Sir John Trollope, 6th Baronet. From this second marriage there was a son, Fairfax, born on 12 July 1842.[1]

In a letter to Horse Guards written in August 1841, the new Mrs Wykeham Martin did her best to promote the future career of her young stepson. Even though he had not yet reached his tenth birthday, she tried 'putting his name down' for a commission in the Royal Horse Guards. She hoped that the Commander-in-Chief, Lord Hill, would consider her request. The reply she received was very considered and tactful: 'Fiennes Wykeham Martin is somewhat younger than those whose names are usually admitted in the lists of candidates for a commission', and 'he would make a memo of her request conveyed'.[2]

Fiennes Wykeham Martin was educated at Eton, where he showed an enthusiasm and prowess for rowing and won the two-oared race for silver sculls with G. Robertson and Ralph Nevill, the latter steering. As well as rowing, he was a keen rider and came second in the Grand Military Steeple-chase at Northampton, even though he was a late entry to the race. At Eton he made friends with young men from similar backgrounds and he would later renew their acquaintance in the Crimea. Young, athletic and a good rider, he was a most suitable prospect for a career as

---

1   *Burke's Landed Gentry 1937* (London: Shaw Publishing, 1937), pp. 1542–3.
2   TNA, WO31/973.

a cavalry officer. In the months before his commission was purchased he had to provide a variety of different proofs to the army. He demonstrated that he had been confirmed by the Lord Bishop of Oxford in 1848, and also produced a tutor's report from Eton. The sum of £850 was lodged with the regimental agents on 10 April 1850 and confirmation sent to Lieutenant General Lord Fitzroy Somerset.[3]

Wykeham Martin joined the 4th Light Dragoons on 12 April 1850 as a cornet by purchase. By 1854 he was the senior cornet in the regiment, which meant that he would be first in the queue if a vacancy occurred, unless a richer candidate appeared. The Adjutant was Lieutenant George Ellis who, as a brass founder, had originally enlisted into the regiment as a trooper in 1824 and had been commissioned into the 15th Hussars in 1847. Ellis then transferred back to the 4th Light Dragoons in the following year. In the Crimea he became ill and his infirmity led to Wykeham Martin assuming the temporary role as Adjutant to the regiment. Officers promoted from the ranks often filled the roles of Quartermaster and Adjutant and, if a soldier was intelligent, sober and literate, there was the opportunity to become an officer without purchase. Officers who did purchase their rank would find these duties an unattractive prospect. A war, though, offered an opportunity for 'a step' without purchase due to vacancies caused by death in battle. A perusal of the *Army List* for 1854 shows this clearly. With the deaths in the battle of Balaklava of Major John Halkett and Lieutenant Henry Sparke, the death from disease of Lieutenant John Marshall and the transfer out of the regiment of Lieutenant the Hon. Hedworth Hyllton Joliffe, there was plenty of movement in the list. Thus, one who was commissioned from the ranks to take up administrative duties was Regimental Sergeant Major Henry Jennings.[4]

By the time Wykeham Martin's regiment sailed, the focus of operations in the east had already shifted. The opening letters [1–7] reveal the hurried and frantic preparations prior to embarkation on the *Simla*. The letters written after embarkation [8–10] begin to point to the incompetence that inexperience engendered. Nonetheless, the letters written after arriving in the east initially reveal a breezy and surprising optimism regarding how the campaign might unfold. Wykeham Martin was preoccupied with receiving necessaries via the post, disgusted with the lack of organisation and also the sickness that afflicted both armies as they languished in the heat at Varna. His last letters prior to embarkation

---

3   Ibid.
4   TNA, WO31/1466.

for the Crimea from Varna reveal doubts about the practicability of conducting a campaign against Sebastopol so late in the year, against a strong fortress and opposed by a large Russian field army.

When the army landed in the Crimea, Wykeham Martin's letters become more sporadic [11–13]. He had much to do and the opportunity for regular correspondence diminished. The choice of vocabulary when Wykeham Martin informs his family that, at the Alma, 'we had nothing to do with it except looking on', shows that the joke that Lucan had become 'Lord Look On' since the affair at the Bulganek persisted [12]. When the army marched again, Wykeham Martin's regiment was in the rear, behind the 4th Division. The role as rearguard was unpopular and uncomfortable. The sick from the army were scattered in such numbers that they gave the appearance of a battlefield. As well as this, the 4th Light Dragoons were in the dusty wake of the thousands of marching infantry in front of them. The rearguard also, because of their position, had the leftovers of any food and forage encountered by the leading troops.

At Balaklava on 25 October 1854 the 4th Light Dragoons were in the third line of the advance and numbered 11 officers and 115 NCOs and men. They lost two officers killed and two wounded, 16 NCOs and men killed, and 16 taken prisoner, of whom six died in captivity. Over half the regiment's horses were killed in the battle or shot for wounds. This loss meant the regiment had fewer than 100 horses left to fulfil its duties; Wykeham Martin describes the 4th Light Dragoons as 'a perfect skeleton of a regiment' [13]. Unsurprisingly, the two leading regiments in the charge, the 17th Lancers and the 13th Light Dragoons, lost most horses. Due to the losses of officers in the regiment there were promotions, Wykeham Martin becoming a lieutenant on 26 October 1854, without purchase. After the battles of Balaklava and Inkerman, Lord George Paget, the commanding officer of the 4th, applied to sell out and returned home. Command of the 4th Light Dragoons went to Major Alexander Low, of whom Robert Portal wrote, 'he makes the army his profession, and though he is not the sort of man I like, being quite an anti-drawing room man, he is about the best cavalry soldier out here'.[5]

Following Balaklava and Inkerman, Wykeham Martin noted that the army still had a 'mild opinion' of Raglan despite holding him responsible for the increasingly uncomfortable position [16]. Apart from the military situation, the men had not been out of their clothes for six weeks, and had been sleeping on the ground and under canvas with the prospect

---

5   Portal, *Letters from the Crimea*, p. 91.

of wintering in the Crimea. Through November and into December [20–3] Wykeham Martin endured the pain of seeing the Light Cavalry Brigade wither away. Correspondingly his opinion of those in command declined. To add to his miseries, Wykeham Martin was detached from his regiment and on duty with the 2nd Division in December and was therefore deprived of the company of his brother officers with whom he could at least commiserate. By the end of the year, Wykeham Martin had concluded that Raglan was not fit to command [24–6].

The winter continued to take its toll though, mercifully, the cavalry were camped in the valley below the Chersonese Uplands so had some small degree of shelter from the freezing winds that assaulted the infantry on the plain before Sebastopol. By the end of February, Wykeham Martin was back with his regiment and enjoying quite a healthy diet, the railway from Balaklava to the siege lines was making good progress and some of the huts had been erected. The improvement in the weather also lifted the spirits of the army and the tone of Wykeham Martin's letters is more optimistic. He mentions the arrival of the photographer, Roger Fenton, and his assistants [36]. One of the assistants was Marcus Fitzell Sparling, a former trooper in the regiment, which may explain why Fenton took a number of images of groups of officers and servants of the 4th Light Dragoons and their camp.

Letters in April and May 1855 were written from Scutari where Wykeham Martin had been sent to join the drafts from England. He was disgruntled at having to leave the Crimea before Sebastopol had fallen and clearly imagined he would not return before this event [39]. He was mistaken, of course, and he was soon at the front again, reporting on the attack on Sebastopol on 6 June [47] and Raglan's death [48]. It is possible that he wrote home to describe the failure of the allied attacks of 18 June, but no letters are extant for the middle part of June. Nor does Wykeham Martin mention the fall of the city in September, conceivably because of the British failure before the Redan compared to that of the French at the Malakov. Wykeham Martin became a captain on 31 August 1855

The regiment went with the expedition to Eupatoria in October 1855 in an effort to attack and harass the Russian lines of communication. The Anglo-French force found the terrain and environment demanding. There was a serious lack of water and the force was insufficient to do much harm to the Russians. The expedition was called off at the end of November and the cavalry sailed for Scutari. Wykeham Martin's letters ceased for this part of the war and he explained later that this was because there was no regular post from Eupatoria [63]. When the 4th

Light Dragoons left the east, Wykeham Martin was not with them. He was acting as aide-de-camp to Lord George Paget, who had returned to the Crimea, and they were among the last to leave. He travelled home with Lord George and Lady Paget [71, 72].

When he returned to Leeds Castle in Kent there was a triumphal celebration organised by the village and Leeds Castle. Wykeham Martin's father wrote to a friend,

> there was therefore a personal wish to shew [sic] him some mark of approbation, and although the movement commenced with our own people it was so well responded to that the whole village was decorated with triumphal arches, flags & flowers, whilst 96 horsemen, 23 carriages & some 1500 to 2000 persons on foot assembled to escort him for the last mile and a half. When they reached the house they presented him with a complimentary address, to which he briefly replied, and afterwards we proceeded to partake of a luncheon which I had provided. To this about 150 persons sat down and 100 more at the refreshments in the servants hall. Of course some toasts were proposed appropriate to the occasion and my guests then moved about the lawn till dusk. We had particularly a very fine day and it was a very pretty sight to those who merely felt a common interest in what was taking place but to us it was as you may suppose, exciting in the highest degree when we considered how great had been the risks our son had encountered and how many amongst our own connections had severely suffered in their families, we felt we could not be thankful enough to see our brave 'Captain' safe at home.[6]

Wykeham Martin changed his name by royal licence to Cornwallis in October 1859. A quieter military career followed the Crimean War. His prowess as a jockey continued and he participated in military steeplechase meetings.[7] He became a major in July 1860. He was a popular officer in the regiment and his friends knew him by the nickname of 'Nick'. There is a story recounted in the 1868 publication of his letters that when he sold out in May 1863 the entire regiment turned out to see him off, and that a court-martial, including the prisoner, suspended their serious business in hand to bid farewell to the departing officer.

---

6   D. A. H. Cleggett, *Leeds Castle through Nine Centuries* (Maidstone: Leeds Castle Foundation, 2001), pp. 110–11.

7   *The Times*, 30 March 1860, 'Grand Military Open Steeplechase, Northampton'.

Fiennes Wykeham Cornwallis married the daughter of John Mott, Esq., of Barningham Hall, Norfolk, on 29 July 1863 and had two sons and a daughter from the marriage. The first son, Fiennes Stanley Wykeham Cornwallis, was born on 27 May 1864 and created 1st Baron Cornwallis in 1927.

His own premature death on 24 April 1867 at Chacombe Priory was preceded by a fall from his horse while out hunting. His horse either trod on or kicked his head. Although he seemed to recover from the accident, some time later he was taken ill with what was thought to be an abscess on the brain. The historian Alexander Kinglake, referring to Fiennes Wykeham Martin, wrote that Thackeray, the novelist, had once chanced to meet this young officer in society, and 'spoke of him as coming up to the very idea which he had formed of a "brave, modest soldier". Cornet Wykeham Martin survived the Crimean War, but died young, and deeply loved.'[8]

---

8   Kinglake, *Invasion of the Crimea*, vol. 5, p. 238, footnote.

I

Wykeham Martin to his brother Philip[1]

[Letter omitted in the 1868 publication]
Yeovil July 1st [1854]
I will pay you the £35 I would do more only I do not think I shall have it to give. I think I shall be able to get a man in Exeter cheaper than 25s a week but if I cannot I must take your friend, I send the old grey up by the next train after having driven him 16 miles because [his?] Master likes me I cannot have a horse box tomorrow on account of the troops going by rail. I took away 1 doz. socks and left ten others in my room so I suppose somebody has taken them. Did you order the shooting boots at Martins the sabretache you can send a servant for. I should like the things as soon as you can send them as then I can see if I want anything more and time is getting short. I do not quite know which animal you have bought but I dare say it is all right. I will write again tomorrow when I see the head quarters fellows and say what else I want. I shall telegraph to you what time the train arrives.

2

Wykeham Martin to his brother Philip

[Letter omitted from the 1868 publication]
Trowbridge July 2nd 1854
I write a line in great haste to say that we have heard from Head quarters that we are to embark immediately and that it will be hard work to get ones service kit in time I shall therefore employ you to get a good many things such as a Deane and Adams pistol sword Wilkinson and if you know of a good strong sound horse that would make a second charger at a moderate price I had better buy it and send my other to you to sell for me. I will write immediately I get the official order and then you can if you will buy these things for me.

---

1   His older brother (1829–78).

3

Wykeham Martin to his brother Philip

[Letter omitted from the 1868 publication]
Trowbridge July 2nd [1854]
I write again to say that you may order me some saddle bags at Peat's [London saddlers] in Bond Street close to your hotel, also a telescope in a leather case with strap to sling over the shoulder also a leather case to hold a couple of knives and forks and spoons a pair of scissors needles buttons and thread razor and shaving brush. They need not put the things in only make the case, the thing I mean is exactly like what the privates have and is called a holdall, it rolls up and goes in your valise, I shall also want a camp kettle and dish to hold what little grub I get and a circle of thick India Rubber waterproof to put on the bottom of my tent about 6 feet from the centre all round. I have written to a man for my bed furniture and will tell him to send it to you so that when you have collected the lot you can send them to me at Exeter where the service troops are to assemble. This is giving you a deal of trouble I am afraid but although they have not actually told me that I am to go I know I shall have to and we are to be off directly consequently
[Letter ends unsigned, presumably the following sheet is missing]

4

Wykeham Martin to his brother Philip

[Letter omitted from the 1868 publication]
Devonport July 10th [1854]
I write you my final epistle to say that I have found the kit and I am now complete. The horse will arrive Tuesday Joliffe will let you know about it. He will also require some money which you can let him have, I have drawn a cheque for £100 which Bills has backed. I had a little difficulty about it so will you see that it is all right, and draw the remainder of my balance to your account and whatever more you want in October and let me know what, I enclose another blank cheque for whatever you may draw in October. [And] now old boy again thanking you for all your trouble and hoping to find you & [illegible] all right when I return and thanking the [illegible] for her final present.

PS If instead of sending the horse on to Leeds you were to sell him for
£100 it would pay you and there would be a surplus over for me you can
do as you like about that. We sail tomorrow afternoon give me a line as
soon as we get there and I will to you.

I like the horse very well only he won't leave the other horses and won't
stand the sword as yet but I will soon teach him my [illegible] is better.

5

Wykeham Martin to his brother Philip

[Letter omitted from the 1868 publication]
[No date or place]
The horse has arrived safe though not understanding your telegraphic
messages I went down about 40 times to the station to look for him and
the kit. Why on earth has it not come having been ordered 1st it is the last
to come, Gardener has telegraphed to me to say that he has sent no pack
saddle Hew Jon got one at Peats if not send one immediately to Plymouth
Royal Hotel it is too bad of them not having sent it before as there is no
chance of getting it altered. What bed have you sent or have you ordered
the bullock trunks, the helper you sent has not got a damn of money was
15s short by his journey and seems not to have the last idea what he is to
do. I shall send my 1st Charger up on Monday morning by the first train,
will you forward him to Leeds unless you know anyone that will give
£100 for him. Cannot you come to Plymouth on Monday. Hamburger
is going to send his bill in to you but do not pay him until the October
dividends are in as I find I shall have to take all that I have got at Hoare's
to pay for things here and in Turkey. With my best love to both & many
thanks for the trouble you have been at although I am afraid I shall start
without a bit now.

6

Wykeham Martin to his stepmother[2]

Ashburton, July 27th 1854 [Incorrect transcription in the 1868 publication, should read July 17th]
I have just time to write a line to say my 1st charger will probably arrive on Wednesday, also some boxes; I shall send one portmanteau back by the Simla, it will arrive about October. Our men marched off in beautiful order this morning, not a man absent or drunk, which is more than other regiments can say. I will write again if I have time.

7

Wykeham Martin to his stepmother

Devonport, July 23rd 1854 [Incorrect transcription in the 1868 publication, should read 18th July]
I write you one more hurried note to say that I have arrived at Devonport, and embark tomorrow morning, and shall sail tomorrow afternoon most probably. I have got everything all right, helper horse and everything. I like my new animal very well, only he will not leave the ranks, which looks as if he has been a charger or trooper before, also he does not like the sword, but I will soon teach him that * * * * *[3]

I must say, although I like going out very much, I shall not be sorry to be back again; if we only stay two years it will be just what I wanted, to see other countries before I settle down; I can see Europe in a wedding tour. I will now wish you all good bye, I hope to find Papa,[4] Maria,[5] Fairfax[6] and yourself as well and strong as you are now; tell the two latter and Papa that I am sorry I have not had time to write to them all, but I know you read out the letters when there is anything in them.

---

2 Matilda, daughter of Sir John Trollope Bt (1798–1855).
3 Asterisks in the 1868 published version perhaps indicating an expletive?
4 Charles Wykeham Martin of Leeds Castle, Kent.
5 His sister (1836–1900).
6 His younger half-brother (1842–58).

8

Wykeham Martin to his brother Philip[7]

Malta July 24th 1854 [incorrect on the original letter; the *Simla* arrived on 26 July, unless the letter was started on 24 July and the word 'Malta' added later]

[*will you go to Peat and tell him he is the worst tradesman in all London. He has sent me a serviceable pair of Douglas bags which I never ordered as I have bullock trunks are [of no?] use I ordered also a brown leather sabretache with deep tache pocket which I ordered also a holdall which he himself sent me Allecs[?] others to buy to the wallets which I ordered and also telegraphed for at the last moment you have not sent, Hamburgers sabretache and Nickey's lamp are not sent but have sent a Bulls eye the which I have already got and is not of the slightest use, if you would but have sent the things to Exeter all this would have been obviated. However it cannot be helped otherwise than by not paying Peat for the wallets which he has not sent or the Douglas Bags and sabretache which I never ordered or Hamburger for his sabretache which he never sent.*]

We had an awful night the day we left England, the ship being very narrow rolled tremendously; the horses were down on every side, the men awfully sick were obliged to stand to their heads and get them up to prevent them falling. We were obliged to kill two, and if it had gone on we should have lost every horse in the ship; I hope never to witness such a scene again, the men behaved beautifully, and won great praise from the sailors, standing at their horses' heads when they were so ill, they could hardly stand themselves. We are getting on better now, and are off the coast of Portugal, we shall be at Gibraltar in about three days and a half, which is very quick from Plymouth. [*I am sorry to say my [illegible] is very bad but I hope the sea will do it good*]. The horse arrangements are excessively bad [*but that is to be expected in a ship fitted up by the government, if they had left it to the company it would have been done very well*]. The part I dislike most is the watches, walking about the deck for four hours day and night among horses, [*stinking like the devil*], the stench awful, biting at you as you pass and making a tremendous noise, we are going a great pace, 15 miles an hour, it is fearfully hot, especially down in the hold where the men and horses are, I will not write any more today, but will send this from Malta as soon as we get there.

---

7   Passages in italics were not included in the 1868 published collection and have been restored from the originals.

Monday. – We have passed Gibraltar and are now well in the Mediterranean, it is very hot, [*and really the cruelty to animals exercised by the government is so bad that I hope it will be represented to the Times. To give you some idea of it I cannot lay on the deck in a flannel suit without perspiring and it would be better if they hadn't crammed the ship*]. They have crammed the ship so full that there is not an inch to spare anywhere, and there are about 20 horses on each side of the boiler, their noses about a foot from it; one is dead already from the heat, no air can get to them, perfectly foaming with sweat. In fact the black hole of Calcutta[8] must have been an ice-house to it. It is a regular case of 'penny wise and pound foolish', as [*in trying to get 20 extra number of horses there, they will lose about 20 each being worth by the time it gets there about £20. Some of our fellows talk about writing to the Times. I hope they will, at all events you can talk loudly about it in the club and elsewhere*] trying to get the extra number of horses in, there will be many lost. I shall try to land at Malta [*and see Charles Trollope*] to have a look at the town. I send this letter to you and you can [*send*] pass it on to Leeds Castle [*when you have read it, but you had better scratch out the part about my little complaint*]. We have made the quickest passage to Gibraltar that has ever been made, and hope to do the same to Malta and Varna [*If we winter in Constantinople I shall want quantities of things sent out which you can send to Rich the Master Tailor at the depot and he will forward them to the regiment, one large parcel costing more than a small one*]. Let me know when they take Cronstadt as it is very doubtful whether I shall see a paper or not. I have just opened my kit and tried to put the bullock trunks on the pack saddle, but find it impossible, as the saddle came from Peats and the trunks from Gardener, and the former is not constructed to carry bullock trunks. The consequence is that I shall be obliged to leave my trunks behind, and as they form my bed I shall not have that important article, and shall have to lie on the ground, the worst thing we can do [*I must say I wish I had made that scoundrel Peat send the things to Exeter when I telegraphed for them as then I could have got it all altered, now I cannot*]. I will write to let you know how I get on.

Ship Simla Tuesday 27th [25th]

July 28 [26th]. It is fearfully hot, two horses gone mad from heat and being crammed up in the hold. We have just sighted Malta.

---

8   A reference to the notorious incident at Fort William in India in 1756 when 146 people were crammed into a tiny room and left for hours in intolerable heat with no water. When the room was opened only 23 had survived.

9

Wykeham Martin to his father

Constantinople August 2nd 1854

We arrived here yesterday having been delayed by trying to tow a Transport up the Dardanelles, everything here is in the greatest state of confusion. We were not expected, and they don't know what to do with us; the Admiral at first said we were to wait till he sent to Lord Raglan at Varna, and then we were to sail last night, now I believe we are to go at 3 o'clock, but it will be probably altered again when we get to Varna. I do not know what they can do with us, as they are going to make a movement in the Crimea to take Sevastopol on the 15th; so if they disembark us we shall have to embark again directly. It will do the horses good to be out of the ship a little while, but on the other hand we shall lose a good many in the operation. It is a pity they did not allow us to bring out Bat horses, as in the hurry and confusion of getting the troops away from Varna it is ten to one that we shall be able to get away these, and so shall lose a good deal of our baggage. A Russian soldier has shot one of the Captains of the fleet, by name Parker, also a Russian steamer contrived to get out of Sevastopol and take two Turkish ships, one laden with coal, the Russian filled herself up with coal and then burnt the ships.

I am sorry to say dysentery and cholera are making great ravages among the troops, at least so I hear. Lord Duplin and some officers of the Rifles have gone home almost dead, I believe it is more healthy in winter, though intensely cold. Constantinople is a magnificent city to look at from the harbour, but when you get on shore it is the filthiest hole, with infamously paved narrow streets, that you can imagine. There is a rumour here that Prussia declared war with Austria, but we do not know if it is true. I went on shore at Malta and we saw Charles Trollope and his wife, he was very well and in good spirits, but Mrs Trollope has had a bad Maltese fever and was not looking well.

Since writing the above we have started for Varna and shall land tomorrow; we have just met an officer from the Guards who gives a very bad account of the Camp, the men are completely done up with dysentery and cholera, and dying like rotten sheep; 45 of the Rifles died in one week, Therapia and Scutari are full of sick officers. The Commissariat is very bad indeed, and altogether the army is so paralysed that the *light division* could not move five miles the other day; so there is not much chance of a move to the Crimea.

The Greeks and Turks about Varna hate us, and officers riding out have been repeatedly shot at, and the other day they fired into the Artillery Camp; the gunners however went out and took them prisoners: so you see you must not believe all you read in the Times of the happy and contented state of the army in the East. I hear all the men who went determined to rough it have come round to making themselves as comfortable as they can. There is also a *rumour* that Sir George Brown and Lord Raglan are going to give it up in the winter, and that General Cathcart is coming out to take command; however, I cannot vouch for this. Send me a letter please as soon as you can, and let me know how they get on in the Baltic. I am going to send Maria a pair of Turkish slippers if I can, they look very grand, I will get you plenty of things *when* I come home. Have you received my little horse yet? you can sell him if you can get him a good master. You need not be frightened by my accounts of the Camp, but I merely mentioned the state of things to let you know that it is not quite the leather and prunella[9] sort of life that the Times made out.

We came up the Bosphorus this evening, and a more beautiful sight I never saw in my life, the scenery was magnificent, a sort of Richmond the whole way up. I think the Turks a most disgusting race of people and not worth fighting for, they take no more notice of you than they do of a dog; the only notice they take of you is to *do* you as much as possible; I would almost sooner fight for a Russian if it was not a treason to say so. We have got two of Omar Pasha's Aides de Camps on board, they cannot speak a word of anything but their own language, and so we are not particularly happy. If I have time I will give you a description of our landing tomorrow morning, but in case I have not, I will wish you good bye and love to all.

3rd part – We arrived at Varna and begun to disembark, you never saw such a scene of utter neglect, no one came off to give us orders for three hours, and at last told us to begin with *one* boat, and gave us no men to tow it, so we have only landed 31 today, with no tents or anything to eat. We go to the Crimea on the 15th. The cholera is very bad here. They have lost over 200 men and two officers died last night; the sooner we get away the better. The names of the officers are Col. March and Cromarty of the Guards, they tell me the men of the latter walk about bent double with dysentery. If there is as much confusion and time lost landing in the Crimea we shall lose every man in the army. Sir George Brown was

---

9   Meaning nothing of any importance. Prunella was a sort of woollen stuff used in the uppers of ladies' boots.

nearly killed by a cannon ball going through the cabin of a steamer, he was reconnoitring near Sevastopol.

The present intention is to make a feint at the North of the Crimea and land at the South. I hope we shall lick them and then go to Constantinople for the winter; though this is a beautiful place, it is very unhealthy. Ponies are very cheap here, the price being about £5, everything else is fearfully dear; they have reduced the rations of beef to 1 lb. and no rum!! I will write again soon, we get letters every five days and can send them oftener.

10

Wykeham Martin to his father

Camp Galata, August 26th, 27th and 28th.

We have not received the mail due on the 21st, so that I suppose we shall get that and the one due on the 28th together, consequently we do not know any English news. We have not sailed for Sevastopol, but I believe we do on the 2nd of September. Both the French and English engineers say it is nearly impracticable; and the fleet say it is much too late in the year, as it is doubtful whether they could even land us, and if they did accomplish that, they declare it would be utterly impossible to take us off again on account of the westerly gales, consequently we should have to land on a rocky soil where we could not entrench ourselves, five miles from an entrenched camp of 45,000 Russians and ten from one of the strongest forts in the world, and in face of all this they are going to attempt it.

August 28th. – The mail has just come in and I see by the papers the English at home expect we have taken Sevastopol, whereas we do not start till Tuesday at the earliest, and shall have as I told you great difficulty in taking it when we get there. The light division of cavalry embark tomorrow morning, the artillery are all on board, the infantry on the 1st and 2nd, I believe; so now we are in for it. I hope when we have smashed the place they will let us come home, as this is a nasty country to live in, all the disadvantages of India with none of the comforts. Always direct your letters Army in the East, as then I receive them. I forgot to say send me out an Indian rubber tub. I see by the Illustrated[10] we are to have a change of uniform.

---

10   *The Illustrated London News.*

For three days after we land in the Crimea we are to have no tents or grub but what we can carry ourselves, which will be very little, as they are going to make us leave our Bat horses behind, which will be a loss of £15 out of my pocket. I wish they had not made us get them. You must excuse this bad writing, as I have no table or anything to write on. I hope you are not bored with my long yarns, if you are you must make Maria read them to you or tell you the pith of them. By the bye I want a compact writing case; you can get them very cheap and hold a great deal, and a lock, so that I can put money in it; and now with my best love to all and hoping you are all well, and likewise that I shall come off all right in the fight, good bye.

I I

Wykeham Martin to his stepmother

Kalamita Bay Crimea September 15th 1854
I have just time to scribble a few lines to tell you my adventures since I left Varna. In the first place we all started from Baltjick on 7th September, the most magnificent sight you ever saw, 32 sail of the line English, besides French and Turkish, convoying about 300 transports; the only drawback from it being that the cholera broke out on board the vessels. We lost three men before we left the bay,[11] among others poor Hunt[12] was taken very bad, but he has recovered a little, however I shall not be able to take him on shore with me, bad luck as usual. Sparke[13] has also been very bad, but I think he will recover enough to *land* tomorrow, although I think it will kill him. The infantry effected a landing without opposition, having dodged the Russian camp that was waiting for us; however I suppose we shall have them down upon us tomorrow. The inhabitants are very peacefully inclined towards us, giving us everything we want, but I'm afraid it will not continue. The French broke into the village (where Lord Raglan had made his headquarters) and broke up the homes, ill treated the women and stole their

---

11 Losses were 1588 Pvt. Walter Blythe, a shoemaker from Norwich, died 10 September on board ship: 1453 Pvt. Patrick Flin, a labourer from Kings County, Ireland, died 12 September on board ship; and 1553 Pvt. William Osborne, a servant from Colchester, died on board ship 13 September. See TNA, WO12/659, Muster Roll 4th Light Dragoons.

12 Cornet George Warwick Hunt, 4th Light Dragoons, from Plymouth, Devon. Hunt died from tuberculosis in Torquay in October 1906.

13 Lieutenant Henry Astley Sparke from Gunthorpe Hall, Norfolk, 4th Light Dragoons. See Canon W. M. Lummis and K. G. Wynn, *Honour the Light Brigade* (London: Hayward, 1973), p. 25.

poultry, which is a great bore for us after we had established a good understanding. The unfortunate infantry were out all last night in the pouring rain, and as we do not take our tents with us they must have got awfully wet, killing more of them than the bullets of the Russians. The French manage this better, as they all had their tents. This is the last letter I shall be able to write to you till we have taken Sevastopol or failed. The light cavalry will have fearfully hard work, there are so few of them (owing to Cobden) that we shall be out every night on picket duty, and as there are swarms of Cossacks here whose tactics are never to charge but to harass the enemy by continually trying to cut off their pickets, we stand a poor chance. The climate as far as I can see is very unhealthy, especially for sleeping on the ground, as we shall have to do, as we land with nothing but what we stand up in, and shall remain so till we take the place. However pluck has it, and I hope we get through. The country itself is very fertile and beautiful. A place we anchored in at first, called Eupatoria, yielded without a shot; it seemed a nice town inhabited by Jews and Germans, I believe. I received your letter of the 25th at 10 o'clock this evening, and the lights are put out at half-past, so you can imagine I have not much time.

You can sell my horse if you can get £100 for him, as I may not get back for some time, and he is getting old. I have not written to Ralph Nevill[14] yet but will as soon as I can. I have left a memorandum in my kit to say that my kit is to be sold if I am *potted*, and the proceeds to go to Papa. With love to all and hoping you are all well as I am at present, and also that I may see you all again some day.

[PS] I land tomorrow morning and shall be sent forward in out-post, nasty work after having had regular meals and a good bed, to be six weeks on shore with no bed and only salt pork, biscuit and water.

12

Wykeham Martin to his stepmother

Camp near Sevastopol, 8th October 1854

I have put off writing to you from day to day hoping that we should take Sevastopol, and then I could have written you an account of the whole campaign, but we have now been here a week and have done nothing

---

14   Ralph Pelham Nevill (1832–1914), the second son of Sir William Nevill, 1st Marquess of Abergavenny, of Birling Manor, Kent, and a schoolfriend from Eton.

except being shot at by the Russians. My last letter was from Eupatoria just before we landed. Since then we have gone through great hardships, I hope I never shall have to again; we landed without tents, and I can assure you sleeping in the open air with nothing to eat is very bad for us, luckily we have had very little rain, otherwise it would have killed the whole of us, as it is, what with the battle of Alma and sickness, we have lost a great deal of the army. We have now been nearly three weeks on shore, during which time I have slept in my clothes, boots, spurs and everything, having no clothes but what I stand up in with me, every one is the same, and I can assure you we look a ragged dirty lot. We had the ill luck to be in the rear division the whole way on the march, the consequence was we had the hardest work of anybody, and being away from our commissariat got nothing to eat for three days and nights, neither men or horses had anything but some biscuit they had saved from the previous day's rations.

You would laugh to see us when we arrive at our camping ground running to the nearest water, while others pick up bits of wood to make a fire, to boil either a piece of pork or excessively tough cow. The Rifles were so hard up one day they killed the bullock that drew their hospital cart and ate him immediately. On our third day without food we came across a herd of bullocks; but they would not let us take them, at which we were indignant. The battle of Alma fought on the 20th, you will see described better than I can in the Times; I can only say that we had nothing to do with it except looking on, for although we were within range the shot never came our way. We had a beautiful view of it the whole time, it was splendid to see the Guards and Highlanders walk up to the fort under the hottest fire Lord Raglan ever saw; they behaved beautifully, led by the Duke of Cambridge in the most plucky manner, also the light and 2nd divisions the only ones much engaged, the 33rd (Thorold's regiment)[15] suffered very severely nearly all the officers being killed or wounded; also the 23rd. Luckily for Thorold he was sick on board ship. It was a wonderful victory, as a letter from Menschikoff to the Emperor will prove: he says, speaking of Alma, 'I would sooner hold it with 40,000 for three weeks against any number of English, than Sevastopol with 100,000 against 40,000 English.'

However, the French say we ought to have taken it with much less loss if we had followed their plan and turned their flank instead of going

---

15   Ensign Henry Thorold of the 33rd Foot, another Etonian, later promoted to Lieutenant and killed at the battle of Inkerman. See Frank and Andrea Cook, *Casualty Roll for the Crimea* (London: Hayward, 1976), p. 54.

at it like a bull as we did; and I, from the little I know, think they are right. We are now in a rather ticklish position, having Sevastopol before us, and a large army behind. They made a small attack this morning, but the French drove them back. I am sorry to say that the heavy Brigade of Cavalry, in crossing from Varna, have lost 280 horses, 200 from Robertson's regiment,[16] consequently our cavalry here is useless; it is a good thing for me perhaps, as I shall have no chance of being killed, unless I am cut off on picket or patrol duty. I always keep a sharp look out, so I don't think it is likely. The Russians amuse themselves with throwing shell at our pickets, but they have only hit two men as yet. One burst close to my picket the other day but did no damage. We are going to winter in Sevastopol I hear, which I am very sorry for, as it is an awful hole. We are still dying here by shoals of cholera. Poor Joliffe,[17] the brother of our Joliffe, was taken ill at 10 one evening, and was dead by 10 next morning – hard lines after getting through Alma. You must excuse the dirt and bad writing of this epistle, as the wind is blowing the dust over this dirty piece of paper as I lie at full length on the ground, with a bad steel pen that won't mark. I received your likeness of the Governor and Maria, and think them very good. Will you send my things to the care of Messrs. Ede and Co., Constantinople, and besides what I have already asked for, some more lamb's wool socks, flannel waistcoats, and quantities of cocoa paste, preserved soup, tea, sugar, soap, and in fact any articles you think good in the eating line that do not take much room, as grub out here is dear and very bad. There is a cocoa paste made up with milk, and which we have found very useful on campaign, as it goes in a very small compass. I should like Miller's lamp out of my kit, and my servants clothes, although I think very likely the poor fellow is dead. I went over the battlefield the next day at Alma; it was the most awful sight, thousands lying dead, and wounded, groaning and crying for water; our men behaved very well to the Russians, taking care of them and giving them water as if they were Englishmen, but the French behaved in a brutal manner, even burying some of the poor creatures before they were dead, *at least so they say*. We have got over 130 guns, independent of the French and the Fleet. They are none of them to be fired till they are all ready, and

---

16 Gilbert Metcalfe Robertson, Eton and Merton College, Oxford, and Lieutenant in the 1st Royal Dragoons, Cornet, by purchase, 1st Royal Dragoons, 12 May 1853, Lieutenant, 20 December 1854. He survived the war. He was also an old schoolfriend. See *Hart's New Army List 1855*, p. 128.

17 Hylton Joliffe, a captain in the Coldstream Guards, died of cholera on 8 October. His brother, Hedworth Joliffe, was a Lieutenant in the 4th Light Dragoons. Both were educated at Eton. See Lummis and Wynn, *Honour the Light Brigade*, p. 24.

then the whole with the Fleet are to begin at the same minute by signal; won't it make a row and astonish the natives. I have just received your letter, no. 6, saying you have received the news of our safe landing, you also say you have sent the boots. I have not received them yet, but I dare say they are somewhere and I shall get them in time. I am sorry to hear of Billy's father; it was only yesterday I had heard from Billy, saying they had cholera there, but were not afraid of it. My private servant, Friend, wishes £5 of his wages to be sent to his father and mother. Now the only way I can get this done is to send a cheque to Philip, asking him to pay it, but I do not like doing it in that way as he never will use the cheque, will *you* see about it?

The attack is to begin in three days, but I hear firing close by, so I must conclude, as we shall most likely be turned out. All the Heavy Cavalry were out this morning to repel an attack in the rear. Best love to all.

13

Wykeham Martin to his stepmother

Camp near Balaklava. October 27th 1854

I write you a line to allay any fears you may have about me, as you will see by the Times that the Light Cavalry Brigade were let into a sort of Chillianwallah trap and cut to pieces. It is unfortunately too true; but I am one of the lucky ones that escaped, although our regiment and the 11th Hussars went further than any into the gorge. The facts of the case are these. Lately the Cavalry have had nothing to do but guard Balaklava, and keep the communication open between it and Sevastopol, and have not been disturbed by the enemy except in occasional skirmishes with the pickets and videttes, when suddenly the other morning at day-break they made an attack on a line of small forts kept by the Turks in front of our position. The Cavalry, who were all out and mounted for the usual morning parade, that we always have an hour or two before day-break, so as to be ready for any attack, went immediately to their support, with a troop of Horse Artillery; but could you believe it, the Turks left all the forts, some even before they were fired; the consequence was a swarm of Cavalry made a dash into Balaklava itself, but they were met on the left by the 93rd Highlanders, who are not in the habit of running away like the Turks, and sent back minus a few men, and on the right by the Heavy Cavalry, who likewise sent them to the right about, the Light

Brigade being too far to the left to pursue. This was a mistake, and now comes the melancholy part of my story. The Light Brigade were ordered to the front, and Nolan, 'my friend', brought an order for us to attack them down a long valley they had retreated into; now to understand why we did this rash and stupid act, you must know that lately there has been some stupid chaff about the Cavalry being afraid of the Cossacks, and Nolan had made some remarks about it to Lord Lucan, he is *rather suspected*, as he was the man sent to make the reconnaissance before we attacked, of having misrepresented to Lord Raglan the nature of the ground and the position of the enemy. Well, the Light Brigade advanced at a trot, and had not gone a hundred yards before we got into a shower of grapeshot bullets, round shot, and in fact every kind of missile from both sides of the valley, the enemy having got a battery on each side, and two or three regiments of sharp-shooters in the bushes. The consequence was we were enfiladed for half a mile by the hottest possible fire at about 30 to 40 yards distance, nevertheless we passed on, got beyond their fire, and captured some guns and drove back their Cavalry. But by this time we found ourselves completely cut off from our own army, about 90 of the Brigade left with a swarm of Cavalry in our front, a regiment of Russian Lancers in our rear, and all the fire to undergo again. Well the only thing to do was to get the debris together, and go at them with all our might and cut our way back, which some of us succeeded in doing, but when we got back and came to count heads we found there were only 190 left out of 700 that went into action. Poor Halkett[18] and Sparke are among the missing; Hutton[19] was shot through both legs and in the back, but will recover I think. We are now a perfect skeleton of a regiment, only having 50 left, and are therefore useless. We live in the hope of being sent home to recruit up again, and being sent out again in the spring, but I'm afraid they will hardly do that. Poor Nolan was shot the first ball.

It is quite melancholy to see the Brigade turn out, the whole being no larger than a regiment was before. The 13th Hussars [*sic*] suffered most,

---

18   Major John Thomas Douglas Halkett, 4th Light Dragoons, was born on 14 April 1816, the son of John Halkett, formerly Governor of the Bahamas. Halkett was educated at Rugby and was Cornet in the regiment in January 1835. He was Lieutenant in July 1837, Captain in October 1842, and Major in March 1850. He was killed in the retreat up the valley after the Charge. He was seen to fall after being wounded by a shell. As the remnants of his regiment passed him he was heard to exhort his men to take the money he had on his person 'for the married women at home'. It is likely he was killed and stripped by the pursuing Russians. He was married to Charlotte Mary, the daughter of Charles Heard Beague. See Lummis and Wynn, *Honour the Light Brigade*, p. 22.

19   Captain Thomas Hutton, 4th Light Dragoons. See Hutton's own account in [197] below.

having only 28 men left. Khyber Pass and Lord Gough was a fool to it, as it was useless waste of life.[20] The Russian troops when met by ours in the field invariably run away. In fact, even in the shattered state we were in, a Pole who deserted, said it was all the officers could do to keep the Infantry in the bushes from running away, for fear we should charge them. If we had waited ten minutes more for our own Infantry and the French Cavalry, we should have retaken all the forts and annihilated their army. The Russians attacked our Infantry about a mile off yesterday, and got a tremendous beating. We do not know when we shall storm the town, but I hope soon, as I am getting tired of lying on the ground with only one shirt, and am getting rheumatic in my joints, turning out at 4 o'clock in the dark; reconnoitring and standing about for hours in the damp night dew without any cloak is killing work. One night when we expected an attack, we stood the whole night with our bridles in our hands, ready to mount at a moments notice; some of the men not having laid down for two nights previously.

I am much obliged for your thinking of the writing case, and will you send me a saddle I left at home as Hunt lost mine when we had to retreat from our position, taking care however to save the brandy bottle with which he got drunk.

I hope that poor little Maria is all right again now, and that you are all well. I am afraid you will think my letters are rather egotistical, all about my own doings out here. It is quite true about poor Hare[21] being dead, Tom Tryon[22] was not at Alma, and the other was not engaged. Tell Philip I have not time to write to him, as owing to Ellis[23] being sick, I have to act as Adjutant for him, and have had lots to do all day, and we have no candles to see with at night. In fact we are glad to go to bed as soon as dark, as we turn out every morning at half-past three. You may as well add my hair brushes and another looking glass, as I have broken mine and not seen my face for weeks; we have all given up shaving, and are awfully bronzed, so that you will not know me when I get back if I do not shave.

---

20 Presumably references to the destruction of a British army in Afghanistan in January 1842, and to the then General Sir Hugh Gough's losses at Chillianwallah in January 1849 during the second Sikh War (see p. 307).

21 Captain the Hon. Charles Luke Hare, 7th Fusiliers, wounded at the battle of the Alma on 20 September and died of wounds on board the *Andes* on 22 September. He was the son of Viscount Ennismore and brother of the Earl of Listowel.

22 Captain Thomas Tryon, 7th Fusiliers.

23 Lieutenant and Adjutant George Ellis, 4th Light Dragoons, sent to Scutari on 7 October 1854 and invalided home in March of the following year. Died in 1856. See TNA, WO12/659–660, Muster Roll, 4th Light Dragoons.

Remember me to all my friends, especially Erskine,[24] and with love to all, and hoping soon to get away from this hole.

PS – Please send me out a Church Service; by some mistake Philip only sent me a Bible, and no Prayer Book. There is one my tutor gave me among my books.

14

Wykeham Martin to his brother Philip[25]

Sevastopol, November 2 1854
[*There's just time to write a line to say I am still alive and well I wrote by the last mail describing the action of Balaklava in which I was engaged.*]
I have no doubt you have seen my letter about the battle of Balaklava, in which I was engaged. The Light Brigade making the most gallant but at the same time most disastrous charge in the annals of warfare [*I have no doubt you have seen the letter. I am sorry to say that Halkett and Sparke were killed and Hutton was dangerously wounded*]. The weather here has changed now, and is fearfully cold, and has caused immense sickness in the camp, in fact we have only 16,000 men out of 30,000 left. One regiment, in fact the whole Light Brigade are mere skeletons of regiments, turning out thirty to forty men [*of a morning*] for a regiment. Will you write a line to Corney[26] [*Cornwallis*], and say I am not dead or buried as he may suppose. We are all very dirty now [*the officers of the Guards even being lousy! What would they have thought if they had been told so in London*]. I have been touched up with rheumatism already from the cold and damp, and I cannot pretend to say what the consequences would be if they intend to keep us through the winter in tents [*which is what the editor of the Times wishes. I wish I had him out here in his shirt at 4 o'clock in the morning, washing in cold water after having slept on the cold ground with one blanket*]. As to Sevastopol, I don't think it will ever be taken, as we are just as far off, to my humble comprehension. I am quite tired of hearing cannon, and certainly never wish to be under such fearful fire as we were the other day again; the old soldiers say Cavalry never were exposed to

---

24 Alexander Erskine, a neighbouring landowner in Kent.
25 Passages in italics were not included in the 1868 published collection and have been restored from the originals.
26 A nickname for Cornwallis. The full name appears in the original unedited letter.

such a fire before, and Lord Raglan said when he saw us start 'those men are going to utter destruction;' and Canrobert said, 'not a man will [*ever*] return,' and they certainly would not had the Russian cavalry been worth [*a damn*] anything. We do nothing but perpetually move our camp. We moved four times last week; no other brigade having moved since they have been here [*only these old infantry generals think it necessary to bully the Cavalry as much as possible*]. The property of deceased officers sells at enormous prices, a pair of common boots fetching 35s., a great coat £10., everything else in proportion. I have no time for more, as I have the unpleasant task of informing Mr. Sparke[27] [*Sparke's parents* in the original letter] of his son's death in my place as Adjutant. Hoping you are all well, and with my love.

15

Wykeham Martin to his stepmother

Sevastopol, November 2 1854

I have just received your parcels by the railway vessels, and hear there is another in the parcel office for me, which, from its weight I conclude is a stove, which I shall not attempt to bring up here as it is too heavy, and I can do without it till I am moved, which I think will be very soon. I have one parcel missing now, the one with the axe and saw in it and Marsh's boots. I have sent one large parcel to England, but still have three times as much as I can carry here, what to do with them I do not know. Tell Erskine his cigars are very good, and that I will write to him by this mail if I can. I wish I could get Marsh's boots, then I would write to him.

---

27 Canon John Henry Sparke, father of the deceased officer and Rector as well as Patron of St Mary's church, Gunthorpe, Norfolk. The letter written by Fiennes Wykeham Martin has survived and is still in the possession of the Sparke family. He wrote: 'My Dear Mr Sparke, I think it my duty to write you a line by this mail (as I believe I have the pleasure of knowing you better than the rest of my brother officers) to inform you that since Major Low wrote to you to tell you that your son was missing, a flag of truce has been interchanged with the enemy for the purpose of enquiring after the officers and men that were missing, & I grieve to say that out of 11 officers missing only 2 were found alive. Mr Sparke must, we all think, have been cut off by a regiment of Lancers that completely hemmed in the remains of the 4th. The Regiment with the rest of the Brigade having passed through the most murderous fire that Cavalry were ever exposed to, only 200 out of 700 returning unwounded in the whole Brigade. The part of his kit that he had with him was sold as we had no means of carrying it, also his remaining horse, the remainder of his property with his papers and writing case were reserved (?) from the sale, will be sent home by the earliest opportunity. Deeply sympathising with your loss in which I am joined by the whole regiment (?) being deeply beloved. And with my kind remembrances to your family, I remain Yours truly F. W. Martin 4th Light Dragoons.'

Charles Trollope has got charge of a brigade,[28] and has offered me to be his Aide, but as it is not certain whether it is permanent or not I have not yet finally settled whether I take it. Will you tell Philip to use my cheque, as if I want money when I come home I will apply to him for some, and at this moment I do not write, as I wrote to him by the last mail, but had not then received his letter. I will deliver the mittens the first opportunity to Col. Reynardson.[29] All the Tryons are gone, so I can give him two pair. I have appropriated Miss Osborn's purple comforter to myself and given the other away. The Ladies Nevill[30] ought to have put their names to theirs. Hunt has taken a pair done by James, and says that he hopes he shall be able to show them to him again some day. The army is much better in health than it was, the chief thing now being scorbutic dysentery. We have got everything in a forward state, and it is expected something will be done shortly. You need not believe half what the paper the Times says, for instance, he says that the French horses are all well: now to prove that is not true, Gen. D'Allonville (who speaks English), came to our camp the other day and told us the French European horses were suffering as much as ours. This was a great deal for a Frenchman to admit, as they never talk about their losses in the French army in public: another thing, the Times says that the 2nd Division were on short rations, now I know from the General and other officers that they have never missed their rations once since they have been before Sevastopol, with the exception of one day, when I believe they had half allowance. They have refused me leave to be Aide to Col. Trollope as there are not subalterns enough here; perhaps it is as well as it is.

[PS] I saw Capt. Reynardson today, and thanked him for bringing my parcel.

16

Wykeham Martin to his friend Ralph Nevill

[Letter omitted from 1868 publication]
November 12th Camp before Sevastopol
I have not written to you since I left Varna for the Crimea so I think I will

---

28 Charles Trollope's brigade was 1st Brigade, 2nd Division (Lieutenant General Sir George De Lacy Evans). See Ron McGuigan, *Into Battle! British Orders of Battle for the Crimean War 1854–56* (Bowdon: Withycut House, 2001), p. 36.

29 Edward Birch Reynardson, 3rd Grenadier Guards.

30 Ladies Caroline, Henrietta and Isabel Nevill, the elder sisters of Ralph Pelham Nevill.

now fulfil my promise of letting you know how I like it. You of course will
have read in the papers better accounts of Alma than I could pretend to
give you so I will only tell you of my own adventures. To begin with we
were landed at Eupatoria with the rest of the army and formed part of the
rear guard, the most fatiguing duty of the whole on a march, as you start
with the others and do not get in till long after them as you have to pick
up all the stragglers and guard the baggage. We used to start at 4 o'clock
in the morning and don't get in till 7 or 8 in the evening and then had to
get wood and water to cook our salt pork, pitch our camp and picket your
horses as we had no tents and no beds it did not take long to find a soft
place on the ground to roll yourself in your cloak and to sleep. At Alma
the cavalry had nothing to do, but at the action at Balaklava my regiment
and the rest of the Light Brigade were completely annihilated owing to a
mistake in the orders. We charged for about a mile and a quarter down
a valley, flanked on both sides with artillery and infantry in masses and
with a tremendous force of cavalry at the bottom. They bowled us over
right and left with grape shot, minie balls and round shot in fact out of
700 that went in to action only 190 came out again and all for no good as
we were not backed up and we have since heard from a Russian officer
who was taken prisoner that one little Brigade charged 22,000 rather long
odds, on Sunday 5th November were again attacked by the enemy at a
place called Inkerman. Our pickets were surprised we found the enemy
in our camp before we knew where we were (lucky for us they were
Englishmen instead of Turks the latter having run away at Balaklava).
The Guards who were foremost suffered fearfully. The Coldstream only
bringing out 40 rank and file and 3 officers. Altogether we are in a very
ticklish position the British Army being all wasted away by sickness and
these frequent attacks and the siege has proved more formidable than was
supposed, in fact we are to winter here in tents, rather a pleasant lookout
as one day you are frozen to death the next washed away by rain. We
are sleeping on the ground with one blanket, never taking your clothes
off many men and officers have not had their boots off since we landed.
Lord Raglan would not allow any one to land any baggage so we only
had what we could carry on our backs. My men have never changed their
shirts or even washed their faces for 6 weeks some of the infantry officers
are the same and they say keeping however we shall get our kits soon
now that we are to stop here and intrench [sic] ourselves so thoroughly
that I hope the Russians will not be able to drive us into the sea as some
people think possible. The Army in general has a mild opinion of Lord
Raglan and think he has put us in a hole. I begin to wish myself back at

Canterbury again driving over to Leeds twice a week or having a days shooting at Birling [Birling Manor, Kent]. How did you enjoy your trip to Switzerland, better than coming to this hole I fancy. I wish I had the man out here who wrote to the Times to say it was possible to winter here in tents. I would have him flank marched and leave him out in the cold for 48 hours every week as I am sure it will kill many men than the Russians with Robertson and Percy out here awfully disgusted with the whole proceeding they both desire to be remembered to you. I am acting Adjutant of the Regiment now and have very little time to myself so you must excuse this short epistle. Hoping that all your family are quite well and write my best wishes to them all.

17

Wykeham Martin to his stepmother[31]

Camp Sevastopol, November 12.
The siege has failed in consequence of the great loss sustained at the Battle of Inkerman on Sunday last. We had on our side 136 officers killed and wounded, among them Messrs. Thorold, Malcolm[32] and Eliot of the Guards.[33] We are now to remain here all the winter in tents, on the top of this hill with little or no water, frozen to death one night, and washed out of one's tent the next. At this moment the mud outside my tent is two inches deep, worse than Chobham; pleasant when one has to sleep in one's boots; to add to all, these perpetual attacks from the Russians, you will have some slight idea how happy we are. [*No one is even allowed to resign his commission, Paget is the only exception. He has sacrificed £8000 for the sake of his wife. Jolliffe tried the same but was told he must wait for a successor.*] I hope you have not sent off my things, as we must alter a good many. Patent leather boots and gold belts will be useless out here, but a pair of thick uniform overalls, leathered at the bottoms, and a pair of long jack calf skin boots with hunting spurs, and my dress jacket, as owing to the alteration of uniform it is of no further use, but they will allow us to wear it here. A thick set of shooting clothes and the India rubber tub, although I am afraid I will not be able to use it, as I have

---

31   Passages in italics were not included in the 1868 published collection and have been restored from the originals.

32   Lieutenant L. W. Malcolm, 2nd Rifle Brigade, killed in action. FWM uses the informal word 'poor' before Thorold in the original letter.

33   Captain the Hon. G. C. C. Eliot, killed in action at Inkerman.

not washed for three days. The provisions you can send. I have never received the boots you sent first, so I suppose they are lost in the boat. [*Tell Mish to send me a new cap also mittens and those sort of things, tell Maria, are very useful, also a small axe and a saw in a leather case, these things you can send to Ridgeway if you have sent the other things as he will be perpetually sending to the regiment.*] Mittens and those sort of things, tell Maria, are very useful, also a quantity of 1s books, a complete set of waterproof things. I have put all these things down in rather queer order, but it is just as they happen to come into my head. Why on earth they keep the [*wretched*] Light Brigade here I don't know, as we have only 200 horses instead of 1500. How are we to reorganise the regiments here on the top of this hill? [*Lord Raglan perhaps may know.*] We never ought to have started from Varna, as it was too late in the year; [*it is the fault of that blackguard paper the Times which writes about things it knows nothing about, as it is*] we expect all the horses to die and most of the men; we have lost already 9000 animals since we landed in the Crimea. I forgot to put down Guernseys, flannel shirts, worsted socks, an air pillow, and an emigrants stove, if not too expensive; not that I think we shall have anything to burn in it, as there is no fuel to be got here. [*Also send out a very light pair of regimental overalls you will find in my kit as they will do to make pantaloons of to wear with the jack boots.*] I will now describe our present life [*for you*]. We get up before daylight, shiver about without cloaks on our horses till it is light, then turn into your lines, get your breakfast, if the wind and rain will let you, then idle about till dinnertime, when dinner is over it is dark, we then stick a bayonet in the ground and a candle in the part that fixes on to the musket, and three or four of us sit and talk on the ground round till about half past seven or eight; then we lie down, I cannot call it going to bed, till the next morning. This is only varied by alarms from the Russians. Tell Maria I would answer her letter, only one has very little time to oneself during daylight, and one cannot see by candle-light. I am glad she enjoyed her visit to my lively and amusing friends, the Miss Derbys.

Tell Fairfax I wish I had his bonfire out here, as we can hardly get anything to burn and it is awfully cold. Fairfax says he was seen walking about with a rabbit on Sunday [*on Sunday with a rabbit*]; tell him his brother last Sunday was assisting to kill 15,000 Russians, and today Sunday, I hear there has been another attack on Balaklava. Philip has not written to me for some time [*send him this letter*]. Ask him to do so, and to tell me how his hunting goes on [*I shall not be able to post this letter as there are no stamps and they won't accept money*]. I forgot to tell you Col Trollope's Regiment[34] is ordered here but has yet to arrive. We want reinforcements to arrive quick, to prevent them driving us out of our position, and the Infantry regiments here are much reduced. We hope by the spring to have got a large enough army here to starve them out. You will see by the Gazette that I am now Lieut.,[35] and I think I shall soon get my Troop. By the time you get this you will be thinking of your Christmas festivities. I am afraid I will not be at your Rent dinner this time; however, I hope you will do for me as you did for Cornwallis,[36] that is to say, 'I wish I was with them,' or even allowed to wait at table, as that would be better than being here. I must now conclude my long grumbling letter, but upon my word it is enough to make a saint swear, to be told he is to remain perched on the top of this rock a whole winter.

18

Wykeham Martin to his stepmother

Camp Sevastopol, November 17th 1854

I wrote to you by the last mail telling you that the siege had failed, but I'm afraid you will not get the letter, as since then we have had a terrific storm, which has sunk or wrecked ten ships, among them the mail that went from here, and the one that ought to have come in, also the ship that had the winter clothing on board for the troops; the consequence is we are in an awful mess, having no clothes to keep off the very cold weather that has now set in here. I told you in my last, but must tell you again (for fear you did not receive it), that we had an awful battle on the 5th November, in which we lost 2500 men and 143 officers killed and wounded; the consequence was we were obliged to stop the siege and wait for reinforcements, and make up our mind to winter here. Rather pleasant in tents, when you are visited by storm that blew down every tent and took away half your kit with it, leaving you to sit in the rain and cold. Colonel Trollope has arrived with his regiment as a reinforcement. There is nothing but cold and wet, sleeping in your clothes wet through, your feet like a snow ball, with perpetual turns out in the middle of the night from perpetual alarms from the Russians, half the army gone

---

34 The 62nd Regiment of Foot. Command of this regiment passed to Major Robert Shearman when Colonel Trollope took command of the 1st Brigade. See McGuigan, *Into Battle!*, p. 33.

35 His promotion to Lieutenant from 26 October appeared in the *London Gazette*.

36 Cornwallis Wykeham Martin (1833–1903), his younger brother, who followed a naval career.

from sickness and nothing done. We do not expect to be in the place till Christmas and perhaps not then. By the time you get this you will be in the middle of your Christmas festivities, you must do the needful for me at the rent dinner[37] if they propose my health, and tell them I should like to be there even to scrape up the leavings. Also tell Stedman[38] that his sleeping out after poachers is a joke to sleeping in your clothes for six weeks; some of the men have neither boots or socks, and are up to their knees in mud. Our unfortunate regiment turns out 20 file instead of 420. The day of the storm we had nothing for 24 hours, men or horses, and it was snowing and raining all the time, and the wind blew so hard it was impossible to keep a tent up. You will think I am a great grumbler, but it is a fact that I am laughed at out here for taking it all so quietly and never grumbling; the fact is, I am afraid I keep it all for you. They talk of hutting us here, but there is no wood; if it is not done soon there will be no horses left to hut. I will now wish you all good-bye, and wishing you a merry Christmas and a happy new year, with love to all.

19

Wykeham Martin to his brother Philip[39]

Sevastopol Nov. 22nd 1854
As yet I have only drawn £35 besides what I drew in England, and that I should not have done if I had had my bullock trunks in which I left £50, or if Government would give us any pay; but in the want of the two latter I was obliged to draw on England. As to my cheques I shall be obliged to get Ridgway to pay for my things if you do not, at all events a part of them, as I see no reason because I am in the Crimea, I should sponge upon you for money, as long as I have any of my own, especially as I may be shot any day, and then you could not get back the money, as you would have nothing to show; so I think old fellow you had better spend my money as far as it will go, and then you can help me when I get back, if I ever do – The horse you gave me carried me splendidly through the severest Cavalry action ever fought, and was much fresher than most of the horses at the end. I certainly must have had [*the devil's own*] immense

---

37 A free dinner twice a year for tenant farmers, who would come to pay their landlords half yearly rents.

38 John Stedman, a worker on the estate in Kent.

39 Passages in italics were not included in the 1868 published collection and have been restored from the originals.

luck, as the only thing I had touched was the curb hook, the top of which was shot away; every one else, men and officers, had much narrower escapes; although the fire at Balaklava was perfectly fearful, destroying the whole of the Brigade I belong to, we were none of us [*in near so much of a funk* in the original letter] so nearly picked off by Russian shots as we were at Inkerman, where they again brought us uselessly under fire, the only thing we could charge being a *ship* nearly a mile off. [*The fact is Cardigan has no head at all*] Lord Raglan's orders in both cases were misunderstood [*if such lives are to be thrown away in this way during the campaign without doing any good to one's country (in fact rather harm as it makes the Russians believe they licked us, although they did nothing of the kind) I for one would rather not serve under such Generals. Poor Henry Tryon was shot the night before last in a skirmish that I believe he himself was the originator of. He certainly was a nice fellow and a very gallant officer. We bury him today I conclude you see all my epistles in due time so I will not repeat what I have put in [illegible] I am sorry to hear B does not make a good husband. I always thought him bad tempered but I likewise thought Fear of the Family would have at least kept him in good order.*]

I saw Gerald Goodlake *the day* after Inkerman, luckily he was on picket, otherwise he would most likely have been potted, as the Coldstreams[40] only brought out three officers out of sixteen that went into action, and fourteen rank and file; rather a [*dent*] gap in the poor old Guards. I hope you are having good sport with the hounds this year, what ripping good sport I should have had at Trowbridge with the Duke of Beaufort, and on leave with you. [*Does Lizzy object at all this year to your showing the noble animal or does she take 14 hours and say nothing about it.*] Tell Lizzie that the Bible was a very acceptable gift from her; but now that I am getting religious I should like a prayer [book] also, as I do not possess that needful article. Owing to my thinking you are going to send me a Church Service, I sent my own Prayer book back again. I cannot prepay these mighty edifying epistles *of mine*, as I cannot get stamps, and the Post Office will not take money. I have written a letter to Mama by this mail, which you had better get passed on, as there are some things in it I have not put in this, and *vice versa*. Remember me *and give my love* to the [*Chacombe Devil Dodger*] Vicar of Chacombe,[41] and all the aunts, tell them I have in prospect some day to give them a line, [*I must say that Uncle Frank would not have looked well in Billy Peareth's Broum* (brougham) *on a certain*

---

40   Her Majesty's Second Regiment of Foot Guards, The Coldstream Guards.
41   Francis William Wykeham Martin was his uncle and was vicar of Chacombe. Chacombe Priory in Northamptonshire was part of the Wykeham Martin estates.

occasion otherwise I should like to have seen him before I started. How does Rude Dick go on [illegible]. Any more young governesses knocking about his establishment. I heard yesterday a man talking about uncle [illegible] as the best [illegible] thing, rather creditable for ones married uncle, scratch this out before you shew it to the ladies. I will conclude but if anything happens before this mail, I will let you know. Hoping you and everybody are quite well and that you are enjoying your [illegible] to his [illegible] her 14 or I should think on cold winters mornings 18 hours and with love to both]
[PS By the by have you seen the gentleman who has nothing to do but walk up and down the deck with his hands in his pockets. I hear he is in England and shall write me a line by the next mail. I forgot to tell you that.] the sword you got at Wilkinson's had a very bad edge, as it turned quite blunt with one cut I gave a Russian at Balaklava.

20

Wykeham Martin to his sister Maria

Sevastopol, November 24, 1854

As I have not written to you for some time, and you have been kind enough to write me a letter or two, I will now do you the honour to answer them by the light of a candle stuck in a porter bottle. I will endeavour to give you the news. In the first place, I have received Mamma's two letters, yours, and Philip's, the former telling me all my kit has started, and as I perceive by the list, that all the principle things are in it that I wanted, you can send the others any opportunity. I am sorry to have to communicate to Mama that poor Henry Tryon[42] in the Rifle Brigade, was shot last night in a skirmish the Rifles had with the enemy's sharpshooters. He was much liked in the Regiment, and was considered one of the best and most gallant officers that that noble corps possessed. One of the Rifles told me that Tryon shot fifty men with his own rifle at the battle of Inkerman, although he was on the sick list at the time; whether that is true or only exaggerated I do not know, but at all events he was a very good officer: he is to be buried

---

42   The second son of Thomas Tryon of Bulwick Park, killed on the night of 20 November. His brother, Thomas, was a captain in the 7th Fusiliers – see note 22 above.

tomorrow.[43] We have not yet received our kits and are still on the one shirt system. How long they will keep us in this state of dirt I do not know, but we are beginning to think it time to make a change: unfortunately the ship with all the government clothing on board for the troops was lost in the awful hurricane we had here on the 14th. Charles Trollop is here as cheery as possible, but his regiment has not yet engaged. I hope the Government will soon send out some more Cavalry. When we first started from England and were complete in numbers, the force was utterly unworthy of such a country as England, but now it is utterly ridiculous and is a mere farce, the weather kills the horses daily. We are now detached from the heavy Cavalry, and are watching the Russian army down in a valley, our business being to charge them if they come up the precipice, a thing we are about as likely to do as you are to take a stroll up the side of the bastion wall; however we get off night duty, which is a great pull, and only turn out with the rest of the army in the morning. Tell Cornwallis in your next letter to him that I will give him another epistle soon. It is getting very cold, and we have got orders to hut ourselves, but how are we to do it without spades, shovels, pickaxes, hammers, or wood, we have not yet discovered; I suppose it will be done by next April when it will not be wanted. The English get on very well with the French; but since the battle of Balaklava we have done nothing but kick the Turks out of our camp whenever they come into it; they take it as quietly as possible. An officer in the Inniskillings saw a Turk passing by his tent, he rushed out and applied his toe vigorously to a nameless part, and after all it turned out to be a Turkish Infantry Officer who took it quietly, never saying a word. At Inkerman, General Canrobert would not bring the Turks up to fight, but we now make them dig trenches, and in that way we save our men. We have heard from deserters that the Russian loss at Inkerman was 24,000, out of which there were about 300 officers and 2 generals, a pretty considerable beating, considering they surprised us in the early part of the morning when we were all asleep, and added to that, the reserve ammunition was not up; consequently our men were without anything to fire with for a long time.

Since writing the above I have attended the funeral of poor Tryon. I am sorry to say Tom Tryon is far from well, but Lord Burghersh[44] has done

---

43   Henry Tryon was buried on Cathcart's Hill and a cross of Portland stone marked his grave. The inscription read: 'Sacred to the memory of Lieut. Henry Tryon, Rifle Brigade, killed in action on 20th November 1854.' See The Hon. John Colborne and Frederic Brine, *The Last of the Brave or Resting Places of our Fallen Heroes* (London: Ackerman and Co., 1857), p. 48, n. 45. It is believed the British cemetery was destroyed during the Cold War.

44   Lord Francis William Henry Burghersh (1825–91), ADC to Lord Raglan.

his best to get him sent on board ship; I believe he will go tomorrow. Tell Cornwallis not to bear hard on my horse's mouth when he rides him, or he will fidget the whole time and it will spoil him as a charger. I see in Mama's list she has not included a lamp, a thing I want very much. It does not signify sending too many things, as I can sell them here at fabulous profit. I forgot to say I met Lord Burghersh at Tryon's funeral, he was very civil and said he recollected me at Leeds Castle. Tell Mama I will send home a blank cheque for £5 for my servant's friends, also for articles bought for me, as I find I can easily live within one's income here, buying every thing you can in the way of luxuries, in which I do not stint myself, as here I consider every one has the right to make oneself as comfortable as possible at any price within one's means, though that is little enough God knows. Remember me to any people about the place that you think would care about it, and wish them a merry Christmas. I am afraid I shall come short of pudding this year. I must now end my twaddle.

21

Wykeham Martin to his stepmother

Camp Sevastopol, November 27th 1854
I will write you a line, as I think in these times you will not mind a 3d to know that I have not been potted up to the date of my letter. I wrote letters to Philip and Maria by the last mail, and to Cornwallis and Uncle Frank by this. I see up to the 4th November by the papers, you had not a true account of Balaklava, but I dare say you have by this time; we are still as uncomfortable as ever, although I hear there is some talk of us getting our kits. The weather is very cold and we have been literally washed out of our tents; some of us being obliged to stand all night as the ground was too wet to lie down on. Hunt[45] wants £2.10s sent to his wife. Will you let me know what you have paid altogether, including the £5. for my servant; he has received no letters, owing to being left behind at Varna ill. I will send you a cheque for the whole; I have given Philip up as he will not use my cheques. I told you all about poor Tryon in my letter to Maria, as also that Lord Burghersh had introduced himself to me. I have never got your parcel, by the 'Faith', but I believe it is with Ridgway's agent in Constantinople, who is a slack

---

45   Possibly 1009 Pvt. Henry Hunt, 4th Light Dragoons. See TNA WO12/659–660.

man in business, as he does not answer one's letters. I conclude by the next mail I shall get a full description of your visit to Eridge, also your condolences on the loss of the Brigade. They are endeavouring to keep us here all the winter, but nearly all the horses are dead of cold, and some of the men, and those that are left have not a go left in them I am afraid, as they tumble down going to water. As to the siege, I think it seems to retrograde, instead of progressing, as the Russians opened up two batteries this morning we silenced a month ago. I have no more news, having written so lately, and with my best love to all, and merry Christmas and a happy New Year, in case I do not write again before that time. Do not forget to send me jack boots, hunting spurs and India-rubber suit in your next parcel.

[PS] Tell Cornwallis, if he is at home, to lick Fairfax for me, and put him out on the lawn every night for an hour, and fire a gun at him, that he may have an idea what sort of life I am passing; also give him my love and thank him for his letter.

22

Wykeham Martin to his father

Camp Sevastopol, November 30th 1854

I see by the papers I am gazetted to a Lieutenancy by purchase, vice Hartman,[46] I had no idea, till I received your letter, that Hartman was going to leave us, and who has paid the money I do not know; however, I think I shall get it back again, as it has happened subsequent to the action of Balaklava, I am therefore entitled to Halket's death vacancy and get it for nothing; will you represent it to the Horse Guards for me, if you do not see my promotion by purchase cancelled before you receive this letter. This is always done, and then I shall be gazetted vice Halket killed in action; they always cancel by purchase when the death has happened *previous*, and ante-date back to the time of the death. We have got a fine day at last but our horses have had nothing to eat for three days, owing to the bad state of the roads, consequently they die by three or four at a time. I believe we go to Balaklava tomorrow, our old place, to be near the forage; we are now before Sevastopol. The new men that come out here are taken sick much easier than the men that are left of the old set; out of

---

46 Gustavus Adolphus Hartman, Cornet by purchase 10 May 1844, Lieutenant without purchase
9 February 1847. See *Hart's New Army List 1854*, p. 31.

100 men that came in a draft for the Grenadier Guards, only three were fit for duty two days after; the laying on the wet ground shuts them up. I forgot to say that in a short time I shall be first for my Troop and to prevent mistakes I shall authorize Hoare to honour your drafts.

The rain has come on again as hard as ever, and we have not been able to march to Balaklava this morning; four days the horses have had nothing to eat, ten have died in forty-eight hours, and the rest I do not think could walk to Balaklava without falling down. *Rather* useful Cavalry we are at present, not 200 effective horses in the Brigade, and the whole unable to walk. It really ought to be known in England, as it would be throwing away lives to charge immense bodies of Cavalry now, as the horses would fall down and we should be cut to pieces; besides, the wet has destroyed the whole of the saddlery, and Sevastopol is rather further from being taken now than it was the first night we got here, and the weather is so much against us that we cannot do anything. I will wind up by reminding you to give Regulation but not any more. I am still in the best of health and spirits, although I should like to be in more comfortable quarters and belong to a Regiment or Brigade that has some use, and not a dismounted Dragoon, as I shall be in a short time. We are still without kits and are with the one shirt we landed with; ragged is no name for the men, walking about in *buff* is nearer the mark. A change is certainly an exciting thing, but this living for months in a tent without your kit, in a wet pond and with nothing to do, is anything but exciting; in fact it is the most tedious work imaginable and requires more pluck than fifty charges. Hoping you are well as I am at present.

23

Wykeham Martin to his stepmother

2nd Division Camp, no date, received in England 18 December
Since writing you my last letter, I have got myself I am sorry to say into a hole; that is to say, I am detached[47] five miles from my Regiment by myself, with twenty men; my duties are simply to find orderlies to go mounted to the advanced pickets, and in case of attack, to send others to other Divisions to say how and in what force we are attacked. I have been here only two days, but I can assure you from spending one night

---

47   He was performing a duty or task away from the regiment.

in a bell tent alone, with no books, and being dark at five o'clock, is very dreadful. The only thing that makes it bearable is that Charles Trollope's Regiment is in this Division, so that I spend the greater part of my time there, but it is an awkward walk at night, being up to your knees in mud and slush. I dined with him last night and rode with him to the advanced picket today. The Royal Albert has arrived, but she came into the Cherson instead of Balaklava, so that I have not even got that parcel yet. The only things I have received (which I got half-a-hour ago), are some muffetees from Aunt Fanny.[48] You do not appear to have got my letters describing the storm of the 14th of November. The old siege goes on as usual, and we have got in much nearer on our side, and have also fortified Inkerman, which we ought to have done long ago. The Infantry are enduring great hardships, short of food, and out three or four nights a week. Last night the Russians took a whole picket, officers and all, they were all asleep and the Russians were on them before they knew where they were and bayoneted some. It was one of the most advanced pickets, they ought not to have been caught napping; if they ever come back they may think themselves lucky, the only excuse for them is being so frightfully hard worked. Will you send me the Times newspaper from the date of this letter, as I am quite out of the world here, trusting to other people's kindness for any news. I am glad you saw Cornwallis, although it was only a few days. I hope he will not come out here, as the only good he could do would be working in the trenches, the hardest work of all. I hear I am in the Gazette without purchase, but I have not seen it yet. I live in hope that if I live through the campaign, I may return a Major. The only sticker I see in my way is Adlington,[49] and nothing would induce him to leave; my best chance would be a good exchange when I get my troop. I hear Joliffe has got a company in the Coldstreams, I suppose because his brother who died was in that Regiment. I left the Light Brigade the morning I got your letter, so had no opportunity of asking about the man Harris[50] in the 8th Hussars, but I will as soon as possible. Will you send me a pair of braces by the post and then I shall probably get them. It is certainly hard lines one should be stuck on the top of a hill working for

---

48   Either Frances Vere or Frances Elizabeth Wykeham Martin, the younger sisters of his father.

49   Lieutenant Henry Smith Adlington, born 1827, the only son of Thomas Adlington of East Bradenham, Norfolk. Educated at Eton and Trinity College, Oxford. Cornet in 4th Light Dragoons, 11 February 1848; Lieutenant, 6 July 1849; and Captain, 26 October 1854. Two horses shot from under him at the battle of Inkerman. See Lummis and Wynn, *Honour the Light Brigade*, p. 23.

50   1159 Pvt. William Harris, born *circa* 1829, Maidstone, Kent. He enlisted November 1850 and embarked for the Crimea in the *Echunga* on 15 May 1854. Promoted to Corporal on 8 November 1854. Died 23 February 1855. See Lummis and Wynn, *Honour the Light Brigade*, p. 100.

one's country and not able to get a parcel from England. Did you ever get my letter asking about jack boots, hunting spurs, emigrants stove, and complete suit of waterproof; if not, please send them by Hayter, as he seems the only authorized Government agent. Tell Papa he is much wanted here as we are all doing engineering for ourselves, either hollowing out our tents or building huts; the latter is out of my power, as it is an impossibility to obtain wood, so I shall try the first. I am afraid that now that I have got up this cold place again it will kill my horses. They tell me my command here is of great importance. I do not quite see it, as the chief use is that the orderly from the picket should bring quick intelligence to the camp in case of an alarm. Now as none of the horses can boil up a trot from weakness, I think a good swift runner would be more useful; in fact, I think I rather endanger the Camp than otherwise. I have nothing more to tell you, and with love to all, and kind remembrances to Gibbons,[51] Erskine, and all the others that care for my existence.

24

Wykeham Martin to his father

Camp Balaklava, December 6th 1854
Since writing you my last letter, which you will receive at the same time as this, owing to private letters being stopped by the last two mails, I have become first for purchase, consequently, if you get a letter from Horse Guards for me, requesting the payment of £2500, will you do so by the means I pointed out in my last letter. I would not let a Troop slip on any account if I can help it; great luck for me getting a Troop so soon, if I do so. I received your letters today, of the 15th November, congratulating me on my escape at Balaklava. There is no news to tell you as I wrote so lately, except that the Russian army has evacuated the forts taken on the Balaklava day,[52] and gone we don't know where. I must conclude, as I dare not risk losing the post, which is just going, and with love to all.

P.S. Our kits are landed at last, but I have not got any of your parcels.

---

51 Possibly William Gibbons, the gardener at Leeds Castle.
52 The line of redoubts on the Causeway Heights taken by the Russians on the morning of
    25 October. The Turks defended the first redoubt on Canrobert's Hill valiantly but were forced
    out by overwhelming numbers. The other redoubts were taken quite easily after this. See Mike
    Hargreave Mawson, *The True Heroes of Balaklava*, Special Publication No. 14 (Ripon: Crimean
    War Research Society, 1996).

25

Wykeham Martin to his father

Balaklava, December 17th 1854

The siege still goes on feebly, and I do not see that we are any nearer accomplishing our object than we were the first day; we want more men and finer weather. The Infantry up at the Fort are actually in want of food; so much so, that the Cavalry are now employed in carrying up biscuit and pork to them, which with pickets gives us a great deal to do; the weather is dreadful, snow, rain and cold day after day, and still we are under canvas with anything but proper clothing to stand it; the number of men sick is something awful,[53] and when I say sick I do not mean slightly ill, but almost dead. Our horses are not yet hutted, although we have got the order to do so, but as we are on duty every day and all day, so much so that the men have not time to wash their faces; how we are to hut I do not know. Neither myself or any other officer that I can hear of have received any of the numerous parcels sent from England to us. It ought to be represented in England that we have no store in Balaklava for parcels from England. The steamers and vessels come in and go, very likely, before we receive letters to say what ship they are in; as in my case, the Faith[54] was in harbour for some time, but I did not know that she had any thing for me till she had gone again. I suppose we shall get them at the same time with the reinforcements, wooden huts, and other comfortable things we hear of, coming. I feel highly flattered at your thinking my letter describing the Balaklava affair as worthy a place in the Times, but I'm afraid the English would hardly have passed muster in public print. I have received very kind letters from the Chacombites. I must also thank you for your kind present [a thick uniform made from pilot cloth, with lace etc. on it] as it is just the thing I wanted, as I find the thieves on board ship have stolen my great coat, among other things, out of my kit: it will also be the saving of my life on picket duty most likely, an amusement I have dropped into again. I can assure you it is very jolly out on a large plain, very cold, and raining or snowing the whole time. We have heard that Austria has joined the Western Powers; I hope it is true; I still continue to hope that we may take this place before long.

---

53   The disparity between the number of men wounded in action and the much larger numbers of sick and ill men was becoming obvious since the army's arrival at Varna. This imbalance continued throughout the war. See TNA, WO12/ 659–660.

54   Transport No. 131, 721 tons, steam powered Commissariat store-ship owned by the Royal Mail Steam Packet Company. See HCPP 1854–5 (283), Return on Transports, p. 18.

You say in your last letter that you did not enter into any gaieties on my account. I hope you will alter this as soon as possible, as life is too short not to enjoy it as much as possible, and if you are under any fears, for me they are groundless, as until reinforcements arrive we cannot possibly go into action, our present strength being 50 horses, therefore my only chance of hopping the twig is by disease, which might equally happen in England; so, for goodness sake, do not stop any festivities or going to balls on my account. Tell Cornwallis, if by any chance he comes out here, by no means to apply to the Trenches, as the night work there knocks every body up and he would probably only make one more; they are frequently four nights out of seven there on duty, which in this weather would kill a horse; and moreover he would never get a chance of seeing me as I am five miles off; people in England have no idea what the Trenches mean, but I can tell them it kills more men than the Russian bullets.

26

Wykeham Martin to his brother Philip

[Letter omitted from the 1868 publication]
Sevastopol December 27th 1854
Many thanks for your intended present, not I am afraid I have little chance of getting it as no one has got anything that has come out from England. I even have not got a parcel sent out on the 20th September. The people of England are certainly impressive in their gifts but they are entirely [illegible, possibly 'misleading'] as the authorities here make no effort towards making a place for parcels to be deposited, the consequence that ships come into the harbour with parcels for officers and go out without leaving them as they have no opportunity of doing it, they then take them to the Commissariat store at Constantinople and leave them there where they stop forever. Old Raglan is about as fit to command an army as my groom and most of his staff (relatives of his own) are as bad. Until we have a new General we shall *do nothing*. I hear there is a rumour of his resigning the sooner the better, I am now on a detachment by myself and I find it very poor fun sitting for hours of a night by myself with nothing to do and the thermometer below freezing. We have got a rumour here that there is to be peace. I hope there is or if not that they will put the Army under a French General as they seem to me to be the only people out here that know whether they stand on their head or their heels. It is wonderful to see the way their army is carried on

and with what little expense, everything very good, whereas with our army the expense is unlimited and we get nothing. Everything is done very bad. The matter is we as a nation do not understand war, now in the instance of the warm clothing we only get it by driblets. Now if the French do anything of the kind the whole army are supplied with it at the proper time and *all together*. You will think this all grumbling but I only tell it you to show you that whatever *the people* of England may do the government will mismanage the business and so make it of no effect. I am sorry to hear that you have had bad sport hunting this year and I hope it improves before the end of the year. Does Madame still object to the noble science. I am very busy making a temporary stable for my horses as it is the only way of preserving their loss. I have no news of any sort.

27

Wykeham-Martin to his sister Maria

Camp, Sevastopol, Jan. 1st 1855

I must, I think, dedicate this epistle to you, as you have written me so many and I have not answered them. In the first place, will you tell Papa I have received his packet at last, by Royal Albert, and am much obliged. The only improvement that could be made would be, if they were larger, as owing to my having grown bigger, and Rich having made them tighter than usual, I can hardly get into them. You cannot have things made too large; there is the same fault in the boots, they are very well made and would look very well in Regent Street, but if there was a sudden alarm I could not get into them. Tell Marsh in future to make them three times as large and twice as thick. I have discovered two parcels for me on board the Cosmopolitan,[55] but I cannot get them out till the huts are landed. The big boots, waterproofs, books and tools are what I want most; I have likewise received letters dated the 12th December from Philip, Aunt Fanny, Papa and Mama. They are getting on with the siege slowly but I hope surely; the great drawback being the immense amount of sick, 13,000 at the present time being non-effective, and the men are a most miserable looking lot. The new Regiments suffer a great deal more than the old ones. The officers, now they have got their huts and are off the ground, do not suffer much, and live very well, only provisions are dear

---

55 Transport No. 157, steam powered, 600 tons, owned by the Thames and Clyde Screw Steamshipping Company. See HCPP 1854–5 (283), p. 14.

and a long way off, but when we come to drinking liquors, I do not think we are much to be pitied, except for the dirt and discomfort of living in a tent. When I get my stove I shall dig mine down, and then I shall be pretty snug. I went with Col. Trollope today to see the Naval Brigade, and found George Tryon,[56] with his messmates, had made themselves a very snug little house. Col. Trollope is building quite a mansion for these parts, with two rooms, the only difficulty being the roofing and flooring without boards or tiles. The French beat us in taking care of their troops; their men, officers and horses, all being covered in long ago, consequently they have few sick. Send me out a strong pair of braces by post, as I am deficient of those articles and cannot get any here, almost the only thing you cannot get now. The warmest thing I find to wear in these parts, is a long coat with a hood, it is called a Greco, used by Greek sailors and Turks. It is almost proof against any wet and very warm; You would think me a very odd figure if you saw me in mine. If ever I come home I shall certainly bring one, as they would be invaluable to drive in. We all hear there is to be peace; I hope it is true. I have got so many things now and so many coming, I do not know how I shall move when I am relieved, without leaving half behind. To begin with, four undress jackets. I think it great nonsense the people of England giving up all gaiety for the war, as after all what is a soldier meant for but to be in the field. The French drove the Russians out of the position they took from the Turks at Balaklava yesterday, and burnt their camp. The whole of the Russian Army have now retreated to the heights above Inkerman, where they have established a Battery, and amuse themselves with throwing shell and round shot at parties going for wood. They sent some at a party Col. Trollope took down (in which I accompanied him for something to do) a great deal closer than was pleasant one coming into the house some of us were in. It is great fun going to our advanced pickets and shooting at the Russian sharpshooters. I watched a man with a picket of the 55th for a long time, and although we shot at him and he at us several times, we did no harm to each other; it would have made you laugh to hear the men say 'Now then, Bill, he's out, pot him,' or 'Look out, Bob, do him,' and a bullet would whistle over your head as you squatted behind a wall of stones. You would think they were rabbit shooting and watching for

---

56 A family friend who was a junior officer in the Royal Navy. George Tryon went on to enjoy a distinguished career in the service, rising to the rank of admiral and also a knighthood. He was drowned in June 1893 when conducting manoeuvres off Tripoli on board HMS *Victoria*. He gave orders that put his ship and HMS *Camperdown* on a collision course. In the collision *Victoria* was holed and sank very quickly with great loss of life. See *The Times*, 24 June 1893, p. 7, col. D: 'Terrible Naval Disaster'.

them to come out of their holes, instead of men shooting; and now having twaddled long enough, I will say good bye, with love to the united happy family.

28

Wykeham Martin to his family

Camp, Sevastopol, January 9th 1855

Dear Family in general, for I have received a letter today from nearly every individual in it, for which I thank you all most sincerely. I have now received some of your parcels; that is to say, those by the Faith, Royal Albert, and Cosmopolitan, and expect to get the others shortly. The Leopard has not yet arrived, but she has to me the most important parcel of all, namely, the boots, saw, axe, books and waterproof leggings. I only hope the long boots are large enough. There are plenty of people coming out at last, so I shall be able to get things without sending home I hope, except uniforms and boots. I have now got such a kit I could not move without throwing away heaps, and as I am not at the front it is more than probable the Russians may make me do so, considering the state of the Army. For the last week we have had awful weather, the first three days a drenching cold rain with sleet, the last three days snow with intense frost, so bad that an officer of the 9th foot froze to death walking home from Balaklava, having previously missed his way;[57] and several privates of the Regiments in pickets have lost their toes. I thank my stars I have no pickets to do now, being in a separate command. The huts now they are come are found too heavy to bring up to camp. I suppose we shall get them by the spring when they are not wanted. I am now living in the lap of luxury with Charles Trollope, who is supplied with every thing of the best by the most indefatigable exertions of Mrs Trollope, from Malta, who appears to me to be the best soldier's wife I have ever

---

57 *The Times* reported that Lieutenant Dent of the 9th Regiment was in command of a fatigue party engaged in carrying up provisions to the camp. He became unwell and could not keep up with his men and was later found dead in the snow. This was Lieutenant Thomas E. Bowerbank Dent, who had served in the campaign in Afghanistan in 1842 and also on the Sutlej in 1845–6. He became a Captain without purchase on 29 December 1854. The 9th Regiment arrived at the end of November 1854 and, like a lot of new arrivals, suffered greatly from the extremes of climate. In the appendix to Colborne and Brine, *The Last of the Brave*, there is a note in the remarks column stating that Lieutenant T. Dent was 'found dead on the road' on 5 January 1855. At the beginning of February the *Illustrated London News* published a version of this story relating to an unnamed British officer who lost his way back to camp and was found dead by the French. See *The Times*, 29 January 1855, p. 9, col. B; Colborne and Brine, *Last of the Brave*, p. 63.

heard of. He is in high spirits and says I must do all the writing for him to Leeds. He is command of a Brigade in the 2nd Division, *pro tem.* in which I think he is likely to be continued. George Tryon is looking very well, and stands his work like a man. I saw Mr. Sheffield the other day. It is my belief if we do not do something soon or make peace, the Russians will be down upon us and clear us up in the spring. Papa's present of the pea coat, fur cap, gloves, and thick suit of uniform, are very good, especially if old Rich had made them large enough. The mail now leaves here twice a week, so I cannot undertake to write every mail to everybody, so I have addressed this to the people of England at large, although I have written it as if to one person, so that all may see it if they like. I wrote to Mr Strange by this mail, thinking he might like to know how his old pupil was getting on, and did intend to writing to Billy Adolphus[58] but was afraid of his marking my letters as he did my themes, thus ═══all over, so I have deferred it to another time. You may tell my servant's friends that he is doing very well at present but heartily wishes himself back in England again. Also tell Harris that his son has made Corporal when I enquired about him, so I conclude he is doing well. I did not see him at the time. I have not received the Maidstone paper, so have not seen my name in print. If you have the other you might send it as I should like to see what is said. I have no news of any kind, so with my usual good wishes to everybody.

29

Wykeham Martin to his stepmother

Inkerman Heights, January 24th 1855

I have received your letter telling me of Mr. Marsh's present; when I receive it I will write and thank him for it, or if I do not receive it at all I shall certainly thank him for his good intention. I have not got the things by the Malacca yet, but I am going to Balaklava tomorrow to see if I can hear anything of them. I had to find an escort for two Russian deserters (Poles), who told us that the Russian Army had got reinforcements to the amount of 30,000 men and 16 batteries of Artillery. Our Artillery are so completely unhorsed by the weather, that no Battery except the one at Balaklava could possibly bring more than three guns

---

58 The Reverend William Adolphus Carter, FWM's tutor at Eton.

into action, and some of them not that. The frost has made great havoc with the men's toes and the horses; of the former many have dropped off. It is awful to see the state some of the Hospitals are in; I went today to see a man of my detachment whose toes have been frost-bitten. I found him crammed in a bell tent with twelve men, one of whom was in the last stage of death, without any one seemingly to know or care anything about it. They have at last got up one tent a Regiment for a hospital, which is a great thing; as to the others I do not suppose the least attempt will be made to get them up till the spring, when they will not be wanted. The great fault of the whole Army is their not having a waggon train the same as other continental nations. I believe Lord Raglan has done as much as was possible with the materials he had. The real truth is that we never had sufficient means of transport or an army sufficient for such an undertaking. Will you thank Erskine for his intended present, and tell him I will give him an *autograph letter* as soon as I can. Adams says in Maria's last that she concludes that she is included in my remembrances to the establishment; tell her I beg to be most particularly remembered to her as well as all the others. I saw a letter from her ladyship the other day, in which she appeared to be in her usual health and spirits. How is Laura? I think I have behaved very badly towards her in not having written since Varna. However tell her I will make up as soon as I have an opportunity, for lost time. Julia and George I have not heard of for some time, so I conclude they are quite well; remember me to them next time you write, and also to little Edith. I suppose the parcels coming with the Navvies[59] will be here shortly. My servant, Friend, wishes £2.10s to be sent to the same address as last time, will you see to it? and mind and send me by the next mail the amount due to you, and I will send you a cheque for it, and one for the Governor for £100 due to him. We have been recommended to get the new uniform,[60] as the men are to have it in April, but I feel rather stingy about it, as I have spent so much already to so little purpose. I hope the long boots will be big enough when they arrive, but I am afraid from what I have received, they will not; what I have got are a perfect fit when on, but take too long to put on and would

---

59 Navvies – originally 'navigators' – were labourers who constructed the canals in Britain and then worked on the railways. They were famous for the prodigious quantities of earth they could shift and infamous for their rough ways, drinking and fighting. They came out to build the railway from Balaklava to the siege lines before Sebastopol. See Cooke, *Grand Crimean Railway*, passim.

60 The old uniform with its pelisse, tight-fitting overalls and barrel sash proved to be impractical for campaigning. By the end of 1854 many of the cavalry were in rags and some were without footwear. The new uniform was looser and less ornate than the one worn when war broke out. See W. Carman, *Richard Simkin's Uniforms of the British Army: The Cavalry Regiments* (Exeter: Webb and Bower, 1982), pp. 149–57.

make my feet swell if I slept in them. I heard today that the Light Brigade of Cavalry were to go to Scutari to be mounted on native horses,[61] but I do not know if it is true or not. I have no news and shall therefore bid you good-bye.

30

Wykeham Martin to his stepmother

Camp Sevastopol, Jan. 28th 1855

I have just received your letter of the 11th, and have likewise received my things from Ede's. Unluckily the portmanteau which contained the writing case and eatables was lost in the Bosphorus so I only got my gun, shot and plain clothes, and shirts, which I do not know what to do with. I wrote to Ede asking him to bring up a parcel of things that I mentioned to him, but it appears he will not undertake anything, but the mere taking care of goods, or forwarding goods consigned to him, so I am overloaded with all these things, which I think I will send back to England at once with some others. I shall have to spend a fortune in clothes when I get back to England, as all my things are worn out or scattered over the globe, and I shall have *grown* owing to living in the open air, too big for any of my clothes. I should like the paper sent direct from Byfield, that I may get the latest news, as those sent through you I do not get till they are stale. The first batch was dated 1st January, the same mail brought out to the 14th. We derive the whole of the information as to what we are about from the papers, so you can imagine how anxiously we look for the latest news, even reading papers before letters sometimes, sooner than lose a chance of seeing them. I have not got the Malacca parcels, but have all the others; I dare say I shall get them in time, the ship having been at Cherson nearly a month. I believe she has got my books on board, for which I would give a great deal. I'm afraid the knitting of the Ladies Nevill and Maidstone Ladies will hardly be appreciated enough by the soldiers, as they have *now* got more winter clothing than they can use;[62]

---

61 The death rate among the cavalry horses meant that the division was not fit for purpose and remounts had to be found. 'Native' horses suggests the small, spirited mounts favoured by the Cossacks. The rumour regarding the Light Cavalry Brigade being sent to Scutari proved to be false.

62 The shipping losses in the great storm of 14 November 1854 included the *Prince*, which was carrying large quantities of winter clothing for the army. Consequently the casualty rate through frostbite and cold rose during the severity of the winter weather. Winter clothes started to arrive in the New Year. See HCPP 1854–5 (283), pp. 10–11.

however I will distribute them *when* I get them. I hear Lord George Paget has not yet left England. I had a letter from the Sailor at Malta, in which he says that they kept it up pretty considerably with the soldiers coming out there, singing, drinking &c. on the forecastle. Charles Trollope is very well, and begs to be remembered to Miss Osborne particularly, and sends his love to the family, I do not know if Miss O. is in the latter. If he does I shall write to his wife. I mess with him now, that is to say, he gives me dinner every night and does not require any payment. I believe he will take me as his Aide de Camp if he is confirmed in command of his Brigade, if so I shall require a Staff suit,[63] and shall acquire the honour of being *abused* in the Times. We hear rumours of peace here, every time the rumour is talked of more than usual, there is sure to be a salvo of Russian guns upon which the soldiers say to each other, 'Is that pace?' [peace]. I see young Tharp[64] has got into the 62nd; he was a very nice young fellow when I knew him at Ipswich, it is a very nice Regiment and a gentlemanly set of officers. I know them all from being quartered there. The mail is closed earlier than usual, so I must say good bye.

31

Wykeham Martin to his brother Philip[65]

Camp before Sevastopol, Inkerman Heights, January 31st 1855
I think it is now your turn for a letter, but owing to the mail going so often I cannot give you all letters every time, but generally contrive to give one or two to the family; this time it is you and Cornwallis, from whom I have received a letter dated about the 28th, at Malta, where he had arrived safe. I have received my air-pillow and long calf-skin boots, by the Malacca; the only things missing now are my portmanteau, which I believe is at the bottom of the Bosphorus, the parcel containing the axe, saw, books, your present of chamois leather underclothing, holster bottle, and the things coming out by [*the Railway*] other vessels [*that ass Ede has sent up by large box from Constantinople although I begged him*

---

63   Staff officers wore a different uniform to the regimentals usually worn by cavalry officers. See Michael Barthorp and Pierre Turner, *The British Army on Campaign. 2: The Crimea 1854–56.* Men at Arms Series No. 196 (London: Osprey, 1993), pp. 37–8.

64   William Montagu Tharp, Ensign 5 January 1855, Lieutenant, 9 March 1855. Laura Trollope, sister to Fiennes Wykeham Martin's stepmother, married Joseph Sidney Tharp on 11 November 1852.

65   Passages in italics were not included in the 1868 published collection and have been restored from the originals.

not consequently here I am saddled with an enormous package that I cannot carry, full of evening ties, servants livery and such other useful articles of wearing apparel in the Crimea. Fancy my appearing saddled in the camp amongst people covered with mud and dirt who have not had their clothes off for weeks together in a white evening tie with patent leather boots followed by Hunt in full rig with his red waistcoat.]

Yesterday we were clever enough to allow a spy to walk through our camp, visit our engineer's yard and go quietly back again; coupled with this, the two Grand Dukes, Nicholas and Michael have returned to Sevastopol, and we expect another Inkerman shortly; but this time they will find Zouaves[66] on picket instead of Englishmen; they have not the English habit of going to sleep on picket, so we shall not be caught napping as we were before, and as the place is so strongly fortified, we shall probably give the young *cubs* a greater hiding than we did before, without so much loss ourselves.

February 1st.

Since writing the above, I have had a thirty two pound shot pitched within ten yards of my tent, rather a pleasant visitor; fancy if it had come into my tent whilst I was asleep, how it would have startled me. Tell Papa I have today received the braces by the post and am much obliged. There will certainly be something done here very soon, although we do not know what; either we shall attack them or they will attack us, it does not much matter which. I shall tomorrow despatch the useless articles of my kit to England, so you can be on the look out for its arrival; among other things you will find a Greco, a stunning thing to drive to cover in; you can have it if you like, as I shall bring a new one home with me *when* I come. The weather has been very fine for the last two or three days, but I am afraid we shall have a change, as it never lasts long here.

February 2nd.

The mail is closing, so I must conclude my epistle. Tell Papa I have received the books this afternoon, but have read many of them before, *unluckily there are 2 or 3 copies of the same work sent.* We, the 2nd Division, are going to be removed, I believe; if so I shall rejoin my Regiment most likely. No time for more.

---

66   Light infantry of the French army dressed in North African style uniforms with red, loose baggy trousers and white gaiters. They were known for their élan and spirit in attack.

32

Wykeham Martin to his father

Balaklava, February 24th 1855

I have just received no. 28 letter. As you will see by the heading I have got back to my Regiment and am in the Colonel's tent, but I am afraid I shall be turned out, as I hear he is coming back tomorrow. You ask me if I want any lift in the Army, it would be a very good thing if they would promote me into either of those two Regiments, the 18th or 19th Light Dragoons, which they are going to organize, as I should get my Troop for nothing if they would do it. I have no claims to put forward over many others; only sometimes people do not like going into newly formed Regiments. I have just received a letter from Philip, in which he says that I am likely to become an uncle shortly. The betting here is even, that we shall be in Sevastopol in three weeks, although I myself do not think it likely that we shall even attempt it till the spring. The weather is very cold, but I do not think there is so much sickness as there was. The Cavalry are quite in clover; to show you what I had for dinner today, and it is a pretty good example of others. Soup, wild duck roasted and boiled, dough pudding with plums, cheese cake, oranges, sherry and porter. I *think* I can exist on that. Tomorrow I shall try and get up Philip's barrel of wine, so that then we shall be well off. As to summer clothing I do not know that we shall be allowed to wear it, so that I cannot order anything; but at all events here one can always walk about in one's shirt and trowsers, except when on parade. If I am not made a Captain in the 18th or 19th, will you tell Rich to make me whatever uniform he is making for the other officers out here of the new pattern. I hear that my portmanteau is somewhere in the harbour, so that now the only things I have lost are the axe and knife, through the stupidity of my servant leaving them in the street. The Railway has made great progress, although not so fast as it ought, owing to the navvies not working as hard as they do at home; the truth is, the native Englishman never will work unless he is obliged. I believe it is partly owing to laziness that the men have died out here. The English soldier is decidedly the laziest and most careless man in the world, although they will fight better than anyone. Charles Trollope is in high force as Brigadier. We hear the Turks at Eupatoria have given the Russians a good thrashing, but I do not know if it is true or not; they are the Danube Turks, and not the lot we have here. Most of the Regiments now have one or two tents up, besides the two for the hospital, and some

Regiments are entirely hutted,[67] especially the Cavalry and Artillery, who have more time than the Infantry. The horses also are in stables, and at Balaklava every thing is in much better order; they have established a bazaar outside the town, which takes away the crowd from the town and leaves the houses as stores for Regiments and Brigades, so we are better than we were; likewise we have had a week of fine dry weather which has cheered people up a little. The Cavalry made a reconnaissance the other night; when they started it was a fine warm night, so they went out thinly clad, but before morning it was fearfully cold, with a tremendous snow storm, consequently many men and officers had their ears frost-bitten.

33

Wykeham Martin to his stepmother

Balaklava, March 1st 1855

I have received your letters of the 9th, and I am much obliged to you for thinking of my pocket by sending out your papers, but as you do not get the papers of the day, and you have to send them back to London, they must always be three days behind, which just makes one mail behind-hand; now a paper of the last mail any one would give you out here, so it is only giving you trouble for nothing. I am glad to see the Sailor is promoted,[68] he is quite a swell and ranks above me for the present, in fact will do so unless I become a Major before he is Commander. I have written to Philip for the things I want for the summer, as he knows the things I had before, but we all expect peace out here, so that I shall not want them. The Railway is getting on pretty well, but the head people say the navvies do not work as well here as they do in England. Lord G. Paget has rejoined and is *pro tem.* the Brigadier of the Light Brigade. Philip asked me if the Bab (that is to be) should have my name or not: I told him he had better give the first one his own name, and if there is another it would be time enough to think about it. Philip is going to borrow my

---

67   The wooden components of the huts had been left on the harbour side at Balaklava for months because of a lack of means to get them to the camps to be erected. As the railway progressed and the labour force increased, it became possible to shift the parts and construct the huts where they were needed most.

68   This refers to the promotion of his brother in the Royal Navy. Cornwallis Wykeham Martin was promoted to the rank of Lieutenant on 3 February 1855, on the screw steam frigate *Arrogant*. See *Navy List*, July 1855, p. 52.

charger when his yeomanry comes out.[69] I see Lord Cardigan is getting immense kudos for his conduct in the Crimea. There are so many fellows of different Regiments smoking and making a row that I cannot write any more. I have written to Peareth[70] to bring me out some Regimental saddlery in the Julia.

34

Wykeham Martin to his brother Philip

[Letter omitted from the 1868 publication]
Balaklava March 1st
I have just received your letter of the 9th and must thank you for your present of wine which by the by I have taken the liberty of changing to sherry and a case of Port amounting to the same money as Rochford told me the octave of Port costs, the reason was that the octave was too heavy to carry and I could not get it up. I am in a bad way with my horses just now, both of them having the mange very badly and obliged to stand in the open air. I do not know what I shall do if they don't get over it. I am glad to see the sailor has got his promotion. I wish I could get mine. Everybody seems to go over my head, even young Sheffield who I suppose is barely 20 has got his company. By the by you want to ride my horse in your Yeomanry Drill, you are perfectly welcome but you must mind what you are at as if you pull on his mouth which is very light at all harder than he likes, he knocks about so and turns round and round so sharp that the devil himself could not sit him, otherwise he is a very good tempered horse and you may do what you like with him in the stable. I must congratulate you on Madame being in the state most ladies should be who love their Lords. As to the name if it is a boy and your 1st one I should call it after yourself and then if you have any more you can think about it when the time comes. Will you if peace is not declared send me out a new canteen, the best you can (not Peat's as it is damned bad) but take care to have a good frying pan of enamelled iron, soup plates I'm drinking lots and something that will boil anything in, Adams of the Haymarket has a very good one only it is rather dear also I want another

---

69   This is a camp rumour that the volunteer cavalry at home, the Yeomanry, were going to come out to the Crimea to make up the deficiencies in the cavalry numbers.

70   William Peareth, 4th Light Dragoons, Cornet by purchase August 1849; Lieutenant by purchase November 1850; Captain by purchase January 1853. Peareth did not arrive in the Crimea for he sold his commission in May 1855. See *Hart's New Army List 1855*, p. 131.

axe as my forgetful fool of a servant left more than a tent in the ship. Whether I told you to use my cheques for Hamburger, if I did not do so I will now. I have made great friends with Hunt of the Enniskillens.[71] He is the man we used to see out with the hounds with light whiskers and a great swell. He was likewise quartered at Maidstone once when he was in the 9th Queens there.

35

Wykeham Martin to his stepmother

Balaklava, March 12th 1855

I was sorry to hear of poor Julia's death,[72] but I have not yet had an opportunity of seeing Col. Trollope. I must likewise take this opportunity of thanking the Governor for his liberality in presenting me with £100. I hear purchase is done away with altogether,[73] but I do not believe it. The last report here is that the Emperor of Russia is dead from an attack of pleurisy, and Prince Menschikoff is wounded in the knee. The English Army is recovering itself gradually; all the Cavalry are in huts, horses and all, except the officers, who remain in tents, in fact we turn out the few we have as clean as if we were in Dublin. Every one declares (Lord Raglan included) that there must be peace now that the Emperor is dead; if so, we shall be home first, having no horses and being of no use here. In case the war goes on, a patrol tent would be a very useful thing to have; a white one, rather larger than the one I had when I came out. My things are on the Bucephalus and will go home in her whenever she goes, but at present she is a store ship at Kamisch. I am glad the Sailor got his promotion and also got through scarlet fever. Another parcel of the concentrated soup would be very useful, as it is not to be got here, other things you can get. We have got up some Race meetings[74] here and

---

71 Edmund D'Arcy Hunt.

72 Julia Reynardson (née Trollope), sister to Matilda, Fiennes Wykeham Martin's stepmother, who died on 16 February 1855.

73 Though often mooted, the abolition of purchase was not effected until November 1871. See Anthony Bruce, 'Edward Cardwell and the Abolition of Purchase' in Ian F. W. Beckett and John Gooch, eds., *Politicians and Defence* (Manchester: Manchester University Press, 1981), pp. 24–46; idem, *The Purchase System in the British Army, 1660–1871* (London: Royal Historical Society, 1980).

74 When the weather improved in the spring of 1855, several horse races were organised with officers riding in silks and money changing hands. See *Illustrated London News*, 26 May 1855, p. 515; Russell, *British Expedition to the Crimea*, p. 234.

the French have some also, so with that and dog hunting we contrive to pass our time. We have everything ready for an assault, which will take place very soon, if the report about the Emperor is not true; if it is, his successor is peaceful, so we shall do nothing. If the bread riots become general, Philip will have a chance of showing his military prowess, by keeping the mob in order.

PS The holster pipe bottle Papa sent out got smashed by the stove coming out. Will you get me glass one from Gardens; I have just got up the big stove, but I cannot sell it, as we are inundated with stoves and the weather is quite hot again; I likewise want a new sheepskin if they are not done away with.

36

Wykeham Martin to his brother Philip

Balaklava, March 14th 1855

From what I can see you are likely soon to be called out to stop bread riots[75] and other turbulent mobs. All you have got to do if you are, is to form your men up so that they take up the whole street, pavement and all, and then trot quietly down the street with drawn swords; one squadron in column division would do it easy, with another in reserve in case you get into confusion. Sir Colin Campbell's battery at Balaklava has just shot a Russian in the plain. All the batteries at Sevastopol are ready for use, but we are not going to begin until we know whether the tale is true about the Emperor being dead, as Alexander his eldest son is a peaceful youth. We have made ourselves comfortable here, every soldier is in a tent and the horses likewise; we have also established a 'Poultry yard' and get fresh eggs every morning for breakfast. I am still in a tent and shall stay there, as I think for one it is quite as comfortable as a hut. You will be happy to hear that Menschikoff was wounded the other night in the knee, we likewise have taken a swell of a prisoner, but he will not give his name;

---

75 There were riots in Liverpool and London in February 1855. The Liverpool rioters were described by *The Times* as from the 'low Irish population', who lived in the poorest part of the city. A severe winter had led to rising unemployment among the day labourers and the poorest sections of society. This, in turn, led to growing distress. Some cities, like Exeter, provided poor relief with soup kitchens. Other places did not and civil disturbances followed. The police usually dealt with local unrest but, if this grew, then cavalry or yeomanry could be called out to 'aid the civil power'.

some people say he is one of the Princes. Starling,[76] a very clever fellow who was in our Band, and is a Pen and Daguerreotype man, has come out here from the Daguerreotype Society[77] to take views and likenesses of the camp and its inhabitants. I will have one done of our camp and send it home if I can. There is a Restaurant established now at Balaklava[78] and a baking establishment, so we are becoming quite a colony here. In fact I do not believe the French will ever leave the country.

37

Wykeham Martin to his father

Balaklava, March 22nd 1855

There is a rumour today that the English have taken the works round the tower. The French have tried two or three times, and have been driven back every time; but if we really tried last night I do not think we should have failed. Our camp begins to assume a picturesque appearance, some people have gone as far as gardens round their tents. Menschikoff is reported dead, and also another general. If there is peace you must have some shirts evening and morning ready for me, as I do not expect to see the others again, or not for a very long time. I am glad to hear the Sailor is all right; tell him I do not write to him because as he is at home he will see this. I am glad he is out of the Calcutta, as I hear his station was or is to be Scotland, a place where there is no honour or glory, and very little amusement to be got. I suppose he will now get a steamer and go to the Baltic. I will now conclude, and add tomorrow anything I can before the post goes.

---

76   Marcus Fitzell Sparling (Wykeham Martin misspelled his name), formerly no. 1242 of the 4th Light Dragoons. After the Crimean War, he wrote a technical work on cameras. On Roger Fenton and other photographers in the Crimea, see Helmut and Alison Gernsheim, eds, *Roger Fenton: Photographer of the Crimea* (London: Secker & Warburg, 1954); John Hannavy, *The Camera Goes to War: Photographs from the Crimean War, 1854–56* (Edinburgh: Scottish Arts Council, 1974).

77   Daguerreotypes were images taken on a silvered copper sheet as opposed to the rival calotype system based on coarse-grained paper. Fenton and his assistants, however, actually used a newer 'wet collodion' or wet-plate process that combined elements of both daguerreotype and calotype by reproducing the image on a glass plate with a finer grained emulsion.

78   This refers to the 'British Hotel' run by Mary 'Mother' Seacole, a Jamaican woman of some character. The establishment provided hot food, drink and herbal remedies as well as a welcome break from the monotony of the trenches and camp. When the navvies arrived to build the railway, they took full advantage of the facilities and were sometimes seen lying all over the road before the hotel in a state of 'unparalleled intoxication'. See TNA, WO28/193, Bundle marked 'Provost Marshals'; Helen Rappaport, *No Place for Ladies* (London: Aurum, 2007); Jane Robinson, *Mary Seacole* (London: Constable, 2005).

March 23.

I hear today that the French were driven out of [one of] their batteries, and were obliged to get the 23rd Fusileers [*sic*] to retake it; the latter, according to report, lost three officers. Today I also hear the Infantry are ordered to sleep all day and be ready for business at night. All this is a shave, as we call it, but I thought I would put it in, as the post is just going, and it may be true. The papers are well worth the money. Tell Byfield to send them regularly. At present rate of living I spend very little more than my pay, barring uniforms and things I get in England. I forget if I mentioned a collar chain, sheep-skin and white cap, in my list of necessaries. The weather is very hot here now. Sheffield is Colonel Trollope's Aide.[79] I have just heard that the shave is true. We lost four officers, and one Engineer officer.[80] They took our trenches, but Colonel Yea of the 7th Fusileers [*sic*], not the 23rd, went down and turned them out.

38

Wykeham Martin to his father

Balaklava, April 2nd 1855

I write you one line today. I have just received your letter, with the sketch of the interesting officers of the 4th;[81] also to say that this morning about 12 o'clock I received an order to pack up my baggage and go down to Scutari tonight, to join the depot coming out from England. I suppose I shall be there about three weeks. You had better send letters to Balaklava as usual, as by the time you get this I shall either be coming home or going back to the Crimea. I have lost the greater part of the kit I meant to send home, but I may find it again some day, especially now that I can ask Ede where it is now I am going to Constantinople. The articles missing are a portmanteau and a box I left at Ede's when we went to Varna. If I do not find them I think I shall come down, as I never authorized him to send them. The stove too I shall never see again, as I leave it behind me in the Crimea. I will write to the aunts and others when I can find

---

79 Lieutenant John Charles Sheffield, 21st Regiment. Sheffield's younger sister, Julia Maria, had married into the Trollope family in October 1847 when she married Lord Kesteven.

80 The three officers killed were Captain the Hon. Cavendish Brown, 7th Fusiliers; Captain Hedley Vicars, 97th Regiment; and Lieutenant W. W. Jordan of the 34th Regiment. Lieutenant Colonel Kelly, 34th Regiment was missing, as was Montague of the Royal Engineers. See Cook and Cook, *Casualty Roll*, pp. 133, 145, 167, 201.

81 A footnote in the 1868 publication explains: 'A caricature out of *Punch* of recruits offering themselves to the recruiting sergeant of the 4th.'

time. Tell Philip, Vann[82] was George Brown's servant, and that he died at Varna.

39

Wykeham Martin to his brother Philip

[Letter omitted from the 1868 publication]
Scutari 8th April 1855
As I wrote to Leeds to announce my departure to this place I will fire you a line to say that I have arrived safely after a rough passage in the most damnable steamer that ever sailed. I was very sorry to leave the Crimea before the business was over as I shall probably lose the medal and I had just made myself pretty comfortable. As it is I was obliged to leave half my baggage which I shall probably never see again and my horses behind me. I likewise think this place more unhealthy although I am in a house and very comfortable. I went to the opera last night but cannot say much for it, since I have seen the hospitals at Scutari I am more than ever convinced that the Times is a liar as I was just astonished to see how much more healthy the men were down here than they are at the front. In fact there are a multitude of shirkers although of course there are many sad cases but that must always occur in wartime. It is a very odd thing but Robertson is the subaltern sent by the Royal Dragoons consequently he and I are in a room together here. We little thought when we were at Eton that we should ever be quartered together in the same room in different regiments at Constantinople. I told them to tell you in my last letter that the man Vann who you wish to know about was dead. He was a very good man and was George Brown's servant after his old servant Abraham died of cholera at Varna.[83] An odd thing a man could lose 2 men one after the other of cholera. I have nothing more to say except that you need not send this epistle to the castle as I intend writing there too if I have time.

---

82 1557 Pvt. J. W. Vann from Leicester. He enlisted on 5 February 1853 and was a clerk prior to enlistment. He died at Scutari on 12 October 1854. The officer referred to is Captain George Brown of the 4th Light Dragoons. See TNA, WO12/659.

83 1114 Pvt. John Abraham, a groom from Hampshire, enlisted 30 April 1840, died Varna 12 August 1854.

40

Wykeham Martin to his stepmother

Scutari Barracks, April 9th 1855

I write you a line to say I am safely landed at Scutari in a moderately comfortable house, and with nothing to do. We remain here till the drafts come out, but as they had not started on the 19th we shall probably be here a long time with nothing to do. I am very sorry to leave the Crimea, as never having been ill I should have like to have said I saw it all through; and likewise, if they take the town while I am away, I lose the medal. By a strange coincidence, Robertson[84] is one of the subalterns sent by the Royal Dragoons. We certainly did not expect, when we were at Eton, to be quartered together at Scutari in the same room. When did the Vestal sail?[85] as I have not yet received the parcel you sent in her, and the forage cap I want. I shall now have an opportunity of going at Ede about losing my box full of gold belts &c. The sick down here are rather stronger and better than the men at the front. I had not time to see Charles before I started, but he was very well the last time I saw him. I shall not want the tunic just yet, but you can tell Rich to send it if the others have theirs. I am not in great want of the overalls; but if he makes me any, tell him to leather them up to the knee, and make them broad at the top of the leg, and small at the foot, as the French overalls are made, only not quite so exaggerated as they are.

41

Wykeham Martin to his stepmother

Scutari Barracks, April 19th 1855

I enclose you a cheque for £50, which I think was the amount of the bills, but I have lost the slip of paper, and am therefore not quite certain. I have found out from Ede that he has lost the large packet of things I left here

---

84 See note 16 above.
85 The paddle-steam transport *Vestal*, 200 tons, owned by James Baines & Co., Liverpool, left that port on 7 March and arrived in Gibraltar on 16 March carrying packages etc. for the British Army and Navy in the east. It left Gibraltar on 17 March and went via Malta and Constantinople to Scutari and Balaklava, arriving there on 9 April. See the *The Times*, 10 May 1855, p. 8 col. F for a letter extolling the virtue of this small paddle-steamer as opposed to the bigger more expensive transports employed by the government.

on the way to Varna, including my gold belts and mess waistcoat; rather a bore. He was sending them up to me at Balaklava without an order, and the lighter upset, so they are now at the bottom of the Bosphorus, a nuisance, as it will cost me money when I return to England. After all, the horses are not to be landed here, so we have had our journey for nothing. The sheep-skin you are sending is the full dress one, and no use here, but you could not know that. I do not know if it is Byfield's fault or my Regiment's, but I never get my papers here; but I have no doubt they keep them with the Regiment to read. Will you look the first time you are in London, at my account at Hoare's,[86] and see if there is a cheque come in, dated about 23rd October. It was one I gave to Halkett for £15, and I'm afraid he had it in his pocket when he was killed; if so, the Cossacks have got it, and it will not be of much use to them; if it has not come in, will you find out Mrs Halkett's address from Ridgway, and I will send her another. I cannot now enquire whether Harris is dead or not, but I saw in the paper that one corporal was dead, and I conclude it was him. The first time I go round the hospital I will try and find out, although I am afraid there is not much chance, as they do not seem to know who they have got in the wards. I will send you an address of a Daguerreotype man from whom you can get any amount of copies of your humble servant, in a group of his brother officers;[87] also of the camp as soon as I return to the Crimea. I hope old Bumble is getting quite strong again. I must write him a letter as soon as I can find something to say. I always forget he is at home; and with love to Fairfax and the rest.

42

Wykeham Martin to his stepmother

Scutari Barracks, April 26th 1855

I have dispatched one box from here by ship Simla, the one I came out in. Mr Stebbing, the Purser, has taken charge of it for me, and says he will see it safe home and through the Custom House. There are two or three little things in it for the female part of the family, but I could

---

86 One of the oldest private banks in the country. Founded in the late seventeenth century in Cheapside. In the nineteenth century it was situated in Fleet Street, where it remains.

87 Fiennes Wykeham Martin is sitting on the ground in the Fenton composition. See J. B. R. Nicholson and Michael Roffe, *The British Army of the Crimea*. Men at Arms Series (Reading: Osprey, 1974), p. 10.

not find any thing to suit the male part except chiboukes.[88] Now as the Governor and Philip do not smoke, they would not be very useful; almost everything else in the bazaar is made in London or Paris, so would be nothing curious. Of course any expense Mr. Stebbing is put to you will repay; his address as far as I know, is Peninsula and Oriental Company's steam ship Simla, Southampton; at all events that will find him. We hear rather bad accounts from the Crimea, but never getting our papers here we are rather in the dark as to general news. Opinions are divided about the Light Cavalry charge, but we must wait to hear Lord Raglan before it is possible to decide. I am going to give Cornwallis a line, so will put the rest of the news into his letter.

43

Wykeham Martin to his stepmother

Scutari Barracks, May 5th 1855

Not having heard from you for the last two or three mails, I conclude some of my letters have miscarried, owing to me being down at this hole. I do not know if it is the fault of Byfield or the Postmaster here, but I have only received one newspaper last month. I got my canteen and things out of the Argo, but I have not got my forage cap yet. I suppose it is at Balaklava. Did it come out in the Vestal? I suppose by the time you get this you will be thinking of going to London. It was about this time last year that we were leaving Canterbury never expecting that we should pass the next six months in this country. They do not seem to me to be making half enough effort to get a Cavalry force here in time to be of any use for this year's Campaign. Were you in London to see the reception given to the Emperor and Empress of the French?[89] We see by the papers it was something superior. Sir Thomas Whichcote[90] is here with his yacht, but I have not been able to drop across him yet. It is becoming quite the fashion to come out here as a show. I have met a good many men and

---

88 Long pipes favoured by the Turks for smoking tobacco. See Lawrence James, *Crimea 1854–56: The War with Russia from Contemporary Photographs* (Thame: Hayes Kennedy, 1981), p. 134, no. 51, for a Fenton photograph of Ismail Pasha with his servants, one of whom is holding the chibouque.

89 Napoleon III and Empress Eugénie paid a state visit to the United Kingdom in the spring of 1855. See *Illustrated London News* April/May 1855.

90 Sir Thomas Whichcote of Aswarby Park, Lincolnshire.

some ladies; in fact it will be a perfect Chobham[91] next summer I believe, with the exception that there were no bullets at Chobham. I have nothing to tell you, and so will say good bye.

44

Wykeham Martin to his brother Philip

[Letter omitted from the 1868 publication]
Scutari May 10th [1855]
We leave this place for the Crimea tomorrow at 3 o'clock not having received a single horse consequently we have had our journey for nothing, I am not sorry to go back for one spends a great deal of money here with a very moderate degree of enjoyment, you will have heard before you get this, in the expedition to Kertch the Cavalry sent 40 men under Low we do not know what they are going to do but we suppose they will cut off the provisions the Russians get into the Crimea from Asia. People are beginning to come out here on their continental tours in fact it is becoming quite Cockney. The cholera has broken out here very bad again with the hot weather. I saw at least a dozen funerals last Sunday afternoon when I was at Pera and they say that in the French camp they are dying 30 a day. I hope we shall not get it in the Crimea. I hear the conferences are reopened but I do not think they will come to much unless they take Sevastopol. The Sardinian Troops have arrived and are the smartest, best dressed and equipped troops I ever saw beating the French hollow in my opinion. How they will fight I do not know but at all events they are broad-shouldered healthy looking men and march like Englishmen, so I dare say they will do if we could but take that damned town, we would soon have all the Russians out of the Crimea. There's no time for more with love to both.

---

91 Chobham had been the site of the camp of exercise in 1853. In fact, Lord Hardinge had pushed for the purchase of land at Aldershot for a permanent training ground and purchase of the first 3,000 acres was authorised in December 1853. See Strachan, *Wellington's Legacy*, pp. 170–1.

45

Wykeham Martin to his stepmother

Balaklava, May 16th 1855

I have arrived here safe and sound again, and find it very hot. We had a field day this morning and eight men went to hospital with slight coup de soleil immediately after. The box I sent you by the Simla contains clothing for the winter, which I shall probably want again next winter if I am here. Will you tell Byfield that he only sends me the latest papers instead of all. It will be better to have them sent by Smith, as his are the only ones that come regularly. The Sardinians have arrived, and appear to be very good troops, and are certainly well mounted and equipped for service. I saw Colonel Dundas the other day, but have not seen the others. They talk of a Campaign in the interior, but I think they have let the time go by, as the heat is too great.

46

Wykeham Martin to his father

Balaklava, May 25th 1855

There has been a large reconnaissance this morning which started at 3 o'clock a.m. I went with it as an amateur, as it consisted chiefly of French, Sardinians and Turks. We have succeeded in establishing ourselves on the Tchernaya, and late this evening we received an order to hold ourselves in readiness to turn out at 6 o'clock, which looks as if they meant to take the heights by Mackenzie's Farm; it will be rather a tough job, I fancy. So as I was up all last night I must take a wink or two, or I shall get none at all, therefore my letter will be short. I received all your letters today dated the 11th of May. The cheque for Mrs Halket appears all right, but if you could find out her address you might write and ask her. I went over the Balaklava plain[92] this morning for the first time since the battle; except for a few skeletons of dead horses you would never know there had been a shot fired there. Will you send out with my

---

92   This refers to the North Valley, the scene of the Charge of the Light Brigade some seven months earlier. Others rode over the same spot and were impressed by its beauty. Troop Sergeant Major George Loy Smith, 11th Hussars wrote on 28 May 1855, 'The whole valley is now covered with flowers and the larks are singing delightfully'. See Loy Smith, *Victorian RSM*, p. 189.

tunic and overhalls [*sic*] (leathered up to the knee like the others) my gold belts, likewise get Rich to buy me a second hand silver pouch, as mine went to the bottom of the Bosphorus. If he cannot get an old one he must send a new one; also I want a new regimental bridle according to the new pattern, but I am not in a violent hurry for that.

P.S. Tell the others I will answer their letters when I come back from the fight.

47

Wykeham Martin to his stepmother

Balaklava, June 8th 1855

There was a partial assault of the town last night. I went up to witness it; the French took the Mamelon, and not content with that, rushed on at the Malakoff Tower without the proper means of taking it, consequently they suffered enormous loss, and have not taken it (between 3 and 4000); at the same time we attacked the Quarry in front of the Redan, and I am afraid we have lost 1300 men and 34 officers; however you will know the true state of the case before I do. Charles Trollope was commanding his Brigade in the attack, but up to the time I left was all right. Will you pay into the hands of John Friend,[93] at Mr. William Eliots, Holyshute, Exeter, Honiton, £20, the savings of his brother out here. His brother will write and tell him what he wants done with it. I recommend him to put it in some bank. I am going up to the front to hear the truth of everything, and if anything is wrong with Charles I will open my letter and let you know.

48

Wykeham Martin to his father

Balaklava, June 28th 1855

I think you are quite right about Mrs Halket's cheque, as it seems pretty clear that she received it, as I did not draw any other cheque for that amount at that time. By this time you will have heard of Lord Raglan's

---

93 Wykeham Martin's servant.

death, which we are all very sorry for he will be a great loss to the army, and I do not know where they will find a better man, his death will defer my getting my Troop for a little while, as they will not have time to attend to such small things till they have got things a little straight. The army has had a great blow – Six Generals hors de combat in one week,[94] three of which are dead. It is awfully dull work here now, and the army are rather down in their luck, what with the loss of Generals, their failure in attack and the cholera also. We know we are in for another winter here, which is not a lively prospect; you might send me out another parcel of books, only tell Bain to let them be good ones, new novels, or something of that sort are the only things read here, as we are not in a humour for serious things. Charles Trollope was very well the last time I saw him, he had behaved very well in the Trenches, I hear, during the first attack.[95]

49

Wykeham-Martin to his sister Maria

Balaklava, July 2nd 1855

I have not written to you to condole with you on your illness. I would have written sooner, only the last two mails I have been busy with money transactions and making arrangements for my Troop. Will you tell Papa to keep copies of the letters I sent him in case they are wanted. They talk of sending us out to the Baidar Valley; but I hope they will not, as the 10th are there now and are losing men and officers daily by cholera,[96] although we have got it here also, it is not quite so bad, and we escape

---

94 Major General Sir J. Campbell Bt, 4th Division, killed; Major General William Eyre, severely wounded; Lieutenant General Sir George Brown, General Officer commanding Right Attack, ill; Major General William Codrington, Light Division, ill; Major General John Pennefather, 2nd Division, ill; Major General George Buller, ill. Brigadier General James Estcourt, the Adjutant General, died on the morning of 24 June 1855.

95 Trollope commanded a composite brigade in the 2nd Division, which was supposed to assault the centre of the Redan. This attack did not take place due to the failure of the Light and 4th Division's assaults. See McGuigan, *Into Battle!*, p. 42.

96 'Up to the last, cases of cholera continued to occur from time to time at Varnootka, one of the latest victims being Sergeant-Major Davis, the paymaster's clerk, a much valued and respected non-commissioned officer. The total number of deaths, including two officers, was nine in twelve days in camp at Varnootka. The regiment did not speedily recover from the state of ill-health into which it had fallen during its short sojourn with the Turkish army in the beautiful valley of Varnootka, and some fatal cases of cholera occurred immediately after the return to the camp at Karani; but by the middle of the month (July) epidemic cholera might be said to have quite disappeared' (R. S. Liddell, *Memoirs of the Tenth Royal Hussars* (London: Longman Green and Co., 1891), pp. 299–300).

pickets and skirmishes with the Cossacks. I hear Lady Augusta is going to get married this month to Mostyn, who was at my tutor's. The army here are all at sixes and sevens, and nothing done now that we are without a head.[97] Tell Cornwallis I will give him an epistle next mail, but now they go so quick I cannot find news for all by every one. When does he go to the Baltic? Hoping you will be quite well and strong by the time you get this, and with love to all.

50

Wykeham Martin to his father

Baidar Valley, July 25th 1855

I conclude my Troop business has gone all right, as I have not received any letter from Hoare or Hopkinson. I am now out beyond Baidar. I was sent here at a minute's notice owing to Marshall's being taken sick.[98] We went out for a reconnaissance fourteen miles beyond here yesterday, the country was most beautiful, but we saw no Russians; we got some coffee at a Count's house, he had only left two hours before for Simferopol. We saw him afterwards about two miles ahead, but as we did not want him we let him go on. I have just received Maria's letters and many thanks. I should have written to some of you before, only owing to this march I have not had time; will you tell this to Philip. I am sorry to say the last time I was on picket I lost my sabretasche, with the silver fork and spoon I took from England in it; it was buckled with two straps to the saddle, so that I am afraid that some man of the picket must have taken a fancy to it and taken it off. I know I had two convicted thieves on picket with me at the time.

PS I am afraid with these new appointments Charles Trollope will lose his Brigade; in fact he has, only he may get another.[99]

---

97 Raglan died on 28 June 1855. With Lieutenant General Sir George Brown also absent through ill health, command of the army devolved to Lieutenant General James Simpson who did not want the appointment. See Sir G. Douglas and Sir G. Dalhousie Ramsay, *The Panmure Papers* 2 vols (London: Hodder and Stoughton, 1908), vol. 1, p. 257.

98 Captain John Barry Marshall, Cornet, 29 October 1849, Lieutenant, May 1852 and Captain, 15 December 1854. He died of disease ('Crimean fever') at St George's Monastery, Balaklava Heights, on 20 September 1855, aged 25 years. He was the second son of William Skinner Marshall of London and Stowmarket, Suffolk. There is a memorial to him at Wetherden parish church, Suffolk.

99 Trollope was given command of the 2nd Brigade, 3rd Division. See McGuigan, *Into Battle!*, p. 50.

51

Wykeham Martin to his stepmother

Baidar Valley, August 2nd 1855

We are still here, but expect to go daily. I am sorry to say that since I last wrote to you I have been bad with Crimean fever,[100] and am still not well, although considerably better. It is unlucky having it out here as we are so far from any luxuries; also I miss all the excursions that our fellows are making almost daily: tomorrow they are going to seize a quantity of champagne, we have already taken one batch, but I have not been able to taste it. I expect if the whole of us are not sent in soon I shall be sent in by myself. The report here is that the whole of the Cavalry go to Egypt for the winter, and that they are going to give short leaves to Officers who have been out all the time. There is some hitch I hear about my promotion; the Horse Guards will not give Molyneux[101] all the money, as he has not served long enough, and having got one step without purchase, consequently he will probably want more of me, but I have not heard from him yet. Will you tell Philip I will write to him as soon as I get better. By the Bye, was my money ever sold out of the funds as Hoare's people have never written to me, so I do not know if they ever got the letter; if they have not, I shall be in a mess.

P.S. I have just received your letter of the 20th. I wanted you to pay the whole £20 to keep for his brother, the parents as far as I know were not to have any. Friend says he can trust Elliot, so that we have no more to do with it except getting a receipt from him, and tell him to write to Friend and say he has got it.

---

100 A general term to describe the type of low fever that afflicted many in the Crimea. Its symptoms include a loss of appetite, diarrhoea, nausea and general listlessness.

101 Charles Berkeley Molyneux, Cornet, September 1844; Lieutenant, April 1847; and Captain by purchase, March 1850. He was listed at the Cavalry Depot in July 1854 and became ADC to the Lord Lieutenant of Ireland from 15 December 1854. He arrived in the Crimea in the middle of June 1855 with a draft of 61 men and 53 horses for the regiment. Portal of the 4th Light Dragoons wrote home that Molyneux had never been in a tent, 'not even had the campaign at Chatham'. (This should probably read 'Chobham' and is an error in the original transcription.) Molyneux left the Crimea at the beginning of July 1855. See TNA, WO12/659–660; Portal, *Letters from the Crimea*, p. 195.

52

Wykeham Martin to his stepmother

Baidar, Thursday Evening August 6th 1855
I am sorry to say I cannot issue a favourable bulletin this time, as I am not much better than when I last wrote to you. I cannot get any appetite, and eat nothing, otherwise I think I should do very well. We, that is the party I am with, not myself, have been out several times on plundering expeditions,[102] chiefly to bring in a quantity of Russian champagne from a chateau about ten miles off. I am sorry to say the privates were not content with this, but stripped the church of all the French had left, and you may see a gallant Hussar swelling it in the Priest's robes about the camp; some of the things taken were very good, but I was not lucky enough to get any not being on the spot, the remainder was quite rubbish, tables, odd volumes of books etc. The last time they went down some Greek Infantry[103] fired into them and wounded two of the Land Transport, and killed two mules. I have no more to say, and hoping that you are all well as I hope to be soon.

53

Wykeham Martin to his stepmother

Transport Belgravia, August 18th 1855
I write you a line for fear you should think I was dead, to tell you that I am alive, and owing to sea air quite recovered. However I stay here for ten days more. The French and Sardinians have had a fight on the Tchernaya,[104] but I have not heard of the particulars yet, except that the Russians were licked. Our Cavalry were there but were not engaged, which I am very glad of as I was not there; they expect they will come on

---

102 A party of 100 Dragoons and 14 Land Transport wagons made their way up the Baidar Valley to plunder the deserted mansion of a Russian nobleman. British and French troops had been there before and much wanton damage was done to the library, children's rooms and other parts of the house. Some 600 bottles of Russian champagne were carried off. See Portal, *Letters from the Crimea*, pp. 214–16.

103 Ibid. Portal states that they did not see their assailants and believed them to be Greeks.

104 A battle on 16 August largely conducted by the French and Sardinians in which the Russians tried to cross the Tchernaya River over the Tractir bridge and were slaughtered in the process. The British cavalry were under fire though spectators. In his journal Paget described the scene after the battle: 'neither the Alma nor Inkerman fields presented more ghastly sights'. See Paget, *Light Cavalry Brigade*, p. 112.

in a day or two, but if they do they will get licked again. I hope to be off the ship before that takes place. I do not see my name in the Gazette,[105] I cannot think what Charley Molyneux is about;[106] I see his uncle, Lord Sefton,[107] is dead, it will be a great loss to him, and will not I am afraid induce him to lose any more money selling out. I must now conclude as I am afraid I am late already. Tell Aunt Fanny I will answer her letter by the earliest opportunity.

54

Wykeham Martin to his brother Philip

[Letter not included in the 1868 publication]

Balaklava [no date, but about August 1855]

As I dare say you have heard from the governor I am at last going to be made a Captain although owing to the death of poor old Raglan I am afraid it will be postponed for a few days till they get things square. We are doomed I hear to pass another winter here, people have abused Lord Raglan a great deal and have wished him recalled and all sorts of things, now that the poor old fellow is gone they do not know where to get another half as good. The Army here are rather down on their luck as during the last fortnight they have lost or rather hors de combat 6 Generals 3 dead and 3 sick including the Commander in Chief and the Adjutant General. This I hope will satisfy the Blackguard Times newspaper making a total of 8 victims with Boxer and Christie. Cholera is very bad in the Balaklava camp but not up in the front. I believe we have lost five men, I hear no news as now the telegraph is in working order you hear everything as soon as we do. Hoping the two are well and with my love.

---

105 He became a Captain on 31 August 1855 and the appointment appeared in the *London Gazette* accordingly.

106 This refers to considerations for promotion. Molyneux had spent hardly any time at all in the Crimea. He needed to sell out in order to create a vacancy for FWM to become a Captain. He appears to have wanted more from the sale of his commission than his career warranted, hence the frustrated nuance in FWM's letter.

107 Charles William Molyneux, 3rd Earl Sefton, and brother to George Berkeley Molyneux, Charley's father. The Earl died in August 1855.

55

Wykeham Martin to his stepmother

Balaklava, August 31st 1855

I have again rejoined my Regiment in a perfect state of preservation, and hope I shall continue so. I have just had my servant in and received his wishes touching the £20. He wants it all paid to his brother at Mr. Elliot's, as he has given him directions to allow his father and mother at the rate of 6s a week; the two brothers keep the old couple between them, so it will not do to give them £5 at any time or they will spend it too quick, but by giving it to the brother he will arrange it. Now for my own affairs, I want two new India-rubber tubs, one small for a wash-hand basin, and one large for a tub; but get them both at some India-rubber shop like Macintosh's; also, when you send Friend's things, you can send the thick Regimental jacket I sent home from Scutari with them. My epistle is exceedingly egotistical, but you must excuse it on the plea of its being a business letter. I have received Cornwallis's letter and the papers describing the capture of Sweaborg.[108] It is expected here that war will be over in six months time from now, as they have got news from Russia by spies in the highest circles, that she is nearly done up, the enormous thrashing they got at the Tchernaia keep them quiet for some time. I hear Ralph Nevill is going to follow his sister's example and take a wife, is it true? I forgot to add a pair of regimental spurs to my other boots. Will you send me how much I owe you, including the £20, as it and Rich's bill will make a difference to my balance.

56

Wykeham Martin to his brother Philip[109]

Balaklava, August 31st 1855

My excuse for not writing before must be that I have had fever, and for a fortnight eat nothing, living in a bell tent in the middle of a plain, with the thermometer at 97 in the shade. I was [*damned*] nearly grilled to

---

108 An Anglo-French naval force bombarded the fortress of Sveaborg (now Suomenlinna) off Helsinki in the Baltic for three days from 9 to 11 August, destroying its walls and guns. See Baumgart, *Crimean War*, pp. 167–76.

109 Passages in italics were not included in the 1868 published collection and have been restored from the originals.

death; however, I am all right now. I was [*very*] sorry to miss the Battle of the Tchernaya, [*as there was great joy and no danger*], it was an awful thrashing for the Russians. I am sorry to say that the other day the French had a frightful accident,[110] they were passing powder into a magazine, when a shell came from the Malakoff and blew them all up, killing 400, at least that is the report. Many people out here believe that the war will be all over in six months. I for one do not think the Russians can hold out much longer. [*I have heard a report but strictly confidential through Robertson that Ralph Nevill is thinking of matrimony I wonder where the sly [illegible] has found a wife.*] I am sorry to hear you have grown so fat; it is bad to have too much flesh when young; you had better come here, as this country is warranted to make even a Billy Williams a skeleton in a month. Remember me to Madame, and box the youngster's ears, as I shall have to do it some day, and as it is well to begin young.

57

Wykeham Martin to his stepmother

Balaklava, Sept. 6th 1855

In your preparations for my winter kit, whatever you do do not leather my overhalls [*sic*] that are at home, as I have plenty here leathered, and they will not be received soon, and are my ball overhalls, and much too thin for winter. There is still some talk of our going to Egypt, I wish they would let us know, as one does not know what to order, as at Alexandria you would require civilised things, it being rather a swell town. You will be sorry to hear that Ross, Mrs. Whatman's brother, has been killed or taken prisoner.[111] They say he turned out a very good officer, and the men had more confidence in him than almost any other officer in the regiment. Tell Maria I do not write to her as I consider this letter does for all, as I cannot make news enough for two. After all it makes very little difference who it is addressed to. I am glad Cornwallis was in time for Sweaborg. Last night they burnt one of the Russian ships.[112] General

110 The French suffered heavy losses at 1 a.m. on 30 August when a chance Russian shell fired from Sevastopol exploded when the French were transferring powder from a cart to their magazine, containing 14,000 lbs of powder. The French lost some 400 men killed in an explosion that shook the ground like an earthquake. See *Illustrated London News*, 15 September 1855, p. 319.
111 Captain Charles Cornwallis Ross, 3rd Regiment (The Buffs), killed in the trenches before Sevastopol, 31 August, was at first listed as missing. His sister, Louisa Isobella Ross, married James Whatman of Vinters, Kent, in 1850. See Cook and Cook, *Casualty Roll*, p. 114.
112 The Russian frigate, *Santa Maria*, was hit by artillery fire and set ablaze.

Bosquet gave the gunners who fired the gun 100 francs; I hope they will repeat the operation tonight. We are awfully worked now; they turn us out every night at three o'clock, which entails the men getting up at two, and keep us standing to our horses till it gets quite light. We hardly get any sleep at all. We have only two subs for duty, myself and Weatherley.[113] [PS] I should like some preserved soup if we stay here, a large quantity and some knives, spoons and forks, (common ones); also some cartridges all ready for use; Denby and Adams large size pistol;[114] they are made up in copper cans.

58

Wykeham Martin to his stepmother

Balaklava, Sept. 16th 1855
I have not written to you since we have had the luck to take this place (by fluke be it said).[115] I went over it today, and you never saw such a wreck as it is. There is literally not one stone on another, not one single entire house in the whole place. The officers of the Infantry behaved nobly.[116] They say we all take the field in two or three days. I think it utter madness, as they say it will take 10,000 men to take Mackenzie Heights, which is a greater proportion that were killed at Sevastopol. They say we are to go to Scutari the first week in November. The telegraph order has come, but everything is so uncertain here, that I think you had better send the things I mentioned in my last letter,

---

113 Lieutenant Weatherley, 4th Light Dragoons, arrived from England 3 September 1855. See TNA, WO12/660 Muster Roll, 4th Light Dragoons, 1855–6.

114 Deane and Adams Model 1851.45 and.50 calibre revolvers were favoured by British Light Cavalry officers and usually privately purchased from Messrs. Deane Adams & Deane, 30 King William Street, London Bridge.

115 On 8 September the allies made another concerted effort to storm Sevastopol. The French attacked the Malakoff and the British, the Redan. The British attack was repulsed with heavy losses. The French stormed the Malakoff and held their gain. After the fall of the Malakoff, the Russians evacuated Sevastopol appreciating that the loss of so significant a part of their defences made their position untenable. See Russell, *British Expedition to the Crimea*, pp. 341–67.

116 The British infantry suffered heavy losses as they advanced into a storm of musket and artillery fire from the Redan. It was said that many of the attacking force were new men who had recently arrived in the Crimea. They hesitated in attack and would not go forward. Consequently, many of their officers stood up to encourage their men to advance and paid for their gallantry with their lives. There were instances of men running away from the attack after witnessing such scenes of slaughter. A total of 12 VCs were won on 8 September, in addition to the 20 won during the failed attack on the Redan on 18 June. See Hugh Pearse, *Redan Windham: The Crimean Diary and Letters of Lieutenant General Sir Charles Ash Windham* (London: Kegan Paul Trench Trubner & Co., 1897), pp. 184–214.

and my servants things, at once, and I will manage with them. I have no time for more, and hoping this will reach you before you start for Paris, and that you will enjoy your trip very much; also tell Maria to be sure and remember me to Miss Boger when she sees her next, and say that I asked after her.

59

Wykeham Martin to his brother Philip

[Letter omitted from the 1868 publication]
Balaklava Sept. 30th [1855]
I have received the note giving a description of the abuse you and the foreman have got for your respective ideas on politics. I do not think the foreman is wise in standing for Maidstone and still less so in putting you up for Rochester as he will now have to entertain the ragamuffins of both towns to keep men in good order. As you will see by the papers poor Marshall of my regiment died the other day of fever, he was one of the nicest fellows we ever had in the regiment and is universally regretted. The Russians have taken to shelling the town and have killed a few men and burnt the [illegible]. We hear a shave [a rumour] that the French have taken six guns from the Russians at Eupatoria but it is not confirmed yet. The tenth Hussars got into a mess at Kertch the other day and were surrounded by Cossacks, had to cut their way out and lost 15 men taken prisoner and 2 killed luckily they were under the orders of a French officer or people would have said it was Mr Stupidity Officer English again. I hope Madame and the baby are quite well and that you will succeed in your election, with love to both.

60

Wykeham Martin to his stepmother

Balaklava, Sept. 30th 1855
I hope you have enjoyed your trip to Paris, and liked the Exhibition. I conclude I shall have a full account of it in your next letter. You will see by the papers that poor Marshall of my regiment has died of fever and dysentery. Rather bad luck for me that my promotion was not delayed

another fortnight; however I do not much care, as I should not have liked getting his troop, as he was a great friend of mine; and also, if I sell out any time soon, they would not have given more than £300 or £400 for it. I am sorry to say I do not see the slightest chance of getting home this winter now; as senior Lieutenant I should have been sure of it, but as junior Captain I am certain to lose it. We go away from here about the middle of next month. I asked you in my last to send me out my warm jacket and servant's clothes. I do not know anything else that I want. Cuff, or whoever you ordered the regimental bridle of [sic], has sent it, and a good deal more saddlery than I ordered to the value of £8; also, now that the head collar has come, it is the wrong pattern, therefore I should not be allowed to wear it. I am going to send it back. If you ordered it, of course I must pay for it. Hoping you are quite well after your arduous campaign at Paris.

[PS] Philip tells me Papa is standing for Maidstone, and himself for Rochester.[117] His letter was very amusing, telling me of the squibs placarded about the Governor and himself. I forgot to say, tell me what I owe you.

61

Wykeham Martin to his stepmother

Balaklava, October 6th 1855

We are off again for a Campaign somewhere, but we do not know where, we suppose Eupatoria. It is rather a bore, as this is not exactly the weather for it, and also we had all made up our minds to winter at Scutari, where I have no doubt we shall go when this is over; one expedition has already sailed for Kinburn. We may perhaps be going to join them, but it is more probable that there is going to be one combined movement to hem the Russians in. Another great bore is, that one will most likely lose all one's kit, as we did when we embarked from Varna, and then we shall be uncomfortable all the winter as we were last year. I am glad you all enjoyed yourselves so well in Paris. I wish I could have been with you, although you did not get beds at Folkstone, I dare say for *once* I could have tried to sleep on the floor. You must not expect any letters from me just yet, as for the next month we shall be birds of passage, but I will

---

117 Charles Wykeham Martin became MP for West Kent in 1857, and Philip became MP for Rochester in 1856.

write if I can, and do not get bowled over by a Cossack. I must write to Ralph Nevill the first opportunity as I have never written to him since his sister's marriage, and hoping you are all well and that the governor, Philip and Fairfax, will all get through their trials.

62

Wykeham Martin to his stepmother

Scutari Barracks, December 9th 1855

I write by this post to ask you to invest my surplus revenue, with the exception of £300 which I may want here at Scutari, and to pay you and buy a horse. Will you pay up everything I owe in England (telling Philip to let me know what I owe him) including Hamburger's bill, Cuff's, Smith's, Byfield's, Baines' and everything you may know of that I do not. In the former letter you received last mail, you will know there are some articles which I sent back, and you can tell him to scratch them out of the bill. Among my wants are two new girths for a plain saddle, one for a regimental ditto, which if you are quick, can come out with a head collar I have ordered at Cuff's, also, I think a new plain double reined bridle and a snaffle will quite set up my stable again. The portable soups you sent in the last package were very good and just came in the nick of time, but they are not what I wanted, as they would be no use in a campaign, the next time you send them let them be the same as the first, in bladders; I have got the tubs all safe. Have you ever received a box by the Bucephalus? it has gone past here some time. Another dozen is novels[118] would help me to get through the time at this stupid place. I consider this quite a business letter. I am glad to hear Fairfax is likely to prove a light to lighten the Gentiles,[119] and also that Cornwallis has come safe home.

---

118 Young men like FWM favoured cheap adventure stories of indifferent quality to relieve the boredom of camp life during the siege. Phillips of the 8th Hussars refers to reading a novel as a distraction. See [174], note 40, p. 223.

119 This alludes to Fairfax having got into the Remove at Eton, the highest place he could take.

63

Wykeham Martin to his stepmother

Scutari, December 16th 1855

I have not written to you since I left Balaklava, as there was no regular mail, and the letters that were sent from there never reached, also we have lost several mails. I sent the saddlery back to Cuff's, but have since heard from him to say that he was not the man who made it. I see by your letter that Hamburger was, so will you get it from Cuff when it arrives, as also the letter I sent with it, as I have no idea of paying £8 for things I do not want and are not regimental. I have also heard from Hamburger that the gold belts he sent me were by Papa's order second hand, and that Papa told him if they were nearly the same they would do; if he did so it was a great mistake, as our present Colonel is more particular than Lord George[120] and will not let you wear a thing that is not strictly regimental, consequently they are no use. Eupatoria was a most disagreeable place, they kept us there for six weeks with scarcely any clothes, and the thermometer at 14, in fact we were worse off than we were last year at Balaklava, as we had no money, and if we had there was nothing to be bought; when we first went there it was on the contrary very hot; we were sent a three days patrol into the country and were forty-one hours without water, and when we did get a little it was so brackish and filthy that it was all we could do to drink it. General d'Allonville, the French General we were under, is a first rate man and would never get you into a scrape. I hope we shall be under him next year again; he has asked for us. Will you pay all my bills and sell my charger, as it is a waste of money keeping him, especially as I shall have to buy another (which he will help to pay for) now that we have a Colonel with different ideas from Lord George. Direct my letters to Scutari, and papers, as I shall get them quicker. I have got the things, but unfortunately, through the carelessness of the people who brought them from Balaklava, the box was broken and the mice eat my servant's coat. Our people are all going home on leave, but being the junior Captain I shall not be able to come. I hate this place worse than Balaklava, as they seem determined to make us as uncomfortable as possible. I shall write again soon.

---

120 Alexander Low (1817–1904) became Lieutenant Colonel and commanded the regiment in December 1854. See Lummis and Wynn, *Honour the Light Brigade*, p. 23.

64

Wykeham Martin to his stepmother

Scutari, December 30th 1855

I am just going to add a few supplementary articles that I am in want of to those I have already sent. Six pillow cases, one pair hunting spurs, six flannel shirts, of a dark colour, (black and white check is very good); these things I hope to have out with the others I wrote for last mail, also two plain saddle pads, to be got at Gardener, if I did not order them in my last. They have never sent my head collars for my regimental bit, you can send it with the other things; also I hope you have heard from Hamburger about the returned saddlery. I also want Marsh to make me a pair of butcher boots, that is to say top boots without the tops. I am ashamed to say I have not yet got your table cover, but will do so soon, also the article you wish for to hold work, its proper use is to carry tobacco in. There are beautiful dresses to be bought here if you like, but I do not know that I could get them any cheaper than you do in England. I suppose by this time you have got the Sailor home; I see he gets a medal and one clasp for Sweaborg.[121] There is a report out here that Omar Pasha and his army are cut to pieces, but I don't believe it.[122] And now wishing you a happy new year and many of them, and with love to all.

65

Wykeham Martin to his stepmother

Scutari Barracks, Jan. 9th 1856

I was truly sorry to hear of poor Lady Trollope's death,[123] and can imagine how much you must feel on the melancholy occasion. I can only say that I have lost one of the best and kindest friends I ever had or am likely to have in this world. I always looked on Cumberland Place as one of my homes, she always treated me more as a son than anything else, I have

---

121 The Baltic Medal with clasp.

122 This refers to rumours from the war pursued by the Russians and Turks in the Caucasus Mountains. In fact, having forced the Russians to retreat from the Ingur River in November 1855, Omer Pasha followed them up slowly only to be forced to retire himself by heavy rains. See Baumgart, *Crimean War*, pp. 177–84.

123 Lady Anne Trollope (née Thorold) married Sir John Trollope, 6th Bt on 24 March 1798. She died on 23 December 1855.

often thought since I have been out here of the many happy days I have spent at her house, and sincerely regret that it has not been my lot to return once more to thank her for her many kindnesses to myself and the rest of us. All her children must I am sure be very much affected by her death, but I do not think they can feel more than I do; as with the exception of my more immediate relations I loved her more than any one else on earth. However at her age it was only what we must all come to, and I only hope I may play as good a part on this earth as she has done. Poor Laura,[124] I am sure she must feel it, if anything more than you do, as she has been her constant companion more, lately than you have. I hope you are quite well after this shock? I suppose by this time you have had a visit from Cornwallis, tell him I have received his letter, and am glad to see he is appointed to a Gun-boat,[125] as it was his wish, although I hear from sailors here they are very uncomfortable things. Hoping that the rest are all well, and with love to all.

P.S. I have got your table cover and will send it the first opportunity.

66

Wykeham Martin to his stepmother

Scutari, Jan. 22nd 1856

I hope you are all over your troubles by this time, and have, I suppose, returned to Leeds. We have just received a telegraphic despatch to say that Peace is proclaimed, but we hardly believe it to be true; if it is I suppose I shall soon be coming home. I forget if I mentioned in my last letter that I wanted a new sheepskin instead of the one you sent me out before, which belongs to my Shabraque. There is a ball at the Embassy on the 30th, to which I intend going. I went to a soiree there the other day, but there is an awful scarcity of ladies. At present I cannot do any thing in the amusement line, as George Brown is sick, and Monckton[126] has gone on leave, so I am left to look after Her Majesty's 4th Light: however, I think the former will be all right in a day or two. I have sent

---

124 Laura Trollope, daughter of Sir John and Lady Anne Trollope.

125 Cornwallis Wykeham Martin became commander of the *Bullfrog*, a Dapper class gunboat built by Pritchard and launched on 6 October 1855 in the White Squadron. See *The Times*, 16 November 1855, p. 10, col. B.; Ibid., 2 May 1856, p. 11, col. A.

126 The Hon. Major Horace Manners Monckton, 3rd (The Kings Own) Regt. of Light Dragoons. He served in the Punjab in 1848–9 and was attached to the 4th Light Dragoons in the Crimea, and afterwards, with the rank of Major, in command of the Sultan's Royal Regiment of Constantinople. See *Hart's New Annual Army List 1860*. p. 138.

you two table covers and four bags by Bryne, our V.S., the latter are not what you wanted, but I will get you what you want the first time I go into the Bazaar. These were got for me by a friend living at Pera, those you do not want you can give to any one you like.

67

Wykeham Martin to his father

Scutari Barracks, Jan. 30th 1856

The items in Hamburger's bill that I object to pay for are the crupper head collar, head stall straps, shoe cases, and pockets for nails, all of which I returned. He has charged me £7. 3s 6d for the lot, which includes a regimental bridle, which I have kept, therefore he must deduct the price of the articles I have returned, also he must take off a heavy per centage on the whole, according to a previous engagement with Rich, who, to save himself the trouble of making out half yearly bills, agreed to do so. I see also he has considerably raised his price in gold lace overhalls [*sic*] of which you can remind him. I see by the papers it is going to be peace, and that we are to return home; if so you need not send out the articles I have ordered unless you have already done so. Have you sent any parcels by the Harbinger? as if you have, all the directions are rubbed off, and they do not know who to deliver them to, so that unless you let me know I shall not be able to claim them. In regard to the charger I think if it is decidedly peace you may as well keep it; if not, get it into condition, and when you go to London either sell it to a dealer for as much as you can get, or put it up at Tattersall's[127] as the charger of an officer gone to the Crimea, who has no further use for it. Hoping that Mama and Fairfax have got all right again by this time, and that the latter will enjoy his little extra holiday.

---

127 The bloodstock equestrian auctioneers founded by Richard Tattersall in 1766.

68

Wykeham Martin to his stepmother

Scutari Barracks, March 8th 1856

I am sorry to say I did not see the box containing my things sent home in the Bucephalus myself. The only things I know ought to be there and are not in your list are a new pouch belt (gold) and a quantity of shirts; there was also, I think, a suit of plain clothes, but I am not sure that they were not in the portmanteau, which has never turned up; it was on board the Pelican, but unfortunately I twice missed her at Balaklava harbour, and since then she has been home, so what she did with the portmanteau I do not know. She is a new steamer belonging, I think, to the South American line; it was put on board this time or a little earlier last year. As I have lost all my shirts, it would be very well to have some made in case I come home, only take care to have them made with wrist-bands doubled back to fasten the studs. Nichols and Housley[128] would know the latest fashion, although they are rather dear. I have no news, and so must conclude, with love to all.

[PS] I have made inquiries about Harris, but his Regiment is not here, so that I may not succeed in case they do not answer; the easiest way is to write to the Adjutant explaining the case, and he will send back the man's number or get the medal for you as he ought to have done before.

69

Wykeham Martin to his stepmother

Scutari Barracks, March 17th 1856

I have succeeded in getting Corporal Harris's number from a Serjeant [sic] of the 8th Hussars, who is employed on the Staff;[129] it is 1259; he died on 23rd of February, 1855; but at the same time I do not think the father will be able to get the medal yet, as they have not nearly distributed them to the living claimants. You never told me which ship you sent the plain saddle in; it has never turned up here, so I think it is just possible you may have been in time to stop it. I sent your bags by post, and hope

---

128 Mercers of St James Street, London.

129 Possibly 989 Paymaster-Sergeant James Lynch. He survived the war but was killed in action at Gwalior in June 1857. See Lummis and Wynn, *Honour the Light Brigade*, p. 80.

they will arrive safe. We are all on the look out for peace here. We expect the telegraph every day; but they seem very slow about these conferences. I hear Hutton is ordered out. I must say good bye, as I have no news or time for more.

70

Wykeham Martin to his stepmother

Scutari, April 21st 1856

I hope you have got my shirts under weigh, as in all probability I shall be starting in a few days. I do not think there were any Regimentals in the box, except a pouch and sword belt. I do not know what plain clothes you put in, but I hope not my best evening coat or the frock. Lord George Paget has asked me to come home with him and Lady George by Athens; but I do not know if I shall or not. You may as well get my charger into condition, as then I shall be able to sell him, if Colonel Lowe [sic] will not pass him, which is likely as he wants every body to get new ones. Philip is going to have Toby back again, and my mare I shall turn out in the Park, or let you have the use of her for quiet work, in place of the old grey, who I do not think will do much more. I am bringing home, if possible, a little Arab pony for Fairfax; if he has grown too big for it we can sell it. I do not know yet where we go to, but will write again if I can find out. We only bring home about fifty horses, the rest we sell to the Turkish Government.[130] Hoping you are all well.

71

Wykeham Martin to his stepmother

Scutari, May 4th 1856

I write you a line to caution you not to send my things to whatever station the Regiment may go to when it reaches England, till you hear from me, as I do not go with it, owing to my being Aide de Camp. I have to remain here with Paget, till the rest of the Brigade come home; it may be

---

130 Paget wrote in his journal that 'the horses were divided into three lots – 1, Serviceable, to be taken home. 2, Such as were worth it, to be sold by auction. 3, some few to be shot.' See Paget, *Light Cavalry Brigade*, p. 158.

tomorrow, or not for three months. The Regiment sailed today. When I do come home I shall probably come to London first, and then have to join my Regiment, till I can get leave, which will take at least a week or a fortnight; and then I hope to join you for some time. Tell Philip to hold his hands about buying horses for me, as our present Colonel is very particular. What is Charles Trollope going to do now that his regiment is ordered to Canada?[131] Will he sell out or take his chance of being made a Major-General? I have never heard from him since I left the Crimea. I will attend to your order as shopman about the bags, if I have time only, and I will vary the patterns.

72

Wykeham Martin to his stepmother

Scutari, May 12th 1856
I find I shall be home sooner than I said in my last letter, although I do not know exactly the day.[132] Will you tell Marsh to have a pair of regimental boots (Wellingtons) not too thick and also a pair of button boots for plain clothes also made thin for the summer, ready for me at Cumberland Place. As this will probably be one of my last letters I shall write, I may as well tell you that I shall certainly come up to London first on landing, and go down to my Regiment next day and try and get leave; if they do not give it me at once, I shall be sure to get it soon. I find Lady George an exceedingly nice person, very good natured, and she has made me excessively comfortable since I have come to live in her house. I find that even out here the difference between bachelors and a married establishment so great that it is quite an inducement to get married. Hoping to see you all soon, and with love to all.

---

131 Charles Trollope went on half pay on 28 September 1856, while his regiment, the 62nd, went to Nova Scotia.
132 He arrived in port on Tuesday 27 May 1856 on board the *Simla* as ADC to Lord George Paget. See *The Times*, 28 May 1856, p. 12, col. E.

Edward Rowe Fisher-Rowe in the Crimea. Detail of a photograph by Roger Fenton (see p. 160). Credit: Library of Congress, Prints and Photographs Division [LC-USZ62-47544].

2

Edward Rowe Fisher-Rowe

Edward Rowe Fisher – the additional name of Rowe was adopted by royal licence in February 1881 – was born on 8 November 1832 at Wilton Crescent in Belgravia. He was the only child of Thomas Fisher (1790–1870) of Thorncombe Park, Bramley, near Guildford, Surrey and his wife Anna Berry, the daughter and co-heir of Lawrence Rowe of Brentford Middlesex.[1] Unusually Edward's mother recorded the development of her son from his earliest years and these observations were included in the opening pages of the edition of E. R. Fisher-Rowe's letters produced by his son in 1907. The first entry records his condition as a two-year-old infant and describes him as 'tall and stout, full of vigour and activity'. Thereafter Edward's development appears to be entirely conventional for a child from a comfortable background and environment. His likeness was painted as an infant. He is depicted attired in a dress, as was the fashion, and beating a toy drum. It was noted that he 'preserved through much illness' when he was eight years old and that, at that age, he could neither read nor write. He was privately educated and, like others of his background, learned Latin and mathematics. He visited Italy before his teens and was at a private tutor's at Hurley in 1849 before attending Magdalene College, Cambridge, in October 1851.

In correspondence between his father Thomas Fisher and the Horse Guards in the summer of 1853, his father revealed that his son's height was 6½ feet and that he 'promises to be a large man'.[2] He added 'I should prefer his being appointed to a regiment of heavy cavalry for which I consider him best fitted ...'. In other correspondence, Thomas

---

1   The original letters have yet to be found and may have been destroyed. Ms M. Paleologo, a descendant, suggested they may have been thrown in the lake at Thorncombe, the country seat until 1937; other members of the family, however, do not concur. The quest to discover the fate of the letters continues. See *Burke's Landed Gentry*, pp. 1958–9.

2   TNA, WO31/1031, Commander in Chief's Memoranda, Papers related to the commission of E. R. Fisher.

Fisher stated that his son had expressed 'a decided wish to enter the army' and would prefer a cavalry regiment. On 10 June 1853 a sum of £840 was paid over to secure the cornetcy for Edward Rowe Fisher and he was duly commissioned as cornet in the 4th (Royal Irish) Dragoon Guards, by purchase, on 17 June 1853. In an essay in 1906, Field Marshal Sir Evelyn Wood, who had served in the 13th Light Dragoons, observed, 'the sons of opulent merchants generally found their way into Heavy Cavalry regiments, in which the expenditure of officers was greater [than the Light Cavalry]. The examinations for entrance to the Army were nominal, the chief qualification being that the candidate was the son of a gentleman.'[3]

In the early nineteenth century, dragoon guards and dragoons were the shock troops of the cavalry. They tended to be men of large stature riding big horses. In set-piece battles they would be used to break wavering formations of infantry or cavalry. In aid of civil power they could be used to intimidate a crowd or disperse a mob. In his book, *Cavalry: Its History and Tactics*, published in 1853, Captain Louis Edward Nolan of the 15th Hussars wrote that heavy cavalry were: 'large men in defensive armour, mounted on heavy powerful horses' and 'held in hand for decisive charges on the day of battle and their horses are so deficient in speed and endurance (being so overweight), that they require light horse to follow up the enemy they have beaten'. He added, 'They are calculated only to show an imposing front in the line of battle, and their history proves them to be more formidable in appearance than in reality.'[4] The ill-fated Nolan, however, was obsessed with light cavalry and it is unsurprising that his book should be chiefly about its potential and capabilities. Moreover, the experience of the cavalry in the Crimea showed that expediency demanded that the historic differences in the roles of light and heavy cavalry were ignored. Though retaining distinctions of precedence and of uniform, the demarcation of duties performed was by no means clearly defined.

The dust-jacket of the second volume of the Marquess of Anglesey's *A History of the British Cavalry* shows a painting by G. Quinton, completed by the artist in 1869, which depicts the departure of the 4th Royal Irish Dragoon Guards for the Crimea. As with the rest of the Army of the East, the Heavy Brigade arrived piecemeal in a combination of steam and sail-powered vessels. Fisher-Rowe was in the *Palmyra*, the last of the vessels transporting the 4th Dragoon Guards to arrive at

---

3   Sir Evelyn Wood, 'British Cavalry, 1853–1903', *Cavalry Journal* 1 (1906), p. 147.
4   Louis Edward Nolan, *Cavalry: Its History and Tactics* (London: Bosworth, 1853), p. 64.

Constantinople. The effective strength of the 4th Dragoon Guards for July was 269 men and 247 horses.[5]

The letters begin with Fisher-Rowe's regiment in Ireland prior to being ordered to the East [73–79], followed by an interesting account of his voyage on the *Palmyra* [80]. There is then a gap of some 26 days in the published letters of Fisher-Rowe. From landing at Varna until his letter of 13 August he either did not write or the letters he did write were omitted [81]. What is clear is that the army at Varna deteriorated. The heat, disease and idleness began to take their toll. On 31 July the 4th Dragoon Guards moved their camp to what Edward Hodge described as 'bad ground, a long way from water'.[6] The following day a trooper died of cholera. Losses from cholera and other diseases or complaints amounted to 22 other ranks in the 4th Dragoon Guards at Varna. The 5th Dragoon Guards also suffered badly from losses to cholera. They had had a miserable time since command of the regiment had passed from the Hon. Sir James Yorke Scarlett to Thomas Le Marchant. The former had commanded with common sense and intelligence and had created high morale in the regiment. The latter, lacking the leadership qualities of Scarlett, transformed the regiment into a dispirited, apprehensive body of men. To add to their woes they lost three officers and 44 men to disease and others were taken ill and in the hospital tent. To the relief of many, Le Marchant went home 'ill' and Raglan ordered that the 5th be attached to the 4th under the command of Hodge, who was now said to command 'the 9th'.

The heavy cavalry were left at Varna when the rest of the army embarked for the Crimea. Consequently they played no part in the advance on Sebastopol, the battle of the Alma and the occupation of Balaklava. Fisher-Rowe was in an optimistic mood when he finally left Varna for the Crimea on the *Simla* [87, 88], but the convoy was hit by a storm that caused havoc on board for the horses. Over 220 were killed and the survivors presented a most wretched condition though the steamers *Simla* and *Trent* appear to have lost fewer horses in the gale than the sailing ships they were towing. Finally assembling in October, the Heavy Brigade was involved in most of the functions that Captain Nolan had claimed they were excused, providing patrols, picquets and videttes [90].

Fisher-Rowe's description of Balaklava poses a number of questions [92]. There is a degree of detachment and inaccuracy that is hard to explain. In the opening moves, Fisher-Rowe confuses the advanced body

---

5   TNA, WO17/656, Monthly Returns, 1854.

6   Anglesey, *Little Hodge*, p. 22.

of Ryzhov's cavalry with the main body, which numbered some 2,000 men. The gentle slope of the Causeway Heights screened the advance of this large body of cavalry from view. The advance guard of some 400 Hussars repulsed by Campbell and the 93rd Highlanders were not 'shot down in heaps' and certainly did not lose the 400, which 'are said to have fallen in the charge'. The bulk of the Russian cavalry advancing with great caution over the brow of the slope was 'the second force' Fisher-Rowe mentions in his letter. There is a lack of clarity in his estimation of the Russian strength and an absence of description regarding the action of the British cavalry when they engaged this vastly superior Russian force. Furthermore the engagement by the British Heavy Cavalry was not as one unified brigade but rather as a series of uncoordinated attacks by the constituent squadrons that composed the brigade. The lack of detail might have been because there was little to report regarding the involvement of the 4th Dragoon Guards in the defeat of the Russian cavalry. Without access to Fisher-Rowe's original letter it is impossible to say if the text has been edited, though why details of such a daring and gallant feat of arms should be omitted would indicate a bizarre editorial decision. The letter suggests that a map or diagram accompanied it. He wrote 'below B on the plain'. One can speculate that this diagram written on the letter or on a separate sheet is still with the missing original letter. Fisher-Rowe observed that 'the Heavy Brigade charged down the same way, but by some extraordinary fortune received hardly any damage at all'. The Heavy Brigade, however, did not 'charge' but, under Lucan, advanced a short distance in support of the Light Brigade and were halted by him after suffering some casualties.

Even allowing for regimental rivalry, letters home from Richard Temple Godman of the 5th Dragoon Guards give a very different account of the action of the Heavy Brigade, claiming that, despite Lucan's despatch that the 4th and 5th Dragoon Guards were led to the charge by Hodge of the 4th Dragoon Guards, 'This is perfectly false: the 4th were not anywhere near us, nor was Colonel Hodge'. Subsequently, Godman was even more dismissive regarding the role of the 4th Dragoon Guards in the battle:

> The Illustrated News account is a very bad one, they put in the Royal Dragoons as having charged. They were not in the fight, all the men they lost were hit afterwards, when we got under the batteries in support of the Light [Brigade]. The 4th Dragoons [Guards] were hardly in it, they executed a flank movement. The Greys got most spoken of, being so easily distinguished by their

bearskins hats and their horses. They and the Inniskillings and the 5th D.G. were the only regiments in the thick of it.[7]

Fisher-Rowe himself later commented again on the charge of the Heavy Brigade some months later [124]. Having dined with Colonel Griffiths of the Scots Greys, the 2nd (North British) Dragoons, he expressed his annoyance that the Scots Greys had monopolised 'all the credit of the heavy Cavalry charge at Balaklava'. He believed the Scots Greys would have been surrounded had not 'the 4th and 5th come to their assistance, and so great was their confusion that they broke our line as they came full speed in the opposite direction'. As it happens, however, lack of detailed description is repeated in other accounts of the charge of the Heavy Brigade.[8]

The letters after Balaklava reveal how nervous the picquets were and also how inexperienced [96]. The Heavy Brigade was not engaged at Inkerman so details are from third parties or 'reports' [97], but Fisher-Rowe did experience a flattened tent as a result of the 'great storm' on 14 November [99, 100]. There is a gap in the letters from 19 November until 2 December, between which dates Fisher-Rowe 'sent in his papers', that is to say he attempted to leave the regiment by the sale of his commission. Godman of the 5th Dragoon Guards reported 'Fisher, 4th D.G., sent in his papers the other day and they were refused; he is not much of a soldier'.[9] Fisher-Rowe, like Phillips of the 8th Hussars, could see no point in staying. Even Hodge of the 4th Dragoon Guards wrote on 24 November, 'The sick are lying in bell tents on the wet ground, and for all this I have spent my fortune! I wish I was well out of it.'[10] In the event, Fisher-Rowe was ordered to Scutari after suffering cramps due to the cold and wet weather. His arrival at Scutari, after a voyage in a patched-up ship that had been damaged in the great hurricane, is of interest [102]. The administrative bungling that had caused so much suffering in the Crimea continued at Scutari. He was kept waiting for hours, there was no room available in the hospital, and orders related to his leave were not readily to hand. Thereafter Fisher-Rowe set himself up in the Globe Hotel at Pera on the Bosphorus. His

---

7 Philip Warner, ed., *The Fields of War: A Young Cavalryman's Crimea Campaign* (London: John Murray, 1977), pp. 83, 102.

8 See, for example, Anglesey, *Little Hodge*, p. 44; and George Buchanan, *Letters from an Officer of the Scots Greys to His Mother during the Crimean War* (London: Rivingtons, 1866, reprint edn, 2005), p. 13.

9 Warner, *Fields of War*, p. 97.

10 Anglesey, *Little Hodge*, p. 61.

health improved and he set about acquiring his property and, with considerable energy and resourcefulness, purchasing materials that would be useful when he returned to the Crimea. Fisher-Rowe wrote that he intended to sell out once Sebastopol fell and this detail was kept in the published extracts [103].

When he returned to the Crimea in the second week of January 1855, Fisher-Rowe was preoccupied with the construction of his hut [111, 113, 115]. As the weather improved, the tone and content of Fisher-Rowe's letters change. In this respect he was typical of many officers in the Crimea who wrote home. The improvement in the condition and organisation of Balaklava, the completion and use of the railway, the arrival of supplies from home, the time to walk to Inkerman and back led Fisher-Rowe to write, 'I was never better or stronger than now' [120]. His forethought, when at Constantinople, enabled him to enjoy the comforts of his hut rather than the misery of a cold and leaking tent. Interspersed with the descriptions of his personal circumstances are comments regarding the condition of the army and those responsible for it such as Lucan, Sir George Brown and, especially, Raglan [130, 134, 135]. Interestingly, the young Gladstone, too, is singled out for overstating the strength of the army before Sebastopol in a debate in the House of Commons; he 'ought to have his tongue cut out' [120].

There were odd flashes of excitement when the Russians shelled part of the camp where Fisher-Rowe was dining with officers of the 97th Regiment and when his charger reared as he tried to remount near Canrobert's Hill after looking at the remains of a Russian who had been left there since the battle of Balaklava the previous October [127]. Some key events of the war pass with little description or comment for his main concern was to get by as best he could and endure the boredom of waiting for the fall of Sebastopol [130, 132]. Though Fisher-Rowe witnessed the French battle for the Mamelon on 6 June, he could see nothing of the British attack on the Redan [138]. Nor is there any description of the assault by the French or the British infantry on the Malokoff and the Redan on 18 June [141] or the final assault on 8 September, Fisher-Rowe referring only to the loss of his friend Major Welsford and the manner of his death [153]. Subsequently, however, he offered some explanation as to his reluctance to describe some of the scenes he had witnessed such as the aftermath of the battle at Tchernaya [156]. There was, too, a sense of resignation at being kept in the Crimea and a low-level scandal operating among some of the officers who desired to quit the discomfort and boredom, which Fisher-Rowe had initially condemned, soon appeared more tempting [158, 162]. Luckily for the regiment, they left the Crimea in December 1855.

After surviving the Crimea, Fisher-Rowe remained with the 4th Dragoon Guards. He was promoted to captain by purchase in July 1860, retiring by sale of his commission in November 1861 following a riding accident that injured his spine and from which he never really recovered. In November 1865 he married Edith Maria, the only daughter of Mayow Wynell Adams of Sydenham, Kent, and there were three children from the marriage. Fisher-Rowe's wife died in October 1871, aged 27 years, and, still recovering from his accident, he went to live with his parents at Thorncombe and also at Wilton Crescent. Fisher-Rowe married again in 1874, his second wife being Lady Victoria Liddell, youngest daughter of the Earl of Ravensworth: there were six children from this match. In the 1880s and the 1890s, he was a regular attender at the reunion dinners held in London by some of the surviving officers of the Light and Heavy Brigades. He died on 8 November 1909.

There was brief and melancholy report in *The Times* that shed light on Edward Fisher-Rowe's last years. There was an inquest at the Westminster Coroner's Court, at which his son, Major Lawrence Fisher-Rowe of the Grenadier Guards, reported that he 'suffered from his nerves for a long time, and sometimes was considerably depressed'. The hunting accident and its consequences were mentioned and that Fisher-Rowe had had to lie on his back for seven years, though, within that time he had married and produced children. What was probably meant was that the injury to Fisher-Rowe's spine was sufficiently severe to cause him considerable pain and to force him to lie down frequently. In 1880 he was a Justice of the Peace for Surrey and later Deputy Lord Lieutenant for the county and a Justice of the Peace for London. At the inquest Major Fisher-Rowe was asked if his father ever took laudanum and he replied that he did not. Major Fisher-Rowe did reveal, however, that his father did use cyanide of potassium to kill wasps and that he was frequently melancholic regarding his condition and the demands it made on his wife. The coroner was informed that the cause of death was cyanide poisoning and the jury returned a verdict of 'suicide during temporary insanity, brought on by insomnia'.[11]

Not all Fisher-Rowe's published letters have a salutation and they have not therefore been given a heading here. However it must be assumed that they were all addressed to his family.

---

11   *The Times*, 11 November 1909, p. 6, col. E.

73

Fisher-Rowe to his father

Dundalk, Feb. 1854

I am very much obliged to you for keeping my servant for me, he is certainly a great advantage. I have not bought the horse I went to see at Belfast, as I think he is too young to buy, when we may be on board ship in a couple of months; he was four years old and six weeks, and a very nice horse indeed. I am going to see an eight year old in a few weeks that I think will answer.

74

Fisher-Rowe to his mother

Dundalk, Feb. 16th 1854

I am very sorry James has not passed his examination, as he will lose some time; however, he well no doubt very soon be wanted, three men appointed to this Regiment have been spun once or twice. I see the report in the papers has been contradicted about the Cavalry going out. The Carbineers are the first for Foreign Service, and we are next; it would be a great shame if they pass us over.

75

Fisher-Rowe to his father

Dundalk, Feb. 23rd 1854

There is a report that the 3rd, 4th, and 5th Dragoon Guards are to be in readiness for Turkey, but nothing official has reached us yet. It is rather a bore for some of the young fellows in the Guards, I hear. At 1.15 p.m. I go out in command of a detachment in aid of the civil power at this disgraceful election. We have 180 Infantry in the Barracks, and they, with nearly all the Cavalry except my detachment, have been in town since 9.30 this morning to keep it quiet, nearly half have come back as there is no disturbance. My detachment is expected to have some work, as we go out in the evening, when the drink will have had effect.

76

Fisher-Rowe to his father

Dundalk, Feb. 28th 1854

I think I had better see about a horse myself when I come home, which will be 1st April if all goes well. You must prepare yourselves for what I am afraid will occasion you great uneasiness: the great probability of our being sent out to the Turkish coast, to some islands, or to Turkey itself, in a very short time. It will be necessary to be fully prepared, and I shall want a very different horse for a charger, in case we get orders to sail, from what would do at home. One thing I want to see about: I want you to go to that shop near Cawthorn's Library, on the right as you walk across the Square, and enquire if they have any revolvers of the same size as the Cavalry carbines (in the bore); please to let me know about this as soon as you can. We shall only be allowed 90lbs. of baggage I hear, so that the principle of little and good must be attended to. You can hardly imagine the joy of the soldiers at the thoughts of going out. It is a very lucky chance for us, as we are the next Regiment but one for Foreign Service, and shall very likely get one year of it instead of 15. I dare say we shall not see any service, as all the Western Powers have joined against the Russians, but still I may just as well have those things which will be necessary in case we do.

77

Fisher-Rowe to his mother

Newbridge, March 25th 1854

There is, I fancy, no doubt about our going to Turkey. I hope that at last Father has succeeded in getting me a very fine horse, and I shall do very well if he is as good as he looks. I am getting my kit as fast as possible, as there is no knowing how soon we may start. I have still hope that I may get over to England for a few days. We only take out 250 horses and 300 men, two Captains, two Lieutenants and two Cornets are to be left at home. I hope you will be able to find me a fine glass, as it is very important to have one.

78

Fisher-Rowe to his mother

Newbridge, April 10th 1854

I saw a letter from the Colonel to the Major today. He says it is decided that we go through France. He has had an interview with Lord Lucan and the Commander in Chief. They told him we should sail very soon. He asked them to give him as much time as they could, but they did not seem disposed to let him have much more. We are to go to Dublin as soon as the 11th are off, and sail from there to Havre.

79

Newbridge April 23rd 1854

It is decided, the Colonel tells me, that we are to go by long sea and not by France, so there will be no bother about the luggage.

80

On Board the 'Palmyra'

June 7th 1854

Two horses rather ill today; applied proper remedies, and tonight they seem all right. We are opposite Cape Clear.

June 8th.

Wind light. Horses all right, but vicious biting at everyone.

June 10th

One horse was seized with staggers at 10 a.m. and fell, and was nearly dead before he could be got up again, the slings are so badly fitted.

Saturday, Sunday, Tuesday, Wednesday, blowing so hard, quite impossible to write. Very ill indeed; very tired by night watches. Sunday night, two horses down; with great danger and difficulty they hauled them out into the space between the horses. Webb came to me at one o'clock that night and ordered me up, said we had just escaped being run down by another ship, which did not see us as our lights were washed out. Those who saw it say it was the most awful sight they ever saw, some of the men got turned and sick by it I got up at once and found one horse nearly dead and two others struggling to leap over the mangers.

June 12th

Two horses dead and were thrown overboard. Wind contrary.

June 13th

Another horse dead

June 14th

Another bad day. Wind still against us. We are in the same place we were in last Sunday – in the Bay of Biscay.

June 15th.

Horses killed for glanders. Pretty well recovered from sickness. Horses quiet. Wind strong and against us.

June 16th

This morning we left the vile Bay of Biscay and are going quietly along, everything jolly.

June 17th.

Ship going through the water beautifully. Suspicion that two more horses have got glanders makes one rather anxious, four gone already, hope they have lost more than us in the headquarters ship.

June 21st.

Another horse died of glanders.

June 22

Wind light, passed Almeria with mountains of Granada capped with snow arising behind. I had a beautiful view of it all, as the Quarter-Master bet me ten bob I would not go to the very top of the main mast and touch the ball. I took up my glass with me, and when I had my hat on the ball, I descended to the royal-yard and had the most extensive view.

June 30

Wind still contrary. Very strong. Five horses down got up again without much harm.

July 1

Wind contrary. Two more horses dead.

July 4

Wind fair but light. Horses suffering from heat very much.

July 8

Arrived Malta. Start again in two hours.

July 10

We sailed from Malta in tow of the steamer 'Tonning', which came in last night at 6 o'clock with mails, and 56 horses on board, a company of the Rifles, under the command of Capt. Rowley and Mr. Churchill. About one o'clock Capt. Rowley came to us in a boat and asked us to dine with them, which however we could not do.

July 11

We dined with the Officers on board the steamer at 5 o'clock, had a first rate dinner, which is the first really good one during the voyage. The thermometer stood at 87 in the cabin during dinner. They told us that there were letters in their mail for the 'Palmyra' which however the Postmaster did not take the trouble to give us.

July 14

Passing through the Dardanelles.

July 15

We arrived at Constantinople at 3 o'clock, and got anchored at 4 o'clock, when all went on shore to our great delight. Bought some tea and a capital Dean and Adams revolver for £8, everything complete, one of the best I have seen, rather a queer thing they should be cheaper here than in England.

July 16

We weighed at 9.30 a.m., but did not get clear till 1 or 2 p.m., on account of the ropes joining us together getting foul somehow. We are now in the Black Sea, and expect to see Varna tomorrow.

Varna

July 17 & July 18

We began to land at about 10 o'clock, and by night were quite clear of the ship and established in our tents.

81

August 13

I have not yet received another letter from you, but write to tell you of an affair of which you have no doubt had full account in the papers (from our own correspondent), viz., the destruction of Varna by fire. I cannot call myself an eye-witness, as I was not there when the fire was at its worst, but after it had been got under, or rather it had burnt itself out. I am sorry I was not there during the night, for the French managed to disgrace themselves as much as they well could in the time. All the shops that were not burnt were completely sacked; their owners struck down and beaten or stabbed, and certainly in the morning it was as pretty a picture of war as could well be seen. The store-keepers I spoke to, told me that 20 or 30 French came into each of their stores, took everything out into the streets and spoilt what they could not take away. One man computed his loss at £600, another at £1300; neither of their houses were burnt. The French have been mutinous for some time owing to the cholera, which has worked us pretty well. They say they came out here to fight and not to die like dogs. The Officers have no control over them, and indeed it was better as it was, for in many instances they were much worse than the men. The interpreter to Sir George Brown told me that he was standing near a building which some French were trying to save, and two Turks were standing close to him. A French Officer came up to them and ordered them to work at the fire; the poor creatures did not of course understand him, and did not move, he got very angry and without more ado by a neat thrust passed his sword through both, and far from being ashamed, was boasting of the way in which he had done it, as long as the interpreter was within hearing. There is not a shop open that I can see since the fire, for the very reason there is nothing left to sell; although not half the town is destroyed by fire, the whole is sacked. Our gallant Generals adhered to their usual policy and did nothing, although there are troops enough to have kept order and prevented plunder in a town 50 times the size. Our Regiment and the 6th Dragoons, and I believe all the Cavalry were ordered out, and after the men had been turned out of their warm tents into the damp, unhealthy night air, what did it all come to? Twenty five file of the 4th Dragoon Guards were sent down to the town, where they were immediately dismounted, and ordered to lie down in their cloaks, here they slept till morning, and then rode quietly back to Camp. Our single Regiment if they had been sent for in time, would have been quite sufficient to have prevented plunder, at any rate in the wholesale way it was carried on. There is little doubt it was the work of Nicholas,[1] indeed it was reported that three Russians were taken in a boat in the Harbour as they were escaping. The French shot several men who they say they caught in the act of firing houses and threw them into the flames. The English, according to all accounts, behaved very well, confining themselves strictly to getting as drunk as possible on the liquor which was wasting all over the town. The fire is hardly out yet, although the fire commenced three nights ago. The ration biscuits[2] burn beautifully, and won't be put out; our clever superiors succeeded in saving 48 bags of them. Our Commissariat General Murray, who is a capital fellow, has got 24 of them. The horses must go without barley, as it has all been burnt. The powder had a narrow escape. The Commissariat chest was with difficulty saved. It must have been a beautifully planned thing, and has answered as well as it could do, with the able assistance of

---

1 Tsar Nicholas I, who ruled Russia from 1825 until his death in 1855.
2 Rock-hard baked biscuits that resembled large cream crackers in appearance only.

our noble allies the French. Nicholas has good reason to be proud of his work. It was a beautiful sight from the hill on which we are stationed, on the opposite side of the bay to the town, which stands within 50 yards of the water. The flames and smoke rising up to the sky were reflected in the bay, and showed the shipping as plain as if it had been day. The large stone gateway stood out with a sheet of flame a quarter of a mile long as a background. There is not a Turk to be seen anywhere. I hear that any of them who have been lucky enough to save a towel have encamped under it, where they sit smoking their pipes, which they did not lose, as I believe they sleep smoking. They seem utterly indifferent as to what they are to do when their 'baccy' is gone. The weather is getting much cooler, and the winter season is no doubt not far off. We know nothing as to where we are going to, but there will most likely be a move on Sebastopol before this season is finished. The shore is covered with fascines and gabions, and the Infantry expect to go immediately.

82

Varna. August 17

I go to Varna very often, and yesterday the fire was still burning and the water at work. I went out with some of the 6th [Inniskilling Dragoons] buffalo hunting the other evening, it is great fun. We take a long pole with the end sharpened and hardened in the fire, and search the woods in a party of six or eight; when the game is started there is a general rush to break the first spear, and a fast pony and one with good strong forelegs is a great advantage, as this is one of the most hilly countries I ever saw. The other day, two French Regiments mutinied, but were persuaded to return to their duty in a few hours; they are afraid to touch the ring leaders lest the mutiny should extend. It was caused by the quantity of illness they have had among them. We are still going on very well, although the sickness has been terrible. Some Regiments are dying off at a great rate; the fleet also suffering severely, the 'Britannia' lost 50 men in one night out of 1000. The men are behaving very badly, and our Colonel is not fit to manage them.[3] Privates and N.C.Os get drunk on escort duty, and the N.C.Os are not broken or the Privates flogged. Both 'Jack' and 'Blood Royal' are doing much better than most horses out here. The 'Britannia' man o'war lost 79 men in 19 hours we hear from the Staff-Surgeon.

---

3   Lt. Col. Edward Cooper Hodge. See Anglesey, *Little Hodge*, passim.

August 30
Something is to be done at last, it would appear. The Guards embarked the day before yesterday, the Light Cavalry are being got on board today, and the Infantry of the line will be all in tonight.

83

Varna, Sept. 8
As you see from the heading we are still in our old position. The Light Division[4] sailed two days ago. I suppose you have seen in the papers of the way in which the cholera has worked us. You can imagine we have been pretty bad when I tell you my troop has been decimated and two over. It carried them off very fast. Men strong and well in the morning, were buried in the afternoon.

84

Varna, Sept. 17
No sign of the vessels coming to take us to the Crimea. General Scarlett cannot understand the continued silence from the Crimea. Pony catching still goes on, and I have achieved a batter pudding. Man murdered last night within speaking distance of the Royals' Camp; he was brought in living, and when they said Bashibazukes[5] he nodded. Hogan, my servant,[6] did an uncommon clever thing. I ordered him to take old '£2.10' the pony, a mile and a half from the Camp and shoot him. He like a regular Irishman, took the animal straight to Lord Lucan's Camp and shot him about 100 yards from his tent. Of course there was an awful smell, and the Staff did not know what to do with themselves. In the morning his Lordship smelt him out and found by the mark on his side that he belonged to the 4th Dragoon Guards, and Hogan has to go down and bury him.

---

4 The Light Division comprised 1st Brigade (7th, 23rd and 33rd foot); 2nd Brigade (19th, 77th and 88th Foot), 2nd Battalion Rifle Brigade; 'C' Troop Royal Horse Artillery; and 'E' Field Battery Royal Artillery. See McGuigan, *Into Battle!*, p. 6.

5 In Turkish *basibuzuk*, meaning 'disorganised, leaderless'; irregular troops of the Ottoman Empire notorious for their lack of discipline, barbarity and savagery. They rode small horses and were armed with an assortment of weapons, especially the long barrelled flintlock musket called the jezail. See E. H. Nolan, *History of the War against Russia* (London: Virtue & Co., 1857), vol. 1, p. 63; Alastair Massie, ed., *A Most Desperate Undertaking: The British Army in the Crimea, 1854–56* (London: National Army Museum, 2003) pp. 66–73.

6 Possibly 1112 Pvt. Patrick Hogan. See TNA, WO12/270, Muster Roll, 4th Dragoon Guards.

85

Fisher-Rowe to his parents

Varna, Sept. 20

I have just returned from the pursuit of the murdering scoundrels, who have been committing fresh outrages.[7] They attacked two herdsmen – cut one's throat and shot him in the stomach and once in the shoulder, and nearly cut the other's head off. The party sent out to search the wood found two more with their hands tied and throats cut. Tonight on shots being heard, the Colonel called me to take the command of the picket and see if I could take them. I proceeded for some distance in the direction of the firing, halted my men on the top of a ravine and went forward to reconnoitre. Suddenly I saw a light like the flash of a flint pistol, or the light of a dark lantern, I sprang down the ravine, but the light was not repeated, nor could I hear anything. I then ordered the picket down, but could find nothing. We proceeded some distance further, when I put the men in some bushes and waited in dead silence for some time, when we heard voices approaching. I immediately extended the men, and took six 'ugly dogs', four of them with horses, armed from head to foot, they luckily for themselves made no resistance or they would all have been killed, as the feeling is very strong against them; two of our men being missing, and one not heard of for ten days past. I brought my friends to the guard tent, and the Colonel sent for an interpreter, but of course nothing can be proved against them. However I don't despair, and if the Colonel sends me out again (which I think is likely, as he was rather pleased tonight with me), and I can catch any of them in the act, I shall save the Government the expense of a halter, and ourselves the bother of trying them. The Transports are coming in today, and the news from the Crimea is most favourable. The troops landed without opposition, and the people of the country most kind, and brought down animals for the baggage, eggs, flour, and everything they could want. They first landed some distance from the town (40 miles, I believe), only a few Regiments though, which they embarked again, and then disembarked again close to the place. They will commence the siege today I believe.

---

7 There was plenty of opportunity for Bashi Bazouks and other irregular horsemen to rob, steal and plunder with so much material at hand related to the armies involved. The murder referred to in the previous letter reinforces the already appalling reputation of these irregulars.

86

Varna. Sept. 21
Hurrah for the Crimea, we are off tomorrow; fine country, people very friendly; take Sebastopol in a week or so, and then into winter quarters for the winter.

87

On Board the 'Simla' Sept. 25
I am afraid you will find this more illegible than usual, but I have met with a rather unfortunate accident. I have had my two middle fingers crushed in the block by which the horses were being drawn up into the ship during our embarkation here; luckily only the tops, about half an inch, were caught, and I was able to drag them out, at the expense of a nail, and barring the inconvenience no harm done. We are uncommon jolly here, you never saw such good living, every possible luxury; it is a beautiful ship. We have got our whole Regiment on board, and 25 horses of the 5th Dragoon Guards. We sail tomorrow morning early, and we expect to reach the Crimea in 40 hours. We have heard today of a general action, which was fought at the first river,[8] 21,000 English and French attacked a fortified position of the Russians, and took it in four hours, and killed 10,000 Russians. The position was expected to hold out against the united forces for six weeks, and was taken in less than that number of hours. The rout would have been fearful if we had had enough Cavalry to follow them up. We shall disembark 15 miles from Sebastopol, and I daresay shall find the army knocking the walls to pieces. We are to winter at Odessa, the Guards at Malta, the line at Sebastopol.

88

On Board the 'Simla' Sept. 30
We passed Sebastopol at a distance of about five or six miles, and had a first-rate view of it. It appears a tremendous place; the houses and palaces are very fine. We saw the ships in the harbour and the streets quite plain. The Fleet are anchored on all sides of it, and a splendid sight. A beautiful day

---

8   The battle of the Alma, 20 September 1854.

and all quiet, there will be a row in the house on Sunday when they start to bombard. The army has marched quite round the town, after severe fighting. If the accounts we hear are true 15,000 Russians have perished, and about 800 English and French. I think more Allies and less Russians must have been killed. We are at present anchored at a place called Balaklava, or something of that sort; tremendous mountains all round, and the bay is a very curious shape. The cliffs are of red stone, perpendicular and tremendous. The Colonel is down with dysentery, and won't be able to land. All my earthly possessions go on my two horses. I find it quite a relief to have so little to look after. The Infantry officers have had nothing but what they carry on their backs all this time, and the quantities of sick who have been sent to Scutari are very great indeed. The first night they landed it rained, and they had no tents – as had been the case all along with them. We shall have a few tents – quite enough to stick ourselves into if we pack tight, and we shall have the advantage of not requiring much night clothing, as the number will keep us warm. They are trying the range of their guns today. We had a very bad passage indeed from Varna here, lost ten horses,[9] cholera quite gone.

89

Camp, near Balaklava. Oct. 8

We are about two miles from the little town. We are living almost entirely on our rations – of which the mutton is first rate. This is a glorious life. We hear the great guns of Sebastopol every hour, but our batteries have not opened yet, we expect them to open every day. The French, I am thankful to say, are not worth a hang compared with our men, and we have to do all the sharp work. You will see a better account in the papers than I can give of the battle of Alma. – our loss was tremendously heavy. I have been on outlying picket the last 24 hours, but am as fresh as a daisy, nothing tires me. The report is now that we do not stay in the Crimea, but return to Scutari as soon as the town is taken. This is a most beautiful country – just like England – the houses are very nicely furnished, quite luxury, and every one that is deserted is given up to plunder. All the people that remain are respected. I have so much to do, and am so ready for bed at night, that I have very little time to write. I have got a great many useful things out of the houses that have been deserted.

---

9   Some 226 horses of the Heavy Brigade perished in transit from Varna to Balaklava. A storm hit the towed transports almost as soon as they left harbour. See [182] below for Edward Phillips's description of his experience.

90

Camp, near Balaklava. Oct. 12

We are still about 15 minutes from Balaklava, guarding the rear of the army, who are working night and day to drag the guns into position. The enemy are very good at their guns, and throw their shells beautifully. None of our guns have opened yet, but are expected to every day. All day long heavy guns are passing our camp towards the front. The ships have furnished more than a thousand sailors to work their own guns. They are the most wonderful fellows, they come along singing and shouting, harnessed to an araba,[10] in which their kits are conveyed; as they come opposite they are received with loud cheers, which they return with a power of lung quite extraordinary. We are turned out and mounted at 5.00 every morning, and remain under arms till 8.30 or 9.00; the early morn is the time for attack. We are, I am most thankful to say, in better health than we have been for some time; another Officer is down (Morgan)[11] with ague and fever, and has been sent to the ships. Webb is, I believe, better. I have heard nothing of the Colonel since we landed, and do not care how long it is before he joins us again. Biggs has been on shore, and is better. Yesterday I was out after forage and came to a village with a very nice little church, it was a square building with a small dome to it, and a porch with a green door. The screen and chapel were full of pictures very nicely painted, and nearly all representing the same subject – the patron saint, I suppose, with a small pickaxe in his right hand raised over his head, and a little black devil held by the hair in his left. I could buy nothing – everything had been plundered by the Turkish soldiers, and the poor people made signs as though some of their throats had been cut. The Russians are remarkably nice-looking people, most polite in their salutations, and seem to like us very well. They are mostly dressed in long white blouses, coats, trousers and caps, quite like Englishmen. Their houses look most comfortable and neat, when they have escaped plunder. They, however bring nothing to sell, and I have got nothing but rations since I came. They give us double rations of rum now, which is a great comfort and beautiful drink. The Cossacks keep us alive, but don't trust themselves very near us. I wish I had a rifle, I could have some capital fun with them; however I am afraid it will arrive too late for human game. Most awfully cold; out every morning at 5 o'clock, and under arms until

---

10   An *araba* was a small light cart popular in the region.

11   Lieutenant George Manners Morgan, Cornet (by purchase) July 1850; Lieutenant (by purchase) April 1852. See *Hart's New Army List 1855*, p. 124.

it is quite light; two pairs drawers, two pairs socks, two jerseys, a red flannel under stable jacket, and a thick stable jacket, which I bought at the auction of Pitcairn,[12] the Doctor of the 5th, who died of cholera, and weighed 18 stone, keep me just comfortable. Horses have got coats like sheep, and are never groomed. I had a narrow escape of being killed in a rather curious way today: I rode to the top of a very high hill to see a hunt after a few Cossacks which was going on below, when suddenly an immense swarm of bees came round me in a most hostile manner. I had sense enough to retreat at a slow walk, and was not stung at all, or 'Jack' either, who did not care at all about it; but for two or three minutes it put me into a fair fright. My fingers are quite well enough to work my sword well; and I have saved the top of the middle finger, which at one time looked like coming off, but owing to the capital state of my health has healed all right.

91

Camp Balaklava. 18 Oct.
The batteries opened on Sebastopol today, one of the Lancasters' guns has been burst.[13] The French have had nearly all their guns silenced during the day, and on the whole the damage seems pretty equal; not much loss of life. I believe one of the immense Russian towers has had a hole knocked right through it.

92

Camp Balaklava, Oct. 26
I do not know when this may reach you, as things are in great confusion just now. Yesterday, about 7 a.m., the Russians made their appearance at the Comora village on our extreme right, and in a very short space of time drove the Turkish forces who were in battery there, head over heels down into the plain. They abandoned their batteries, I believe, from what I now hear, that some, if not all, the guns were spiked. The Russians brought their own, and turned them on the Cavalry who were drawn up on the

---

12 George Kincaid Pitcairn, MD Edinburgh 1830. Died on active service at Varna 16 August 1854. See Alfred Peterkin and William Johnston, *Commissioned Officers in the Medical Services of the British Army, 1660–1960* 2 vols (London: Wellcome Historical Medical Library, 1968), vol. 1, p. 290.

13 The 68-pdr rifle muzzle loading (RML) Lancaster artillery piece had a tendency to burst.

plain. The next position was abandoned by the Turks the moment a shell fell near them, and was seized in the same way as the first; the Cavalry had to retire very fast, and the Russians came down into the plain between no. 1 and no. 2 positions, and by the Comora village. Our batteries at it, and some behind them, kept firing on them, but without much effect. A large force of Russian Cavalry now charged the Highlanders' position, which was the key to Balaklava. The Highlanders, only half a Regiment (93rd), received them with the greatest coolness, firing separately and very fast; they shot them down in heaps; 400 are said to have fallen in the charge. A second force of Cavalry, about the same size, (rather more than our Heavy Brigade), made for our camp and baggage, which were in great danger. The Heavy Brigade, however, were loosed at them, and rolled them over and over and cleared the plain. Our Regiment lost only one man in that charge.[14] Now comes the recital of an affair almost too grievous to put on paper. Reinforcements of Infantry having come up, the Russians were driven from the 2nd position and plain, and nothing was left them but the 1st position and Comora village. About 2 p.m., the Cavalry being under no. 3 position, an order was brought to charge the enemy who were below B on the plain. The Light Brigade went first and were completely destroyed by the Russian batteries all around; still they passed on and took the battery above B, but as they had no spikes and could not bring the guns away they did no good. The Heavy Brigade charged down the same way, but by the most extraordinary fortune received hardly any damage at all. Of the Light Brigade, out of 800 who went down into the valley, 40 or 50 returned mounted, and about double that number straggled up after. I believe the Light Brigade is now about 190 men. Very little is known of the melancholy affair; it appears that Lord Raglan sent a written order to Lord Lucan to charge. This ended the day's work. The forces came into camp about 9 p.m., and were not disturbed during the night nor up to the present hour, 2 p.m.

93

Camp Balaklava. Oct. 27
Nothing has happened to us since yesterday. The Garrison made a sortie[15] in which they were completely beaten, 750 left for dead on the field and

---

14 Pvt. Thomas Ryan, from Clonmel, Ireland, formerly a carpenter, had enlisted in January 1853. See TNA, WO12/270.
15 This refers to 'Little Inkerman' on 26 November 1854.

quantities of wounded. They spiked a gun or two, but so badly that they got them to work again. The first time that I was engaged[16] with the enemy was on the 6th of this month. I had command of one of the outlying pickets, and was not disturbed through the whole of the day or night. On the morning of the 7th I patrolled to the front at daybreak with 10 men of the picket – the horses of which had had no water for 24 hours, and were very soon beat. I patrolled for some distance and had stopped to listen for about two minutes, when suddenly a Regiment of Lancers, I believe Polish, charged over a hill on our left front, so steep that an English horse weighted as ours are must have walked down. I retreated on the picket at once, and gained our heights with the loss of three men, who could hardly get their horses to canter, and were run into and speared in the most merciless manner. I stayed behind with them as long as I could but could give no assistance, as 10 or 12 Russians closed round each the instant his horse stopped. They now made for me, and one got within a spears length when I stopped him with a shot from my large pistol. I caught my men on the ridge and began a skirmish, and managed to keep the hill till the pickets came up, and in the course of an hour the whole of the Cavalry were on the spot. The enemy fired very badly, all the shot passing over, a yard or more. I don't think our men did much harm either. I saw none fall, though the French said many fell in the plain afterwards. Sebastopol will soon be ours now, and these are their last efforts.

94

Fisher-Rowe to his parents

Camp, near Sebastopol, Oct. 31
Nothing of importance has occurred since my last of the 27th. I don't see any complaints in your letters of mine not reaching you regularly, so that I hope they go as well one way as the other, yours come to hand capitally.

---

16   This refers to an incident that resulted in quite a degree of negative criticism of Fisher-Rowe. According to Kinglake, 'It was a patrol under Cornet Fisher which first felt the presence of the enemy in the country of the Tchernaya. The Cornet was surprised in the early morning by finding himself in contact with part of a powerful force which had come down into the valley, and three of his men were made prisoners.' See Kinglake, *Invasion of the Crimea*, vol. 4, p. 242. Godman of the 5th Dragoon Guards was also critical: 'Fisher ... made a bad business of that piquet when his men got speared, for which he got tremendously blown up ... I believe his piquet was surprised when watering, and the men dismounted, so report says.' See Warner, *Fields of War*, p. 97. For the three troopers from the 4th Dragoon Guards who were captured see David Inglesant, *The Prisoners of the Voronesh:: The Journal of George Newman, 23rd Regiment* (Woking: Unwin, 1977).

On the 26th, the day after the action, the Cavalry moved some distance nearer Sebastopol, and more out of reach of the enemy in our rear, who, if they had any heavy guns, might have thrown shot into our camp. On the 27th nothing was done, but the camp was awoke at 10.30 by the cry that the enemy was advancing upon us in force. We turned out with all speed, but were only half ready when we heard the galloping of horses advancing. I ran out of my tent with my coat in one hand and my sword in the other, and found my horse with one rein only and Hogan struggling to undo the knot that fastened him to his post. The galloping was within 50 yards of us. I cut hard at the rope with my sword, but it was too tough; a horse was now ridden over by the advancing troop, when suddenly it was discovered that it was our dirty pickets commanded by Captain Webb, who had run away in the most disgraceful manner and deserted their post, merely because they had heard a shout from the camp of the enemy.[17] Captain Webb got fearfully abused by the Colonel and by Lord Lucan, and was ordered not to come back to camp until relieved, whatever happened. We were again turned out at 2 a.m., and thrown into a state of alarm by 30 or 40 horses belonging to the enemy who galloped into camp with their reins tied to their saddles, and some with their nose-bags on. They got loose owing to the French throwing shell into their camp. They are very good horses indeed, and will mount the men whose horses were shot, capitally. It is a horrid sight to see the way in which men and horses sink into the ground under round shot practice. We were very lucky. I saw shot that passed over our heads strike the troop behind, and again plump into a Regiment in front and the Horse Artillery within 20 yards of my right, but our Regiment only had one man struck, who was hit in the mouth with a piece of shell. I have got an Officer's handsome saddle and a sword, which I will try to send home. It is reported that a grand assault will be made on Sebastopol on the 1st November, in which case I should hope our hardships, which it is no use disguising are considerable, will come to an end. It is almost impossible to stir out of camp for fear of something happening, and the cold is very great just now, accompanied with rain. One can hardly get enough firewood to boil a kettle of water, and the water is the colour of pea soup. The ground is so hard it is impossible, or next to it, to drive a tent peg, and I have been obliged to cut up my bedstead to supply these useful articles. I am turning all my ingenuity to the erection of a fireplace in my tent, and sit on the ground quarrying

17   Webb, who commanded the pickets on the night of 27 October, believed the Russian were advancing in strength and panicked. He galloped back to camp and the entire cavalry force turned out for what was a false alarm. See Anglesey, *Little Hodge*, p. 52.

through the rock on which it stands. The Turks are found out at last; they are a blackguardly, cowardly race, without honour amongst the Officers or honesty amongst the men. They are treated in a very different way since the action; instead of a nod and a 'Bono Jonnie' from everyone, if one comes near a well when any soldiers are there he stands a good chance of a blow across the mouth from a heavy dragoon's fist and curses as long as he is in sight. I hear they get still rougher treatment from the French. The 93rd, who like all Highlanders can bear malice, swear, if they get a chance to drive their bayonets through the whole lot. They stole all the Highlanders' kits while they were actually defending them from the enemy. And when the work was over, about half a Regiment of Turks marched across the plain with their trumpets and drums, sticking their weapons into the dead. The French bands strike up at daybreak, and sometimes play 'God save the Queen', which sounds very fine in the early morn, with the accompaniment of the heavy batteries breaching Sebastopol, and gives one a thrill of pride and gratitude to think one is a British Officer in spite of the '46' and the Sunday Times.[18] Although cold and uncomfortable, I think the air healthy. The poor horses are the great sufferers in the cold nights which we have here, without cover or clothing. I have kept a blanket each for mine through the whole campaign. Letters have been intercepted from Sebastopol to the army in our rear, to say that unless reinforced they could not hold out two days more, and last night a large force was seen moving away from our rear towards Sebastopol. I hope we may winter in Sevastopol. I should think it is a very nice place indeed. I am afraid I may never see my handsome mule again; great nuisance having to leave her at the depot. That is the bore of being a junior. However there are lots of beasts on shore, and if only I get one quick I shall do pretty well.

95

Camp Balaklava, Nov 2

I write again before my last letter is sent, so that you may get the latest news. Nothing much has occurred since the last was written, except an attack on some of the batteries round Sebastopol by the French, which, however, did not succeed. It continues very cold, and I have had to cut

---

18 It is likely that this refers to a public scandal over the bullying of a junior officer in the 46th Regiment by other officers. The newspapers reported it and it did little to enhance the reputation of British officers. See *The Times*, 14 July 1854, p. 10, col. B for an account of the court martial.

up my blanket to line my blue coat and trousers, which makes them somewhat more comfortable. About a quarter of a mile in our rear the French have constructed a ditch and parapet to preserve us from attack in the rear. Our rations are not so good as they used to be; we get salt meat every other day,[19] which is so unwholesome I do not touch it, and make the ration of fresh meat serve me two days. The preserved soup is a great thing, when it is to be got; it is very dear – a pot holding enough for two days five or six shillings. However there is no doubt that this sort of thing cannot last much longer and that Sebastopol will fall, and we get into comfortable quarters. The early morn is the trying time on account of the extreme cold, but on the whole the army enjoys good health. The Light Brigade have just marched off to a new camp, but I am in hopes we shall be allowed to stay where we are, as shifting is a terrible nuisance, and the first night we get in without wood and water near, very hard work.

96

Camp Balaklava. Nov 7.
I write to tell you that our side of the house is all right. The mail, I believe, goes out tomorrow, so this is all the news I can send you, especially as I am at the present moment on outlying picket with the Russians two miles off, and well in sight. November 5th was a bloody day for us.[20]

97

Camp Balaklava, Nov 8.
I wrote in a great hurry yesterday, as I was on outlying picket, and should have got into a terrible row if I had been caught. You will of course have heard of the battle of the 5th November by Electric Telegraph. From what I hear today it has been more bloody to our side than I could have believed – 2,300 are said to have fallen on our side, killed and wounded, 800 dead; and between 10,000 and 15,000 Russians are lying between the town and our Camp. The attack was commenced by a new army from Poland, which was kept from all intercourse with the troops in

---

19 The provisions of the army had begun to deteriorate before this date. The Commissariat was unable to procure enough good quality meat and food from suppliers in Constantinople and, consequently, rations were second or third rate. Difficulties in supply were predicted by Captain Simmons in May 1854. See Simmons to Lord De Ros in TNA, WO1/368.

20 The battle of Inkerman.

Sebastopol, and were told by Prince Minschikoff [*sic*] that we had always been beaten, and that if they went bravely in, the campaign would be over. The consequence was they came on very bumptious, drove the pickets in, and got to the camp before the men were dressed. The tents are full of holes. One Major – I heard his name but have forgot it – had both his legs taken off by a round shot while he was in bed.[21] The night was terribly foggy and wet, and the pickets say their muskets would not go off. As our men came out of their tents in their shirts, or whatever they had on, they were shot by the Russians, who were accustomed to the light. However, in the course of ten minutes or so, two or three companies got together, half-dressed, and charged our gallant foes, who bolted back to the main body – 45,000 strong – which was advancing with an immense force of guns. However our men were all right by this time, and manned their lines, which they defended in the usual British style; 6,000 I believe in all, till we were reinforced by 5,000 French. Then I hear they went down to them, and insinuated at the point of the bayonet that the Russians had better go home, which little bit of advice the Russians eagerly followed – leaving some 15,000 either killed, wounded or prisoners. All the prisoners I have seen are evidently very glad of it, and were laughing and eating in great glee. They are a dirty-looking lot, and always fight in their great coats, which is the only dress I ever saw them in. The colour of the coats is a dirty dark yellow, and the cloth is so tough that a sword jumps off like indiarubber. The army of General Sacken is said to have gone by sea from Odessa to Upatoria, and to have been conveyed in Arabas to their present camp; if it is so, I should mildly propose that Dundas lose his head.[22] However, we will hope that such is not the case, it is merely a report in the camp at present. It is said Lord Raglan and the Duke[23] have quarrelled; the Duke having said that if the precautions in the way of trenches had been taken which he had recommended to the General Officer Commanding, the loss of men would not have taken place. Raglan pooh-poohed it, and the Duke resigned; but that is all idle talk bandied about from mouth to mouth, and may or may not be true. It is certain that trenches are

---

21 Major Sir Thomas St Vincent Cochrane Troubridge, 7th Fusiliers. See *Hart's New Annual Army List 1855*, p. 158.

22 Presumably Admiral Sir James Dundas, commanding the British Fleet in the Black Sea.

23 The Duke of Cambridge, commanding the 1st Division, went on board ship to recuperate from fatigue on 7 November 1854 and was formally ordered home on sick leave by a Medical Board at Constantinople on 27 December. The Duke was not uncritical of Raglan but defended him against press criticism. See Giles St Aubyn, *The Royal George: The Life of Prince George, Duke of Cambridge, 1819–1904* (London: Constable, 1963), pp. 81–8. The Duke was to succeed Hardinge as Commander-in-Chief at the Horse Guards in July 1856, remaining in post until 1895.

being made where the attack took place. It was a most extensive affair altogether, and when the Russians were driven back the French on the left near the sea got into the town with them, but not in numbers sufficient to make a lodgement. If you recollect reading Lord Raglan's despatch after Alma, in which he states that not a murmur did he hear at ponies being left behind, you are very much deceived. The remarks of an Officer of a Highland Regiment were very good. 'I can't make out', he said, 'where he got to if he did not hear them', especially as his Lordship had plenty of arabas to carry his own things, so he told me, which was pretty well. If the case has left before this reaches you, I wish you would send another small one with three bottles of medicine for my complaint.

Last night, Nov. 10th, there was a great row in my house; it rained torrents and blew great guns. At 2 a.m., when I was pretty well undressed and in my bed, my tent was blown clean down, and I was out in the dark with the rain pelting my bare neck and arms. I slipped on a great coat, picked up my blankets, and bolted through the mud for some other tent, into which I bundled in no very ceremonious manner, rolled myself up in the blankets, and lay revolving the pleasing thought if the enemy made an attack that night where my boots might be, or my trousers, or my coat, and what might be the state of my sword and pistols. However nothing luckily happened, and next morning I found my clothes in remarkably good state of preservation, as an antiquary would say, having got under the protecting wing of a mackintosh. Certainly the sight of the tent and appurtenances was not elevating to the spirit, considering that it has been raining all day and no chance of drying anything.

98

Camp Balaklava, Nov 12.
A much better day. I wish you would get my name put down for the Army and Navy Club, as I think it is better to belong to it. The chestnut horse is very well; 'Jack' has had a fever and is not worth anything; they have all got coats like sheep. I am now very comfortable in a bell tent, and my servant in mine, which he expects down at any minute. Sebastopol in much the same state as at first; a rather tougher nut than our Chiefs expected. Now that we have the full details of the battle of the heights of Inkerman, it appears we have lost 2400 killed and wounded; the Russians full 20,000–5000 or 6000 of whom were killed, and a great many taken prisoner.

99

Camp, Near Balaklava, Nov 17.
We have had a pretty fair taste of winter the last few days.[24] Two days ago, after we had mounted at daybreak and sat still on our horses for about an hour in a tremendous rain, about ten minutes after we had got to our tents, a hurricane of wind and rain struck the Army and blew down every tent nearly through the British force. I succeeded in throwing a mackintosh over my bedding, which I look on as the most important thing to keep dry. You can hardly imagine the misery of our position, sitting on the remains of our tents, without a house, a tree, a wall in sight; the mud half way up to our knees; nothing to eat, no rations all day. Eleven transports were lost, and upwards of 500 men. Several vessels went on shore on the Russian coast and were burnt by the enemy. I do hope the case will come soon, also the small case. There has been no more fighting on a large scale since the bloody battle of Inkerman. Lord Raglan is in great discredit with the Army, as no generalship has been shown throughout the whole campaign. The general feeling is that if any honours are bestowed upon him for Alma it will be most undeserved; the day was gained entirely by the pluck of the men. More confidence is placed in Canrobert than any one else; I am sure I don't know why, probably because he is the only one who has not made a fool of himself. I have not had a letter or a paper for a long time now, though I think there are some about the camp. Lord Raglan yesterday sent for all the mail bags, and when he had chosen his own out of them, he told the Postmaster he might send for the rest. The Postmaster has no means of conveyance, so I suppose our letters must remain at Lord Raglan's to light fires with.

100

Camp near Balaklava, Nov. 19
You can't think what pleasure it gave me to received your delightful letters dated Oct.23rd and 27th, and Nov. 2nd. I can assure you that I was delighted to hear that the case was on its way. How many subalterns do you think are with the Regiment now? Three: Dean, Macdonnel, my noble self, and a precious time we have of it, on some duty every day; no

---

24   He describes the 'great storm' of 14 November. See Russell, *British Expedition to the Crimea*, pp. 180–6, for a description of the hurricane and its consequences.

time to go to Balaklava to get anything; no time to wash; tooth brush very low in the market; hands like a hedger's. I have lost half the nail from one finger, which was torn beyond the quick and won't grow again. I was sorry to see no mention of a woodman's axe and a good billhook in the list of things in the case, they would be most useful here. I suppose the letter in which I spoke of them went wrong, do have them put in the next case, and some large and small nails. A very strong little spade would be most useful. We shan't move much more I hope, in fact the Turks are hutted, and I hope we shall be before long. I hope they will knock the confounded place down before Christmas. Cold begins to work the men a great deal; men are taken from their tents senseless, and get compression or eruption on the brain, or something. Sentries are found dead at their posts – this is not so much owing to the climate as to the want of proper clothing; the men have nothing but what is on their backs, or very little else, which if it gets wet, dries on them. Last Tuesday, that day and night never to be forgotten, when all our tents were swept off at one blast, and the rain fell in torrents, no food was served out all day, and the men turned in with their wet clothes and blankets and lay in a puddle of mire. That night we had some bad cases. Our list of Officers away is very large: D. P. Webb, the Adjutant, is going home; Morgan, at Scutari; Gunter, so bad, expects to go home; Burn, the Veterinary, who swore the night before Balaklava he could not cross his tent from weakness, as soon as a shell burst in our camp, turned out of his tent and bolted to Balaklava, got on board a ship and has never been seen since. Wilkinson, at Scutari, very ill indeed; Muttlebury, on board the 'Sans Pareil' with dysentery; Capt. MacCreagh, on board the 'Victoria'. There will be a good deal of promotion this winter, which I don't think will benefit me much, as unless the Cavalry has a chance of being sent home next spring or the war is over, I feel much disposed to quit the festive scene. Living in a tent in November is capital fun, but, in my humble opinion, living in a house with the certainty of something to eat is much better. I forget whether I mentioned that my baggage, which was lying under the remains of my tent, was plundered during the night. I lost a quantity, or rather not much, but all my wine and liquors of all sorts, preserved soup, and am now the proud possessor of an odd sock and glove, and a few articles, certainly not too numerous to mention. I have ordered up the rest of my things from Scutari to refit myself, and have ordered a fur coat and a little stove from Constantinople. Of those young fellows who were with me at Burton's – one, Boothby, lost his leg at Alma;[25] another Clutterbuck, was shot at Inkerman.[26] A Polish Major has come in to us to state the total loss of the Russians that day to have been 25,000 killed, wounded and missing. I suppose you heard about the absurd conduct of Lord Duncallen of the Guards;[27] he was sent with a fatigue party to bury something beyond the lines; he is very short-sighted, and contrary to the advice of everybody he started off by himself, lost his way in the dark, and walked straight to the enemy's picket, and was heard by our own demanding whose picket it was. The Russians were very frightened for a moment, but perceiving it was only one man, and armed with an eyeglass, they closed round him and took him; and the general verdict is serve him right. The Duke of Cambridge was on board 'Retribution', which was nearly lost. He was most undignified, and held the Steward's hands in his, bewailing his fate, saying 'Oh! is it come to this? Oh! Oh! We shall be lost.' I believe his conduct was not thought very much of on Alma day. I was in a Turkish Officer's hut last night, it was most comfortable. The hole about 6 ft long and 9 ft wide, was dug out 4 or 5 ft deep, and the roof put on. You go down steps and find two or three dirty fellows squatted down smoking, a large round tin full of rice boiling on a capital fire, with a chimney which passes through the roof. I have dug out a place 6 ft long and 4 ft wide, which I shall cover with mackintosh, to retreat to next time all the tents are blown down. All our tent ropes are rotten, the Government of course has made no provision for any more; we have hardly any tent pegs, no more to be got. The French have everything comfortable, we have nothing. The British spend five times as much on their soldiers; their soldiers are five times worse cared for. After an action it takes two days to collect the wounded, because we are short of transport. Mr Guthrie's ambulances are beginning to make their appearance, and a few are to be seen about now.[28]

---

25 Ensign Basil Charles Boothby, No. 6 company 95th Regiment, right leg amputated. He went home on the *Cambria* in December 1854. See H. C. Wylly, *The 95th (The Derbyshire) Regiment in the Crimea* (London: Swan and Sonnenschein, 1899).

26 Ensign John Hulton Clutterbuck, 63rd Regiment, 4th Division, killed at Inkerman. He was the son of Robert Clutterbuck of Watford House, Herts. There is a memorial to him in the chapel of Harrow School.

27 Captain Lord Dunkellin, Coldstream Guards, eldest son of the Marquess of Clanricarde, a former British Ambassador at St Petersburg. Dunkellin's capture was comic in many ways. He was out with a party just before dawn and despite the warnings and protestations of his better-sighted men, rode up to a party of Russians and demanded, 'Who is in command of this party?' He was taken without a shot and in December exchanged for a Russian artillery officer who had been captured by the British.

28 George Guthrie was President of the College of Surgeons and devised a form of two- or four-wheeled cart for the transport of the wounded. Unfortunately they were left in Varna when the army sailed for the Crimea and were not available after the battle of the Alma.

The accounts we have heard of women coming out to wait upon the wounded does not give half the pleasure it appears to give in England. The Doctors say that women nurses give an immense amount of trouble in all hospitals, and that when they become used to the wounds and horrors of a Military Hospital they become more hardened than the men and less tender to the sick. The attendance at Scutari is thoroughly bad, so our Officers write. The place is full of rats, fleas, lice and everything bad. The Army are beginning to think Lord Raglan is not fit for his post; I don't know whether that is the opinion in England or not. Canrobert is considered a good man, but I'm afraid we have no one very good, indeed nothing tip-top. Our commissariat is undoubtedly the worst branch of the Service, because in time of peace we have no commissariat at all, and the men are not trained to it. I consider it very hard when they keep us without food for a day, never give us the back ration next day, so that we lose it altogether. The one thing that I consider perfectly wicked is, instead of ground coffee or tea, they give us coffee in the green berry. The men have no means of roasting it, and when it rains so that they can only get the pot to boil, the men who might have a breakfast get nothing at all. At the best of times it is so badly roasted that it makes a most unwholesome and unpalatable drink, without any sugar very often. The men say it is wet and warm, and take it to fill their stomachs. It produces more dysentery, cholera and diarrhoea, than any other cause. It's an infamous shame. I wish some paper could have this little bit – that the gentlemen of England, as they read the paper by the fire after breakfast, might have some idea of the state of their Soldiers at the same moment out here, sitting on their blankets with an inch of soft mud all round them after their precious breakfast. I am thankful to say that mine is quite a different affair – two or three good cups of tea or coffee, some fried beef or pork, French bread and butter; although I may be occasionally content to feast on biscuit and rum and water when no fire can be obtained on account of the rain, or the wind blows the tent down, or the Commissariat gives us no meat. Sorties take place every day on the French or English side, or we make an attack on some fort or rifle pits. The whole of the sky over Sebastopol is lit up at night by the flashes of the guns or the houses on fire.

101

Camp, near Balaklava, Dec. 2
Another actor slowly sheaths his sword and quits the tragedy in which

up to the present time he has played his part. I look back on a dark and dreary stage in which stand men night and day in trenches full of water, holding their muskets in their cramped and half frozen hands ready to repel the enemy, the rain soaking them through the only clothes they have in the world, which I speak from experience, once wet will remain damp forever in this climate. Look at these men in their tents next day, they are at dinner, you would think that after a night like the last, they would have a good mess of soup and an extra ration of rum. Let's see what they have got: the men are quickly devouring their biscuit; but what is in that pot? it looks good rich soup, it is not though: it's good rich mud and water, used by Officer and Soldier alike. The poor Soldier gets his green coffee baked in a shovel, bruised between two stones, and boiled in this water. Fresh meat has not been heard of for a fabulous time in the Army. The pork is awful stuff. I must direct your mind's eye to another portion of the camp. The wind howls across the plain and throws storms of rain and hail against the tents, which shiver and tremble as if in pain, and let through streams on the men inside; the mist and the clouds seem close to the tents, not a star, not a patch of sky anywhere. It is a dreadful sight; the floors of the tents are inches deep in mud, half the horses of the Regiment are lost, having dragged up their posts. They walk over the tent ropes and round the tents to keep themselves warm. What has happened now? A tent is opened and three or four men drag out another. What is the matter with him? He is cramped all over. They won't call the Doctor, cramp in the stomach is far too common for that; he will get a stimulant, be left till morning, when perhaps he may be alive, perhaps dead. The road 2 ft deep in mud and covered with dead and dying animals, some having been driven over so continually as to become part of the road themselves. Loads of meat with broken wheels are a good witness that some Regiments get no rations next day. I have now taken you round the Army and shown you a trifle of the hardships endured in this awful siege. I have not shown you a Hospital with all its awful horrors, the heaps of dead Turks, or the nightly sortie with its 80 to 100 pieces of Artillery let off in about two minutes, the crash of musketry, and all over in 20 minutes. Then the Russians may be found in heaps; they can't thrust them in two lines like the English, but bring them up in square, so that a round shot kills a good lot; with us it only takes two at a time. By the bye I have not told you what is the matter with myself. I was on outlying picket on Monday last, and when I came back on Tuesday my left arm

had stiffened at the elbow, with intense pain. Cooper, our new man[29] –
Pine is promoted – said it was an inflamed suffusion of the joint, and
that the joint might permanently stiffen. He held a board of two other
Officers, who taking into consideration that I have had awful attacks of
cramp, and that this was a thing I should be laid up some time with,
they have ordered me to Scutari. The cause of this is a month's exposure
to fearful weather, with no proper clothes, scanty food of the worst sort,
and lying in wet things night and day. I will tell you the disgraceful way
I have been treated, and how I have been kept rotting in a wet tent for
four or five days when I might have been sent off at once.

I have just heard from Biggs that the last mail did not take our letters,
as the monster, Raglan wishes to get his a start of the other letters, which
might state that his right division got no food for two days and meat for
three. You ought to get both letters together.

102

Globe Hotel, Pera, Dec. 8

After the greatest misery and danger, I am at length at rest at the address
you see above. I have thrown off my disease in a most surprising manner,
and although the Doctor could give me no medicine, which of course he
would have done had I been under a roof, I was much better by the 1st,
when I heard that I was in orders the two days before. But for a merciful
Providence I might have been a dead man through the delay of nearly a
week – 25th to 30th. Then, owing to some neglect, the Order not being
copied, delayed me two days more. However my dwelling on all this will
not do any good. I got on board on the 3rd and sailed on the 4th. The
'Sovereign',[30] the vessel I got the order to, had suffered most severely on
the 14th. She had a large hole in the port bow, and the stern covered with
matting to keep the wind out of the cabin. She had no ballast on board
and rolled awfully, so much that the hanging stands from the roof of the
cabin touched it in the rolls. I daresay you can understand what I mean.
The night after we started it blew a moderate gale, we were struck several

---

29 Robert Cooper, born 24 May 1818; Assistant Surgeon Staff, July 1843; Staff Surgeon 2nd class
18 March 1853; Surgeon, 4th Dragoon Guards, 6 October 1854; half pay, 22 September 1862. Died,
London, 4 December 1864. See Peterkin and Johnston, *Commissioned Officers*, vol. 1, p. 324.

30 Steam-powered transport no. 68; 602 tons, had previously sailed from Constantinople to
Balaklava with Turkish troops. She sailed back to Constantinople for repairs. A note in the House
of Commons Transport report stated that she needed 'extensive repairs'. See HCPP 1854–5 (283),
p. 21.

times by waves in the stern and shipped a great deal of water, and were, I believe, in danger of the ship not righting, but turning over. Altogether we had a very long passage, and did not arrive till the 7th. I went to Scutari Hospital and reported myself to the Medical Officer, who told me to get a room. I went to try. They told me the Hospital was quite full, but that I could have a room in an empty house some distance from the Hospital – rather a good look out for a sick man without a servant. I mildly objected, stating I should die if sent to an out-of-the-way place where I could get no assistance. He seemed much of the same opinion, but politely stated that was all he could do for me. I then told him I should be very glad to go to an hotel and live at my own expense, he said he could not give me leave, but if I would wait a quarter of an hour Lord W. Paulet[31] would be there and he would speak to him; it was then 11.30. I waited till 3.30, when I saw his lordship, who could not find any order for my being sent down to Scutari. After three quarters of an hour this was discovered. I got leave and was dismissed. Now having lost seven days of my precious leave owing to the blunders of my chiefs, I intend to have a good run at grass. My leave was from the 30th November to 31st December. I hope to get my case out of the hands of Grace tomorrow. I shall be lucky if I do. Elliot, or whatever was his name, was most careless, and it was not down in the ship's papers; please tell him of it, it's too bad. I shall also be able to get my winter clothes from Scutari. It is almost impossible to get anything forwarded to Balaklava, and if I had not come down I doubt if I should have got my case or winter clothes. I shall leave orders with Oppenheim to send the next case straight on to me by the same vessel, if possible, as it comes in.

103

Globe Hotel, Pera Dec. 13

I am getting on capitally here, eating awful breakfasts and ruining the proprietor in dinner. I have succeeded in getting my things out of store at Scutari. I have got a change of everything, and washed all over. The former I have not done for six weeks, the latter not since leaving Varna. The terrible itching of scurvy has almost entirely left me and my skin is getting smooth again. Hurrah for Pera! I shall be ready to take the field again in no time. I have got my Russian saddle here which I wrote about and will send

---

31   Among his responsibilities for the administration of British forces in Constantinople, Lord William Paulet was Commandant at Scutari. Previously he had been Assistant Adjutant-General to the Cavalry Division.

home at the earliest opportunity, also a Russian sword taken on the day of my skirmish, which by-the-bye, I find has preceded me here and made my name known. I have just had a capital lunch at a Greek coffee house – ham cutlets, woodcock and bitter beer. But I shan't go there again in a hurry, 7s. 6d. is too dear. Woodcocks have not so much taste as pigeon. There is a Capt. Benson[32] staying here who was six years in the Peninsula war, and says he would sooner serve six years in the Peninsula than one month in this campaign. He says no comparison could be drawn between the two for the horrors of war. I am determined to make myself independent for the future at Balaklava, and shall lay in a stock of preserved meat and everything else. I shall buy a stove and a quantity of charcoal. I fear there is a great chance of my case being lost: Grace, it seems, has let it get into the Custom House, where the Turks plunder everything with impunity, boxes strewn all over the place with lids off. When I get back to Balaklava I will bully the Turks a bit more than I used to. I have ridden over one or two already to teach them not to run away, and have caught every Turk who came near me and flung him into the most muddy place I could see, but if my case is lost I will buy a whip and beat every one across the head; how I hate them. The Russians are angels compared to these dogs. I have ordered a pair of boots here, as it is so uncertain when the next case may arrive. As soon as Sebastopol falls, I think I shall sell out, for another campaign like the last neither my temper, which I am sorry to say has got almost beyond control, nor my constitution would stand. My temper is not worse than others; we have all become most awfully morose and selfish. I have not yet touched a circular note or letter of credit, but will have to draw on the letter of credit here I expect. I should think I was never so cheap a son as I have been since I came out here. The hotel is excellent and very moderate, 12s. a day for board and lodging.

104

Globe Hotel, Pera, Dec 19

I am very well with the exception of my left arm, which is weak and not much good, but will be all right by the time I go back. I have laid out a large sum in boots, preserved meat, a fur coat, a stove, and, would you believe it, a house 9 ft long, 7 ft wide, 6 ft high in front and 7 ft behind,

32   Capt. George Thomas Benson served in the Peninsula War from 1812 to the end of the war. He also served in the Anglo-American War and was severely wounded in the right breast by a ball at Plattsburg. He was the Paymaster of the 28th Regiment and had been an officer for 35 years by the time of the Crimean War. See *Hart's New Annual Army List 1855*, p. 179.

a door, a window and a floor of boards, mat bed quite comfortable. The boards dovetail into one another and make it nice and tight. I am to have a shelf and a table, the price is £14.

105

Globe Hotel, Pera, Dec 20

I have been to look at my house again, and it will be most comfortable. I am almost disposed to send to England for a piano, only the fireplace will be too close to it. I am in the most extraordinary spirits; Brown who was, according to those who were in the house with him before I came, a very quiet and melancholy man, is in wild spirits. We go out every day together, and to the Opera every night. My appetite is extraordinary, only we are both ill owing to the quantities of Turkish sweets we both eat. We go to a grave, lazy old Turk, who sits in the bazaar in the midst of beautiful silks, embroidery and lovely things, and quietly ask him what he will take for his beard, to the great delight of the Greeks, who are as lively and clever as the Turks are dull and stupid. I went to see the 100-and-1 Columns, which are the finest sight I have seen yet in this town. It is an immense cellar, supposed to have held water, but now full of rope makers. I went to the Custom House yesterday and was disgusted at the sight: one thing on top of another, some broken and the goods coming out, and everything in disorder. I, however, hope I may get my case before I go.

106

Globe Hotel, Pera, Dec 27

I am glad to tell you I have been as lucky with the last three cases as I have been unlucky with the first, which has never been found. Mr. Grace promises to forward it as soon as he gets it; I have been at him every day. The last three I never heard of till Mr. Grace spoke of them, and the 'Balbec' came in the next day. I got a boat and took them ashore, when a Custom House man prevented their being carried off, the graceful warning of my whip in his face soon gave them passage. The Crimean business looks black enough at present; all the harm I wish the Ministers is that they had a Cornet's Commission for the last three months out here, just to feel the misery their neglect has caused. The Infantry are suffering severely from mortification of the feet, and the deaths are said to be 120 a day. A very unfortunate occurrence took place a few nights ago in the trenches. The enemy made a sortie[33] on the most advanced work and bayoneted 20 or 30 men and their Major asleep, very disgraceful to their Major, poor fellow; but they are so hard-worked that no endurance can stand it. The scurvy is very bad, and I am most thankful that I have none to apprehend for the future from that fearfully painful and annoying disease. There has been another gale and the 'Royal Albert' has injured her rudder and screw. I hear there has also been a good deal of snow, which I fear will increase the illness of those not under cover. I shall return to the Crimea either tomorrow or next day as strong and healthy as ever, after having devoted my attention to making myself [as] comfortable up there as during my stay here, with a most satisfactory result. I have not forgotten the horses. I have got the framework of a shed and a quantity of second-hand canvas, for which I paid 6s., and two splendid Turkish horse rugs, the best things in the world. I wish they would send out some potted carrots or preserved green grass for them, and some waterproof boots to keep their feet out of the mud.

107

Globe Hotel, Pera, Jan. 1 1855
I have not yet quitted Constantinople, as I am to take a draft of men with me, and shall most likely go the day after tomorrow. I am very anxious to get back on account of the horses, for whom I have got warm clothing and a capital house. I suppose there is no doubt the 'Tamar'[34] took the case, I have not been able to get it so far.

108

Globe Hotel, Pera, Jan 2
I have been over to Scutari today to see about a passage; I shall go by the

---

33 This refers to the surprise attack on the pickets of the 50th Regiment made by the Russians on 20–21 December The men were asleep and were bayoneted as they slept. The Russians were eventually driven out by men of the Rifle Brigade who then declared, 'The Russians relieved the 50th and we [The Rifles] relieved the Russians'. See *The War in the Crimea by a Staff Officer* 3rd edn (London: John Murray, 1858), p. 205; *The Times*, 25 December 1854, p. 7, col. A.
34 A Royal Mail Steam Packet Company steamer of 1,963 tons. See HCPP 1854–5 (283).

'Lidney' tomorrow.[35] I have spent a most pleasant time at Constantinople; all the ladies who have been staying there have been most kind to me. I have got a regular stock of medicine and different comforts. A Mrs. Benson and a Mrs. Ives, one has come out with her husband, the other, who has just come out from England, has followed her boy, who has just joined the Guards. She has given me a great deal of useful things. I am sorry to say things are quite as bad, if not worse than before: food very scarce and weather dreadful, sickness terrible. I do not think there is a single thing that I could require that I have not got. I have taken a pair of warm socks to each man in the troop and plenty of tobacco, and a great many other things for the Officers.

109

Jan 3. 1855
I am on board the 'Lidney', a good large vessel, with about 15 Officers on our return to the Crimea. There are some reports that we are to have peace. I wish they would make it, but I do not believe in it at all myself, at any rate until Sebastopol falls.

110

Jan. 8 1855
I am still on board the 'Lidney'. We did not start till yesterday as the weather was very bad and stormy. We had a capital passage and shall arrive tomorrow, when I hope to be in time for the mail.

I am rather in a fix as to what to do with my large stock of goods on landing, and in great anxiety about my dear horses, whose miseries I hope to alleviate greatly when I get there. The houses they made so much fuss of in England, and which were to be ready in such a wonderfully short space of time, have arrived, but are useless for want of nails, which they say have been forgotten. The Railroad will be a great thing if it is done and fit for use before the middle of the Summer. We have on board two gentlemen from

---

35   This should read *Sydney* and is a mistake in the original transcription. Transport no. 76, was a 1,250 ton steamer and was in Constantinople at the time. The ship had previously transported sick troops from Balaklava to Constantinople arriving on 18 December. See HCPP 1854–5 (283).

England: Mr. Glynn,[36] son of the Banker in London, and Smith, son of the member for Middlesex. They have brought out two or three ship loads of things for the Army – the Crimean Charitable Fund,[37] I believe, it is called – and will be a great blessing to their perishing countrymen. The things are sent out as a present, but, I believe, will be sold, which is much the best way of disposing of them. I hope the Commissariat will not get hold of them. It is a pleasure to think that if the authorities have forgotten us, the people still think us worth keeping alive. We hope to get in tomorrow early, but I shall not most likely get up to camp before the next day.

III

Kadekoi Camp, Jan 12

I have only time for a line. I have got up to camp, which is a very good place at present. I have got so many stores, pray don't send any more at present. I am quite comfortable and have got everything possibly necessary. It is freezing very hard indeed; my poor, dear gallant 'Jack' is freed from his troubles and misery, and I can't help crying at his loss, and the warm clothing and house arrived too late. In a day or two I hope to have my house up, but even the tent is quite comfortable with warm clothing as I now have.

112

Kadekoi Camp Jan 14

The snow is a foot and a half deep. The carriage very difficult. I broke down with an araba and my house on it yesterday; luckily I got ponies and have it all safe. I have been so hard at work getting things up from Balaklava, that I have no time to send more than a line. I have got such an immense supply of things, that I can hardly get into my tent. The lock-up cases are a great thing. It freezes very hard night and day, and any thing that gets wet freezes too and won't dry; snow will not melt a

---

36   One of the many sons of George Carr Glyn, MP (later 1st Baron Wolverton), banker of Glyn Mills & Co., established 1753.

37   Following *The Times* coverage of the war and the vivid descriptions of suffering and deprivation various charitable funds were set up to help the army. The Crimean Army Fund was administered by *The Times* and sent supplies and food to the troops before Sebastopol. Similarly, the Royal Patriotic Fund raised funds for widows and dependants. See Massie, *A Most Desperate Undertaking*, pp. 216, 230.

foot off the stove. I do not want any more rifles, as unless we cleared the Crimea of Russians, we could not go out, and there is no prospect of taking Sebastopol, much less the Crimea.

113

Kadekoi Camp, Jan 20

I have been so much occupied during my leisure moments in fitting my little kennel, that I could hardly find time to write even a line. I am at last located, and very much more comfortable I am than when in a tent. The difficulties I had getting it up were very great, the road was awful. I got it put on an araba, which very soon broke down, and then it appeared as if it might all be lost; however with the kind assistance of the Commissariat, I got it carried up in mule carts. I got it put up as soon as possible, but it was freezing so hard it was difficult to do any work. The iron stuck to the fingers and made mine so sore that they are not well yet, and when I got hold of a nail I could not get rid of it again. I have now got it up, and am now employed papering up the cracks and covering the walls with matting, the floor with floor-cloth. The country has made me a present of my Lieutenancy,[38] which is nearly a £1000 in my pocket, a large sum to save and which will pay me pretty well for all the outlay in this expedition: for the mere rank, I would as soon be Cornet as Lieutenant out here. Did Morgan say whether he was going to leave the service? I wish you could hear whether Gunter is getting better, he is the only one of the three who ought to have gone home, so I understand, at Scutari. Godman has got the filter, I believe for me, but although we are close to each other, the ground is so deep in mud that it is quite impossible to get about, and one Regiment never visits the other, or very seldom. We are fully employed: we take biscuit to the poor fellows in the front, who look awfully worn – that is, the style of face. I am sorry to say our men are deserting in great numbers,[39] and there are horrid reports that two Regiments at least have run away at the first attack, and I fear it is but too true. Poor shadows, who have to sit down two or three times as they crawl to the trenches, are not the same men who fought at Alma and Inkerman.

---

38 He had been promoted without purchase, from 29 December 1854. Other subalterns in the 4th Dragoon Guards similarly promoted were D. P. Webb (8 December), B. E. Wilkinson (8 December), Hon. F. M. Deane (29 December), and J. A. Bragge (29 December). See *Hart's New Annual Army List, 1855*, p. 124.

39 This is an exaggeration. At the end of hostilities in September 1855 there were about 93 deserters who remained in Russia. See TNA, FO/493, No. 93, Wodehouse to Clarendon.

114

Kadekoi Camp, Jan 26.
I was horrified at the size of the large case when I had to get it up to camp, and it required a good deal of ingenuity to get it there. 'Blood Royal' took it up, however, all safe by unpacking it on the wharf and putting the contents into a sack on one side and the case on the other. I am now employed in making another hut, just at the door of the present one. I shall dig 4 ft deep and then roof it over with boards we get from Ordnance, it will be the dining-room and sitting room, and I shall go up a ladder to my hut as the bedroom. It will be so jolly. The stove I shall have in the lower room and carry the pipe through the upper one, which will be sufficient to warm it.

115

Kadekoi Camp, Jan. 28
I am now comfortably settled in my little hut, with a beautiful fire in the stove, a nice floor-cloth down, and very nice indeed. My horse will have a very comfortable stable in a day or two, and I shall have a second room to put my things into. Everyone here talks of peace, I hope it may be true, but I don't think there's much chance of it till Sebastopol falls. All the Marines have been ordered to join their ships, and all the Officers belonging to the screw steamers have been recalled to their ships and their places supplied from those in sailing vessels. I have by no means done with Orderly work, and I get no advantage by promotion except the rank and saving of money. I should hope there is no chance of the Cavalry being reduced again when the war is over, which will soon be the case if all we hear is true, as I hope it is. We have had a capital road to Balaklava made by the French, which passes our Camp and makes it much easier to get to town. Glanders and other diseases are killing the horses daily; the men are more healthy here, though very seedy and miserable up at the front. The heavy breaching batteries are firing as I write, and very likely a fierce hand-to-hand fight is going on. Thank heaven no longer does one spring out of bed, tear on boots and overalls, and rush to horse in instant expectation of a charge of Cossacks, striving to cut the picket rope with one's sword.

Here we live in a deep valley with steep hills and precipices all round, with the French in our front behind a good rampart, which will keep out any amount of Russians.

116

Kadekoi Camp, Feb. 1

I am very comfortable indeed now; I have got a woman to cook my dinner instead of doing it myself, which gives me much more time. My handsome mule has arrived from Varna, and is, I understand, looking very well. You ask me if it is true that the French men and horses are taken better care of than ours, and that they have not half so many sick: it is quite true. When our men's cheek-bones stuck through the skin, the French were fat; when our men looked sick and yellow and dirty, the French looked red, healthy and clean; as to sickness, while we Cavalry bring down dying men without shoes and stockings on, clinging to the horses' necks, the French lend us their ambulance mules. Our pensioners were a dead failure,[40] as anybody who knows what Pensioners are might have foreseen: drunken, riotous old fellows, who, if they were willing, were past work. Ah! everything is true of the miseries brought on by ignorance and neglect; if you set to work and invented the most horrible stories of privation you could not come up to what has happened here. Just to show you how they are going on at the front even now, when they are supposed to be much better, I will tell you an anecdote as Capt. Benson[41] of the 28th Regiment told it to me. One of their Captains in going round the tents about 11 o'clock in the morning, found seven poor wretches coiled up in a heap; not recognising one of them, he asked his sergeant who he was, one from the heap stuck his head up and said 'Sure, your honour, it's Pat McKew, he died last night at 10 o'clock and they haven't removed him yet': poor Pat was lying on his back gazing upwards, and the living were so like the dead, the Captain did not perceive the difference. Balaklava is now assuming a different aspect: instead of mud and filth, streets like sewers, through which the baggage animals could hardly drag themselves, the closely packed mass of people, fighting, swearing, crushing, through which it was hardly possible to force one's way till some heavy Artillery waggon crushed through the throng, driving men and horses into the little holes of shops: the water-side with no piers to land goods, everything in the greatest confusion. The Railroad people have now established a good wharf, and are working at an extraordinary

---

40   When news of the plight of the wounded reached home there was public outrage and the authorities quickly responded. The Director General of the Army Medical Department, Dr (later) Sir Andrew Smith, raised a corps of 300 old army pensioners into an Ambulance Corps. The measure proved a failure. The pensioners were too old and frail to carry out their duties. Many died from cholera and disease, while others succumbed to the comfort of alcohol.

41   See note 32 above.

pace, and will soon have the Railway going. Good roads are being made, and we have a capital one as far as our Camp, made by the French, which will soon be as good as a turnpike in England, they are carrying it on to the front at a great pace. The comforts for the Army are beginning to pour in: Glyn, the son of the banker and manager of the Crimean Fund, called on me the other morning and told me the 'Sir George Pollock'[42] had begun selling off her stores; she has been freighted from Fortmun [*sic*] and Mason with all sorts of good things, but it is a matter of little interest to me, as I have more already than I know what to do with.

117

Kadekoi Camp Feb. 16
[A letter about clothing he wants, and mentions that the cases he sent home with loot had arrived safely.]

118

Kadekoi Camp, Feb., 24
We were all excitement last Sunday night, orders being given to turn out at 11.30 to march and surprise the enemy by daybreak. I luckily did not go. The night, up to the time of starting, was very warm, quite oppressive, so that no one wrapped up much; about 12 it began to rain and hail, at 1 to freeze and snow, the wind got up from the North and there was a terrible snow-drift. The 4th Dragoon Guards took nearly two hours to go a mile and a half, it was so dark; the whole thing was a failure. The French, of whom 20,000 were to have gone, never came at all; they saw us the other side of the plain next morning. There was no fighting, but by some mistake the spare ammunition was left behind and the Cossacks got two barrels. They got back at 11 next morning. We have five men with their ears frost bitten from it.

---

42 A ship appointed by the government to sell government stores at cost price and thus avoid the exorbitant prices for necessaries charged by the throng of peddlers and rogue merchants who followed the army. See *The Times*, 20 February 1855, p. 7, col. D.

119

Kadekoi Camp, Feb. 26

I receive both *Times* and *Mail* regularly, but I think the *Times* alone will be quite enough, there is very little to please me in it: people in power seem to behave badly there as well as here, and I greatly fear we shall be as unprovided for the Summer as for the Winter Campaign: old tents, old saddles, everything knocked to pieces. The Railway is getting on capitally, and they are beginning to use it. There was a severe affair two days, or rather nights, ago, at the front at Inkerman. The French with two battalions, tried to surprise a 14 gun battery of the Russians, but found them all ready for them with a very large force, they succeeded in getting into the battery but very soon had to quit it with heavy loss. It appears there is some traitor who mars all our schemes. Of course we have heard of General Forey, who has been sent home to France on a charge of treachery; if it is proved I hope they will send him back to be shot here.

120

Kadekoi Camp, Feb 28 1855

I was determined to have something to tell you in my next letter, and as 'Blood Royal' is still unfit for service on account of cracked heels, I walked all the way to Inkerman and back with Armstrong, we went into the very advanced trench of all, where our sharpshooters and the enemy keep up a continual fire at each other. We have a little hole made to fire through of four sandbags, and the Russians have little stone walls, behind which they keep very carefully and send their bullets pinging over our heads every minute. We walked over the field of the battle of Inkerman, the cannon shot lie all over the ground, little ones, and big pieces of shell, a little bit of one of which I picked up and will send you if possible. The Russians are buried in long trenches, one on top of another; our men are buried where they fell, and their humble little graves are scattered all over the ground, marking the different lines of fight. One scattered line shows the place one of the pickets was killed as they ran for the Camp in a scattered line, and were shot down one after another. We walked along the whole line of defences to the rear, which seem fairly strong. I hope you will soon see Mr. Sym, he has started on his return to England, and has the old gold watch which he promised to give you. We have had some beautiful weather lately, but today it is snowing and raining again. We were to have been inspected by the General, but it was counter-ordered. This is a most extraordinary country: one hour so hot you want your summer clothes, and the next a cold north wind and hail. There is a biting wind just now. Wilkinson went out with me this afternoon to cut some roots for firewood, and came back with his mouth quite stiff, so that he could hardly speak. We have had the nicest coats possible served out to us, made of grey cloth lined with rabbit skin, so very jolly, so light and warm. We are most comfortable now, and I never wish to be more so: lots to eat, plenty of clothes, and plenty of time to sleep. The tents are very cold just now, but my little hut most comfortable. I was never better or stronger than now; my walk to Inkerman was, I should think, from 15 to 20 miles, and except that it made my feet sore, had no effect on me. I hope they will look sharp about sending out some more troops, we have got very few, 10,000 perhaps. Mr. Gladstone ought to have his tongue taken nearly out for saying there are 30,000, it is such an impudent lie. I think England is in a very ticklish position, and unless she looks very sharp she will lose her character as a nation; unless we want Sebastopol to become the strongest place in the world, we had better leave it, for the more we besiege it the stronger it gets. The Garrison, besides, are very different from what they were, they are much more plucky, and by no means look on us with the same respect they did after Alma. If Prussia joins Russia, I wish they would send us home, and then to the Rhine 1000 strong, it would be very different work from this, where we get double allowance of kicks but no half-pence.

121

Kadekoi Camp, March 5

All's well. The Railroad has reached our camp. Yesterday, two of the navvies, who seem a drunken, hard-working set of rascals, had a fight for an hour, to the great amusement of the French. I have made the acquaintance of some of the French Officers, they are a very civil lot. Major Welsford[43] called the day before yesterday, he seems a very nice man. He said the Artillery were to commence firing again on the 10th, but he did not think they would be ready. It's quite a toss up whether we silence the Russian batteries or they ours, but I expect they will get the best of it. I would not give a hang to be in the trenches when the fire commences. We had a parade a day or two ago, and it was said there was

---

43   Augustus Frederick Welsford, 97th Regiment. See *Hart's New Annual Army List 1855*, p. 249.

a chance of the Cavalry going home to re-organise, but I doubt it; still, it would be the best thing to do, they will never get men to volunteer to a Regiment out here, but they could get the Regiments at home recruited to 500 and send them out, and 12 months of home service would make us fit for work again to a certain extent. The 17th came to parade without a horse, the 8th had three, I believe. It is quite a relief to get rid of Lord Lucan, poor old man, he was a horrid old fellow.[44]

122

Kadekoi Camp, March 7
You ask how many men we can mount? We can mount 90, Officers and all, and are the strongest Regiment out here. I shall have to buy a second horse for myself, the Government are not quite so liberal as all that; I get £37 compensation for poor 'Jack'. We had some pony races here a day or two ago, which were very amusing: in the middle of them the alarm was given that the Russians were advancing, and away we all scuttled to get mounted, with the expectation of Balaklava no. 2; however it turned out to be some deserters, and we returned to our racing. Today, the 8th, we hear the Emperor of Russia is dead, the Ministry out again, and London in a riot; a very cheerful state of things when the efforts of the whole country ought to be bent on sending out soldiers to continue the war.[45]

123

Kadekoi Camp, March 20
There is nothing new here. The Russians are making tremendous sorties, but only lose a great many men themselves and do no good. I hope to be able to buy a good horse in the course of today for £60; horses are now very dear indeed. We hear the Light Brigade is going to Scutari. The chestnut is much better of the mange, and the mule too.

---

44 Lucan was recalled from the Crimea over the question of culpability for the destruction of the Light Brigade at Balaklava. See Anglesey, *Little Hodge*, p. 86.

45 Fisher-Rowe refers, firstly, to the death of Tsar Nicholas I on 2 March 1855; secondly, to the ministerial crisis within the Aberdeen government over the conduct of the war that led to Aberdeen giving way to a new administration under Palmerston on 6 February 1855; and, lastly, to bread riots in London. See *The Times*, 3 February 1855, p. 6, col. F; ibid., 23 February 1855, p. 7, col. D.

124

Kadekoi Camp, March 24

I have bought a new horse, which I think will do very well. He is very strong and well broken, he belonged to an Officer of the Greys, who was shot at Balaklava. I gave £70 for him: he is a very dark grey, almost black, and is very good-tempered and quiet. The chestnut is very well again and I can ride him. The day before yesterday I dined with Colonel Griffiths,[46] Scots Greys, and had nearly as good a dinner as I used to have at mess; he brought the mess cook out with him as his private servant, and has lived in great style. It is rather annoying that the Scots Greys should monopolise all the credit of the heavy Cavalry charge at Balaklava, and it is curious no Officer should have thought it worth while to contradict it. The only credit they had was, that they happened to make the first charge, in which they failed to rout the Russians, who outflanked and would have surrounded them had not the 4th and 5th come to their assistance, and so great was the confusion that they broke our line as they came full speed in the opposite direction. Men who were looking on from the hills around speak much more strongly on the subject than I do here.

125

Kadekoi Camp, March 25 1855

It's getting very hot indeed, and last night an aide-de-camp rode into Camp and ordered us to be ready to turn out at 4, and we were all ready at the time but were not called out. I am going to Kamish today, as I have not seen it yet. The fighting at the front at night is very severe, we are doing nothing, and the Russians are getting the same moral influence over the French that we have over the Russians, which is bad, but shows how superior our men are to any other nation. I should think, next to ourselves, the Russians are the bravest Army in the world.

126

Kadekoi Camp, March 28

I mentioned in my last letter that I was going to Kamish to see whether

---

46   Henry Derby Griffiths, Lt. Col. by purchase Aug 1852. He had been a cornet in the regiment from
     November 1828. See *Hart's New Annual Army List 1855*, p. 129.

the French are so far before us as they are supposed to be, and certainly there could not be a better regulated little town. There are very fair native houses. They are almost all wooden huts built by the French, in streets, and numbered so that you can find any shop that you want without difficulty. Things are rather dearer than at Balaklava: fowls 4s each, and a lunch of a stale patty and two bottles of the smallest beer 8s. 6d. The country between Balaklava and Kamish is the most ugly and horrible it is possible to conceive, it looks as if it was cursed. It is a continual succession of hills with great ragged rocks sticking through the surface like the bones of a starved horse, and valleys full of large stones. I should think it is a ride of some ten miles from our Camp there, and only one and a half from Balaklava to us. I am sorry to say that the report that the French are beginning to give way before our enemy is confirmed daily, and the difference between the English and the French is so marked, that one day after taking some rifle pits from the Russians and holding them for some time, we handed them over to our allies. The Russians immediately came out and drove the French out without difficulty. There are races continually going on here, and we are certainly in capital condition at present, but greatly fear the sun will develop a great deal of disease. However, it is hoped that we shall be in very different health here from Bulgaria, the most pestilent place possible.

127

Kadekoi Camp, April 6.
I dined and slept at Major Welford's yesterday. I had a good view of the Russian works, which are very strong indeed; there was a great deal of firing going on at the Mamelon, and we could see the shell bursting inside the work with a jet like a volcano. They live a very exciting time up there. As we were smoking after dinner, the enemy began firing very fast, and presently the bugles sounded the turn-out and everyone seized his sword, and in the space of ten minutes they were all paraded and ready for action. The enemy shelled our Camp and threw them on each side of us; it is a strange state of affairs that the Camp should be under fire, and that they should be liable to be shelled out at any time. The shells are very easily seen on a dark night, you see a small fire rising gradually into the air, going slower and slower as it reaches its utmost height, and then coming down with a dead thud as it reaches the ground. Major

Welford is commanding the 97th at present.[47] The affair was soon over and we returned to our brandy and water. General Campbell, who lived very comfortably in a cave all winter, has an amazing story related of him. A snake was found in his habitation nearly 6 ft long, and was killed; as the General was asleep the next night, he was awoke by a noise in his room, and on getting a light the female was found. The General has not slept there since. When I was sitting in my hut on my return from the front this morning, Armstrong's servant began to shout for help, and on going out I found the miserable man squeezing himself into the furthest corner of his underground hut with a drawn sword in his hand and a snake 4 to 5 ft long lying on a ledge in the passage down into the hut: the passage is about 1½ feet wide and 4 ft long and 3 ft high, so that he crawls in and out and could not get past the snake, who lay quite at his ease in the entrance. I got a pistol and shot the snake in the head, greatly to the man's relief. I was on picket a night or two ago, and had a very comfortable night's work. I patrolled close to Canrobert's hill and found the body of a Russian who had lain there since Balaklava. I dismounted and looked at him, it was a horrid sight, his face had the same expression as when he had fallen, and was bleached by the snow and winds: to my great disgust, when I tried to mount, 'Blood Royal' reared and fell on his haunches, broke away and went off leaving me in a perilous position, so near the Russians and on foot. I was glad when I got hold of the horse again. Welsford told me that one of the Officers being ill, a shot had to be heated and put to his feet, one was picked up and warmed, fortunately not very much, for it proved to be a shell full of powder.

128

Kadekoi Camp, April 9 1855

I have sent home almost everything I do not want, as I may move out of here soon: there is a Russian tea urn which Capt. Biggs plundered out of a house near here, a cannon ball from Balaklava, and a piece of shell from Inkerman. I have never sent you a full account of the saddle sent home:

---

47   Major Welford commanded the 97th instead of Bvt. Col. Henry Lockyer. The 97th had arrived in the Crimea from Greece on 20 November 1854. See McGuigan, *Into Battle!*, p. 36.

it belonged to Prince Kabrun or Chabrun,[48] a Captain of the Russian 12th Hussars, the Regiment who fought best at Balaklava. He was a brave young Officer, and rode to the charge like a hero, waving his sword and encouraging his men; he fought well and was cut down by a man in our Regiment. His boyish face, without beard or moustache, created a feeling of pity as the troopers passed him in the pursuit, when the charge was over he was dead. His belts and watch were sent to the Russians; his saddle came into my possession, his name is on the pommel in Russian. He was stripped as he lay on that bloody field by (I am ashamed to say and hardly believe it) two of the vile women we brought out with us. His boots are worn by a Corporal in the Regiment. His trousers, drawers, everything were stripped from him as he lay on the damp ground; such are the fortunes of war. This morning we opened fire after the long suspense and continual delays. I hope we may be successful, but it is a great toss up, the great guns have been booming away all day and are shaking every timber in my hut as I write. It has been pouring torrents of rain all day, which is lucky, as it will prevent the Russians bringing down great guns on our rear here, they may bring as many troops as they like, they will soon be disposed of, but heavy guns are quite another thing. Of four men, myself and three others who were at Barton's together,[49] two were killed at Inkerman, one shot through the foot at Alma, and I alone remain. I shall have the medal with two clasps, Inkerman and Balaklava. I wish they would send us to a nicer country, where there are some good cattle to eat and houses to plunder. I made a rather lucky hit today and bagged two sheep, very fine and fat, a very good catch, for we have not had any fresh meat for a long time. We seem to have got into a regular pest of snakes, and very big they are. Major Welford told me a good story of the sailors at the beginning of the winter, one of them boasted that he had his winter clothing served out to him, his friend asking what it was, he replied, 'three oranges and a night cap'.

---

48 There were four officers killed from the Russian 11th and 12th Hussars during their battle with the Heavy Brigade on 25 October 1854: Gorelov, Yabukov, Veselovski and Voinovitch. Fisher-Rowe may have made a mistake reading the Cyrillic script or the saddle in question did not belong to the young dead officer. Information regarding this question was supplied by Mark Conrad, an expert on the Russian Army in the nineteenth century. None of the descendants of Fisher-Rowe have any knowledge of the saddle or its present location.

49 Spelled Burton's in [100]. Possibly either his house at school, or the private tutor at Hurley in 1849.

129

Kadekoi Camp, April 19 1855

I was on picket last mail and did not write to you. We had rather an exciting picket: about 10 o'clock at night we saw a most brilliant light from the Russian lines beyond Kamara, which assumed different forms and continued for about three-quarters of an hour, then about 2 o'clock we saw the flashes of some muskets from Kamara, and immediately started to patrol to see what it was, and we went close to the village with 15 men, but saw nothing. Just as we started returning, however, a volley was fired in our rear, we immediately wheeled right about and were thrown into the greatest confusion by the rear guard galloping right into us at full speed. We all thought the enemy were close behind them, especially as one of them as soon as he reached us rolled heavily off his horse and lay on the ground as if he had been shot. However, nobody followed us, and we found that our hero's saddle had turned round with him, and he was soon all right again. Still, we could not make out what the volley was fired at, and by whom. The 10th Hussars have just arrived,[50] they are a very fine Regiment and nearly double as strong as our whole Cavalry force. This will make the work much lighter than it was before. They are hard at work at the bombardment, but doing little good we hear. They say now that Lord Raglan has commenced the firing he does not know what to do next. The 10th Hussars are encamped just above us, and are a beautiful Regiment; their Colonel will take the command of the Cavalry, and is said to be a good man. Our horses are getting into good condition, and everything looks well, we could not possibly be better off. The duty has been hard, but one is quite used to it and does not care for it, and a night on picket leaves one quite fresh next morning, neither tired nor sleepy. Omar Pasha has arrived with 20,000 Turks and 30 guns; the Turks, who wear green turbans, are very fine men indeed, they are called the Holy Band, I believe, they are camped at Karani. I was up at the front and saw all the men-of-war in position all round the town, they have done nothing yet, but will attack, I suppose, when we go in, if we go at all. It will be a horrible affair when it does take place, and many a gallant fellow must perish.

---

50 This regiment arrived from India on 17 April, under Lt. Col. William Parlby. See McGuigan, *Into Battle!*, p. 54.

130

Fisher-Rowe to his parents

Kadekoi Camp, April 24 1855

I am sorry to say I have sustained a most vexatious loss, the horse I bought has died of gripes, which came on in the night and left him so weak that nothing did him any good next day – £70 gone clean without the Government giving me any remuneration. I hope I shall be allowed to buy one of the remounts when they come out. You have heard, of course, that the bombardment has failed, which, of course, is not a pleasant thing for we people out here; however, I don't suppose the Russians can hurt us more than we can them. We hear they have taken Upatoria, but I don't know about the truth of it. We made a reconnaissance two days ago, but saw nothing and did nothing. Omar Pasha has been here with 20,000 Turks, and went out with us. I saw him the other day: he is ugly, and looks worn, very different from our fat old Generals.

131

Kadekoi Camp, April 28 1855

Nothing new has occurred, in fact there seems to be nothing going on. I am very anxious to hear what you think in England of the failure of the second bombardment, in that we were all ready to go in, but the French could not be trusted, as they are so dispirited. I don't think there is much chance of our taking the place left, it is so strong. We are taking quantities of guns every day, and every sort of stores. The Camps are in beautiful order, and the men in first rate condition and spirits; we look as much better than the French as we did worse in the winter. Omar Pasha has returned from Upatoria, it appears that it is threatened by a large force. I thought I told you I was on 'Jack' on 7th October. These horses are the plague of one's life. I don't know where I shall get another; however, I suppose one will turn up. The chestnut is well; the mule has a sprained leg.

Fenton's photograph of Fisher-Rowe's hut. Credit: Library of Congress, Prints and Photographs Division [LC-USZ62-47839].

I enclose one of the photographs of my hut[51] on the left is my lumber room with a French Officer of the 27th, next is Biggs, next Drake, next self, Muttlebury, Macdonnel, Murray, my servant, 'Blood Royal', a Frenchman, and a sheep my servant found (viz., stole), a cooking hut in rear.

---

51   These images were among the many of the Heavy Brigade taken by Fenton. Several were taken of the officers and men of the 4th and 5th Dragoon Guards. There are fine studies of Captain Adolphus Burton, who commanded the 5th Dragoon Guards, and Godman of the same regiment standing next to his charger with his groom. Fenton also took views of the now hutted camps of the cavalry, both heavy and light. Almost all the photographs taken by Roger Fenton can be found on the Library of Congress website, www.loc.gov/pictures/item/2001696100/.

Fenton's 'Camp of the 4th Dragoon Guards, convivial party, French and English'. Credit: Library of Congress, Prints and Photographs Division [LC-USZ62-47544].

132

Kadekoi Camp, May 1 1855

There is no news whatever, nothing seems doing. I dined at the French Camp, 27th Regiment, the day before yesterday, and had a very amusing evening. I can keep up a conversation without difficulty, though I daresay my accent is bad enough.

133

Fisher-Rowe to his parents

Kadekoi Camp, May 4 1855

I am glad to hear that you have seen Mr. Sym, and hope he has given you the different things he had charge of – my gold watch and the Russian sword. I hope he succeeded in getting hold of the sword at Pera, as, if not, it is lost, which is a pity. Godman has gone with a large force of Infantry and ten steamers, the whole under the command of one of the greatest old fools out here, Sir George Brown, on some expedition, the object of which is not known. There are not more than 50 Cavalry sent, under the command of Colonel Lowe, of the 4th Lights. It is something to think about, Kutch [Kertch] is supposed to be the destination. I have always forgot to ask you to get me a good map of the Crimea, if you could send one by post it would be the best way. I had a very nice silver watch sent in this way, which has just arrived. I dined with Major Welsford the day before yesterday, and with Capt. Gaulton[52] of the 50th yesterday; we had a turkey beautifully roasted by a candle stove, which the Crimean Fund sent out. Every branch of the service is in fine condition at present, which I trust will continue to be the case. I am glad to say I shall be allowed to purchase from the remounts, which will soon be out. We expect this will be much better than getting a horse from anyone here, both on account of price and because almost all the animals which have wintered here are touched in the wind, and are greatly shaken altogether. Mr. Sym is no authority as to the privations of the soldiers, he came out when their sufferings were over, in great measure, got among the Artillery and Commissariat, who always live well, brought every comfort with him that he could require, and his only night work was playing cards and drinking brandy and water. These sort of men are rather disgusting, especially when they go so far as to apply for a medal because they have been three weeks in the country for their own amusement. Last night I went up after dinner to see the firing, which was pretty heavy on the left attack. The Russians threw a great many Bouquets, as they are called, they consist of a quantity of small shells, which are put into a barrel and fired out of a large mortar. They are very pretty of a night, all in the air together, they go on exploding for half a minute, and are very destructive on account of the difficulty there is in dodging them. The rockets also look very well, they fly into the town, leaving a long tail of fire behind them.

---

52   Herman Ernest Galton. See *Hart's New Annual Army List 1855*, p. 201.

134

Kadekoi Camp May 9 1855

It is raining very hard, and has been doing so the whole of yesterday, night and day; the ground is in a very bad state as you may suppose, about an inch of mud in all the tents and huts; the horses stand with their legs altogether, their heads down and ears back. Picket becomes a great bore under such circumstances; fancy choosing the dirtiest and most boggy place down by the pond at Marshall Vale, when the wind was blowing hard and the rain coming down in torrents, holding a horse there from 10 in the morning to 10 the next morning; occasionally when it is pitch dark, riding out 200 to 300 yards in advance to see if any of the enemy are about. There is a great deal of ill feeling and disgust felt on account of an expedition of some 14,000 men which was sent to Kutch and did nothing at all.[53] As soon as they came in sight of the place they wheeled round and came back. Sir George Brown was in charge, an old imbecile bully. Twelve of our men and horses are gone and not come back yet. The horses have remained on board ship all the time, which has been long enough to see them safe in England. The 12th are landing at present and look very well.[54] We had a magnificent field day three or four days ago, all the English Cavalry in the Crimea. I had a capital view of it all, as I was acting Aide-de-Camp to the Colonel,[55] who, as you know, has the command of the Heavy Brigade, in which I expect he will be confirmed soon. I hope he will, he is every way fit for it. In the middle of the winter I bought a wretched horse from a sailor for £1, the poor beast had the mange so badly that I should have shot him if my servant could have found time to bury him, he has got well now and is beginning to look rather well, and has, I am told by some Officers who know it, got Nolan's brand on him, which shows him to be an Arab.[56]

---

53 The expedition to take Kertch was recalled on 4 May before any troops landed. Emperor Napoleon III interfered and forbade any distraction from the main French effort before Sebastopol. A second expedition later in May took Kertch without resistance. See Baumgart, *Crimean War*, pp. 148–50.

54 The 12th Lancers arrived from India on 8 May. See McGuigan, *Into Battle!*, p. 54.

55 Anglesey, *Little Hodge*, p. 103.

56 This refers to horses purchased by the late Captain Nolan, who was sent to buy horses in the Middle East before the campaign. See David Buttery, *Messenger of Death: Captain Nolan and the Charge of the Light Brigade* (Barnsley: Pen and Sword, 2008), pp. 77–90. The size and quality of the horses prompted some critical observations.

135

Kadekoi Camp, May 20 1855

It is really quite difficult to find anything to tell you, there is as little incident here as in a country house at home. One of our new drafts has arrived with very good horses indeed, but miserable little boys; the Regiment will look very different when it returns from what it did when it came out.[57] There is another expedition going to Kutch tomorrow, we hear, and it is most likely true, as the Russians will have had time to make it very strong, and will be well prepared, which they were not last time, so, of course, we would not take such an advantage of them, and came back till they could complete their little arrangements for killing us. Our talented General is said to take great interest in the culture of the vines round his house, having them tended and watered carefully; who can accuse him of want of forethought after this? The old Duke never displayed so much providence, he evidently expects to be here in the autumn, which is gratifying indeed. The Sardinians are arriving daily and are very fine troops in appearance, we shall be able to say more about them when we see them fight.

136

Kadekoi Camp, May 26 1855

I have sent four letters today with seeds, which, if they arrive safe and grow, will be interesting next year. I have also sent a centipede, of which I am sorry to say there are a great quantity here, the one I send is rather a small one, they sometime reach great size. The night before last I was awoke by a noise close to my head, something crawling over the matting with which the hut is lined. I found it was a very large centipede, so ugly, it made my flesh crawl, and kept me awake most of the night, as I could not succeed in catching him. I did not know what moment I might find him on my bare flesh. If you had heard the noise he made in biting a piece of wood I tried to kill him with, you would not have enjoyed the idea of such a friend in the dark. We are going to do something at last. Another expedition has gone to Kutch, and today, at 2 a.m., all the French down here advanced upon Thergum, beyond Kamara, and after some fierce fighting have, we hear, taken four guns and a quantity of prisoners. I was, with my usual ill luck,

---

57   The transport, *Crest of a Wave*, arrived from Kingstown with 50 horses and 31 men. Hodge also described the new men as 'An ugly set of little dogs'. See Anglesey, *Little Hodge*, p. 107.

Orderly Officer, and could not get out of camp, or I should have bagged something. The Russians were surprised and two Officers taken in bed. The Colonel captured a sentry's musket and pouch, which he had thrown away when he had bolted. At the moment I write we are all saddled and pistols loaded ready to turn out in a moment for what I do not know. The night before last the firing at the front was pretty heavy, an average of 45 cannon in the minute for two and a half hours. Father will easily calculate how many shots were fired altogether. I have just been ordered to visit the sentries twice during the night, which will rather stump sleep, great bore; however, this is better than doing nothing. The Russians showed in large force today, and it was so clear that I could see a man on horse-back with a bow and something like a glove. All this is very amusing, but out on the plain where the French were under fire of two large guns is, perhaps, more exciting, with rather less pleasure. I hope to get a good horse out of the next lot of horses, for which I shall have to pay £40.

137

Kadekoi Camp, June 2 1855

Nothing has occurred since I last wrote; we are still in our old position, but the French and Sardinians have moved to the Tchernaya, to a beautiful and sufficiently strong position. I have been all round it; I had some punch with some friends in the 27th French Regiment, and then walked down with them to the picket, which the Russians vainly endeavoured to shell. They threw a 30 lb shot (solid) while I was there, which one of the servants dug up and brought to us. These big shot are very useful to grind coffee. With a glass the men in the Russian batteries were to be seen with the greatest ease, and on riding along the river, the enemy's videttes were so near that we could see the lances and all the horse traps. The advance of the French was so rapid, that one Russian Officer is said to have been taken in bed, reading; in another house, breakfast was laid and the tea found in the cups. The whole of an Officers' baggage was taken, and altogether it was very successful for us. Kutch [Kertch], also, has been very satisfactory; we hear that 150 Russian ships have been taken since we took the place, as they come in not suspecting anything and cast anchor in the Harbour. The day before yesterday I went to the first parallel, where the sailors batteries are, and had a very good view of the whole affair. The French have run their advanced trench into the middle of a grass field, and the Russians have got one opposite, about as far off as from our malt house to Vanhurst; you may be sure they keep a sharp look out on each other, and take pretty good care not to stick their heads up, in fact a stranger would not believe there was a soul within a mile, all is so quiet. Mrs. Jones, the Major's wife,[58] has come out, and, I believe, went up to the front in a carriage today. I hope she will favour us with her company for as short a time as possible, she will be an unbearable bore in camp. I am beginning to hope we shall have very little illness this summer, we have done very well so far, and should think it must be naturally a very healthy place. We are to make a third try in a day or two, and they say we shall then go in. It would be a terrible blow to Lord Raglan if we took the place after all the trouble he has had with his vines, and I should think it would rather put the Government out, they would not know what to do next.

138

Kadekoi Camp, June 9 1855

The third bombardment is at present taking place, and I should hope it will be the last. On Thursday, at 6 o'clock, after heavy fire all day, the French rushed from the trenches and hurried across the space that separates them from the Mamelon, so sudden was the attack, that they got in without difficulty, and the Russians ran out the other side as hard as they could run; away went the French after them, and got to the edge of the Malakoff ditch, which, however, was too deep for them to cross without gabions to fill it up. All this I could see very plainly through my glass, but it was not good enough for me to see the men fall as the shell burst among them, which they did in great quantities. All this time our batteries kept up a heavy fire, as did the Russians, who fired so wildly and high as to cause a good many deaths among the spectators. I spent two or three hours preceding the attack on a little hill in the rear of Gordon's battery, which commanded a view of the Mamelon, Malakoff, and Redan, the whole of the left of which, however, nothing could be seen on account of the smoke. The hill, although covered with round shot, was pretty safe, as there was a deep ravine between the battery and it, in which most of the shot and shell that missed the battery lodged, if a shot did happen to ricochet across the ravine, it was pretty well pumped and only hopped slowly along like a big cricket ball. Soon after the French

---

58   The wife of Captain Thomas Jones, who was Brevet Major until his rank was confirmed in 1860. Other officers' wives came out to the Crimea and such arrangements were by no means popular. See Anglesey, *Little Hodge*, p. 110; Rappaport, *No Place for Ladies*, pp. 195–210.

got to the edge of the Malakoff ditch, I could see, first two or three, then six or seven, then twenty, and at last the whole of them rush back again to the Mamelon, the Russians after them, and then out of the Mamelon back to their own trenches. This looked very bad, however they got up their pluck again and retook the Mamelon, which they were content to hold and leave the other alone. Of the English attack, nothing could be seen through the smoke, but there must have been a very severe struggle from the continued rattle of musketry. They remain in possession of the Quarries in front of the Redan.

If you could hear of some Officer who is coming out, I should so much like to have a large and first rate single glass, one about 18 inches long when shut up, with a large focus, the double glasses are no good at all. I was up again yesterday, the cannonading goes on much the same, and there is great discontent among the Infantry as not being allowed to follow up the success and take the Malakoff and Redan by assault. I have not yet heard what was the result of last night.

139

Kadekoi Camp, June 14 1855
Nothing has taken place since my last of much importance. I have not got a horse, so shall wait until the next draft arrives, they are all poor beasts and most of them quite unbroken. There was an armistice on the 11th and Capt. Biggs got into the Mamelon. He says it is a most curious place, and that the Russians must have suffered dreadfully from our cannonades, quantities of their guns were overturned and men lying half buried under them, as if they had been there for days. The wounds of the storming party were of a dreadful nature, inflicted by round shot and shell. Major Welford, who is thought a great deal of here, was placed in charge of one of the supports, he is a most deservedly popular man in his Regiment. The expedition under Sir George Brown has done something it appears, though no doubt it is Sir E. Lyons who does it all.

140

Kadekoi Camp, June 16 1855
Yesterday I rode to the advanced post of the French, about 12 miles, I should say, just above Baida, through one of the most beautiful countries

I ever saw, very much like Wicklow. If you look at a good map you will be able to follow my root. I went through Kadekoi, crossed the plain to Kamara, where the Sardinians are posted and have thrown up some pretty field works, and where are the remains of quantities of Cossack huts, to build which they had pulled down every house of that formerly beautiful village. The little church, which formerly contained many very good and curious pictures, and was so quiet and retired, is now a cattle pen. Through Kamara we took the road to the right, which leads to the Camp of the Marines, on reaching which, we turned to our left along a road parallel to the sea and rode on about three miles, when we came to the French Camp, pitched by a couple of large villages, the names of which I do not know, which the Cossacks completely sacked before leaving, even pulling off the roofs. From there we pushed on along the Baidar road, which is a beautiful piece of engineering, running through a very mountainous country covered with oak, ash, birch and very fine grass. Not a sign of cultivation, and the inhabitants must depend entirely on their cattle for subsistence. Our ride terminated at the advanced picket of the French, which is posted at a curious looking building with a high tower and round top, it is said to be the shooting lodge of some nobleman. The flies here are quite extraordinary, in millions. The other night Biggs felt something crawling on his foot in bed, and throwing off the clothes discovered a large centipede and a mouse, both of which interesting creatures bolted before the horror struck Biggs was sufficiently recovered to interfere. The taste those brutes have for blankets and clothes is very annoying, their viciousness and powerful poison renders them extremely dangerous to life, and from our exposed state, men are frequently bitten in their sleep. The other day I succeeded in catching a snake by the tail as he disappeared in a tent, and flinging him into the open he was speedily dispatched.

141

Kadekoi Camp, June 23 1855
You have heard before this of our repulse and great loss in the assault. It was certainly most annoying. Pelissier does not appear to be a better man than the last. The whole thing was completely botched. Major Welsford, who was assembled with the rest of the Commanding Officers of the Regiments the night before the attack, says it was intended to have all the men in the trenches before daybreak, and the moment it was light enough to commence bombarding, and to continue it for three hours,

by which time they hoped to pretty well silence the enemy's guns and then to assault. This the impatience of Pellissier completely defeated. The Russians made a sortie at the Mamelon, which the French then repulsed, and instead of returning to their trenches when it was over, they followed the enemy across to the Malakoff supported by fresh Regiments, and the attack commenced. The Russians stood on the parapet four deep and poured down a terrific fire on the French, who had reached the ditch but could not cross it, as it was said to be 30 ft deep. Our attack on the Redan now commenced. Some sailors went first carrying woolsacks and ladders to cross the ditch, they were almost all killed with grapeshot at the abattis, which was very strong and difficult to cross. Sir J. Campbell[59] fell here. Our loss altogether was very heavy. The 38th and 18th did not come back till next night, they had penetrated into the town by the Cemetery, and could not get back owing to the enemy's fire during the day. Send no more beer, always send tea or coffee; all eatables should be in tin, otherwise they are not fit to eat.

142

Kadekoi Camp, June 28 1855

I have got a beautiful horse, Captain Robertson's were sold by auction, and I gave £87 for one, which, although aged, is a thorough good horse. Horses are very dear indeed, ponies that cost in Bulgaria £3 or £4, fetch £15 or £20 here. My mule I shall sell, as she has never recovered the use of her hind leg after the cracked heels she had in the winter. The pony is as brisk as a bee, and a capital one, 'Bob' he is called. 'Blood Royal' is in fine going condition and can do his 30 miles against any horse. The drafts, men and horses, are miserable compared with the old nails, as the veterans are called. I suppose you saw an account in the paper of an Officer in the Russian Army, 23 years old, with 24 years' service, every month in Sebastopol counting a year, better treatment than we get; if the Russians get a year for being inside the town in winter, we ought to have two for living outside without cover. On Saturday night we had the strongest storm, as far as rain goes, that I ever saw. I was dining with Godman at the mess of the 5th,[60] about 8.30, when up came a thunder storm, it was as dark as pitch in five minutes, beautiful lightning was succeeded by the clouds opening and dropping some tons of

---

59   Major General Sir John Campbell commanded the 1st Brigade, 4th Division. He was killed in action.

60   For Godman's version, see Warner, *Fields of War*, pp. 165–7.

water on every square foot of ground. The water streamed through the roof on to the mess table which was a bore, for the dinner was first-rate and the champagne beautifully cool. The unfortunate possessors of house property immediately decamped to look after their dwellings, most of which consist of an excavation of about 4 ft roofed over, leaving me to enjoy chicken and champagne inside, and cold water out; now cold water is a first-rate thing in its proper place, but not down one's back in the middle of dinner. I soon found that I must find a place of retreat, and no other being at hand I crawled under the table, where I waited the end of the storm. Godman presently came in to say he had 4 ft of water in his hut, and every stitch in the world floating about in it, bed and all. His horses had a most narrow escape, his servant having to go up to his neck to cut them loose. Most of the others came in with much the same story: some with their trousers off altogether, others turned up to their knees. The evenings amusement seemed pretty well come to an end, so I took my departure to look after my own country seat. The hall had about 4 ft of water, but the Best Bedroom in which I generally sleep, being above the level of the ground, was all right. I found nothing wet but the blankets: of my stores, however, there was very little left worth much, and all the saddlery and harness were fathoms deep beneath the wave, and will take some time to get to rights again. Poor Biggs was the greatest sufferer, he had not only water but earth and large stones washed in, so as to cover his things a foot and in some parts 3 ft deep, so that two men were at work the greater part of next day in digging out his goods. He was undressed at the time it happened, and so sudden was it, that he did not even save a pair of trousers, but had to bolt out to prevent being smothered, and went about next day in a pair of Capt. Webb's trousers, a flannel vest, and another man's boots. All this is very good fun, but I fear that some lives have been lost. Some men were picked up in the Harbour, who had been carried considerable distances, several huts were washed away and all the water troughs, which is a great pity, as our talented engineers take an immense time to execute so difficult a work. Tea and coffee are always acceptable, and I should like some saltpetre.

143

Kadekoi Camp, June 30 1855
I sold the tent for £11 at Pennefather's sale, so that not much was lost by it. Two or three dozen of port would be always acceptable. Don't send out any more beer in cask, it goes so fast; bottles of beer in three or four

dozen cases, so that they could go by Hayter and Howell, would be very acceptable, and much cheaper than buying it out here – 24/- a dozen is the price here. I expect we shall stay here for the next winter, there are no signs of a move. Raglan died last night, and General Brown has gone home very seedy. I fancy that the thoughts of another winter have an injurious effect on these swells, just as it did the last. Sebastopol is a nut which is by no means cracked yet. If they will only leave us alone we shall be quite comfortable next winter. I shall have my hut covered with felt and tarred all over. I like the cold best, though the heat does not at all disagree with me. I saw Major Welsford today, his drawings and paintings of the Crimea are capital. Brooksbank,[61] who I daresay father recollects at Francis' when he dined there one day, is in the 38th. I went to see him on the 18th, and was told he was lying in one of the houses by the cemetery, wounded by a grape shot, and could not be brought away till night. He, I am glad to say, [is] all right, though he had some narrow escapes. Some of the 18th found a quantity of ladies' bonnets with which they adorned themselves and went into the drawing room, in which were some beautiful pier glasses, seeing their own ugly faces with the bonnets on in the glasses they thought they were the enemy in another room, and fired on them.[62]

144

Kadekoi Camp, July 10 1855

The firing is heavy today, for the first time since the 18th, and I heard yesterday that the French are going to attack some small work in front of the Malakoff Tower. Major Foster is going home sick; Brigstock has sold out; Wilkinson has gone home for three months' leave, and will try and come and see you – he has two muskets for you. Always send out tea and coffee when you send a case. In the next case you had better send a plane, gouge, chisel, and a hammer with a flange to draw nails.

---

61   Arthur Brooksbank, ensign by purchase, November 1851; Lieutenant by purchase October 1853. See *Hart's New Army List 1855*, p. 189. Brooksbank was probably wounded when the 18th, 38th and 44th Regiments advanced down the Picket House Ravine on 18 June, as part of the support force, left attack.

62   As well as the women's bonnets, the Irishmen of the 18th Regiment found liquor and wine in the house and, despite being under fire, had a party and even a bare-knuckle fist fight. See Pemberton, *Battles of the Crimean War*, pp. 204–5.

145

Kadekoi Camp, July 17 1855
Here we are still in the same place, and likely to remain here for another winter at least, so everyone thinks. I'm sure I don't care much, it is quite as good a place as we could expect to be in, and if there was only something to hunt or shoot I wouldn't mind at all. However, as it is, I never feel dull and find plenty to do. Those dirty Turks can't hold their position at Baidar, and returned without saying that was their intention, to two or three squadrons of the 10th who were under Omar Pasha's orders, and who were left there all alone. I am afraid we shall be boxed up on our own little bit of land like last winter. There are lots of foxhounds coming out, which I am afraid will not be much use. I have sold the pony I bought in the winter for £1 for £15, and the mule which never recovered and could not go at all for £10 10s. I have bought an Arab at the sale of the Turkish General's Aide-de-Camp – an Englishman, Colonel Balfour,[63] who died a day or two ago – I paid £35 for him, but as I hear his master valued him at £60 or £70 I suppose it is a fair price, he is a stallion, but very quiet. We have a thunder-storm two or three times a week now, and the wind very strong, so that the heat is not so oppressive as it was, and makes one think of winter. The number of sales is quite curious, so many leaving or dying; they answer the same purpose as a flower show at home; you go there, lounge about, talk to your friends, and buy any little thing that strikes you. There has been a great deal of rain, which will be a good thing for the men at the front to fill their water tanks. Brigstock's papers have been sent to England to be approved, and leave refused to permit him to go till they are answered, which is a great bore for him as he has taken it into his wise head that if he goes into the sun without an umbrella it will be the death of him. He has 197 pots of preserved meat to be sold at his auction, and 12 or 14 cases full. Young Webb has arrived some time, fat as butter, he has not been received with any loud demonstrations of affection.

146

Kadekoi Camp, July 25 1855
I am very well off for horses now, the pony is a capital one, and Captain

---

63 Actually, Colonel Balfour Ogilvie, attached to the army of Omar Pasha, who died of cholera, 12 July 1855, aged 41 years. For details of his work, see *The Times*, 27 July 1855, p. 10, col. A. There is a memorial to him at St John's Church, Forfar.

Robertson's horse very good indeed. The Camp was disturbed this morning by a mad dog, which ran through our Camp, and finally located himself in Armstrong's tent next to mine, luckily the owner happened to be in my tent at the time, or he might have stood a bad chance. I took my gun and planted a shot behind the ear, which brought him down without a groan – he was a fine wolf-dog. The thermometer stood at 96 in the Colonel's hut, the coolest place in the Camp today – rather a caution. I had a beautiful bathe this morning, but the water was so hot it put me into quite a perspiration when I came out. There has been a pretty fair murder committed by the Turks close to us. A Tartar family and two traders were living in a small house that had escaped destruction on the plain, and a night or two ago were invaded by twelve Turks, seven stayed outside, five went in. They took about £150 from the traders, and then hacked the whole party to pieces. An old Tartar woman was found next morning, the only one of the six alive. She was cut across the jaw, and her head nearly taken off, still she is expected to recover, and she says she knows three of the Turks by sight, as they used to come for water close to the house, so I hope we shall find them out.

147

Kadekoi Camp, July 28 1855
Major Welsford was down here yesterday, and says the next (fifth) bombardment will come off in 10 or 14 days, and that it is possible the place will fall. I am glad the *Times* is giving Lord Cardigan a touch or two, no one deserves it more.[64]

148

Kadekoi Camp, July 31 1855
I rode to Baidar in the 27th, leaving the villages of Vanutka and Kaita on the right, which have been completely unroofed and plundered by the enemy. The road is quite new and beautifully made. It is not marked in my map although it is the main road, and the one that is marked is quite a

---

64 In the late spring and summer of 1855, *The Times* published letters relating to the conduct of Lord Cardigan and Lord Lucan in the Crimea. Both lords responded to the criticisms and these letters were also published. Added to these was a pamphlet by George Ryan entitled *Was Lord Cardigan a Hero at Balaklava?* The correspondence began to take the shine off Cardigan's good reputation which he enjoyed on his return from the Crimea at the beginning of 1855.

small one, so that no doubt it was finished very shortly before we landed. The map is an excellent one. We started at 11 a.m. and reached Baidar at 3 p.m., and dined in some beautiful meadows full of fine oak trees, which are the abode of quantities of wood pigeons and doves. A small stream runs through the middle of this plain, which is full of dead cattle, which I suppose the enemy killed on our approach. All the inhabitants have not left Baidar, and there are some shops open where they sell champagne, bread, tobacco etc. They are not at all a pleasant looking lot of people, and I thought did not seem to like the look of us very much. We passed through the town, and reached the English Cavalry Camp, where there are four Squadrons: 4th Lights, 8th, 11th and 17th – 400 in all. Our Assistant Surgeon is out with them.[65] He gave us a bottle of Russian champagne, of which they had taken 20 dozen – it was strong wine with a taste like perry. They have also taken 50 pictures. They have not seen much of the enemy. When they first went out, Colonel Peel of the 11th, who commands the whole, and Wilkin (11th) were chased by a Cossack for some distance as they stupidly went out without any arms, as Englishmen are fond of doing. In patrolling one day, a party of twelve Lancers came to a house, and some of them entered by the front door, a Cossack walked out of the back door, mounted his horse, and galloped off in spite of them. There is some talk of sending the Cavalry to Egypt or the Bosphorus this winter – I wish they would, one might get some good shooting. It is a great bore doing nothing here, when we might go out into the country and have some fun, and get a little plunder. I saw the French bring some mule loads in, they are not treated the same as us, they take what they can, as do Turks and Sardinians, while we get nothing but our share of the blame from the enemy. We are getting much more healthy than we were: a short time ago we had 60 in hospital out of 240 or 250, now we have very few indeed.

149

Kadekoi Camp, August 12 1855 [mistranscribed from the original; should read August 22]

We have had rather more excitement the last day or two than usual. The Russians attacked the French and Sardinians in force and were beaten back

---

65   Charles John White became Assistant Surgeon on the resignation of William Bruce Armstrong in May 1855. White was previously with the 3rd Dragoon Guards. See Peterkin and Johnston, *Commissioned Officers*, vol. 1, p. 366, though this entry does not mention his service with the 4th Dragoon Guards.

with great loss. We were out from 2 a.m. on the 16th till 11 p.m., and again on the 17th were under arms at 3.45 a.m. I expect it is the last fight this year, except the trench work, which there seems no end to. I am a mass of flea bites and kill as many as seven at a time of a night, they are increasing very rapidly and will soon become almost as bad as the flies and mice. We have got out another draft with Cornet Richardson,[66] 6'6" high. Send more spirits of wine, sometimes the little stove is most useful for early turns out. The bit of bread I enclose I picked up in the battlefield today.

150

Kadekoi Camp, August 25 1855
I have completely changed my habitation and gone up to Brigstock's place, which is in a much better situation than my old one. I had my hut carried up by 25 men without taking it to pieces. I have got a fine view from the room from which I am writing, I can see the Turks Camp at Kamara and the advanced battery of the Russians on the other side of the Tchernaya, and can occasionally see the smoke of a gun as they fire on some cattle party or watering party of the French. We are all on the alert now since the battle of the Tchernaya. We were turned out this morning (25th) at daybreak and remained under arms till 8 o'clock. Some 32 lb guns were sent for from the front, so I suppose they expected an attack. There is undoubtedly a large army before us but they can do nothing, and I am afraid we (the Cavalry) have no chance of a row. We are up at daybreak every day and once or twice have been turned out at 2 a.m. I am getting a good carpenter and have made first-rate tables, sofa, chairs and a bedstead, all strong enough to bear a ton weight, but the wood is so rough that splinters get into all parts of the body, when I get a plane I shall be all right. I am eaten with fleas, which are in hundreds here, I kill four, seven, ten of a night, there are also plenty of rats and mice.

151

Kadekoi Camp, Sept. 4 1855
They are working us pretty hard just now, because there happen to be some Russians on the other side of the Tchernaya. About twice a week

---

66   Henry Thomas Richardson, Cornet with the 4th Dragoon Guards, February 1855. See *The Official Army List 1856*, p. 199.

an Aide-de-Camp gallops into the Camp at 1 or 2 a.m., turns us out in a great hurry, and away we march to the plain as if a second Balaklava was going to come off, we wait there till daybreak and then march home again. I am almost always up at 4 a.m. and very often much earlier. If the Russians would come on what a licking we should give them, we turn out at 3 a.m. tomorrow. The day before yesterday I went out before breakfast and killed four couple of quail and a pigeon, that was the 1st September, they were uncommon good.

152

Kadekoi Camp, Sept. 11 1855
On the night of the 8th the Russians, finding the south side of the town too hot for them, set fire to all that was left and retired in good order across their bridge of boats, which they then broke down. Their retirement was followed by a series of tremendous explosions, Forts, Magazines, and public places being sent into the air, and also they say a good many little Frenchman engaged in picking up anything the Russians had left behind them. I got down there about 11 o'clock, the 9th, and passed all the pickets on various pretences, till I got down to the Battery at the Creak on our right of the Garden Battery, here an Officer of the 10th Hussars shouted to one of his men to nail me and send me back, but I had reached the great ditch and jumped into it, crossed and crawled through one of the embrasures and stood in the town. This Creak Battery is a most beautifully built one, there are bomb proofs in each traverse to hold all the men employed between it and the next one, so that when they saw us fire they ran into these and were quite safe. Every thing stood as if all the gunners had left their different occupations at one moment, the powder bag just ready to put into the gun was flung down with the rammer alongside, and the sponge leaning against it on the other. I walked up a street torn on all sides by our shells with great holes in the walls, every place was on fire and the smoke blinding. A dozen little French suddenly rushed out of one large house, of which the roof immediately fell in. The noise and roaring of the fire was tremendous, with continual falling roofs. I could not stay to make any plunder, of which altogether there was not more than would fill about a dozen good houses in the whole place, and which was soon snapped up. I picked up a piece of music, a Russian newspaper and a leaf out of a Bible, and got a capital piece of cloth big enough to make a shooting coat, and on my

return I cut a large piece of rope off one of the guns for the horses. The Russians are said to be leaving the north side as well, today and yesterday a great many fires have been seen.

153

Kadekoi Camp, Sept. 12 1855

The south side of Sebastopol has fallen with terrible loss of life; many a gallant fellow has gone to his account, among them one who was a most kind friend, a first-rate Officer, beloved and respected by all who knew or were under his command, Major Welsford.[67] He was in command of the storming party and was killed many yards inside the Redan, he was the first man across the parapet, far in front of his men. A Russian put a musket close to his head, which took the upper part of it off, his body and sword were saved and brought back to the Camp; he was buried next day at 3 o'clock. Captain Woods,[68] Mr. Fletcher, a cousin I believe, and myself were the chief mourners. He was followed by hundreds of his men, who poor fellows knew they had lost a friend indeed. The Country has lost a gallant soldier, who understood his profession better than any man I have met out here, and who has been most shamefully neglected by the authorities out here and at home, as every good soldier who has no patronage is. I have requested to be allowed to join in the putting up of a monument to his memory with the rest of his Regiment.[69] The Colonel, Senior Captain and Adjutant were all killed in the same attack. I intended to have written you a longer letter, but I shall be able to give you a better description in another letter of the inside of Sebastopol when the memory of our brave friends is a little less fresh.

---

67 Welsford's regiment, the 97th, was part of the assault force in the attack on the Redan on 8 September The regiment, along with the 90th, made up the 2nd Brigade of the Light Division. Their casualties were heavy. As well as Welsford, Lieutenant Colonel Henry Handcock, the Commanding Officer, Captain John Hutton, and Lieutenant Douglas Alexander McGregor, the Adjutant, were killed. See Cook and Cook, *Casualty Roll*, pp. 122–3, McGuigan, *Into Battle!*, p. 56.

68 Henry George Woods, Adjutant of the 97th Regiment. See *Hart's New Annual Army List 1855*, p. 249; *The Official Army List 1856*, pp. 58, 627.

69 This was done and a monument put over Welsford's grave. It read: 'Sacred to the memory of the Late Major Welsford 97th regt., who fell on the 8th September 1855 Leading the Ladder Party at the Assault on the Redan.' The grave and monument were located in the cemetery of the 2nd Brigade, Light Division. See Colborne and Brine, *Last of the Brave*, p. 7, no. 13; also an illustration of the cemetery between pp. 6 and 7.

154

Kadekoi Camp, Sept. 20 1855

Captain Brooksbank, who takes this home, is one of my greatest friends in the Crimea. He says he will try to come and see you when he reaches England; if he sends this to you, ask him to bring his gun with him, he will treat the birds in proper style. I hope you will be able to give him some good sport, you will like him extremely. We have had some good shooting together here: one day we got 34 brace of quail in less than four hours. He brings home a Russian flag taken at the fall of Sebastopol. He has promised to send me a dog. I should like 'Duck' and 'Jessie' too, if they can both go.

155

Kadekoi Camp, Sept. 23 1855

I went into Sebastopol on Thursday and had a good hunt all through it. The French have pretty well stripped it of plunder – a helmet or two were all I got. I went into the St. Nicholas, which is an immense fortification, but a good deal burnt, it was completely undermined like Fort Paul, but the enemy had no time to fire the mine, and the French are removing all the powder from it: it is a very fine Barrack and must have held a large quantity of men. I went to the Garden Battery and Crow's nest, they are fearfully knocked about. The English Engineers ought to be ashamed of themselves when they look at the Russian defences; there is a traverse between each gun, or two guns, in which is a bombproof big enough to hold all the men connected with that part of the work. In these bombproofs were chairs, tables, and even ladies' dresses, so that I daresay many people lived in those places in safety under the heaviest fire. We are under orders to winter in the Bosphorus, where the shooting is capital. I do very well here myself, much better than most people. I seldom kill less than four or five couple in two or three hours, which is very pretty work indeed. I shot two landrails the other day. I have got a shooting coat made of a piece of cloth I got in Sebastopol. Brooksbank has got a Russian flag and the spike of a Cavalry helmet. Henry Wight[70] has got three bayonets and a helmet for you. I missed seeing him the day he left,

---

70 Henry Arthur Wight, a Cornet in the 6th Dragoon Guards. See *Hart's New Annual Army List 1855*, p. 126. The 6th Dragoon Guards landed in the Crimea on 14 August 1855. See McGuigan, *Into Battle!*, p. 54.

as my servant who I sent over said he left Camp at 12 o'clock, instead of which he sailed at that hour, and when I rode to his Camp he was gone; however, I saw him the day before. I got two goats and 13 or 14 cocks and hens, so I am pretty well off for eggs, and I have two or three geese and so on, which help out the rations in very good style. The barrel of beer is in Harbour, and I shall most likely get it tomorrow. I can speak French well enough, but as for grammar, I may as well tell you at once, I have hardly time to write a letter much less learn grammar, which I get on very well without. I dined with Timson[71] a short time ago, and he dines with me the day after tomorrow. I see him continually and like him very much, he is in one of the nicest Regiments out here. Jones and Shaw are miserable creatures out here,[72] as indeed are most of the Depots. Henry does very well, and old Bragg[73] is a capital fellow; he hardly ever stirs out of Camp, so that I can get leave every day, which, taking into account going to Kamish, dining at the front, shooting, going into Sebastopol, riding out to look at new positions, batteries and such like, is very lucky, and could never be got through if the other subalterns were lazy, but it is quite fair that the young fellows should do the work, and let the old ones enjoy themselves. Sidney Hand[74] is here in the 82nd; he has been ill, but is getting better. Yesterday we had a parade, and speech and distribution of medals. Today I am wearing a bit of ribbon with a heavy half crown and two gin labels attached.

156

Kadekoi Camp, Sept. 26 1855

I have had some very good quail shooting: I killed 16½ brace, but they are leaving this, there are not so many as there were. I wish I had 'Duck' here, already she would be a great comfort. I was on picket yesterday at 9.30 a.m. to 9.30 this morning, very different 24 hours from those I spent last winter. I saw the field of the battle of the Tchernaya, and wrote you a full account of the scene the day after, but when I read it over it told of so many nasty

---

71 Lieutenant Henry Timson, 6th Inniskilling Dragoons. See *Hart's New Annual Army List 1855*, p. 132.

72 Captain Thomas Jones and Lieutenant Charles Fleetwood Shawe, 4th Dragoon Guards, neither of whom had gone out to the Crimea with the regiment in 1854. See *Hart's New Annual Army List 1855*, p. 132.

73 Captain Robert John Henry, 4th Dragoon Guards; Lieutenant John Arthur Bragge, 4th Dragoon Guards. See *Hart's New Annual Army List 1855*, p. 132.

74 Lieutenant John Sidney Hand, 82nd Regiment. See *Hart's New Annual Army List 1855*, p. 234.

sights, I did not think it fit to send. The bread I picked up alongside a dead Russian, and there were dozens lying all around so thick that I saw one lying balanced on top of another. All around the bridge, just above which I picked up the bread, they were killed in heaps. The French were not so thick by any means, they were all lying in rows as they were picked up and separated from the Russians as soon as the battle was over. It seemed to me that most of the enemy were killed by a ball in the head or upper part of the body. I was not allowed to cross the bridge, as the Russians were throwing shot and shell pretty freely just there without any regard for their own wounded, but I could see them lying as thick as if two or three regiments had been in skirmishing order and then killed in an instant. I am delighted father takes to shooting and does it so well: I should like to shoot the covers. Perhaps they will make peace now. The other day I rode into Sebastopol with Mrs. Forrest, and in going into the Garden Battery we rode close past a dead Russian, who was lying close to the road. Luckily she did not see it. The Crimea is not a proper place for Ladies.

157

Kadekoi Camp, Oct. 5 1855
We are still in our old position, though I hope for a short time longer. I should hope by the 20th we shall be out of this. There is a report that our Regiment is to go down to Pera, which would be a nice quarter for the winter. Some movements are taking place here. A Brigade has been sent to Nicolai,[75] and some of the Light Brigade have orders to embark, it is supposed to Upatoria, where there has been some fighting and some Russian guns taken by the French. The quail are getting scarce, and I am truly miserable for want of 'Duck'. Perhaps Wilkinson could bring him out; don't miss the chance; lots of Officers have got dogs out, and it makes me quite melancholy to see them. *Parlez-vous Francais* – I should rather guess I can a few. I dine with the French about twice a week, and talk at an alarming rate. They say the English will never learn because they won't talk. Nobody could accuse me of that. One of them gave me a medal of St. George, nice little thing enough. I will have to behave all

---

75 After 6 July 1855, the cavalry had been reorganised into three brigades under the command of Sir James Scarlett. The Light Brigade, under Paget, consisted of the 6th Dragoon Guards, 4th Light Dragoons, 12th Lancers and 13th Light Dragoons. They landed on 18 October and departed on 27 October after very little action. A detachment of the 6th Dragoon Guards went with the expedition to Kinburn on 4 October See McGuigan, *Into Battle!*, pp. 54, 61; Paget, *Light Cavalry*, pp. 118–29.

correct if Colonel Wood calls. I wish someone would make me his Aide-de-Camp. These recruits are a great nuisance. They know nothing at all, and we have drills and parades continually. I got a piece of Russian cloth in Sebastopol the day it was entered, which makes a capital shooting coat. Yesterday I went out with six other guns and 15 beaters beyond Kaitu, on the road to Baidar, and tried for deer but found none. The French are a long way beyond there, about nine miles. There is some talk of a forward movement when the different forces which have sailed reach their different points. What fun it would be if we bagged the whole Russian Army. I hope, if anything is to be done, it will be soon, for it is getting cold, much colder than this time last year. You have, of course, heard the sad news of poor Henry Wight's death.[76] I don't think he was sent away soon enough; he bore up against his illness like a man – very different from the ordinary run of fresh comers. He was a fine plucky little fellow, and thoroughly good-hearted. He was most grateful to Mr. Shrub for all his kindness, and had a great respect for him. He took some three bayonets for me, and a helmet, but they will no doubt be lost. Miserable death to die away from his Regiment in a strange hospital.

158

Kadekoi Camp, Oct. 12 1855

In my last of the 11th, I forgot a rather important matter. Except Macdonnel, Muttlebury and myself, all the old subalterns have gone home on sick leave or urgent private affairs. M'Creagh is the only Captain left of the old lot. As it appears that the Government is not going to be just enough to give leave to all the old men for a month or two in the winter to see old England again, and I trust there is no fear of my requiring sick leave, of which Dean went away today with four months, my only chance for a month or two is urgent private affairs. If you can make out a case and send me a lawyer's letter requesting my presence, I think I should have no difficulty in getting three months' leave of absence to come home, which I think would be no loss, as there is no chance of any work this

---

76 Wight died at Scutari of Crimean fever followed by dysentery, aged 19 years. He was the eldest son of the late Major Arthur Wight of the 23rd Regiment, of Braboeuf Manor, near Guildford. *The Times* reported that Wight had been nursed by Florence Nightingale 'to the great comfort and eternal gratitude of his mother'. See *The Times*, 9 October 1855, p. 1, col. A.

winter.[77] The places in the Bosphorus being fixed for winter quarters, one at Scutari, one 14 miles from Pera and the other in the sea of Marmora. If you can manage anything it will be just about the time five weeks hence, by which time you could send the letter out. It must be written so as to show to the Colonel, who I know will be delighted to let me go.

159

Kadekoi Camp, Oct. 27 1855
As soon as I know I will write and say where we are going, at present it seems we are going nowhere. If you like 'Duck' so much keep her by all means, and send me a good setter, well broke and steady, you can easily pick one up, but don't send me any but a really first-rate dog. I don't want a fast one but a good one at cover, try her in Colonel Wood's bit of cover. I was out on the 22nd with three other guns and killed six couple of woodcock. I killed two and a half myself and lost three more for want of a dog. The whole of the front of my trousers was completely gone and my skin pretty sore, the cover was so rough. If you send a dog have a strong iron collar put on with my name in full cut right through, let the collar have a coat of leather on account of the cold in winter.

160

Kadekoi Camp, Oct. 30 1855
Nothing new has happened up to this time: we have no orders about sailing, in fact, there seems to be more chance of our remaining here altogether.

161

Kadekoi Camp, Nov. 11 1855
A day or two ago when I was riding with the Colonel he asked me if I wished to go home, and when I said I did he said he expected I should

---

77 Fisher-Rowe is describing a scam to get leave from the Crimea. 'Urgent private affairs' were often used by officers to wave before their colonels in order to get leave. From the tone of this letter it appears that this malpractice was not uncommon. See *The Times*, 9 November 1855, p. 6, col. C; ibid., 20 November 1855, p. 7, col. C, for comment and discussion regarding this practice.

get a month or two without difficulty. I am tormented with fleas I cannot write at all. I was in the Malakoff today and my trousers covered with them. I have killed about 150 today.

162

Kadekoi Camp, Nov 16 1855

I am very glad you take the view you do of getting leave on the plea of urgent private affairs. I should never have felt comfortable if I obtained leave in such a manner,[78] not that I care a bit for the country which treats us in such a miserly manner, or for the Commander-in-Chief, who no doubt is a fool, but one's own self-respect would be undoubtedly damaged. Don't be led away by that curse to the country, The Times newspaper, and think that the Officers view with any other feeling than regret the removal of General Simson and the appointment of Codrington. Sir C. Napier said in India that General Simson was equal to any command, and his opinion was as good as Mr Russel's, I should fancy. Before I would take the command of this army I would turn out every reporter out of the Camp. Yesterday I had a great escape and was witness to one of the most terrific explosions we have had during the war. I had just been up to Major Welsford's tomb, which is very neatly arranged, and put a small stone in my pocket to give to Mrs. Irby, when the Right Siege Train and the French Magazine blew up.[79] I was about 500 yards off, and of course out of danger of the explosion of gunpowder alone, but in about ten seconds the sky above me burst out in fire and smoke and about 1000 shells flung their iron hail on all sides of me. I luckily escaped without a scratch, but many a brave fellow was sent to his last account who a short time before had been engaged in building a little hut for the winter. As soon as I had shaken myself after the first explosion, I galloped off to the place where it had taken place and got within 150 yards. The huts and tents were all in a blaze and, horrible to relate, the French had a large hospital and we had many marquees full of sick and wounded close too. As many as were able ran away in their shirts. I stayed about these places for a minute or so, when a magazine of rockets or shell, or some beastly thing, went off and made us leave that pretty quickly. I then

---

78 See [158] above. Fisher-Rowe clearly had qualms about the malpractice on grounds of integrity rather than considerations of loyalty.

79 The magazine in the French artillery park accidentally ignited on 15 November 1855, causing heavy casualties in both armies among the men in the vicinity of the explosion. British losses were among the Royal Artillery, the Field Train Department, infantry regiments and the Rifle Brigade. See Cook and Cook, *Casualty Roll*, pp. 215–17.

went to the 88th Hospital and found one man with a piece of shell about 5 lbs. in weight in his back, and a great many more wounded less severely. I stood outside this hospital for some time watching the explosions which were very frequent, when a Frenchman came up to me and asked me to go to the hospital and interpret for a little French doctor who had just found an immense French Lieutenant of Artillery who was struck in the head, breathing heavily and quite insensible. The little doctor took off his cap, bowed politely, and said, 'Sir, I beg to inform you that this man is lost' he then begged to request that I would put myself to the trouble of asking for some cold water and for one of our own medical men to give his opinion, I did both and found that there was no hope after everything had been done that could be for the poor fellow. We went outside and the little doctor was very talkative until a piece of shell came tearing through the air towards us, when suddenly the little man disappeared and I felt a hand grasping the calf of each of my legs, which the little villain pinched ferociously as he stuck his head between my thighs, as soon as the piece pitched, which it did about 30 yards off, the little man was up again and not a bit abashed at his conduct, the dirty little coward, but I had had enough of him and went away. Wilkinson, who is sitting opposite to me as I write, has been up today and saw 11 men and one officer going to their graves, and heard that 17 men were killed and 50 wounded in one Battery of Artillery alone. The French who caused it suffered still more heavily.

163

Kadekoi Camp, Nov. 23 1855
You may direct the wine and beer to the Army in the East, if the Regiment is gone it will be sent to Scutari immediately. It is by no means certain we shall leave the Crimea, although most of the regiments have gone. I am sure I don't much care, the Crimea is a very nice place, and a pleasant climate, and I am very comfortable. I have built a first-rate chimney and fireplace, with a great chimney corner. It draws very well – it is much warmer this year than last. We have had a little rain and snow, but nothing to speak of. Timson applied for leave of absence, but his Colonel (who is a great brute)[80] would not forward it. He then went to the General, but he snubbed him. He is very indignant indeed. I went to our Colonel yesterday and asked about it, he said he would send in my

---

80   Lieutenant Colonel Henry White, 6th Inniskilling Dragoons.

name for leave as soon as we get down to Scutari, so that if we get down there I shall most likely get it, though not for long. They expect to begin the next campaign early in March.

164

Fisher-Rowe to his parents

Kadekoi Camp, Nov. 29 1855

I have received your letters of the 11th November. I will try and get more photographs. Chapman – and Driscoll is the other man's name.[81] He received five wounds, and his horse was run through the head by a lance, a Hussar Officer saved his life. The socks have not come to hand yet, but I daresay will turn up in time. The winter has set in with a vengeance – rain, snow and frost. This morning I am Orderly Officer. When I got up at daylight it was raining in torrents, and looks as if it would keep it up all day. The soil is the most beastly I ever saw – it is a greasy clay, and 24 hours of rain will hardly wet an inch. It is impossible for horse or man to stand on a slope. Men and horses are down every five minutes. I believe the 6th Dragoons go next, and then we shall get away. Of course I shall try and get home if I can. Sidney Hand is quite well – I dined with him about a week ago; they have a very good mess, the whole regiment live together. He had half of one of the large huts, and is very comfortable indeed. Our Depot Officers[82] complain bitterly of the cold and wet here, while those who have been out the whole time, and know what last winter was, only feel too glad to have their heads under wood instead of canvas. My little hut does beautifully. I have an old tent nailed round him, which makes him very snug. I keep my self warm with the pickaxe and spade, and the fire does very well at night. I never thought of my birthday till I received your letter – time slips away so fast.

---

81 Fisher-Rowe is referring to the incident on 7 October 1854 and the men captured by the Russians when he was in charge of the picket. See [93] and note 16 above.

82 Unsurprisingly, there was a bond between those officers and men who came out to the Crimea at the beginning of the war and endured the appalling hardships of the first winter. Fisher-Rowe appears to be contemptuous of the officers from the regimental depot who joined the regiment in 1855.

165

Fisher-Rowe to his parents

On Board the 'Oneda' Dec. 9 1855

As you will see from the date, we are on board the 'Oneda',[83] on our passage to Scutari, where we expect to arrive tonight. I am going to try for leave the moment we arrive, so you must not be surprised to see me walk in some day in three weeks time from the receipt of this. I shall have plenty to do for the short time I shall be at home. I will try to get some more photographs when we arrive at Constantinople, but I am afraid they will have been all bought up by the Officers already there. It was a beautiful passage – no wind at all – very different from my last journey to Scutari in the 'Sovereign', which was knocked all to pieces in the harbour on the 14th November, she had even the wheel carried away, and a great hole in the bow. I shall go by Marseilles, if I can get away, as it is much shorter than by Gibraltar. I shall bring nothing home that I can help. I daresay you will not hear from me again until I either come, or write to say I cannot. The Colonel will do his best I know.

166

E. Harran[84] to Fisher-Rowe

Scutari Barracks, Dec. 30 1855

My Dear Fisher, – Poor old 'Bob' died two days after you left this. Macdonnel's horse died also, and he applied for compensation, which I think he has a reasonable chance of getting. I enclose you a form which you can fill up as required, and I will get old Chambers to make out a good strong case, which I hope will have the desired effect. The mess is working very well so far. There is no excitement here of any sort. I have not been over to the other side of the water yet, although my hair requires cutting very badly. Poor old Shaw has rather unpleasant recollections of his visit to the barber's shop, which is to me rather a caution. I think I shall wind up now as I cannot think of anything worth telling you

---

83 The regiment left on the *Oneida* on 8 December 1855. See Anglesey, *Little Hodge*, pp. 138–9.

84 Cornet Edward Harran, 4th Dragoon Guards, commissioned without purchase, gazetted 23 February 1855. Harran had served in the ranks and was commissioned from Regimental Sergeant Major. As Cornet he served as Adjutant to the regiment.

about. By the way though, these are Christmas times, I ought to say something about wishing you many happy returns of the season, etc. etc. Well, I have no doubt you are happy to be in old England again amongst friends – still, not more happy than I wish to be. This time last year, in the Crimea, to wish a man many happy returns of the season would be taken as an insult – and very justly so, too. I only hope that we never have to return to such a season again.

Major Edward Phillips, c. 1860, Adjutant of the Ayrshire Yeomanry Cavalry.
Credit: Mr Jeremy Phillips.

3

Edward Phillips

Edward Phillips was born on 22 April 1830 in the parish of St James, Westminster, London. He was the son of John Edward Phillips, gentleman, and Elizabeth his wife, who had married in June 1827. John Phillips became a member of the London Stock Exchange in 1840. In 1847 the family moved to the elegant splendour of 44 Westbourne Terrace, Hyde Park. John Phillips invested in railway companies in the 1840s and made enough money to live in considerable affluence.

On 8 February 1850, John Phillips wrote a letter to the Horse Guards requesting that his son should be considered for the purchase of a cornetcy in the cavalry in India. He also committed himself to provide a 'liberal allowance' for his son and to 'purchase him on' in the service. If a reference was required, he cited Major General R. B. Fearon CB as a source. Another letter in support of this application came from a Mr Arthur Talbot. The letter is undated but requests that Edward Phillips be considered for a cornetcy in the 12th Lancers, pointing out that it is said that all the officers of this regiment are about to 'sell out' because the regiment is 'ordered to the Cape'. Talbot requested, 'Could you stitch a point and provide for my youth Edward Phillips who is dying for glory?' Talbot's point was an exaggeration. The *Army List* reveals that no such volume of resignations from the 12th Lancers occurred. Talbot may have used the misinformation as a ploy to draw attention to Edward Phillips's quest for a commission.[1]

A cornetcy arose when Lord Fitzgibbon of the 8th (The King's Royal Irish) Regiment of Light Dragoons (Hussars) purchased a lieutenancy in June 1851. His previous rank of cornet became vacant. Phillips's father paid the sum of £850 to Cox & Co., the agents for the 8th Hussars, on 4 July, the purchase price for the rank. Edward Phillips's military career started

---

1   TNA, WO31/990, Gazette 11 July 1851, Records of the Commander in Chief, Memoranda and Papers.

on 14 July 1851.[2] He presented himself for examination at Sandhurst to be scrutinised to see if he was fit to be a cavalry officer in the British Army. The regiment was at Hampton Court with billets in and around Hounslow. It was inspected by Major General Brotherton on 6 August and found to be 'well commanded and in excellent order'.[3] In the spring of 1852 the regiment marched off to the Midlands and was scattered in barracks and billets in Nottingham, Mansfield, Loughborough and Sheffield. More inspections followed. When the Duke of Wellington died on 14 October 1852, the regiment provided a band and a squadron in the funeral procession in London. The following year saw more moves around the country and inspections, hardly the stuff of glory for a young cavalry subaltern.

At the end of March 1854, however, Phillips's regiment was one of the first to embark for the east. The regiment had assembled in Exeter in March 1854 and proceeded thence to Plymouth for embarkation. Two light troops were to form a regimental depot at Newbridge Barracks in Ireland and were removed there after the regiment had sailed. The government hired five large sailing ships to transport the regiment to the east: the *Echunga*, the *Medora*, the *Mary Anne*, the *Wilson Kennedy* and the *Shooting Star*. The question of how cavalry and artillery horses were to be transported to the east was raised in the month before the declaration of war by Cardigan in the House of Lords.[4] Cardigan regretted that passage in sailing ships inevitably meant a longer voyage and, therefore, greater stress for the horses. The government's response was that to hire the requisite number of steam-powered ships would lead to a serious disruption of the postal arrangements of the country. Some steamers would tow the sailing vessels when appropriate and where available. A fellow officer of the 8th Hussars, Lieutenant the Hon. Somerset Calthorpe, Raglan's nephew, who was acting as his uncle's aide-de-camp, was equally critical of the decision:

> It is a very bad policy of the Government sending out the cavalry and artillery in sailing transports: many horses die on the voyage, and almost all arrive in bad condition, and are not fit for service for some time after they are landed. Some of the horse-transports have been sixty and seventy days coming out.[5]

2   Ibid.
3   Murray, *History of VIII Hussars*, vol. 1, p. 402.
4   See *The Times*, 24 February 1854.
5   The Hon. S. J. G. Calthorpe, *Letters from Head-Quarters* 2 vols (London: John Murray, 1857), vol. 1, pp. 37–8.

Calthorpe was of the opinion that it would have been better to wait until such time that sufficient steamers were available so that the horses would not lose condition due to the shorter voyage time. In the event, only six horses were lost on Phillips's passage to Constantinople on *Shooting Star* but 46 were lost when a storm hit Phillips's sailing vessel, *Rip Van Winkle*, which was being towed by the steamer, *Trent*, between Varna and the Crimea [167, 168, 182].

Of the four correspondents, Phillips was the first to arrive in the east. His letters reveal a realisation that the organisation of the Army of the East was chaotic, not least the lack of transport [172]. As W. H. Russell of *The Times* observed of the disbandment of the Royal Waggon Train in 1833:

> The people of England, who had looked with complacency on the reduction of expenditure in all our warlike establishments, ought not to have been surprised at finding the movements of our army hampered by the results of injudicious economy.[6]

The problem was partly resolved by using local provision of horses and wagons. Phillips was specifically mentioned in one of Russell's despatches in July 1854 as having just returned from Tirnova, where he had purchased 494 horses [173, 174]. In turn, however, assembling some 16,000 horses meant additional problems in finding sufficient forage.[7]

When the army embarked for the Crimea in September, the pack and draught animals and the ambulance carts were left at Varna because there were not enough ships to take them. Phillips himself also remained behind as he was too ill with a low fever to accompany the army [180]. There followed his traumatic journey on the *Rip Van Winkle*. By the time he arrived, therefore, the routine of the cavalry acting as the early warning system against an expected Russian attack against Balaklava and its harbour was already established.

At the beginning of the battle of Balaklava on 25 October, the morning parade of the 8th Hussars recorded 11 officers and 104 NCOs and other ranks. When the Light Brigade advanced, the 8th Hussars were in the third line and on the right of the 4th Light Dragoons. Both regiments trotted towards the guns at the end of the valley. By the time they reached them, the first line of the Brigade, the 17th

---

6 Russell, *British Expedition to the Crimea*, p. 45.
7 *The Times*, 8 August 1854.

Lancers and the 13th Light Dragoons had already silenced the eight guns of the Don Battery. In covering the distance, the 8th had lost half its number mostly from the fire on their flanks. Trotting beyond the battery, Lieutenant Colonel Frederick Shewell, the Commanding Officer, saw retreating Russian forces before him. Those on foot were the surviving gunners from the Don Battery, the cavalry they saw were Rijov's, who had already suffered at the hands of the Heavy Brigade earlier in the day. Both had been driven back by the remains of the Light Brigade's first line and part of the second line made up of the 11th Hussars. Despite their losses, Shewell's squadrons kept their order and advanced at a brisk trot some three to four hundred yards beyond the guns and then halted. Before them they saw only small groups of the regiments who had been positioned in front of them at the start of the advance down the valley. One such group belonged to the 17th Lancers, some 15 men strong and under the command of the Brigade Major, George Wynell Mayow. This group joined forces with the 8th and Shewell took command. There was no sign of Cardigan and no orders had been received on what to do next. The decision was made for them. As the 8th and the 17th joined together, three squadrons of Jeropkine's Lancers started to deploy from concealment at the foot of the Causeway Heights. They advanced across the valley and two of the three squadrons wheeled into line. They waited for the completion of the third squadron's manoeuvre. Shewell quickly appraised the danger to his formation and, as described by Phillips [186], they charged the Russian Lancers. The audacity of the British reaction stunned the Russian cavalry and they broke to the left and right as Shewell's Hussars and Lancers galloped through them. Phillips himself was almost cut off at one point. Having escaped entrapment by Jeropkine's Lancers, Shewell's horsemen were now exposed to the mortal danger of the fire from the Russian batteries and infantry in the Causeway Heights. This fire would have been worse had not the Chasseurs d'Afrique executed a brilliant charge that silenced the Russian battery on the Fedioukine Heights which bordered the north part of the north valley.

The regiment had lost two officers (Captain George Lockwood and Lieutenant Fitzgibbon) and 19 NCOs and other ranks killed. Two officers and 17 other ranks were wounded, and one officer was a prisoner (George Clowes), as well as seven NCOs and other ranks. The total casualty list, therefore, was five officers and 43 NCOs and other ranks: Phillips records the loss at 44 NCOs and other ranks. Some 37 horses were killed in the battle and a further nine were shot because of their wounds.

The remnants of the Light Brigade were positioned near the windmill at Inkerman, an exposed location which exacerbated their plight. Here they were some eight miles from Balaklava and as the roads became impassable because of the mud the supply to the brigade diminished. The problems were exacerbated by the aftermath of the 'great storm' [190]. Phillips was particularly critical of Cardigan, 'the noble yachtsman', living on his yacht in Balaklava harbour [190, 193]. Well might Phillips write: 'When we shall take this place, goodness only knows' [188]. By December, the condition of the 8th Hussars, like other units in the army, had deteriorated still further [189, 190, 193]. The returns for the depot at Scutari, where the wounded and sick were taken first, show some 61 men of the regiment listed. On 12 December an order was issued that the cavalry were to perform the work of the Commissariat and provide 500 horses every day to transport provisions to and from the army on the plain about Sebastopol.[8] Unsurprisingly this role was bitterly resented. Against this general background, many subalterns considered 'selling out' including Phillips [192] though he did not go through with his intention.

If Phillips wrote letters from the Crimea in 1855, none have been discovered or survived in any form. Phillips served 'on duty with service troops' throughout the whole of the year and went on leave in December 1855. After losing 15 horses dead in December 1854 returns for the regiment show only 103 horses 'fit for service' in January 1855. This was barely enough to mount two troops. February was even worse. Forty-four horses had died in January and the state of the regiment amounted to 58 horses; 45 fit for service and 13 recorded as sick. The 'regiment' now amounted to one weak troop. Though these figures are dismal, the 8th Hussars actually had a higher number of horses at their disposal than the other regiments of the Light Brigade as one troop was detailed as Raglan's escort and enjoyed marginally better conditions.[9] Shewell wrote on 15 January:

> We are doing nothing against Sebastopol, the snow is nearly a foot deep on the ground, and seems likely to continue. Our horses are dying daily, but our men are bearing the cold better than could be expected.[10]

---

8   Anglesey, *History of British Cavalry*, vol. 2, pp. 114–15.
9   TNA, WO17/665, Monthly Returns to the Adjutant General.
10 Murray, *History of the VIII Hussars*, vol. 2, p. 429.

When Roger Fenton arrived in the Crimea in March 1855, he took several views of the cavalry. On 8 April 1855, for example, Mrs Duberly recorded, 'Bob & I, & Henry were photographed yesterday. I on Bob & Henry at his head – a very good picture.'[11] Fenton took other photographs of the 8th Hussars including a group of officers with Phillips in his Hussar's jacket in the centre. It is likely that Phillips was duty officer of the day as the others are far more casually attired. Phillips was later photographed on horseback, wearing the new blue peacoats recently issued as a substitute for cloaks, in the company of Yates, the unpopular adjutant of the 11th Hussars.

The 8th Hussars provided troops for the expedition to Kertch but Phillips was not one of those despatched there. The 8th Hussars also provided the escort when Raglan's body was taken from his headquarters to the steamer *Caradoc* to be returned home for burial at Badminton. The 8th also accompanied the allied expeditions to Eupatoria and Kinburn in October and November to harass and disrupt Russian lines of communication and supply to the Crimea. The 8th Hussars with the rest of the cavalry went into winter quarters at Scutari in early November. Phillips was granted leave of absence from 9 December 1855 until 29 February 1856, on 'urgent private affairs'. He rejoined the regiment on 28 February at Scutari. Phillips's regiment returned to England from Scutari in May 1856 and was inspected at Portsmouth by Queen Victoria and Prince Albert. Following the inspection the regiment immediately re-embarked for Kingstown. They disembarked on 17 May and then marched to Dundalk arriving on 21 May. Of the 293 men of all ranks who had set out with the regiment, two were promoted, 42 were invalided home, 68 died of diseases and wounds, 26 were killed in action or died immediately after, one deserted to the Russians, and 154 returned with the regiment to England, including 68 who had been on the Danube.[12]

At the end of 1856 Edward Phillips's military career was temporarily suspended. He had been absent from the regiment from 1 August on 'private affairs' and returned to duty at the beginning of October with the regiment still quartered at Dundalk. With the war in the Crimea over, the government decided to reduce the size of the army and consequently there was no troop for Phillips to command. Like many other officers he went on half pay, starting on 10 November 1856. Phillips rejoined on 3 April 1857, shortly before the outbreak of the Indian Mutiny, which saw the regiment ordered to India in October 1857. The 8th Hussars did not

11   Kelly, *Mrs Duberly's War*, p. 162.
12   Murray, *History of VIII Hussars*, vol. 2, p. 433.

achieve its full complement of horses until the second week in February 1858 but then participated in the campaign in Central India.[13] Phillips was at Nusseerabad in April 1859 and the following month was granted leave for one month for 'private affairs'. In April 1860 Phillips bought the vacant majority in the regiment for £1,400.

Phillips retired by sale of his commission on 11 May 1860 to become Adjutant in the Ayrshire Yeomanry Cavalry. On 25 September 1861 he married Mary Ann Freeman, a gentleman's daughter, at the parish church at Lugwardine, Herefordshire. There were 13 children from the match. In the summer of 1873 Phillips retired from the Ayrshire Yeomanry and moved to Earley, near Reading, Berkshire. He lived out the rest of his life here, first at Earley Hill on the Wokingham Road and then in a much smaller dwelling at 2 Marlborough Avenue, Reading. Apart from raising his large family, Phillips was active in the local church, St Peter's, Earley, and the Church Missionary Society. He died on 18 April 1915 and was buried at St Peter's Church, Earley, on 22 April 1915. When he died he was the last surviving officer of the 8th Hussars who had participated in the Charge of the Light Brigade. The informant on his death certificate was his daughter, Minnie, who died unmarried in December 1933. According to members of the Phillips family today, a great deal of material related to Edward Phillips's life was then lost or destroyed.

---

13 See Frances Isabella Duberly, *Campaigning Experiences in Rajpootana and Central India* (London: Smith Elder & Co., 1859).

167

Phillips to his father

Mediterranean 60 miles from Gibraltar.
Date: 3rd May 1854 on board the SS 'Shooting Star'.[1]
I have not felt inclined to write before, but think it best to begin, as probably if an opportunity occurred of sending letters, I should not have time.

I suppose you all want a true and particular account of our voyage. To begin at once, we sailed from the Sound at 6 o'clock A.M. on Wednesday 26th April, with a fine N.E. wind, and had an excellent run till the Friday morning. This left us about the middle of the Bay of Biscay. During Thursday night, the wind freshened considerably, and running nearly before the wind, the vessel rolled very much. The rolling increased by the morning, and about 8 o'clock (blowing pretty strong), we carried away both our main and mizzen top gallant masts. Several men were on the yards at the time reefing the sails, and one, in falling, broke his leg, another one having the narrowest escape of going overboard possible, falling on to the main yard, and clinging with his legs only, with the head down.

All this detained us considerably, and obliged us to run about 60 miles right off course. Towards evening, things being got to rights somewhat, we stood in again. During the evening, the wind rose very much, with a tremendous sea on, and at night blew a regular gale. We ran before it all night, the vessel going fifteen knots, with but three sails set; she rolled and pitched awfully, and not a soul slept a wink that night; the scene in the hold was indescribable, half a dozen horses down at a time, and the rest plunging and kicking. The consequence was that two of those who were down and suffered most, died the next morning, and were thrown overboard in the course of the day. Having once broken their slings,[2] it was impossible to keep them on their legs, and throwing themselves down they got under the other horses and were dreadfully knocked about. After a storm a calm, and I hardly know which is the worse; with a dreadful swell, we lay without a breath of air almost, rolling our gunwale under. Since then we have had but light winds. However, we passed Gibraltar

---

1   The *Shooting Star*, a clipper sailing ship, built at Quebec by Thomas C. Lee in 1853, 1518/1362 tons (old/new measurement); one deck, elliptical stern, scroll figurehead, re-registered 8 April 1854, no. 233. See HCPP 1854–55 (283).

2   These slings were attached to the sides of the wooden stalls where the animals were stabled during the voyage. The idea of the slings was to reduce the wear and tear on the horses' legs as the ship rolled and pitched at sea.

about ten last night, greatly to our disgust, in the dark, and are now again becalmed, about 60 miles to the Eastward of it, not a breath or a ripple, and broiling hot. We have one great consolation; our vessel has as yet beaten everything we have come near; vessel after vessel, have we passed,[3] without the slightest difficulty; even now that we are crippled in some degree (not yet having our masts up again), none of them have a chance, and had it not been for the light winds and the accident, we could easily have made Gibraltar in four days and a half. However we must expect this sort of weather now, and we must be a fortnight or longer getting to Malta yet. How this will reach you, I do not know as yet, we have had no chance of sending anything, and may not have till we reach Malta. I am getting alright now, but was very seedy at first; not so ill as feeling so.

Mrs. Duberly was very unwell for some time, and wished herself out of it over and over again; she is getting better. We passed a vessel yesterday with some of the 17th Lancers on board,[4] at least that is what we made out from her signals. We lost another horse yesterday, the rest are alright. Fairy goes on very well. I shall, of course, add to this before sending it, but thought it best to pull up a little. We have rigged out an awning and white covers to our straw and glazed hats, and now sit broiling in sight of the coast of Spain; the snow on the mountains there looks delightfully cool.

5th May. A westerly wind sprang up on the evening I last wrote (Wednesday), and blew all day yesterday; we have made a fine run of it, being nearly half way to Malta by this time. It still continues, and promises to blow harder; should it not, we hope to reach Malta by Sunday night; this making the fastest passage known by a sailing vessel. It is however, rather early to talk about that. Another horse died yesterday morning; he was almost mad, and struggled furiously. We have been running in sight of the African coast almost all the time since leaving Gibraltar; it is very different from what I had pictured it; I fancied a low sandy looking country, the sight of which made one thirst, whereas, it is rather mountainous in its whole course, and altogether a bold looking coast. The deep tint of the Mediterranean is certainly very striking, and the evenings deserve all that has been written of them.

---

3   Paymaster Henry Duberly's wife, Fanny, was also on the *Shooting Star* and shared Phillips's exultation regarding the speed of the clipper: 'I could not but exult in the magnificent sailing of our noble ship, which bounded over the huge waves like a wild hunter springing at his fences and breasted her gallant way at the rate of 16 knots an hour.' See Frances Duberly, *Journal Kept during the Russian War* (London: Longman, Brown, Green and Longman, 1856), p. 3.

4   Almost certainly the *Blundell*, Transport no. 30, carrying a troop of the 17th Lancers. It departed from Portsmouth 23 April 1854. See HCPP 1854–55 (283), p. 10.

Passed a large steamer early this morning, steering West, supposed to be a P&O boat with mails to Gibraltar, and hope if so, she must be catching it now, as it blows hard right in her teeth; just after breakfast, it was rather squally, and all of a sudden snap went the fore top mast stun sail boom, just like a walking stick. We set our main topgallant sail for the first time since the accident this morning, having rigged out a new spar yesterday. Seen no fish today; the porpoises and whales seem to have deserted us. Our captain says when he can add another 100 to the 270 miles we ran yesterday, he shall be satisfied. We certainly are most fortunate in the sailing powers of our vessel. We logged fifteen knots one night, and averaged ten more, and not on her fastest point of sailing. The hold is cooler today than it has been yet, but there are two horses still very ill; a trooper and Mrs. D's horse, both look very like dying before long.[5]

Monday 8th May, Arrived last night in Malta, after 11 days and a half splendid run from Plymouth all well; ordered off immediately, and shall leave in an hour. As we are before the mail, there are no letters from you. We hear from the Admiral that Odessa is taken; a man killed, and ten wounded.

168

Phillips to his father

Monday 8th May Malta

A line in the greatest haste by pilot to say we arrived at 3 a.m. this morning after altogether a beautiful passage, and leave now, 11 o'clock. I have written a long letter (but forgot to put 'via Marseilles', so send this); you will get it a week later. We sail for Scutari, to touch at Gallipoli for active service immediately. Have lost six horses, two from violence in a storm, and the others sickness; mine are, thank goodness, still well. Excuse this writing, my hand is still so shaky from being on shore in the heat; just the first of it is trying. We shall, I hope catch up the 'Echunga' and 'Marianne';[6] they left yesterday; only came in the morning. Odessa is

---

5   Fanny Duberly took two horses with her: a grey and a large black gelding named Bob. She recorded in her journal entry for 5 May that their servant, Pvt. Connell, woke her to tell her that her grey was very ill. Mrs Duberly's grey died as the clipper arrived in Malta on 8 May.

6   The *Echunga*, a sailing ship built in 1853, 1,007 tons, owner James Johnson, Liverpool, Transport no. 44. Entered into government pay 13 March 1854, capable of accommodating 578 men and 54 horses. Sailed with one troop of the 8th Hussars under Captain Longmore 19 April 1854. The *Mary Ann*, Transport no. 6, owned by Edward Oliver, Liverpool. Left Plymouth 21 April 1854 with detachments of the 8th Hussars under Major Rodolf de Salis. See HCPP 1854–55 (283), p. 14.

taken; the Admiral showed the letter [and] arrived by steamer last night. We lost 1 killed and 10 wounded.

[PS] A letter for Erin[7] with your other one.

169

Phillips to his mother

Wednesday 17th May

As we expect to be at Gallipoli by tomorrow, it is almost time for me to send you an account of our progress. Today makes the three weeks since leaving Plymouth, and we are now just off Tenedos, not far from the mouth of the Dardenelles. We have certainly had, taking it altogether, a splendid voyage, and have been very comfortable, at least as much so, as one can expect at sea. It has been a great pleasure to us passing every vessel we have seen, and almost every day has afforded us a little excitement in that line; to crown all we have just passed the 'Echunga', the first of our division (that is the regt.); she left Plymouth 10 days before us, and the 'Marianne' whom we passed the day before yesterday, left 6 days before; we were only a day behind them at Malta, and should have caught them before, had it not been for light winds, calms, and then a heavy gale right in our teeth. The light winds prevailed for three days after leaving Malta, when the wind changed to dead ahead, and gradually freshened to a very heavy gale; it blew in squalls for two days and nights, and we did not make the least progress; fortunately, as we had no sail at all on, nothing was carried away, which was more than we expected, as in spite of her being such a fine vessel, she is badly rigged; some of her spars too heavy. I was just as ill during the gale as at first, and am informed that it would be the same whenever it was blowing hard. Mrs. Duberly and the Quartermaster[8] have been fellow sufferers of mine; these last few days of fine weather have set us up again; had we had the same winds since Malta we had before, we should have been in Gallipoli 4 days ago, but have not had a really good breeze since leaving. A few hot days but nothing really oppressive; at sea whenever there is a breeze, it is always cool. The day at Malta was really hot; I thought I had never felt anything like it, and the glare was frightful. We were sent off in such a hurry, that

---

7   Most likely Phillips's younger brother John Henry, born in 1847.
8   Henry Fletcher Lane (1812–59) served in the ranks before promotion to Quartermaster on 17 March 1854.

an hour on shore was all I could smuggle. What I did see, was greatly pleased with and should much like to have quartered there for a month or so. The last few days have been passing all along the shores of Greece and up the archipelago; of an evening the shores look beautiful, all we have passed as yet being very mountainous; the sunset is generally very fine. I have greatly regretted being carried past these classic shores without an opportunity of visiting them; it seems almost sacrilege. We are now just about opposite the famed site of Troy, and for ought we know, it might be a thousand miles off; it seems a pity to be so near what many would give their ears to see, and yet pass it. I believe though, I am the only one who regrets it. I, and the others are very matter of fact passengers. The horses have done very well since Malta. Up till then we had lost six. The 'Echunga' lost three; they told us this morning. I believe the Marianne none; this will be a great crow for the Major.[9] They say the two vessels with part of the 17th Lancers lost fourteen between them. Mrs. Duberly's horse died the morning we reached Malta; it was a great blow to her. I was very glad you did not come to see us off; your kind letter was very acceptable; believe me, my dear mother, I shall take every opportunity of letting you know how we progress; you must, however, be satisfied with one letter in the family at once, at least sometimes, as I may not have the chance of writing much. I wrote to Erin at Malta, and will, if I can manage it after landing, but you must let him know. Be sure and remember me very kindly at 'Burntwood'; on arrival I may probably learn whether my chance of farming 'Daylesford'[10] is quite put out or not; as we arrived at Malta before the mail, have heard nothing since leaving; possibly something must have happened somewhere by this time; shall just leave room for any news of destination etc.

At anchor off Constantinople. Friday May 21st. Since writing the above, we have had no opportunity of forwarding it so resume. We were then about ten miles off the Dardanelles, with a fine breeze, which deserted us at the entrance, and the current, running three knots an hour, meeting us there, we drifted right away to the island of Lemnos (you can see it on the map) where we found ourselves at daybreak. About

---

9 Rodolf de Salis (1811–80), son of Jerome Fane, Count de Salis. Cornet 17 December 1830, served throughout the Crimean campaign, commanded the cavalry on the Kertch Expedition in 1855. Assumed command of the 8th Hussars in 1856 and led the regiment throughout the Indian Mutiny. Lieutenant General, October 1877. See Lummis and Wynn, *Honour the Light Brigade*, p. 72.

10 Burntwood Lodge and Burntwood Grange, Wandsworth Common, Surrey, the home of Henry Grisewood. Phillips's sister, Anne, had married Henry Grisewood in November 1850. Daylesford was land owned by the Grisewood family, formerly in Gloucestershire (now Worcestershire).

eleven o'clock a breeze again sprang up, and we started for another trial; it took us up to the entrance, where we again had the satisfaction of being drifted away for about a mile, where just as we were going it, up the breeze freshened again, and to our great delight, we got in, and made about eight miles up the straits; everyone in high spirits at being again on route, and admiring the scenery, when for the third time, it fell calm, and away we went with the current, not bringing up till after dark, and five miles outside the Castles at the entrance. These repeated failures, and having lost two days in vain efforts, sent us all to bed very out of temper; however 'fortune favours the brave', so the next morning getting again under way, the breeze this time held, and freshening as the day advanced, we rapidly passed all the points of failure, and raced up to Gallipoli at the rate, in some places, of 15 knots an hour, our splendid vessel passing everything. The scenery is very striking all the way up (a distance of about 35 to 40 miles), and I would not have lost it for anything; It quite repaid waiting for two days, and everyone congratulated themselves on not going through in the night. The Castles are strong, defending the Straits at so many points, that if well manned, no vessel could pass and escape getting sunk.

On arrival at Gallipoli about 4, not an English ensign to be seen, and the Navy agent[11] going on shore, we got orders to proceed straight to Scutari, which we did. The roads were full of French Men o' War steamers, and the tents of the French Army crowned the heights in all directions, making it look excessively pretty. Five regiments of ours are quartered there, The Royals, 50th, 28th, 44th, and another. We did not reach Constantinople until last night (Saturday), as the wind dying away after leaving Gallipoli, it took us all day to get across the Sea of Marmora. In case you might be ignorant of it, Scutari is only about a mile from Constantinople, but across the Bosphorus. We are at anchor between the two, and are to disembark tomorrow. The 'Echunga' and 'Marianne' both came up with us, while becalmed off the Dardanelles, and getting more favourable starts of wind, the 'Echunga' arrived here yesterday morning, and they are now disembarked, and, I believe, in barracks. I was sent ashore this morning too, with Macnaghten[12] from the 'Marianne', to report our arrival; we fell in with one of the 17th, who also arrived last night, and we landed together at Scutari, and ferreted out our way

---

11 Mr Coull. See Duberly, *Journal*, p. 16.

12 Lieutenant Francis Edmund Macnaghten (1828–1911), served throughout the Crimean campaign and the Indian Mutiny. Commanded the 8th Hussars in 1865. See Lummis and Wynn, *Honour the Light Brigade*, p. 75.

to Lord Lucan, reported ourselves, and heard the news; nothing seems to be known here, and until Lord De Ros went to Varna, we had no communication with the Turkish army at all; he has come back, I believe, and Lord Raglan has now gone to meet Omar Pasha and the Admirals. The Fleet is said to be blockading Sebastopol, but nothing fresh seems to have occurred on either side since Odessa. All the Infantry are pretty near together at Scutari, the greater part in barracks, and some in tents; the Cavalry are to be some five miles further up the Bosphorus, and in barracks; Lord Lucan told us we should not like them much, as they are dirty enough; he is living at present in a marquee outside the infantry barracks. After hearing all we could, Macnaghten and I started to come back; we were greatly amused coming to the landing place, although but a short distance; crowds of old Turks sitting outside the cafes, calmly smoking, while a conglomeration of all sorts of uniforms were passing up and down the hill. We fell in with a boy who sold us a small Turkish and English vocabulary for a shilling, and both bought one. Having sent our boat back to the ships, we had an immediate opportunity of testing our proficiency in using them, so out came our books, and shouts of Barka and something else I forgot, at last brought one to us; after a lot of vociferation on both sides, he agreed to take us off for a shilling in Turkish money, and we started. In the middle of our bargain, I could not help stopping to laugh at Digby; when he had exhausted his string of Turkish words or could not find any applicable to the moment, roared out to the fellow in English as if he were deaf, to my immense amusement; on getting into the boat and pushing off, we were as near over half a dozen times as possible; the boats are so narrow and crank. We plied the old Turk with words strung together all the way back, not above one in half a dozen of which he could understand; however, at last, we reached our vessel and paid him, much to the amusement of all on board, who envied us our first visit to the City of the Turks. You will see this letter has been opened, for on reaching Gallipoli, there was a chance of sending letters on shore, but the muff of a Navy Agent went without them, and also never called at the Post Office, so that we received no letters, papers or news since leaving England; we were hurried off so from Gallipoli, that no time was afforded us of sending again. We are now going to send down and have them forwarded from here. I do not know about the mails, but when you write, direct to 'the 8th Hussars, British Army,' wherever the place may be we are at, as the French may have an 8th Hussars here also, I believe they are coming. Passed lots of French transports the last part of the voyage, principally loaded with cavalry; 40 horses in a small brig, we

could put in a cuddy; all of them are very small. Everybody says you hear and see a great deal more in England than here; so that any conjectures as to what is likely to happen would be ridiculous, especially as I have not seen a paper since leaving; you had better send this to Erin, in case I should not have time to write to him before the mail leaves. We are only 24 days out altogether, out of which, one detained in Malta and two off the Dardanelles, making 21 sailing, at least a weeks calm out of that; we never had anything higher than top gallant sails set after carrying away our masts in the Bay, until two days before reaching the Dardanelles. I think I have now almost taken the worth out of the paper, so just having a small space in case of anything between this and the mail leaving, shall say goodbye. I forgot to say my first experience of climate is a rainy, blowy day, the coldest we have had yet; got wet through coming back this morning. Have heard this evening that the mail (French via Marseilles) leaves tomorrow, so I really must close, with all my love to everyone
[PS] Tell the Gr. his piece of carpet has been of great service to me;[13] I should never have thought of it myself. I hope to hear from some of you soon. The letters will, no doubt, be forwarded from Malta or Gallipoli or wherever they are. We are all growing tremendous beards, and look as dirty as possible; goodbye. E.P.

170

Phillips to his father

25 May 1854 Barracks near Scutari.
We disembarked here the day before yesterday, and embark again for Varna today; this looks like war. I believe seven regiments of infantry, composing of the Light Division, leave with us, a troop of Horse Artillery, and our squadron. The 17th who have been here longer than we have, are not yet under orders. The whole of the division will not be ready until tomorrow night, and we are to start either then, or on Saturday. We shall be towed all the way. Pack horses are, I believe, to be provided for the officers, who have not had time to obtain them, and will be carried on deck. It will not take more than a day and a half towing to carry us to about thirty miles beyond Varna. We are delighted to get away from this horrible place; it is indeed a whited sepulchre. The barracks we are in

---

13   Likely to be his sister's husband Henry Grisewood, hence 'Gr.'

have just been left by Turkish Cavalry, and are filthy beyond description; fleas, &c, swarm in great numbers, and I am pretty well tormented as you may imagine, although only two nights here. Nothing can be more beautiful than the views of Constantinople from the Bosphorus, but do not try it any nearer. As long as I was on board, I thought it delightful, but directly you approach the place, the illusion vanishes. Nothing could have been more picturesque than the scene at our disembarkation. A body of Bashi Bazouks,[14] just arrived from the interior of Asia Minor, were being ferried over to Constantinople on their way to the Danube, and every possible Asiatic dress was there. Some of them enormous negroes, others ferocious looking Arabs, all armed with long guns and mounted on very small horses. They look much under horsed, but, I believe, as far as work goes, would kill us. Our horses all disembarked without accident, and looked uncommonly well; I only hope they will get over the next stage as well. They have curtailed our tents a good deal; all the officers excepting Field Officers are doubled up. Our pelisses and stable jackets to be left behind, the valises to be packed in a new way, taking as few things as possible. The men to manage with the horse blankets, and everything showing that we are to be a light division; no field batteries to go with us. I received Annie's letter the day before yesterday (many thanks for it; had no idea of leaving so soon or would have answered it) and saw a paper in Pera of 3rd May, but that is all; you have heard of the 'Tiger's' misfortune of course, before this time.[15] When you write give me always the latest events, and probability of Austria and Prussia joining us, or not, as nothing whatever can be heard here. This is being written in a great hurry, as the Artillery are embarking, and we go next; only received the order at 6 this morning. The mail goes this afternoon, and I am not sure I can send this, as we are three miles up the Bosphorus (on the banks the vessels come alongside), so the chance of paying it is but small; I hope it does not come very hard on you, but cannot help it. It is tremendously hot here already; we have white covers for our caps[16] and busbys thank goodness. Something must have occurred to send us off at such short notice, and not giving the horses time to recover themselves, but any place is better than this hole of a barrack. Could write for a week

---

14 See p. 121, note 5.

15 HMS *Tiger*, a wooden-hulled paddle sloop refitted as a frigate ran aground while patrolling off Odessa in a fog in March 1854. When the fog lifted, the ship was bombarded by coastal batteries, set on fire, and captured. One of its guns is still displayed in Odessa.

16 White linen button-on covers fastening at the side, much in evidence at Varna because of the heat. See John and Boris Mollo, *Into the Valley of Death: The Cavalry Division at Balaclava 1854* (London: Windrow and Greene, 1991), p. 116.

as to what I have seen here, but have not the time, so with begging you to let me know how things go as often as possible, (there are mails every few days, one way or another, and a letter is invaluable), must conclude. I trust the intended visit to Paris has come off, and that mother is better for it. My kindest love to you both, not forgetting all at home and at Wandsworth. God bless you my dear father, and believe me.

Let Erin hear of this.

Sunday 28th May.

I was too late for the mail, to embark, and could not get down in time; the Artillery took so long that we could not embark till Friday, and then instead of sailing immediately, heard it was put off for a day or two, why I do not know, but believe in consequence of the difficulty of procuring provisions at Varna; however, we are now ordered off tomorrow. Lord Lucan says that on arrival, we are to march for three days before encamping, if so it will come very hard on the horses, as they were only on shore three days. Reports are rife as to &c.

It is no use sending newspapers; there is a rumour afloat that they are stopped; however, no one, not even those longest here have received a newspaper since their arrival; the best way will be for any important bit to be cut out of the paper and enclosed in the letter you may be sending. The best way to see and enjoy Constantinople is decidedly to live on board ship, and go ashore every day; you then escape living in a constant stench, and keep out the fleas &c., Whatever they may say the Turks certainly are a very dirty people, and not worthy of such a beautiful situation for a city as this. Constantinople from the Bosphorus is very beautiful, but when you approach it, the beauty vanishes. They have a very light boat here, a caique, which they send along at a great pace in their own style; they are beautiful rowers, and nothing is more delightful gliding along laying at the bottom of a caique. I have been up the valley of the Suret Waters today, the resort of the elite of Constantinople on a Sunday and Friday. Today is the great Armenian and Greek day, crowds of them were there; plenty of Turkish women, with their dreadful 'yashmaks' also; they are horrible things certainly, and enough to spoil any woman, but what you can see of the Turkish women, they all look pasty sort of countenances. On leaving our room in barracks, it was taken up by Lord Dupplin (you remember him I dare say, he is on Lord Cardigan's staff); he was rather disgusted with the dirt, &c., but tried to make the best of it. I hear that 15 baggage horses are to be taken up to Varna, on board one of the steamers; I hope to get a chance of one. I fancy you will have a better chance of receiving letters than I shall as yet; Annie's is the only one received, and many of our fellows have not received any since leaving; there is no better direction than 'British Army, Turkey' or something of that sort. Very contradictory orders have been issued lately; we are now to take our stable jackets and pelisses, the men also to take their blankets; two days ago they were all to be left behind. As we leave early in the morning, I must close this again tonight. Write as often as you can on the chance of one reaching me.

171

Phillips to his father

4 June 1854 Sunday Evening Constantinople
You will, no doubt, be surprised to see my letter dated from this place still, but the truth is, that I have just returned from Varna. We left this, as was intended, last Monday, in tow of the 'Megera', but from a variety of mishaps, too numerous to mention, did not get clear of the Bosphorus till the Wednesday.[17] We arrived at Varna the next morning (Thursday), and disembarked in the afternoon, not reaching our encamping ground, two miles from the shore, till after dark. We found no such thing as a pack saddle was to be had at Varna, and as almost all have got ponies, but no saddles, we were in a fix. Our money could only be changed at a great sacrifice, and very often not at all; notes no good whatever. Under these circumstances, the Major determined to send someone down here to buy saddles, and change money if possible, and as Duberly has his wife with him, he has sent me. I was only asked at one o'clock yesterday if I would go, and was down at three, looking for a ship. The 'Victoria'[18] was leaving at seven in the evening, and they gave me a passage, so here I am. Should I be fortunate enough to fulfil my mission, how I am to get from Varna to join the division again, I do not know. They expect to march tomorrow morning on their road to a place called Devna, about half way between Schumla and Varna, and when another division of ours arrives, or a French one or two, it is reported that we are to raise the siege of Silistria. Omar Pasha has sent several despatches lately to Sir George Brown (in

17 *Megera*, a Royal Navy iron screw troopship steamer, carrying the 7th Fusiliers, was to tow the *Shooting Star* to Varna. The latter attempted to weigh anchor on Monday 29 May but the cable broke, injuring two Hussars. They eventually cleared the Bosphorus on 31 May, arriving at Varna on 1 June in the afternoon. See Duberly, *Journal*, pp. 24–5.

18 *Victoria*, Transport no. 72, an iron steamship, 1,130 tons, screw driven and chartered from Robert Marshall. See HCPP 1854–55 (283), p. 20.

command of the Light Division) saying that the Russians have again attacked Silistria, and have been repulsed with great loss, but the place much wanted relieving. I shall have to make the best shift to catch them that I can with a bullock cart. The whole of the Army will shortly remove to Varna. The 17th [Lancers] had arrived there before I left yesterday, but not disembarked. The French are also pouring in great numbers. The heat is something dreadful in the tents of a day, and the dews at night wet them through, but no harm done as yet. I am sorry to say Fairy has been and still is very unwell. We were obliged to bleed her here last Monday on board ship and although better, she is still very weak and cannot be ridden for some time yet. I have bought two ponies, one very strong one, if he will only let the baggage be placed on him, the other one of them to ride and lead the mare. As I do not fancy we shall go far for a week or ten days, trust she will be sufficiently recovered by that time to march. Devna is only 16 miles. Lots of very large black ants at the camp, but as yet mosquitoes have not, thank goodness, made an appearance. We are worried quite enough without them. Nothing has been heard as yet of the 'Medora'[19] or 'Wilson Kennedy', unless we passed them last night on our way here, which is not improbable, as several steamers went up yesterday towing. Do not run away in England with the idea that everything as to the Commissariat &c. is to be so well arranged and different to what it had been formerly, quite the contrary, everything is confusion, and I believe while we are haggling about the price, the French stepped in and took all the best supplies. The Turks believe that the Sultan has ordered ourselves and the French here, and take every opportunity of robbing you right and left, asking three times the value of everything. Oh that such a beautiful country should be in such hands! However, the post leaves tomorrow, and as I got here (the hotel, such as it is, Bellevue Pera) late, am very tired. Goodness knows what arrangements will be made for sending letters from the Army,[20] so when you will hear again I do not know. Love to you all; have only received Annie's letter as yet.

---

19 *Medora*: Transport no. 45, 642 tons, rejected as being too small for further use. See TNA, WO1/368, Raglan to Boxer, 29 June 1854.

20 The plan was for letters home to go through France, six times per month in closed mails. See TNA, WO1/385 Sir George Brown, Out-Letters, April 1854, no. 23; Peter Boyden, *Tommy Atkins's Letters: The History of the British Army Postal Service from 1795* (London: National Army Museum, 1990), pp. 8–11.

172

Phillips to his mother

Saturday 10th June Camp Devna

Ah, how sorry I am that a letter of mine should have gone without a message to you; it is not for want of thinking you every happiness I am sure; however accept this, a double portion of love, and in case through inadvertence, I might leave out any one, read the same to the whole family. We were all greatly delighted at receiving our first letters from England this afternoon. I may say, our first, as Annie's is almost the only one that has reached us all through the regiment. However, now for our proceedings. My last letter was dated last Monday, Constantinople, and could explain why I was there. Having executed my commissions, I left on board the 'Wilson Kennedy', on Tuesday morning; she and the 'Medira', having reached there the day before. We were towed to Varna by the 'City of London',[21] all on board very glad to see me and hear the news. The 'W.K.' is an old tub compared to ours, as indeed are all of them, but our ship, having been rigged and fitted in such a hurry, our cabins &c., were not quite so well fitted up as some of the others. Still, I would not have changed on any account. The W.K. lost four, and the 'Medira' one horse, making twelve troopers and two officers' horses in all. They disembarked the same day, and have remained at Varna since. We expect them, however, on Monday. Now for myself: having twelve large pack saddles and a carpet bag with one hundred pounds in silver, and which I dare not leave, with not a soul to help or look after things was a decided nuisance. After a deal of trouble I obtained an order on the Commissariat for a bullock cart, but so late in the afternoon, as to leave little hope of reaching the camp, distant 16 miles, that night. They had moved from Varna on the Monday previous. In spite of the order the lazy brutes of drivers had all disappeared in consequence of a thunder storm. So there I was stuck in the middle of a Turkish town (the dirt and filth of which must be seen to be appreciated) with a cargo of saddles, lots of money and the camp 16 miles off, to add to my misery, wet through. However 'it's a long lane that has no turning', and fortunately a young Commissariat Officer saw me in the street, and having heard a young Hussar Officer was wanting to get on, spoke to me, and offered, as he was going with some carts, half way, viz, – to the Infantry camp, to put my pack saddles on some of them, saying at the same time, he

---

21   *City of London*: Transport no. 66, 1,116 tons, 231 ft long, built for the Aberdeen Steam Navigation Company. See HCPP 1854–55 (283), pp. 13, 18–19.

would give me a shake down in his tent and a bit of dinner on arriving. As you may imagine, I jumped at the offer, and we started at 5 o'clock. After numerous mishaps and breaking of wheels &c. we arrived at the Infantry camp at 11, and delighted we were indeed at reaching it. The C.O. gave me some coffee, beef and bacon, and lent me a cloak to sleep in, and the next morning started me off here. I arrived about 2, and found Tomkinson[22] just starting on a reconnoitring party[23] about thirty miles off, to enquire in to the circumstances connected with the burning of a town called Basardchyk. He returned yesterday and reported its having been done two months ago, probably by Bashi Bazouks. We have lots to do here. In this camp as yet, there are only the 17th [Lancers], and ourselves. Cardigan is here and has pickets and patrols as if in front of the enemy. Indeed, it was reported that the Cossacks were within twenty miles the other evening. I was out on patrol this morning and precious cold it was, turning out at 3 in the morning. Went about four miles and returned by 6 o'clock. We expect the Head Quarters and the rest of the Regiment tomorrow. When we first disembarked the heat was dreadful. But since the thunder storm, it has been rather colder than otherwise, blowing and raining, more like Chobham, for which I am very thankful. It is a very good place for a camp, this, close by a stream. Indeed the whole country seems well adapted for fighting, as the country is all open with large plains stretching towards the Danube. This country is entirely inhabited by the Bulgarians, and with the exception of soldiers, not a Turk is to be seen. They are however, what I have seen of them, a lazy race indulging in as long smokes as the Turks, and nothing can be got through without it. On leaving Varna I sent one bullock trunk back to the ship, and now place my air bed on the ground, but sleep comfortable enough notwithstanding. Heneage[24] is my companion. He has an air bed also. Altogether I am disposed to think two in a tent is much more sociable than one. Forget if I told you that Fairy was very ill in my last. She is, thank goodness, getting round again, although not fit to be ridden for 10 days or so. I am the possessor of two ponies., one purchased, pack saddle and all, for five pounds, carried no end of baggage here. The other I obtained in a swop yesterday. When at Varna I had bought a grey pony for twenty five pounds off the Consul, and paid for him by bill of

---

22 Captain Edward Tomkinson (1825–70), son of Rev. H. Tomkinson of Reesheath, near Nantwich. See Lummis and Wynn, *Honour the Light Brigade*, p. 73.

23 Leaving on 7 June, Tomkinson, with Lieutenant Clutterbuck and 16 men, was ordered to make a reconnaissance near Basardchyk. Tomkinson returned bearing a bouquet of roses for Mrs Duberly when they returned on 12 June See Duberly, *Journal*, p. 34, and note 49 below.

24 Lieutenant Clement Walker Heneage (1831–1901) survived the Crimea and won the VC at Gwalior during the Indian Mutiny. See Murray, *History of VIII Hussars*, vol. 2, p. 455.

exchange. But he would not let a saddle come near him and was so much bother, besides having cut and lamed himself with a heel rope, that I was too glad to make an exchange yesterday for another one. I shall want to have twenty five pounds off Cox's to meet it. I wish the Gr. could ascertain how much money I have at Cox's, and would send him a cheque to draw it out, as it is no good to me, or anyone else there. Our rations here are nothing but a pound of beef and a pound and a half of bread, with some tea. I certainly have never tasted tough meat until I came here. It is awful, only killed in the morning, it will stand more boiling than anything I ever saw, and then won't come tender, your jaws really ache after it. The bread you might almost call black, so very dark a brown it is, and they seem to have a disagreeable habit of kneading it on the ground, it has rather more sand than is pleasant or nutritious. Everyone is excessively savage because Sir George Brown has stopped the beer coming any further than Varna,[25] and the consequence is, the division gets none of it. This is too bad, and the idea that people in England fancy we are enjoying every luxury, while we are not a bit better off than others, makes matters worse. You may tell Harman[26] from me that the English Commissariat has certainly not advanced with the age. When with the Commissary Officers the other night, I had the opportunity of hearing about it, and they said themselves it was badly managed. The conveyance of the country is so bad, the bullock carts so slow, and will not always work when you want them, but one would think Government ought not to have undertaken this war without some arrangement for carriage or organising some train. Everyone is writing home about this, and the beer, especially the Infantry, so you will no doubt see plenty of it in the papers. The beer is not left because of the difficulty of bringing it, but merely to please Sir George Brown, the Commissaries told me so. Reports are rife as to our moving, but not believed until another division arrives. Also whether Silistria is really invested or only partially, or whether the Russians have not re-crossed the Danube, but nothing really known. We managed to get some eggs here and geese, so do very well with the latter and our rations boiled or stewed, if it was not for that, should be badly off. Brandy is invaluable here, and the Gr's case most opportune. I have hardly drunk any of it as yet, and keep it for the troop. Some of the fellows shoot a good many doves and they make a capital stew, but no vegetables are to be got here. There is yet no regular post to and from this,

---

25 A deeply unpopular decision, especially in the fiercely hot weather. It was said to have been taken because of the lack of transport but believed to be because of the puritanical disposition of Sir George Brown and the poor record of the troops for drunkenness when in Constantinople.

26 Harman Grisewood (1821–1871), Henry Grisewood's older brother.

so cannot say when I may have a chance of sending this; shall keep it open; no chance of paying them here. Write some of you as often as possible, and there will be a chance of my receiving them. You must not wait for me always. This is my fifth letter since leaving England, counting the Malta one as one. Received a letter from Erin with yours, and he tells he has given you a list of the mails. I was excessively pleased to see yours dated from Paris at last, and hope you will return as intended in the Autumn. Let me know the last dates of mine whenever you write. An order has just come for me to proceed South of the Balkan, to purchase horses, to be ready at a moments notice.[27]

Love to all of you, in great haste.

173

Phillips to his father

20 June 1854. Tirnova, in Bulgaria, just North of the Balkan.

In my last letter (the last words), I told you of an order just received for holding myself in readiness to proceed South of the Balkan, to purchase horses. I was much astonished and not very agreeably so, as having just returned from Constantinople, did not imagine I should be called upon again so soon. However, it appeared that the Colonel had been applied to recommend an Officer to purchase horses for the use of the Army, and wanted me (why, I don't know; Head Quarters have been kept at Varna, until Saturday last, so that we at Devna, 16 miles off, knew nothing of it) on Friday last. I started at 7 to ride into Varna, to receive instructions from Sir George Brown. On reaching Varna, I first went to the Colonel and tried all I knew to get off, but the General, having ordered me in, it was too late, so went off to his quarters. The General then told me that he was going to send me to Tirnova, about 130 miles off, and North, instead of South, of the Balkan. He gave me an order on the Commissariat for five hundred pounds, which I cashed, and after consultation with two of the Engineers,

---

27   Mrs Duberly noted on Saturday 17 June, 'Mr Phillips left today for Tirnova, where he was sent to purchase 500 horses.' See Duberly, *Journal*, p. 35.

Major Dixon[28] and Captain Simmonds,[29] I obtained an interpreter, and started at 7 for Devna, where I should sleep in my own tent, and getting my baggage, start finally next morning. Reached the camp about 10, and started again at 8.30 in the morning. I was riding post (they have such things in Turkey) mounted on small ponies, and changing every four hours or so, at least for the first part of the journey. To give you an account of my train then: first comes a cavass, or sort of mounted policeman, dressed in Turkish costume and armed with a melee of weapons, stuck in the voluminous shawl which serves for his belt. Then a guide mounted and armed in the same way, leading a pack horse on which is placed a pair of saddle bags, a waterproof case containing my air bed, blankets &c., a waterproof tube and canteen, a bundle belonging to the interpreter, and a small saddle bag of his. Then came the interpreter mounted on one pony and my servant Brown[30] on another, and your humble servant on a third pony. I rode on my plain saddle, and was dressed in a frock coat (Regt.), forage cap with white cover, and over all, I had my sword, on the belts of which were placed a case with my Deane's revolver loaded, and the other side a pouch with ammunition, my telescope over my shoulder. I carried the money in the saddle bags, and being all gold was heavy enough for me the night before, although nothing for a horse.

So behold us starting for my evenings destination which was Shumla. Away we went, much faster than you would fancy such small ponies could go to keep it up, and after a hot days hard riding, reached Shumla about 6. On arriving there, after a little difficulty, found out Captain Fearons, one of the English Officers attached to Omar Pasha, who most kindly gave me a shake down on a divan, a dinner, and the next morning took me to Omar Pasha and presented me to ask for a letter to the Pasha of Tirnova, about buying horses. We found his excellency outside his courtyard, looking at some horses which were being ridden up and down by Kurds and other Asiatics, and what with the mixture of dresses &c., presented as strange a scene as could well be imagined. He was dressed quite plainly in a grey

28 Actually Major Collingwood Dickson, Royal Artillery. Born 20 November 1817; entered the Royal Artillery as a 2nd Lieutenant, 15 December 1835; served in Spain in the Carlist War, 1837–41. Served on Raglan's staff throughout the Crimean campaign and was awarded the VC for his actions on 17 October 1854 when he commanded the night siege train. Major General, 1866; Lieutenant General, 1876; General, 1877; GCB, 1884. See TNA, WO76/359–372.

29 Captain John Lintorn Arabin Simmons, Royal Engineers, was Queen's Commissioner on the staff of Omar Pasha from October 1853 until December 1857, and went on to become a Field Marshal in May 1890 at the end of a long and distinguished career.

30 887 Pvt. John Brown, born *c.* 1823 Ballycastle, near Antrim, Ireland, a servant prior to his enlistment on 13 March 1845. He was wounded in both hands during the charge of the Light Brigade and died of his wounds, 17 December 1854. See TNA, WO12/844; Lummis and Wynn, *Honour the Light Brigade*, p. 90.

frock coat, dark overalls &c., fez; no one would ever have imagined he was speaking to the man all Europe is talking of. He asked my opinion as to which horse he should buy, but I am not sure whether he took it or not. We then went into the garden and sat under a sort of temple where he receives all his visitors &c. Fearon then told him my business, when he said he would render every help in his power and wrote a letter to the Pasha of Tirnova, desiring him to assist me in every way. After that we sat a long time and tasted the little cups of Turkish coffee being handed round. It seemed all so strange and sudden, I could hardly realise my being actually there, quietly sitting with Omar Pasha. He is very fond of having a good chat with English and French Officers, so Fearon told me, as he doesn't seem to have much in common with the Pashas and others around him. There is no ceremony whatever to bore you, and there you can be as much at your ease as in England. We remained about two hours, and at last he let us go. I was already to leave by two in the afternoon, when I started again, but must now stop to give you an account of what I heard about Silistria.

The siege has now lasted some time and by all accounts has been a most gallant one. Captain Simmons, who gave me some directions at Varna about my journey, and had just returned from there, and Fearon had gone with him. The place is not thoroughly invested, but desperate attacks are continually being made on one side, and as constantly repulsed with great loss. The Russians have come within 50 yards of the walls and breached them with 32 pounders, then attacked and been beaten back. They say the Turks fight splendidly and only want leading. I am sorry to say the Officers are as bad as the soldiers are good. The whole credit of this unparalleled siege, is due to two English Officers, both in the Indian Company's service, who were travelling for pleasure about the country, and just as it commenced, entered the city, and then thought that having come there they ought not to leave it, and so remained. They have done everything. The Turks look up to them for directions, and indeed they intended to give up the place if they left. Their names (they deserve to be known everywhere) are Butler[31]

---

31   James Amar Butler (1827–54), fourth son of the Hon. Henry Edward Butler, uncle and heir presumptive to the Earl of Carrick. Butler was educated at Paris, Sandhurst and Freiburg. He was Ensign by purchase in the 90th Regiment, 13 October 1843, and served in the Cape Frontier campaigns, 1846–7. Lieutenant in the Ceylon Rifles, 9 January 1847 and helped quell an insurrection there. Promoted to Captain in August 1853 and travelled to England in early 1854. He joined his father in Rome and volunteered to help the Turkish forces resist Russian attacks on Silistria. He was hit by a spent ball on the forehead at Arab Tabia whilst making a reconnaissance of Russian positions on 12 June 1854 and died of wounds on 20 June. Omar Pasha described him as the 'Saviour of Silistria'. See Calthorpe, *Letters*, vol. 1, pp. 61–70; *Illustrated London News* (hereafter *ILN*), 29 June 1854, pp. 96–7.

and Nasmyth.[32] Butler has been wounded three times. Nasmyth was at Shumla, at Fearon's while I was there, having come down for two days for a few things for them. He left Shumla on his return to Silistria the same evening I was there. He is a very pleasant fellow indeed and told me all about the siege. Some of the stories of the Turkish Officers would astonish you. They hope to hold out some time longer (as yet the Russians have taken nothing), but wish earnestly for the advance of our Army. Unfortunately we cannot move without pack horses, and as I have come to get them (as well as others on the same service in different towns), you can form your own idea of when we are likely to move. Omar Pasha is not strong enough to raise the siege without help. They are told the Russians will meet us with 90,000 men this side of the Danube. If we are in time to raise the siege and be at the Russians, it will be at least a campaign saved, and here we are stuck because proper Commissariat arrangements were not made beforehand. All these troops of horses should have been organised before we set foot in Bulgaria. They had plenty of time. This will give Harman an idea of the Commissariat.

To resume my journey: on starting from Shumla, we ascended a tremendous hill, and then descending, traversed a series of beautiful wooden ravines, and after six hours ride, reached a place called Jimap Bazer about eight. I had intended pushing on to the next place, but a thunder storm coming on decided me to stop. The Turkish Officer sent a soldier on to find a house, or rather a room in one of the smallest, closest rooms possible, just like an oven. Like a fool I made down my blanket in it, just taking off my overalls, but soon found that I was almost eaten up; struck a light, found my blanket covered with fleas, and the walls, painted white, nicely spotted over with the finest specimens of the larger tribe I ever saw, they were really in dozens. After trying to make up my mind to it a little longer, I was obliged to give in, so took my blanket and laid it in the open gallery all the houses have (like the Swiss cottages), with a saddle for a pillow. However, got up at 3.30, after driving these lazy Turks

---

32 Charles Nasmyth (1825–61) entered service in the Honourable East India Company in 1843 and the HEIC Artillery in 1845. Served in Bombay until 1853 when the work and climate began to tell on his health. He was ordered to return home to recover his constitution. Proceeding to the Mediterranean for his health he joined Omar Pasha's forces at Schumla and also sent regular reports from the field for *The Times*. He sent valuable intelligence to Lord Stratford De Redcliffe from Dobrudscha and joined the Turkish forces in Silistria in May 1854. Here, with Butler, he assisted the Turks in a clever defence against Russian assaults. Following the Russian retreat from Silistria, Nasmyth transferred to the British Army and was present at the Alma and Inkerman. His health though was in decline and he was invalided home. He served in Ireland on the staff and later in Australia but declining health still dogged him and he was invalided home in 1859 from Sydney. He retired from the army on his way home in Pau, in the south of France, and died there on 2 June 1861. See *ILN*, 11 July 1861, p. 36.

about, managed to start finally at 4.30. After an hours ride, came on a ridge of mountains running right across our road. You soon discovered a narrow valley running right through them, and for another hour our road lay in the bed of a mountain stream, with the most beautifully wooded mountains rising almost perpendicularly on both sides. If in Scotland, how it would be run after to be sure. I never saw anything more striking. Reached Oman Bazar about 8 to breakfast, and stopped till 11.30. The next stage was eight hours and uncommonly good ones they were. A very bad but very pretty road, continually crossing some of the lower slopes of the Balkan; awfully hot, but with a large fold of white linen placed like a turban round my forage cap, managed to keep it off pretty well. Reached our destination for the night about 7.30. and stopped at the post house. The owner of the house killed a lamb for our supper and cooked it over the ashes of a wood fire; such a picturesque scene. I was lying down in the raised verandah (about two feet from the ground), while the Turks were squatted on their mats outside, smoking and enjoying their coffee. The Greeks (owners of the house) seated in a group on my right, watching my proceedings with great interest. Presently one of the Turks would spread his carpet facing to Mecca, and begin praying. That consists of a great number of prostrations &c. and lasted about ten minutes. They all seem very devout while praying.

I did not attempt sleeping in a room again, so spread my blanket at once on the verandah and after twelve hours ride slept soundly enough as you may imagine.

Woke at 4 and managed to start at 5; only six hours more to Tirnova, which I reached at about 10. Went to Caravanseray and sent out for some breakfast; directly afterwards sent my interpreter to the Pasha, saying that there was an Officer from Omar Pasha and wishing to know when we could see him. He came back in about a quarter of an hour with a horse and an Officer of the Pasha's to conduct me to him. So behold me parading through the streets of a Turkish town on a Pasha's horse with fine strappings, an Officer and Zaftie[33] going before me, and a groom by my side. I was received at the entrance to the Pasha's house by several Officers (the guard presenting arms), and the Pasha's interpreter. I was ushered with great ceremony into a large room, in one corner of which sat the Pasha on a divan. He immediately came forward to meet me and took my hand. After conducting me to a seat by his side, he read Omar Pasha's letter and began the conversation. Of course my own interpreter

---

33   Zaptie, a type of Ottoman policeman.

accompanied me, so it all went on through him. The old fellow was most polite and promised to do everything for me, sending letters to the different places around, ordering the horses to be brought in. After a short time a tray of sweetmeats was brought in, of which I partook and followed it with a glass of water, then came the long pipe. It was much the longest I have seen in Turkey, over six feet, at which I puffed away for about five minutes and sipped my cup of coffee. How you would all have laughed to see me calmly smoking a long pipe in company with an old Pasha, sitting crossed legged on his divan, and surrounded by heaps of servants. He sent his Officers out to find a house for me, and promised to send my breakfast, dinner and supper every day as long as I stayed. Of course I did not like to refuse. After taking leave I was conducted with the same ceremony to the house he had procured for me, belonging to a Greek, and certainly very clean and nice it looked, quite refreshing after the flea begotten holes I have seen lately. Two rooms and a kitchen are to be for my use and that of my suite. The one I am in is ornamented with pictures of Greek and Bulgarian religion, with a small lamp suspended in front of them. A sort of sofa with cushions and pillows forming the divan, extends round three sides of the room. Outside is a large gallery, open and extending round the sort of courtyard belonging to the house, a delightful place in hot weather. I had not been in the house ten minutes before sweetmeats were again brought to me, followed up by coffee. About 7.30 my supper appeared, sent from the Pasha's. It consisted of a dish of kebabs, a dish of meat in small balls rolled in vine leaves, some beans stewed in a pod and a basin of curds.

The Pasha has ordered a Cavass, or sort of orderly to remain in my house, and anything I want he fetches immediately. So here I am living in grand style, but nothing can compensate for the loss of society. What a dreadful thing it is to have no one to speak to. How soon one gets hipped. Do all I can, it is impossible to help being low, with not a soul (except my interpreter and servant) that can speak either English or French nearer than Schumla, two days journey. As to illness, that is not to be thought of, for no help could be had here. I have fortunately brought some quinine pills with me and am now taking some. The heat has been so great lately as to make me quite languid. I have now been here two days and have bought 22 horses, averaging three to four pounds each. It is the most dreadful thing possible bargaining for these horses. The Turks invariably ask twice as much as they mean to take, and beating them down is most annoying. They wrangle away at a dreadful rate, and keep you an hour, where in England it would all be settled in five minutes. What with the purchasing, engaging grooms, buying forage, taking them to the Pasha's stables, paying for the horses (the calculation is peculiarly annoying, in Piastres, as here twelve and a quarter go to the shilling),[34] and keeping accounts, it is more than one person can do well; but like everything else with us, it is left to the last, and then done in a hurry. They ought to have sent an escort with me, instead of sending me riding about the country with five hundred pounds in gold in my saddle bags, and when I have bought fifty or sixty horses, they are to be sent down to Varna directly in charge of these wretched Turks, not a soul else to look after them. Whether they will ever get there or not goodness only knows, but such are my orders. I have brought away with me by chance two old papers sent by you, the 'Illustrated' of April 29th[35] and 'Observer' of May 21st, (they only arrived the day before I left camp). I cannot tell you what a blessing they have been as yet. Unfortunately I have spelt them both quite through, and now have nothing to look at in my leisure hours (not many by the bye). You must excuse all the painting &c., you may find in this scrawl, for unfortunately the day after arriving here, my ink failed me, and the stuff I have bought here would not mark for a long time. My candles also give such wretched glimmer (my only time of writing being in the evening) that I see I have wandered all over the paper. I made a dreadful mistake too last night for, as you may perceive, I wrote over the back of the paper, the very sheet the direction should be on, and am obliged in consequence to send it in a half sheet as an envelope.

My great luxury here is my India-rubber tub. What I should do without it, I do not know. I use it twice a day and really, could you see me going into it, you would think I had the Scarlet Fever or something of that sort. I am most dreadfully bitten, much worse than ever the Harvest Fly served me in Dorset. Tell Sally that unfortunately I have no Harts Horn in revenge. I truly wish for a bottle long promised but never sent. Give my love to her. I wear nothing but flannel shirts now. They are much the best. Through the whole camp you will hardly see a linen shirt, at least among the Officers, and the variety of patterns is quite amusing. Bargaining in this country is dreadful work certainly, such noises, vociferation and confusion, it is hardly possible to know what you are about. I have just returned from a visit to a large fair held every Friday and Saturday, about an hour from this. It begins, the horses part, at sunrise on Saturday morning. I bought 15 horses before breakfast, altogether brought back 29,

---

34   Making one piastre about equal to one penny.
35   Presumably *The Illustrated London News*.

and these with what I have bought here will comprise my first batch to send to Varna, 60 in number. When at this village I was put up at the house of a Bulgarian gentleman, such I learned was his station in life, although from his appearance you would never have guessed it. However, he fed me very well and behaved very hospitably. One advantage of this trip is that I shall have greater advantages of seeing the people and their mode of life, than perhaps any of those who are always in camp.

It certainly is a wild country. To give you an idea of it: my interpreter, whose habits are everything but in accordance with English or French ideas, and whose only notion of civilised life is Constantinople, exclaims 'Oh what people are these!' Fancy my pitching into the same dish with a Bulgarian and two interpreters, who all three dispense with the use of knives or plates, and tearing off pieces from the meat, convey it at once to its receptacle, or a pillow [pilau?] (by the bye a very good thing) into which all of us plunge with broad wooden spoons, and yet this Bulgarian is what they call rich, and it would be insulting him to offer him anything in return for keeping four of us for a night.

This town, Tirnova, is the most curiously situated one I ever saw or heard of. In a very mountainous country, it is built on sort of peninsulas, formed by a river winding about in the valley, so that the town is divided in streets, each of which, as it were, fits into an opening opposite, forming a whole. Were it in a civilised country, all the world would rush to see it, the scenery about is so peculiarly bold and striking.

The Pasha showed me a Journal de Constantinople the other day, just arrived with news from London (teleg. Via Marseilles) that Austria was going to march with the Western powers. I wonder if it is true or not. They have said in the papers so often that she would join us, that when I left no one would believe it. Shall try to send this with letters to Major Dixon [Dickson] by the Turkish Officer, who takes the horses down tomorrow, so I am not sure whether you will ever get it. Send it to Erin when you have finished. Tell him with every kind remembrance that I find it impossible to write the same account twice, so hope he will consider it a letter. I had more than half finished one at Devna, but this has knocked it on the head. The date is up to the 24th June. God bless you all my dear Father, and with kindest love to Mother and all the family at Wandsworth and elsewhere.

174

Phillips to his mother

June 27th 1854 Tirnova

This will be more a continuation of my last letter than anything else. How astonished you all would be to see me in a sort of procession visiting the villages. First come cavasses of the Pasha's, then I appear mounted on one of his horses covered with a splendid shabraque, but a most uncomfortable saddle, then two interpreters, my own and the Pasha's, followed by several men guides leading baggage horses, among them Brown, looking most wretched in a Turkish saddle.

10th July. I have had so much to do lately that I have not had much inclination for writing. You will see by the date that some time has elapsed since the first paragraph was written. I am still here buying away, and have now obtained 460 horses in the three weeks. 360 have already left for Varna. Last Sunday, Lieutenant Maynard[36] of the 88th arrived here, sent to my assistance by Lord Raglan. He brought me up one thousand pounds, which, with another five hundred left me by an Artillery Officer who passed here on his road further up, makes two thousand pounds, and it is almost all spent. I sent off Maynard this morning to Schumla for six hundred pounds more to clear us out of this.

On Saturday evening last, the Pasha invited us to dine with him at a country seat belonging to his Lieutenant, a short distance from this. So we started about 5 o'clock with a French gentleman who happened to be here. It was not more than half an hours ride, but the road leads through a gorge by which the river, running by the town, finds its way from the Balkan, and is about as striking a bit as could be seen anywhere. The house we went to is situated on the banks of the river and surrounded by mountains, a really beautiful place (not the house, which is most rickety). We sat for some time (after the arrival of the Pasha) in the garden, where sofas, chairs and tables were laid out, smoking long pipes, and eating the most curious melee previous to a dinner possible. Fruit, young cucumbers eaten with the skins on, some sort of pepper in pods, followed by cherries, and lastly a sort of sweetmeat. They drank, at least the Turks, copiously of small glasses of, as they called it, 'eau de vie', the Raki of the

---

36 Edmund Maynard, son of John Charles Maynard of Harlsey Hall. The brother-in-law of the photographer Roger Fenton, Edmund Maynard was an officer in the 88th Regiment, the Connaught Rangers, and was severely wounded in the arm on 7 June 1855 in the attack on the Quarries. He survived and retired by sale in 1861/62 and died on 9 June 1896 in San Jose, California. See Gernsheim and Gernsheim, *Roger Fenton*, pp. 91–7.

country,[37] washed down by draughts of cold water. We declined the Raki and took the water. About 8, dinner was served in the garden, to which nine of us sat down. A Turkish dinner consists of a number of dishes served one at a time in no particular order, as far as I can see. As to the contents &c., ours consisted of about 20 dishes, every one of which we all partook. There was rice, fowls, meat, plenty of vegetables, beans, French beans, and peas, all cooked in the pod, pumpkins, artichokes, &c., and other dishes the contents of which I did not know, and as dessert, plenty of cherries, and wine, of which the Pasha partook as freely as anyone else. The whole of dinner, Bulgarian musicians, the best in Tirnova, played away, making to my ears a dreadful noise, but which occasionally seemed to rouse an enthusiasm in their auditors. The dinner lasted at least an hour and a half, when we adjoined to our sofas on the banks of the river, pipes and coffee the order of the day or rather night. It had been awfully hot all day and was most delicious sitting there in the moonlight by the river. After dinner, the old Pasha got very sociable. And talked away through his interpreter and some Turkish Officers, who speak French to myself and the Frenchman at a great rate. By the bye you would be amused to hear me since my arrival here, for the first time in my life, I try to speak French, but having forgotten all my grammar, it is horrible. However, as long as there is no Englishman who can speak it here, I do not care. Maynard is worse than I am, and cannot speak a word. I talk away to the Pasha's interpreter half the day in some way or another. To return to the Pasha, he would have me sit next to him on the sofa, and we being four on it, we were rather close. Once he put his arm round my neck and I thought that in his enthusiasm for the English, he was going to embrace me. Fortunately for me he did not, or I must have kicked him. I must tell you that here I am always called 'Monsieur le Colonel' not that I ever gave myself out as such, but of course, they thought that no one under a Colonel could be trusted with so much money up here to buy horses. The Colonel in command of a Turkish Regiment of Infantry here is most polite. He asked me to a review the other day, at which the Pasha was present, and when I meet him coming from drill at the head of his Regiment, about three times a week, he always makes them carry arms to me as they pass. Just fancy, a whole Regiment saluting a Subaltern! I see the 'Journal de Constantinople', a French paper, every week. The Pasha lends it to me, so that I know nothing very extraordinary has occurred. I have also the 'Times' occasionally up to 9th June, sent by Simmons the

---

37   Possibly an error in the original transcription as it would make more sense as 'small glasses of, as they called it, "Raki", the eau de vie of the country'.

Engineer attached to Omar Pasha. The last journal, in which is an article copied from a Paris paper, the 'Constitutional', seems to explain what I previously was much surprised at, viz, – the retreat of the Russians. According to that article, the Emperor is going to stand out against the whole of the four powers, indeed against Europe. I should think his subjects would surely never stand that. However, it is evidently not likely to be over so soon as I thought when I first heard of the retreat. How surprised everyone in England must have been at the non marching of the French Army towards Silistria[38] when they landed at Varna, not knowing of the impediments of moving without any conveyances. However, now the great necessity is removed for the moment, I am ordered to procure as many Arabas as possible, besides horses, and hope to send off 100 to Shumla tomorrow. As yet my horses have averaged 411 Piastres each, about 120 Piastres to one pound, just three pounds, eight shillings and six pence, and are supposed to carry about 200 lbs weight each. The pack saddles are 42 Piastres each, just seven shillings. A pony complete for four pounds is not dear certainly, and they are hardy little brutes. I am organising brigades of 300 each, one groom to three horses, one Zaftie, a sort of non-commissioned officer, to every ten grooms or thirty horses, and one Yuz-Bashi or sort of Captain to every three hundred horses – one hundred grooms and ten Zafties. It is hard work, what with buying horses, finding grooms, Zafties, and getting pack-saddles, barley &c., and now they give me Arabas to look after. Unless Maynard brings more money than the six hundred pounds, and fresh orders for more Arabas or horses, I hope to leave this by the end of next week. I did not like it at first, it was so dull by oneself. I never felt what it was to be alone before, but have now, especially since Maynard arrived, become more used to it, indeed have every reason to be thankful that I am in a house instead of a tent this dreadfully hot weather, or fear I should have been laid up before this. I have not received any letters since leaving the camp, but have written to ask Major Dickson if anyone should be coming by there now to Schumla, not unlikely, to let them ask for letters for me. I hope you will never wait for a letter before writing, as so many things besides my not writing might occur to delay the arrival of mine. Your last letters came from Paris, but, no doubt, there are others waiting for me at camp. I was greatly pleased to hear of your trip. Hope Trollope has found you

---

38   Like the British Army, the French were also inhibited by the difficulties of acquiring transport. Their difficulties were exacerbated, according to Russell, because they did not pay the natives in cash. Instead they tried to give the vendors 'orders on their military chest', which turned out not to be understood and, therefore, not trusted. See Russell, *British Expedition to the Crimea*, p. 59.

a place somewhere by this time. Be sure and give my kindest love to all at home and at Wandsworth. How are all the young ones and my Godson Harry?[39] The writing case you sent me has been the most useful thing, with all this writing and accounts, possible, and I thank the Gr. for it every day. My pistol, tell Erin, I always keep loaded, of course, with so much money about me. I fired it the other day after being loaded for a month and having come all the way here, the balls were not in the least shaken, and not even a cap missed. I was much pleased at this. It is meant as a general one. Pistols are necessary in this part of the world. There are so many robbers, or as they call them, brigands. The other day the head of a notorious one was exhibited in the public street. It was dreadfully gashed and was to be sent to another town some distance off. They say he had killed 100 persons during his career, and four at his death. However robbers do not generally like to attack people with government zafties with them, although it is well to be prepared.

Tuesday 11th July. I have heard a rumour of an English Officer being attacked by robbers, and wounded, between this and Schumla, but do not know the truth of it. Must go to the Pasha to ask. He is reported to have had plenty of money with him. My dress here would amuse you could you but see it and astonish the Generals if they only knew it. On a holiday, I have nothing regimental on, but my spurs. I certainly wear my forage cap, having nothing else, but it is so smothered up, no one would recognise it. It has a white cover with a large peak in front and a curtain behind. That is allowed in camp, but in addition, I have covered it in folds of white linen like a turban. It is great protection to the head. Turbans are not worn on the top of the head, but bound round in a line with the forehead. That is the part to protect. So much for my head. I wear a flannel shirt (the most comfortable thing in a hot climate, possible), and a brown holland kind of dressing gown, very loose. I had it made on my arrival here, having nothing but uniform to sit in the house. Overalls, very large and loose of the same material, that is my costume, and I perambulate the streets on horseback twice a day on my way to my market and stable a little out of the town in this airy costume, when I go to the fair at Rakowitza about an hour and a halfs ride from this, which I do once a week. If very hot, I put up an umbrella in addition. The heat makes my nose bleed at times, but thank goodness as yet nothing worse has happened. The people here, at least the majority, being Christians, are always having fete or Saints Days, on which it is impossible to get

---

39   Henry Edward Grisewood (1851–86), Phillips's nephew.

them to do anything. This is a great drawback to me and makes me proportionably angry. Brown amuses me very much at times. He is under the impression that he can make people understand him, and he goes on talking to them in English in a measured tone, as if explaining something to a child. He was not at all happy here until Maynard's arrival, having no one but the interpreter to speak to, and they did not get on very well together, but now he is much better, as Maynard brought a servant with him, and being one of the 88th, of course, is an Irishman also.

Oh what a luxury my India-rubber tub is. I would not be without it for any money. Numbers have them now. Maynard has left me a book: 'The Robber' by James,[40] and I am husbanding up in case I should finish it before his return. You do not know in England what a treasure one book or an old newspaper is. I was always fond of a newspaper, but now I read every word, advertisements and all, and find myself taking the greatest interest in all sorts of things I never heard of before. They want places now. I am as anxious to hear if the young woman as nursery maid, whose age is 21, has an objection to go into the country, as I used to be to know if Austria had joined us or not. My maps also are the greatest boon possible when so short of paper at first here. Had it not been for them, I feel sure I would have done something terrible. A troop of Bashi-Bazouks arrived here the day before yesterday. They are a lawless set of ruffians and I believe at first were guilty of all sorts of atrocities. Now they have them in better order, but no doubt, if they got a chance would kill you as soon as look at you. Omar Pasha was not allowed to hang any of these fellows, so he very coolly had them flogged to death, by sentencing them to more lashes than they could stand.

I heard in a letter from Simmons the other day of the death of Butler, who behaved so gallantly through the siege of Silistria. He was wounded in the forehead with a Minie ball, and after lingering some time, died. Everyone regrets that he did not live to receive a reward for his gallantry. I met the other man, Nasmyth, at Schumla.

What are you going to do this Autumn? Where do the little ones go to? How is Nell,[41] riding still? Give my kindest love to her and all of them, Sally and the young ones. Could buy plenty of ponies for them all here, if they could only get them home. I hope the Gr. and yourself have not suffered much from the heat this Summer. Has he had any more attacks of gout? I hope to get a letter from him soon, perhaps when Maynard

---

40 *The Robber: A Tale* (London: Parlour Library, 1850), by George Payne Rainsford James (1799–1860). James was a minor somewhat second-rate author. See also [62] note 118, p. 97.

41 Eleanor Grisewood, Phillips's niece.

returns. The paper is just finished my dearest Mother, so with all love and kind wishes to yourself and Father, believe me,
P.S. Tell Erin he shall have a letter from me when I get back to camp and have more time.

175

Phillips to his sister Anne (Annie)

14th July 1854 Tirnova.
It is very kind of you to write this second time, that I feel called upon to send you a letter, or rather write you one, as when it will be sent is quite another matter at this end of the world. It will be of little use, I fear, writing from here, as the only way of communication is by what they call the post in this country, but as that consists of going to Schumla, where it waits an indefinite time until a number of letters are collected, when they are forwarded to Constantinople or Varna as the case may be. It is not, however, in the least connected with our postal arrangements, therefore its ever reaching England is a desideratum not to be looked for, for these reasons. I have not troubled it. I sent one letter by one of the Turkish Officers in charge of one of my parties of horses, but having since heard from Major Dickson's at Varna, in which he makes no mention of its having arrived, fear the letter is lost. I cannot say how delighted I was this evening at receiving through one of the return Turkish Officers, two letters, one yours, the other my Father's. You, who have only lived in England, cannot appreciate the pleasure of hearing from home in this barbarous and uncivilised country. As I told you before, I felt your kindness in writing to me so much, that I immediately sat down to pen this, as I intend my letters from here to form a sort of continuation one to the other. It will be necessary for the right understanding of this for you to read first one to Mother then send for one to Erin. Perhaps you will not mind letting this travel about in the same way. The reason is this: I find it impossible to write an account of my proceedings twice over, so think it best that where there is so much to tell, all may read. Your letters are of the 8th June. I have received orders to stop buying horses and have dispatched my last party this morning, 130. Thank goodness they are all gone. You cannot imagine the trouble and bother of starting them. The lazy wretches of Turks sit and smoke their pipes while the horses are kicking their pack saddles &c. to pieces, and we are riding fit to break our

necks to catch them. Maynard and I had a run this morning for certainly half an hour as hard as we could go without a check after a loose horse. It was the best gallop I have had since hunting. I have now to collect arabas, the bullock carts of the country, the only means of conveyance, and was promised 100 on Monday last. It is now Friday evening and I am still 20 short. These Zafties are not to be trusted out of your sight. They directly begin to smoke and take it easy, and goodness knows how many days they may take on an errand.

Since coming here I have been adopting the custom of the country in a great measure, and have been living a good deal on rice and vegetables. They are less heating than meat in this country. I drink the wine of the country, and like it much, a sort of light red wine.

It seems that a report the other day of an English Officer having been attacked (in the middle of a town while buying horses) by robbers, is partly true.[42] He was knocked over, but have not heard of his having been wounded. I always carry my pistol in my belt now. It is as well to be prepared, there are so many Bashi-Bazouks and other ruffians about.

You would be surprised to see what weights the girls here carry of water. I mean in coming from the fountains, as much as they can stagger under. I cannot say that the Bulgarian women are a good looking race, not having seen a pretty girl yet. The women of the country, not the towns people, wear a most singular head dress. The best idea I can give you of it is to suppose a large plate, placed almost upright from the back part of the head, and covered with white drapery reaching over the neck and shoulders. It has a very picturesque effect when seen in a body of them.

This town is certainly one of the most strikingly situated places I ever saw. Now our horses are all dispatched and we have more time, Maynard and myself take long walks into the country, after the heat of the day is somewhat passed, and from whatever point you view it, there is always some fresh beauty.

When I received your letter, I heard from Major Dickson at Varna, who informed me of the arrival of my first two parties of horses, making 120. The first Officer had, however lost three on the way. They had broken away in the night. It had nothing to do with me, however, as when sent off, I had nothing further to do with them. I already begin to miss my occupation, and up here, nothing to do is indeed a calamity. I am supposed to be collecting Arabas, but as I cannot do much towards this (as they have

---

42   The roads and tracks were dangerous. Calthorpe wrote of meeting a Maltese who was robbed
     of 1,700 piastres by two Turks, one of whom was apprehended and duly hanged. See Calthorpe,
     Letters, vol. 1, pp. 85–6.

225

to come from different villages around and the Pasha's Zafties are looking after them, they can do it much better than I can, if only when you sent them on an errand you could in the least make sure of their executing it in double the time allowed) am obliged to remain here idle.

There is fortunately a Bulgarian Doctor in the town who speaks French, having been educated at the College of Constantinople. He, by some chance, has a few English books in his possession and has lent me some. One, a novel, although just now an instructive one, 'Anastatius' or the memoirs of a Greek.[43] The other one, an account of Turkey and the Turks, published as late as 1842. This has been a great haul for me.

I an sorry to hear of the unsuccessful trip to Herefordshire. I quite agree with you, indeed rather think it is you agreeing with me, when you say you will not get a place without renting it first, much the best plan on many accounts. As this comes to you, be sure and give my kindest remembrances to all at the Grange. Tell Harry I only hope the Buffer will turn out well for him, but do not think he will answer for his purpose, but by this time, no doubt, things have changed, and being flush of horses, as I hope he is of cash, it will no longer be a matter of any importance to him. Remember me most kindly, and kiss my dear little Godson for me.

Let me hear of him whenever you write. I do not know what you think about the war, for my English news is so old, there is no knowing what might have taken place. They report here today that the Russians are again in Little Walachia, this after raising the siege of Silistria and being threatened by the Austrians, I cannot make out at all, unless they are going to try at Ralafat again. As for us, I somehow fancy we shall not do much this year. It is already the middle of July, and no move. I dare say people at home are much surprised at our remaining stationary, but they do not know how long it takes to organise the means of not only moving an army but provisioning them also. I have seen something of this difficulty this time.

Camp Varna 21st July.

The order to return reached me on Monday last, and I started on my homeward journey on Tuesday. The old Pasha was much alarmed for my safety on my road to Schumla, as so many robbers were about, so sent me down through the bad part of the road under an escort of 15 Bashi-Bazouks. How you would all have laughed to have seen our party, every possible variety of dress under the sun. If you remember in any book a description of a part of Asiatics, Toorkomans, Koords &c. it will just do

---

43 *Anastasius, or Memoirs of a Greek at the End of the Eighteenth Century* 3 vols (London: John Murray, 1820), by Thomas Hope (1770–1831).

for us, I mean as to the manner in which they suddenly dart forward at a gallop, and after performing all sorts of warlike movements, pull short up, or else are pursued by others of the party, where the attack or defence takes place.

Varna 24th July.

I was ordered in here my dear Annie on my arrival at camp, to report myself, and give up my accounts; have been so busy since, have not had time to pen a line. The Mail leaves today, so thought I would give you the last news of me. I am stopping at Colonel Dickson's, who tells to my sorrow that the letter I sent down to him to be posted never arrived, so that this mail will bring you three at once. I have received all your letters now I think, except those that might have come yesterday. They have gone to Devna. Nothing seems positively known here as to what is to be done. They talk of Anapa and the Crimea. Sir George Brown has gone to make a reconnaissance there in the fleet. We shall probably hear something when he returns.

Love to all at home, and excuse in great haste.

176

Phillips to his father

Wednesday 26th July 1854 Varna

You will have seen by my last (the one to Annie) that I arrived here once more, to give up my accounts. It takes some time to do that, as the expenditure incurred is rather large, and everything has to be made out in duplicate. My horses, I am happy to say, have turned out very well, and in his last letter to me, Colonel Dickson sent me a message from Lord Raglan, through the Military, to say he was much pleased with the manner in which I executed my mission. Out of horses (495), all arrived, but 4, three of which were lost on the road (breaking away at night), and one was left ill.

I have been staying here since last Saturday with Colonel Dickson, who very kindly put me up. Russell the 'Times correspondent' has been staying here also. He is a very amusing man, well known now with the Army, and much liked. He is recognised here now and claims rations, has a tent and stops with the Light Division.

As you have of course heard of it through the papers, there is no harm in mentioning the fact that Cholera has broken out here and at the several camps, and they have in consequence changed several of them. The Light Division has gone from Devna about six miles further, but the Cavalry, for want of water, remain. Till Monday no cases had occurred with them. I have been unwell two or three times during the last week, probably after my journey and long exposure to the sun during the last month, but have succeeded in stopping it as yet very soon. I called on Calthorpe[44] the other day, when he gave me some of Hodgson's cholera powders,[45] saying how successful they had been in curing himself and others. I had occasion to use one yesterday and found them answer admirably. Pray tell Mr. Hodgson they are far superior to what we get out here from the Doctors. I am very thankful that my health was preserved so well during my five week absence up the country at Tirnova, for being started in such a hurry, I had nothing with me whatever, should have had no chance. The Turkish Doctors are not worth having. Thank God I was perfectly well all the time.

Sir George Brown started with the fleet to make an armed reconnaissance of the coasts of the Crimea and Anapa. He was expected back at the beginning of the week, when a steamer came in to say that it had been blowing so hard, the steamers could not tow the fleet, had therefore never stirred from Baltchik Bay. He has now started I believe. Since he has gone, however, it has become evident that the Russians are as strong as ever on the other side of the Danube. The Turks also, who were undoubtedly thrashed [at] the last affair at Giurgevo,[46] when Burke and the others were killed, are not strong enough to advance against them alone. It is evident then that we cannot leave this until Austria advances into Walachia, and as an advance on our part is not very likely from the

---

44 Lieutenant the Hon. Somerset John Gough Calthorpe (1831–1912), Cornet in the 8th Hussars, 23 May 1848, ADC to Lord Raglan. Author of *Letters from Headquarters, or the Realities of War in the Crimea*. Calthorpe was sued for libel by Cardigan as a result of the allegation in the book that he had ridden back to the British lines prematurely at Balaklava. The case was non-suited in 1864 on the grounds that it was time-expired, five years having elapsed since the publication of the third edition. See Massie, *Most Desperate Undertaking*, pp. 371–2.

45 A preparation believed to help rectify the symptoms of cholera. The real cause was not discovered until 1884 by the German scientist Koch, who identified the cholera micro-organism under a microscope.

46 Captain Bent and Lieutenant Burke, both of the Royal Engineers, were sent to Silistria to assist Butler and Naysmith in their efforts to defend the town. According to Calthorpe they arrived, much to their chagrin, on the morning the Russians raised the siege. On 7 July a column of Turkish troops from Behrim Pasha's division crossed the Danube at Giurgevo and were met by a large force of Russians. Leading the main body of Turks, Lieutenant Burke with Sergeant Anderson and a private, (all three from the Royal Engineers), accounted for five of the enemy before Burke was shot dead. Lieutenant Meynall of the 75th Regiment and Captain Arnold of the 3rd Madras Light Infantry perished in similar fashion. The Turks were victorious, forcing the Russians to retire. Turkish losses were 500 dead and some 800 wounded. Russian losses were estimated at some 1,500 killed and wounded and some 500 carried from the field. See Calthorpe, *Letters*, vol. 1, pp. 90–1; *ILN*, 9 September 1854, p. 243.

difficulty of carrying supplies and the dreadful nature of the country in front of us, there does not seem much probability of anything being done this year. If the Austrians advanced in time, we should probably try Anapa or the Crimea. Everyone is sick of this kind of life, all the inconvenience of a campaign with none of the excitement &c. of one. As for fighting for the Turks, such humbug is long past. A lazy set of ruffians, who would rob us all if they could; somehow or other it really seems as if nothing would fall to our share, and to be stuck here doing nothing is dreadful, especially with disease flying about in all directions, and there are few indeed who do not own themselves tired of it altogether.

Lots of fellows have gone home ill already, and the number is being increased every mail. Lord Dupplin went home by the last (Cardigan's aide). He was settled by that reconnoitring party of Cardigan's.[47] You have no doubt heard of Mayall, the other one, is they say so ill that he is to go too. I do not know whether you may have any details in the papers, but it was a dreadful affair.

One squadron of ours and one of the 13th, were out. They were told they would be out three days, and took nothing, no tents, and only one baggage pony to about three fellows. They were out sixteen days and suffered all kinds of hardships. One of our men died, several have never been out since and the horses are perfect skeletons, with so great a number of sore backs to be almost unrideable. I believe we returned 95 horse unfit out of 122, and the 13th, as many in proportion to the number taken. We had the largest number out by 20 and more. Some of the backs are awful and will not be well for I cannot say when. Our troop, fortunately, was not in this squadron, and only made up the number for them. Instead of coming back when he could not find the Russians, he went round to Silistria and Schumla, days out of his way and knocked up half of ours and the 13th in consequence. Do not show this letter except in the family, and to Erin, as what I tell you I do not wish to be published to everybody, at least in regard to news of this kind. Glyn[48] was laid up until my return in consequence and hardly a fellow but what is the worse

---

47 Lord Dupplin, one of Cardigan's ADCs, was examined by a medical board on 22 July and was ordered home on 24 July. Mayall, another of Cardigan's ADCs, was sent home along with Assistant Surgeon Davidson of the 42nd Regiment, Surgeon Young of the 28th Regiment, Assistant Commissary General Watt, Captain Pearson of the 63rd Regiment, and Paymaster Macdonnell of the 55th Regiment.

48 Lieutenant Sir Richard Riversdale Glyn, fourth son of the second Baron Wolverton. Cornet in the 8th Hussars, 16 April 1852; Lieutenant, 27 April 1854; Captain, 1st Battalion, the Rifle Brigade, 10 August 1855. Served with the reserve at the storming of the Redan, 8 September 1855; and served with the 2nd Battalion, the Rifle Brigade throughout the Indian Mutiny. He died 11 December 1859 off Aden whilst returning from India. See Lummis and Wynn, *Honour the Light Brigade*, p. 76; *Hart's The New Annual Army List 1860*, pp. 343, 347.

for it, as you hear, both his own aides are done. Tomkinson was sent out at the same time to Silistria with twelve men[49] and a subaltern, Clowes.[50] He was away a week, had a very pleasant trip and brought back twice as much news as Cardigan.

I found our fellows had built themselves arbours on my return, delightful places in the heat of the day, indeed, the only place to live in. Our letters that might have arrived by the last two mails have gone to Devna, so shall get them when I go out. Your last was dated the 3rd Inst. If people desire a peace, I am sure we must not attack the Crimea. Anything like the taking of Cronstadt and fall of St. Petersburgh, or the fall of Sebastopol, and taking the Crimea, would exasperate the Emperor to the last degree, and also all the Russians. He would only shut himself up in the centre of his country and laugh at us. We should be put to enormous expense for years and always have to maintain an army for the occupation of the Crimea.

27th July.

I have got all my papers approved and signed by Lord Raglan, and am now happy to say quit of the whole affair, at least trust and believe so, except receiving a one pound a day the period that I was at Tirnova, 27 days. I was away altogether just 5 weeks.

It is reported here, and I have heard from a good authority, that a Russian steamer painted like an Austrian Lloyd, with their colours and the name of one of their vessels on her, has got a way from Sebastopol in the night, entered some harbour near the mouth of the Bosphorus, and burnt two Turkish vessels laden with coals. If true, what a row there will be about it, but of course unless a whole fleet was kept in front of the mouth of the harbour, such things are always likely to happen.

During my late journey, and coming on here without things as I did, I am got quite accustomed to sleeping in my clothes and not taking them off for two or three days, coming down and always sleeping out in the verandah wrapped in my blankets.

It is a great consolation to me to think that should I be taken ill tomorrow, I have done something toward the campaign, for as all acknowledge, buying 500 horses and equipping them was hard work

---

49   Tomkinson's orders for the patrol, dated 25 June 1854, can be found in TNA, WO1/368, Despatches from Lord Raglan, no. 169, instructions for Captain Tomkinson, 8th Hussars.

50   George Gooch Clowes, son of Colonel Clowes of Broughton Hall near Manchester. Cornet 8th Hussars, 11 March 1853; wounded and taken prisoner at Balaklava. Lieutenant, 19 January 1855; Captain, 17 September 1857. Served in India and retired by sale of commission, 11 February 1862. Died, 7 November 1899. See *Hart's New Annual Army List 1860*, p. 144; War Office. *The Army List April 1862–63*, p. 753.

in three weeks and three days, and is more than a good many can say. I find that I bought more than any of the parties out except Gambier[51] at Schumla, but he had several others detached from him, all of which were included in his number.

I found this morning that the Cavalry have moved from Devna, and gone further up to Jeni Bazar, one of my posting stages, about 40 miles from this. There is no shade near I am sorry to say, so do not know how they will manage for arbours.

The house I am stopping in, although small, is well situated, close by one of the bastions, looking on to the sea, tolerably cool and gets the sea breeze. I hear that the 'Shooting Star' has been sent home, together with a number of other transports.[52] On leaving her, we all left a number of things on board, with instructions as far as I was concerned, to bring them to England if sent back. They consist of one bullock trunk, a canteen, a black portmanteau and a stable chest or two, containing sundry articles. Would you write to the owners of the vessel at Liverpool and tell them (as the vessel must have arrived long before this reaches) to send them up to London. The trunk and canteen have my name on them, the portmanteau: 'E.P. 8th H.', and as for the chest I am uncertain, but there may be the remains of a direction on it, however it is broken in the lock. If you can get them, have them opened and the things in them taken out and aired &c. I forgot all about keys. She left Constantinople, I hear, about a fortnight ago, and would be home by the time this reaches you.

I am delighted to hear Nell's mare kicks so well. I found Fairy alright on my return, as well as the other horse. I fancy I have received all your letters now. The last were from Nell and Mother, except the last two mails, they no doubt are at the camp. One mail, the long one I fancy, reached this on Tuesday, and another with news to the 12th from England, came yesterday. Calthorpe tells me today that they hear that the Russians are retreating, although but slowly, in consequence of the number of sick &c., at Bucharest, therefore if Sir George Brown reports favourably of a landing place, we might still go to the Crimea or Anapa. From what

---

51 Gloucester Gambier (1812–72), Royal Artillery, 2nd Lieutenant, July 1831; Lieutenant, July 1832; 2nd Captain, April 1842; Brevet Major, June 1854; Lieutenant Colonel., July 1854. Wounded by a round shot to the right chest whilst in command of two 18-pounder guns at Inkerman. Invalided home, December 1854. Brevet Colonel, July 1857; Colonel, February 1861; Major General, March 1868. Died, 29 March 1872 at Gosport, Hampshire. See *Hart's New Annual Army List 1872*, pp. 164, 189; TNA, WO76/359–372.

52 Raglan considered the *Shooting Star* too large and unwieldy and its captain incompetent. Despite his poor opinion of both ship and master, the former was kept on as a transport and used to convey supplies and Turkish troops from Varna to Eupatoria. See TNA, WO1/368, War Dept. In-Letters, Crimean War, Raglan, no. 173, 29 June 1854.

I hear Cardigan does not like our Regiment, although he gained all his steps to a majority in it.[53] He has been bullying the Colonel or trying to do so,[54] and Winter quarters would be anything but agreeable.

28th July

The 'Agamemnon' arrived this morning with Sir George Brown, and on my going to Calthorpes, he told me there was good news. From what I can learn, a good landing place has been discovered, close to Sebastopol, where the fleets can cover the landing by cruising within a quarter of a mile of the shore. All the transports are to be here by tomorrow, so that in all probability, something will at last be attempted. Anything is better than inaction in this climate and a change to active service will do us all good. If we go, there will be plenty of fighting you may be sure, for besides the landing being disputed, the fleet will probably come out to engage ours and distract their attention. The mail leaves tomorrow, and I also if possible intend to leave this for the camp. They have moved off on sanitary grounds, but where I do not exactly know. Some say it is only for three days. However, we are not likely to go far with this hanging over us.

I hope you will be, if not already, successful in finding a house in the country. You seem to have visited numbers. In your last, you express surprise that the Regiment is not mentioned, or passed over in the Brevet. There is no passing over in the matter, all Brevets extended, they are done away with now. To the end of a certain year, all whose commissions for their last rank, bore date previous to the end of that year, were promoted, and the reason why we are not mentioned was because the Colonel, Major and Senior Captain were all junior to the date fixed upon.

The young ones wish to know if I have met young Ewart yet.[55] I have not even seen the 93rd, or that Division, except at a distance, and very probably shall not do so. The divisions as yet, have been encamped 6 and 7 miles apart. That, in this howling country is a long way, besides which, since we landed here, I have not been more than a week with the Regiment. Altogether, during the short time I have been there, the Light Division, being the nearest, is the only one I know, but do know several fellows in the different Regiments there, several who were at Staines with

---

53   Cardigan was gazetted a Cornet on 6 May 1824; Lieutenant, January 1825; Captain, June 1826; Major, August 1830; Lieutenant Colonel, December 1830 and on half pay. All these ranks were purchased. See *Hart's New Annual Army List 1855*, pp. 17, 31.

54   Lieutenant Colonel Frederick George Shewell (1809–56), a deeply religious man who was nicknamed 'The Old Woman' by his detractors.

55   William Salisbury Ewart (1835–90), 93rd (Sutherland Highlanders) Regiment of Foot. Ensign, July 1852; Lieutenant, August 1854; Captain, March 1855; Captain and Lieutenant Colonel with 1st Grenadier Guards, June 1862. Served with the 93rd at the Alma, Inkerman and Sebastopol. See *Hart's New Annual Army List 1865*, p. 210.

me. I saw Sherlock Henning[56] before starting for Tirnova, but Maynard, who was in here yesterday, tells me he has been very ill indeed, and looks so still, rheumatism and fever I think he said. There are about a dozen who will have to go home to recover. I hear it is next to impossible to pick up strength, so the Doctors say, in this country. The Cholera is reported, I am happy to say, in the town, on the decrease; and the change of quarters had also, I am happy to say, a good effect in the several camps.

I heard from Calthorpe today that the 'Shooting Star' was to bring out Infantry again, and would have left England before this reaches you, but think it must be a mistake. However you can but write to the owners and see. I am glad to hear that you are much pleased with Daylesford, but I fear Mr. T. will never let Harman take possession of it. Love to all of them. From what Erin says, I am sorry to see that all my letters to you have not been sent to him. Pray send them, as I write generally but one, that all may see it who wish. Am glad the Buffer has proved useful to Harry, it is more than I thought he would.

29th July

The mail leaves this afternoon, but not having been out, have not heard any news. Awfully hot, and this next month is always the worst of the year. By the bye, what I told you is corroborated in some degree by Sir George Brown's letter to Colonel Dickson, that he was coming to live in Varna again. He has, since Lord Raglan's arrival, been living in Devna with the Light Division. Love to all of you. I hope to get your letters tomorrow. I intend starting for the Regiment this evening. I suppose you have not left W.T. yet. Many thanks for the credit you have given me, it may prove useful, although not just now, as what with the pay since leaving England and for the time I was at Tirnova together, which came to thirty pounds, received the other day, besides the twenty seven pounds received for my Tirnova trip, and a little money left, it all comes to about sixty pounds, so I am well off in this respect. Something must come to stir us up, but if not, if this campaign is passed here without doing anything, I shall be thoroughly disgusted with the whole affair. My kindest love to Mother and yourself.

---

56   Sherlock Henning (1829–98) was a friend from Dorset. Ensign, April 1849, 88th Regiment; Lieutenant, June 1854 (without purchase); Captain, March 1855; Major, November 1860, 26th Regiment; Lieutenant Colonel, July 1865; Colonel, July 1870; Lieutenant Colonel, May 1871, 38th Regiment; Half-pay, September 1877; Major General, December 1880; Retired, 26 December 1885. Served in the Crimea, the Indian Mutiny, and the Abyssinian Expedition of 1868. See *The New Annual Army List 1885*, pp. 8, 14.

177

Phillips to his mother

Friday 6th August 1854. Camp, Jemi Bazar
I have received a letter from my Father (date 18th July) the day
before yesterday, so I am in possession of the last dates from home,
and was delighted to hear you had received my first letter from
Tirnova, as I feared it was lost, in which case you would not have
heard from me for 6 weeks, however it is alright now. I joined the
Regiment here on Thursday last, after stopping a day or two at
Devna. We are about 10 miles from Schumla, camped on a large
undulating plain, no shade near and fearfully hot. You have no doubt
by this time heard a great deal from the papers &c. of sickness and
Cholera. There has been a great deal about, but as to Cholera, as
yet, thank God, our Regiment has escaped, and indeed, the whole
of the Light Cavalry Brigade has been very much favoured. The
17th lost two men and the troop of Horse Artillery one man since
it began. Other camps have lost dreadfully I believe, but we have
a great deal of sickness, diarrhoea and its companion, low fevers
&c., very prevalent. Our troop alone has 22 sick including those
left or put in hospital at Varna and I do not think we are worse
than others. As to horses, they are still suffering from the effects of
Cardigan's patrol, and will be for a long time. Many never will be
fit for anything, about six horses have died.

We are all much amazed at the telegraphs in the last papers saying
20,000 troops, Anglo-French, were at Rustchuk at the battle some
time ago. Why the move, if any, is all the other way, to the Crimea,
but it is getting so late in the season, the Black Sea will not be safe
after the middle of September, that no one expects that we shall do
anything this year. I feel sure the Austrians will throw themselves
sooner or later on the Russians flank in Moldavia, and then they
must retreat.

Our present life is most sickening; hard worked by Cardigan in
a hot climate at Field Days, just what we should do in England, no
wonder the men are so knocked up, so give you a specimen of him.

Water is a very long way off here, about a mile and a half. There
is however, one fountain under some trees, where he has pitched his
tent, about 100 yards from our tents. He placed a sentry over it, and
no one could touch it, so the poor fellows toil in the sun to the other

places or go without.[57]

You will find this a short but dull letter, but I have exhausted all my news, and must now fall back upon one's dull camp life. We have just heard that the men, indeed all, are to have half a pound more meat, and half a gill of rum a day. The meat the men do not care about, but the rum is a good thing.

I have just heard from the Colonel that there is a strong report in the Light Division that Sebastopol will be attempted very shortly. They say 70,000 men are to be landed there and that General Canrobert has guaranteed the capture within six days after opening the trenches. It can only be looked on as a report, but from what I told you in my last, am inclined to believe the attempt will be made. As to what the French General says, I do not see how he can guarantee what he has not visited, except by sea. Whether Cavalry were to go or not, was not known, but with such a force, some cavalry must go, I should think. It would be a dreadful thing if the expedition was to take place without us.

You have never told me what you all think of the Crystal Palace at Sydenham. From what the papers say, one would imagine it is a failure, at least as far as the Directors go. What are you going to do this year? Where will this find you I wonder, as you have not got a house. In case my Father should not be able to find out the name of the owner of the 'Shooting Star', it is Currie of Liverpool. I told him in my last that I did not stand in need of his kind credit at Constantinople at present. Since my journey, have received thirteen pounds more as another month's pay, so that it keeps me up pretty flush, with sixty pounds still. It is, however, agreeable to know that I can always have what I want by drawing for it, and am greatly obliged to him. I am sorry that for the first time since coming here, I am quite out of anything to tell you, and as regards myself,

---

57 This episode became notorious and earned Cardigan widespread disapproval. The Light Brigade had marched some 14 miles in sweltering heat on 27 July and had been on the move for nearly six hours without water. At Yeni Bazaar they approached a well and the horses smelt the water and started to become uncontrollable. Lockwood's horse almost jumped down the well. When it became known that there was a spring under some trees nearby, many of the riders immediately abandoned the well and went intent on enjoying its water and finding relief there. They were stopped in their tracks by one of Cardigan's ADCs who reported the orders that the spring was not to be used. Some apologists for Cardigan have suggested that there was a concern that the water might have been contaminated but this excuse becomes unconvincing when one considers that Cardigan had his own tents erected by the spring. One tent was for sleeping, the other for dining. The enraged reaction of the disappointed men and horses is not hard to imagine. Some of the officers of the 8th Hussars had erected a tent for Mrs Duberly but it was ordered to be taken down and Cardigan's tents erected instead. During the night the spring overflowed and flooded one of Cardigan's tents, much to the satisfaction of those who were not allowed to use the water. They still had to fetch their own water from some distance away and over demanding terrain. See Kelly, *Mrs Duberly's War*, pp. 42–3.

nothing occurring, why, it remains a blank. An awful thunder storm the other night; it poured in torrents. Not a soul in the Brigade had a trench cut, some, like myself have no bedsteads and who sleep on the ground, got very wet as the streams of water perversely ran through the middle of their beds. I turned up the corner of my warerproof sheet (always spread under my air-bed), and escaped very well. On leaving Varna Saturday week, by the bye, half an hour after, a most heavy rain came on; wet through in two minutes or would have turned back. As it was, took me 5 hours and a half to reach Devna, raining all the time, and such a rain as we hardly see in England. I fortunately got into an old house where a Commissariat depot was, and there one of them lent me a blanket and a cloak, which in the room did admirably on the floor, in spite of my wet things. It was a miserable ride, and what made it worse was I was quite ignorant of where I could put up, knowing that the whole camp had moved. We have no paper later than the 17th July, so that the last letter is our latest news. It is almost time to shut up. The letters must be in the Brigade office shortly, so with kindest love and wishes to yourself, Father, and all of you.

[PS] Tell Father I have just signed a bill of exchange I told him of some time ago. Duberly gave me a bill at the same time that he bought also; it is worth twenty five pounds; it goes by this mail.

178

Phillips to his father

12th August 1854, Camp Yeni Bazar
I have only just heard that the letters leave this evening at six, and have only an hour and a half before me. I do not like, however, to let the opportunity go by, so step in from a ride to send you a line. Everything has gone on just the same since my last; the same dull do nothing life (except one's camp routine, which is hard enough in all conscience under Cardigan).[58] We have had, I am sorry to say, a great deal of sickness about, and have lost several men. It is a horrible, unhealthy climate at this time of year, all[59] say, more so, than India, as the men are much more exposed.

---

58 Cardigan's insistence on parades and exercises inappropriate in the heat and injurious to the men and horses, together with the lack of adequate forage and water, meant that the condition of the Light Cavalry deteriorated. See Albert Mitchell, *Recollections of One of the Light Brigade* 2nd edn (Tunbridge Wells: Richard Pelton & Hamilton, Adams & Co., 1885), p. 30.

59 Officers with Indian experience.

We are, however, much better off, I believe than other camps, but have not heard any details for some time.

We are all much annoyed at the misrepresentations in the newspapers as to the heat, climate and many other things. Goodness knows it is bad enough without people in England imagining we are living off the fat of the land, in a delicious climate. One paragraph said: 'the weather here is very fine, but no hotter than a fine summer's day in England'.

Now I assure you, for the last two months, the heat has been so intense you would not if you tried ever so, remain in bed after six in the morning. The last fortnight has been intolerable, not merely heat but accompanied with a strong hot wind that produces a dreadful lassitude, and clouds of dust filling every crevice.

One of our chief annoyances is fleas. They are in millions. Everything you eat covered with them. They are common English ones but sting tremendously. Every tent swarms with black ants, but one gets so accustomed to them that you no longer think anything of a dozen or two in your whiskers. I fear you will think this rather a complaining letter, but I only wish to let you know the real state of things. One thing more, and I have done on this subject, our ration bread up here is very bad, so sour I really cannot eat it, fortunately can buy better in the village. There is still great talk about Sebastopol, but it is getting so late, I almost question it. If not done this year, I do not think it will ever be attempted, as they will no doubt patch up a peace during the winter. There is nothing we should all like better than going back in the spring.

I feel confidence in Austria, unless negotiations are being carried on, and fancy if we are to have a war, that we should see her in Moldavia before long.

The date of your last letter is 18th July, and have had one mail within 3 days after with papers to 23rd July, expect another tomorrow or next day. By the bye, would you always send me the latest 'Times' by each mail. Papers are difficult to get, although they arrive now very regularly. We take the 'Evening Mail' as a newspaper, and do not always get the latest date, as sometimes it is not out. The latest 'Observer' would also be very acceptable, any agent in the City would send them if you could not. It is a wonderful boon getting a paper. I do not know if I told you that just before leaving Devonport, I bought a chair, the most portable and convenient you ever saw. It has proved to me in camp the greatest luxury possible, and everyone has been trying to get one made like it, but there are no hinges to be had.

Both Cardigan's aides having left, done up, he has taken one of our Captains, Lockwood,[60] but do not know if for a permanency or not.

Should much like to see you all, and know what you are doing. I cannot imagine where this letter will find you, whether at Brighton in W.T., on the Continent, or in the country.

The horses have been picking up again since coming here, as we have been fortunate in obtaining grass for them, but the men have dropped off sadly. One fourth of the Regiment are sick, and the 17th as many I believe. The 11th, are the best off, but they came out much later than the others, and had not any of the work to do. We have been much the hardest worked Regiment here, and the Officers have had also much more work than the others. Of course in a climate like this, it tells, and we are not therefore surprised.

You must excuse all irregularities in the writing, as my chair, although comfortable enough to sit in, does not make a good place for scribbling letters, and my blotting case not being stiff enough, bends as I press on the pens.

Several fellows constantly go over to Schumla from here, starting very early, but it has no attractions for me. Now Omar Pasha is up at the Danube, it is very different. Everything has risen enormously since we got here. What horrible intelligences the newspapers must have, to have lain under the impression that our Division and the Light with French troops were up at Rustchuk and to have thought so for a week, and the 'Times' give a leader.

Having been interrupted two or three times, it approaches the hour of departure, must close, and with the kindest love to Mother, yourself, and all of them, believe me, my dear Father to be, Your affectionate son

179

Phillips to his mother

22nd August 1854 Camp Yeni Bazar
Another mail leaves this today, and as I know you like to hear from me, send you a line, but it is really to let you know we are still in the land of the living, thank God. We are still in the same dull state as when I last wrote. There have been numerous reports of Sebastopol &c., but the

---

60 George Lockwood (1818–54) of Bishops Hall, Essex. Ensign, 75th Foot, July 1837; Lieutenant, August 1840; Lieutenant, 8th Hussars, May 1844; Captain, December 1851; See *Hart's New Army List 1854*, p. 34. Killed at Balaklava: his body was never found.

Cholera breaking out in the fleet, and the burning of the stores at Varna, stopped it for some time, and now I should imagine it would be too late in the season for such an undertaking. If not tried this year, I do not think it will be at all, as I have every confidence in Lord Aberdeen's making peace somehow by next year, and how earnestly we hope he may succeed can only be appreciated by those who have witnessed and endured the misery and suffering of this year or campaign if you like.

I have received by the last mail a letter from my Father, dated 3rd August, but have received no letters from you, or anyone, except my Father and Erin, since the one dated 2nd July. I then had one from Annie and Nell, I forget which, and one from yourself. You will have seen my last letters that I have received my Father's of 18th July, and by the next mail had one from Erin. I am sorry now I ever stopped the papers, it is so difficult to get hold of one. In my last I asked for the 'Times' only, but really the best way would be to send them regularly between each mail, or at any rate the last two or three previous to the mail leaving. I should be satisfied with that, as it would be a great boon. I must confess that hearing you were both pleased with Warnham, I had hopes that something would come of it, and fully sympathise with you, my dear Mother, in your disappointment. I fear it is as I always said, that question of soil would spoil every place, and you will go to Brighton innocent of the country for the next ten years. I might as well direct this to you at Brighton, I expect, as it is pretty sure to find you there. By the end of this month I trust the hottest and worst time of year will be over. Where we shall go for winter quarter, I cannot imagine, unless to the Bosphorus, as all the grain stores of the Commissariat were burnt at Varna the other day. I hope it will be there instead of some inland place where we should get no supplies to render the time more endurable. Does Harman and Mrs. Grisewood enter Daylesford this October. My love to all at the Grange, Annie and Harry. How are all the young ones? Quite French by this time I suppose. My letters, you see my dear Mother grow shorter and shorter, even though writing to you, but the dullness of this place is infectious, and must be part of my excuse, added to which my position is extremely uncomfortable, but cannot improve it.

We get very badly supplied up here and are sadly off for anything to drink. In this climate, some sort of stimulant is really necessary. The brandy they sell here is horrible, you cannot drink it. For a short time we could get Marsala, but now it is all out and not a drop of anything drinkable is to be had. General Cameron, who is in the Turkish service, came through the camp today, saying that as far as the Turks were concerned, the fighting was over, as the Russians were retreating fast and the Austrians would occupy Wallachia. Whether it is fear of the Austrians cutting them off or whether they are really evacuating, I cannot imagine. However, I really think I have written myself out, and must conclude in spite of the shortness of this letter. That is, however, what in future I fear for some time at least you are likely to complain, as there seems no likelihood of our doing anything to write about.

My kindest love to all of you, particularly yourself my dear Mother, and believe me to be Your affectionate son

[PS] To show how little chance some fellows have of meeting, I was only one day in Devna (on my return from Tirnova) in the same camp with George Burnand,[61] and that day was not well, and kept quiet. On my return from Varna, the whole camp was broken up and regiments dispersed, and have never been within twenty miles of him since. Yet his regiment was quartered not 500 yards from us for more than 6 weeks, but I never had a chance of seeing him. As to young Ewart, it is never likely that we should meet. I have not seen the 93rd yet. Please do not forget about the newspapers, send the last three before the mail leaves.

180

Phillips to his father

Sunday 3rd September 1854 Varna

I am sorry to have to inform you of a real calamity that has befallen me. I must first inform you that I have been laid up with an attack of intermittent fever since about the 10th August. I was taken ill while at Yeni Bazar, and after a short time was sent down to the village with the Assistant Surgeon, Towers,[62] who was also suffering from the same complaint. We lived in a wretched place called a house, eaten up by fleas, and until last Monday, 28th August, when the Brigade, having received

---

61 Lieutenant George Sapte Burnand (1829–76), 5th Dragoon Guards. Cornet, April 1850; Lieutenant, February 1853; Captain, December 1854; Major and retired by sale of commission, 25 March 1869. Burnand's father, also called George, was a successful stockbroker from Finsbury, Middlesex, and it is likely he was acquainted with Phillips's father as they both lived in Paddington and were members of the Stock Exchange.

62 Misread in transcription as 'Towers', this is actually Henry Somers, FRCS (1819–61). Medical degree from Glasgow, 1845; Assistant Surgeon, 73rd Foot, October 1845; Assistant Surgeon, 8th Hussars, February 1846; Staff Surgeon, 2nd Class, August 1854. Noted as remaining at Varna in the muster lists for September 1854. Surgeon for the 55th Regiment of Foot, June 1860. See TNA, WO12/844; Peterkin and Johnston, *Commissioned Officers*, vol. 1, p. 331.

orders to march to Varna for embarkation to the Crimea, had left on the Saturday before. We determined to make only two days march of it, in order to save the nights on the road, and therefore left in an Araba on Monday, reaching Varna the same day as the Regiment, viz, – Tuesday. I was getting better of the fever, but the weakness consequent on it is so great that the Doctors, both our own and the Staff one attached to the Brigade, declared it would be madness for either of us to go, and ordered us into Varna for house accommodation, and here we are. This is my calamity that has befallen me, not being able to go with the Regiment. They say they will have to endure great hardships at first, no tents, and as each Officer only takes the horse he rides, can only have with him what his valise will hold, and a blanket, which they must carry under their saddle. Taking this into consideration and our very weak state, the Doctors declared it impossible that we could gain strength enough in the short time they would be on board ship for us to stand even one night of it. So unfortunate, by circumstance over which I have no control, at the very time I most wish to be with them, am I separated from them. There is one hope we have; at first they cannot do more than land and seize a position, so that not much will be done, especially by the Cavalry for some days. In the meantime, the vessels are to come back, first, I believe for more French or Turks, and then they say for Officers' led horses &c., and by that time we hope to be able to go also.

They say the heavy Cavalry, which also stopped behind at first, will also follow, so we might get a passage with them. However, as soon as we are strong enough, shall use every means to rejoin. The Regiment is on board the 'Himalaya' and still in harbour. I have just heard of the death of Longmore, our senior Captain.[63] He died of Cholera on board this morning. Poor fellow, the morning they embarked, he rode up and asked for some brandy, complaining of diarrhoea. I had none to give him, and fear he has been unwell ever since; that was Thursday, and was taken off suddenly this morning. Saltmarshe of the 11th,[64] and Colonel Boyle of the Guards[65] are also dead after short illnesses from the same cause. It makes

63 Charles Joseph Longmore (1816–54), born Antrim, Northern Ireland. Ensign, 47th Foot, May 1834; Lieutenant, August 1838; Lieutenant, 8th Hussars, May 1839; Captain, August 1844. See Lummis and Wynn, *Honour the Light Brigade*, p. 73.

64 Arthur William Saltmarshe (1830–54), born Halifax, Nova Scotia, the only son of Christopher Saltmarshe of Saltmarshe, Yorkshire. Cornet, 8th Hussars, November 1850; Lieutenant, September 1851; died at Varna, 3 September 1854. See TNA, WO12/844, Muster Roll, 8th Hussars, 1854.

65 Lieutenant Colonel the Hon. Robert Edwin Boyle, MP (1809–54), Coldstream Guards. Ensign, November 1826; Lieutenant, July 1829; Captain, August 1833; Brevet Major, November 1846; Captain and Lieutenant Colonel, December 1847; Liberal MP for Frome, 1847–54. See *ILN*, 30 September 1854.

no difference in promotion, as Reilly,[66] the Riding Master at home, being senior, will I suppose get the step. He was not for purchase before, and unless he sells immediately, which being a man with a family and old in the service, he is not likely to do, it will make no difference. Should he sell, McNaughten gets it, and that gives a step, but by that time, goodness only knows where we may all be.[67]

Lord Raglan and Sir George Brown embark tonight, and indeed everybody, and all rendezvous at Rustchuk, where the Fleet is tomorrow, if favourable. I suppose they will then sail. Everybody is surprised at the lateness of the season not stopping such an undertaking. After all one has heard of the Black Sea after the middle of this month, one would have thought it was too late in the season for the Fleet to have supported the Army. My view of the case was: that as the Emperor had evacuated the Principalities and Austria had joined us, so far as to say, she would require the same guarantees as ourselves; he was (the Emperor of Russia) prepared to make further concessions, which, had we remained quiet, would have terminated in a peace this winter. But if Sebastopol is taken, I am quite sure he will not treat, and we (those who are left of us) may remain here for an indefinite period.

I received your letter and newspaper for the 8th August but have received no letters from Mother or anyone else by the 13th, as you said. Today the mail came in again; in spite of my having left my name at the post office, in a hurry, it was overlooked, and the letters, if any, all gone to the Regiment. We may by some chance get them before she sails, but fear not. We have sent to see if we can get one of our servants on board. In future, please send me newspapers. They always arrive as safe as a letter, and I cannot say how acceptable they are. The last 'Times' and as many others as you can. Never mind an evening paper because it is later, real information is what we want, and that is best in the 'Times'. I do not object to any others, 'Observer' or 'Illustrated' you can send, they are the greatest boon you can conceive. At this moment I would give any money for a 'Times'. I have received three letters from you at different intervals, and one from Erin, but none from Mother, Annie or anyone else, since those dated 2nd July.

---

66 Captain Joseph Reilly, Riding Master of the 8th Hussars and Senior Lieutenant at the time. Born at Cavan, Ireland *c.* 1801, he had served in the ranks from October 1821 to 1833. Commissioned as Cornet, April 1833 by purchase; Lieutenant, March 1834. On the day that Phillips wrote his letter, Reilly's son, John (1822–1858) was gazetted Riding Master of the 8th Hussars to replace his father.

67 Reilly did not sell out but continued to serve with the 8th Hussars. Joseph Reilly's promotion to Captain was dated 3 September 1854 and he retired by sale of his commission, 4 September 1857. Apart from his son, John, he also had two daughters and another son, all of whom were with the regiment at home. Thanks to Bridget Geoghegan, a descendant, for genealogical details.

Monday 4th September.

To our great delight, last night our servant managed to reach the 'Himalaya', and we have received our letters; one and a parcel of powders from you, a letter from Mother and one from Annie. They are most acceptable. I was delighted to receive them. Many thanks for the powders, although I trust I shall not require them.

Our servant brought word that two men of ours, on board the 'Himalaya', were very bad and not expected to live.[68] I much fear it may break out on board. Had the things you speak of, brandy and [?] arrived at Varna now I should have got them alright, but it is impossible to say where we might be in another fortnight, and therefore it is no use sending anything until we settle in winter quarters. Then, perhaps if I am spared, [I] shall ask you.

I feel better and stronger, thank God, this morning, and hope to be tolerably well in about 10 days. We are in a very comfortable house in Varna, and being close to the ramparts, get a view of the sea and vessels in the harbour, as well as sea air. I yesterday managed to get to the beach, and enjoyed the breeze much. The whole of the expedition has not started yet, and I cannot help thinking they are keeping some back on account of the Cholera, which is evidently showing itself on board some vessels. I am sorry to hear that Harry has been bored with the Buffer's tricks. I never thought him fit for harness, and what ought to have been done with him, was to have him ridden in the park of a morning by someone who knew how to make him show himself off, and if properly looked after, he would have fetched at least seventy pounds. I am sure I would, had I been in London, have sold him for that.

My last three letters will have been, no doubt, not so satisfactory as the former ones, but that and any little crabbed expressions in them, you must set down to illness. I do not like to let the mails go without writing, in case you should imagine me ill, although at the time hardly able to hold a pen, at the same time I did not like to mention it, as I hoped to get better, and fear Mother would only frighten herself about me. However, now I trust the fever has left me and that the weakness which is present, is all I have to contend with, will disappear before better living and sea air. How they make you pay for things here to be sure. 5/- a bottle for very bad Sherry, and bad Brandy at an equally great price. Hams 1/9 to 2/- a pound, and 11d for a loaf of white bread, French baking. This is

---

68   Three 8th Hussars died on board the *Himalaya*: 1206 Pvt. Thomas Lewis, died 4 September; 1138 Pvt. George Jarvis, died 10 September; 901 Pvt. Timothy Connell, died 13 September. Connell was buried at sea. See Duberly, *Journal*, p. 79; TNA WO12/844 Muster roll, 8th Hussars, 1854.

the last mail to pass through Varna, as the post office moves after today, I suppose to follow. However, I hope to be with them before a fresh batch of letters arrive; never mind, write away and send newspapers. Pray give my kindest love to Mrs. Grisewood and Harman, and say how pleased I am to hear that at last they are so near taking possession (if indeed by this time they have not already done so) of their beautiful place. I wish I could get 10 days at Daylesford, and do not doubt it would make me all right for the Crimea. However, I hope to date my next letter from there with the Regiment. It will I doubt not make you comfortable to hear that Cholera belts have been served to the men. I wear one.[69] Only fancy my taking to rum. On board ship, when I had to see it served out to the men of a day, it almost made me ill to smell it, but since then, when up at Yeni Bazar, and nothing in the shape of wine or spirit to be had, with sickness and fevers prevailing all around, then when the order came to open rum to the troops, and no order about the Officers, who were of course equally in want of it, I was one of the first to get up an agitation about it, and now how I enjoy my ration of rum, and such really fine rum as it is too. I must do the government the justice to say that when we do get the groceries and those sort of things, they are first rate, but the bread and meat is anything but.[70]

Your letter of the 16th only arriving on 3rd September is not so good, as you say mine was, reaching you in 11 days, but I think you must have written too early for the mail, as it ought to bring letters and dates of the 18th August. Thank Annie very much for her letter. I am glad to hear my Godson grows so strong and well, dear little Jack too having kept so well this year, will I trust grow up quite strong. Boyish notions sometimes grow up with them. Do not encourage him in the idea of ever being a soldier. I earnestly hope never to be far up this wretched country again. It was dreadful at Yeni Bazar, such sickness, strong men dead in a few hours, others so reduced in a week from fever you do not know them. We lost a great number of men from fever. The number of funerals every night was quite disheartening, and then on our journey down, the meat we had cooked for the road turned out to be tainted, and for two days, at the very time we most wanted nourishing food, exposed in an Araba for

---

69 Belts made of flannel worn round the abdomen in a futile attempt to ward off cholera (it was believed that keeping the abdomen warm would have a protective effect).

70 The army relied on local provision for its victuals and these proved difficult in this part of Europe. Barley, cattle, sheep, bread and meat were contracted to be supplied by Messrs Samange Oglou and Falanga, who were based in Constantinople. The quality of the bread was frequently criticised as was the meat. See TNA, WO62/13, Miscellaneous Correspondence from the Commissariat Headquarters, Crimea, 1854.

10 hours a day to the sun and dreadful jolting, of which no description can give you an idea, we had nothing but hard biscuit and coffee, no milk, that was our breakfast and dinner. When it comes to that with sick people, hardly able to stand on their legs, it is past a joke that I hope is over now, unless the Crimea gives us a taste of something worse.

God bless you all. My kindest love to yourself and dear Mother, whom thank a thousand times for her letter, and hoping soon to tell you of my recovered health and strength.

[PS] The post leaves directly or I would finish the other sheet.

181

Phillips to his father

Thursday 21st September 1854 Varna
I have only just time for a line, having heard that a bag will be made up immediately. I am happy to say that I am now, thank God, quite well again and feel alright; have been waiting impatiently for the last week for the steamers return to rejoin. They have fortunately arrived last night. This morning I have been to the Generals, and shall have a passage in one; expect to leave in a day or two; run there, with favourable weather, is 48 hours. As yet I lost nothing by the last account, and earnestly hope to reach them before they are engaged. They move forward on Tuesday morning, but I believe only for seven miles to a river. Indeed cannot imagine they will attempt anything serious until the arrival of our heavies and the French Cavalry, as the Russians are said to be strong in that arm. Of course you will have much better accounts than I can give you from this, so will not attempt it.

I hope you have set down my silence to its right cause, the want of mail. Since the expedition left, only one bag has left for Constantinople, and that, the day after. We have had no chance of writing. In like manner all our letters have gone to the Crimea, so have not heard since my last. However, hope to get them all on joining. How extraordinary that there should have been no opposition to their landing. It has left an impression in the Army. I hear that the Russians did not expect us this year. I hope you have all kept well this sickly time, and not frightened yourselves about me. There has been a great deal of sickness about here since their leaving.[71] They say they are also sickly where they landed, but as they advance it gets a different country, and hope more healthy. I trust my next will be from the Crimea.

[PS] For once, you must excuse a hurried epistle.

182

Phillips to his father

Sunday 1st October 1854. At sea, on board the 'Rip Van Winkle'

Wherever I go, I am sure to fall in with something to relate to you, so now for an account since my last. I reported myself to General Scarlet, commanding the Heavy Brigade as soon as the steamers came in, when he told me off to a ship, and as some of the Light Brigade horses left behind were to be sent on, put me in command of them. I embarked on Sunday 24th, left on board this vessel in charge of 15 horses with part of the Royals on board under the Colonel Yorke.[72] As we were to sail in a convoy, each vessel in tow of a steamer, and as the French who was to tow us was not ready, could not start until Tuesday afternoon at 6 o'clock. Our convoy consisted of the 'Simla' (4th Dragoon Guards), 'Jason' (5th Dragoon Guards), 'Trent' (Enniskillens), (all Heavies) and the 'War Cloud' (Enniskillens), 'Pride of the Ocean', ' Wilson Kennedy' and 'Rip Van Winkle' (Royals), all sailing vessels. There was another steamer with some Artillery on board, all under the convoy of HMS 'Spiteful'.[73] The weather up till this had been beautiful, no signs of the equinox, but the day we left, became very heavy, damp weather. As it was for a short distance only, we were carrying 120 horses, ponies and all. All the Officers horses were placed in stalls on deck to the number of 10, one trooper and some ponies filling 16 stalls. We placed them on deck, as having been so long exposed to the air, fancied the heat below

---

71   Cholera remained with those at Varna, broke out on the ships, and came ashore with the allied forces when they landed. See Trevor Royle, *Crimea: The Great Crimean War, 1854–56* (London: Abacus, 1999), pp. 175–8.

72   The ship was supposed to sail on 25 September from Varna. On board with Phillips was the headquarters squadron of the 1st Royal Dragoons under the command of Lieutenant Colonel Yorke. With him were Captain Campbell and Cornet Hartopp, five sergeants, one trumpeter, one farrier, 58 rank and file, one woman, eight officers' chargers, and 61 troop horses. See Ainslie, *Historical Record*, p. 185.

73   HMS *Spiteful* was a paddlewheel steam-powered sloop, number 463, built by Scott and Sinclair at Pembroke Dock and launched 24 March 1842. A 'Driver' class steam vessel, 280 horse power, 180' x 36', 1054 builders measurement (pre-tonnage) units. See *Navy List 1855* (London: John Murray, 1855), p. 171; TNA, ADM 53/5657, log of HMS *Spiteful* describing the storm.

would do them harm. None of the [horses of the] 4th Dragoon Guards embarked, the first having died before we left Varna. On the top of the stalls covering them in, the spare spars belonging to the ship were lashed and with them, the long boat over all. They seemed very merry, and I thought myself fortunate in taking both Fairy and the Chestnut,[74] when all our fellows were allowed one before. We all steamed out at 6 o'clock in the evening, it then raining hard and looking dirty; about 9 or 10 came on to blow and gradually increased to a gale by midnight. About 2.30 a.m. one of the hawsers to the 'Trent' broke, the vessel rolling, pitching and plunging about to such a degree, that the only wonder was both had not parted long ago. It now blew awfully, the sea running tremendously high, everything in the cabin of course in a smash, and about daylight, 5 o'clock, the Captain startled us all by saying that the long boat spars and stalls had all been carried away, and every horse on deck was killed. We scrambled out as well as we could from the frightful rolling of the vessel, and discovered that it was only too true. Half the horses were buried under the ruins smashed and others, among them both of mine, were swept down the hatchways into the lower hold, where they lay piled up one on another. Poor Fairy went down one and the Chestnut down the other hatchway, and of course were killed almost directly. After all it was fortunate that it was so, as the vessel continued to roll so badly that we could do nothing to those in the hold until Thursday morning. Some of the other chargers (two I think) survived on deck for a few hours, but only to die by degrees, having been too much injured by the crash. Up till this, 5 o'clock, our other hawser had held, and the steamer still towed us, but shortly after, it parted, and we went adrift. We were some time hove to under a close reefed main top sail, but towards the middle of the day the wind, somewhat abating, we got another sail up. It continued to blow until the Thursday, when it moderated and we were able to get the dead horses up. On examining the hold, numbers of troopers were discovered dead, and in two days after sailing very nearly 40 horses were dead and thrown overboard, including all the officer's chargers (10). I do not imagine that four Cavalry Officers were ever so completely dismounted in such a short time before. Up to this time, the number of horses dead

---

74 These were Phillips's two chargers. Officers whose chargers died or were killed on campaign received compensation. Most officers took two chargers, the best being classified as no. 1 and the second as no. 2 and their compensation value reflected this. First chargers for officers were valued at £45 and second chargers at £35. Phillips received the going rate for the loss of his chargers at sea and again for the loss in battle of his replacement first charger at Balaklava. See TNA, WO60/5, Commissariat Dept. Accounts, Crimea Warrant Book, 1854–55, entry 642, Compensation for losses, 7 February 1855.

on board is 46, and two ponies. Four of my detachment are gone and two more very doubtful, but the Royals are worse: out of 61 troopers, 32 are dead. What an awful loss is it not, and all because things are left so late that at last it all comes to a hurry and you are sent off in any weather. The fittings were said, by the Inspecting Officer of Transports, to be only intended for short passage and fine weather, but what can you expect in the Black Sea the last week in September. We ought never to have come to sea that night, the Captain and the Mate both say so, and no doubt the Captain of the 'Spiteful' will catch it for sending us. The chances are it has buried the Heavy Brigade, and all the steamers were full of horses on deck &c., and when we parted from the 'Trent', several horse boxes and stalls were carried past our vessel, showing she must have been as badly off as ourselves. Indeed, that is proved by her leaving us, or else she would have stayed by us until the gale abated, and then taken us in tow again. The other vessels must have suffered much; one had 100 horses in her hold without a stall up I believe, and how could they have come off. There is one thing, when I reach the Regiment, can always have a trooper to ride, as they always mount Officers, but by that time Sebastopol may be taken through all these unfortunate delays, and I see nothing of it. Fate seems against me as to that.

It is very annoying after taking so much trouble with ones horses all the summer to lose them so. However, I try to think all is for the best, and shall manage to bear up with it. Poor Fairy though, I did hope I should have ridden her in England again. I have had a foot taken off in remembrance of her. Of course, our horses are hardly to be replaced out here, but do not buy anything for me until I see what is likely to be done, as it is no use having horses sent during winter quarters. And I might pick up one here. The allowance is forty five pounds for a first, and thirty five pounds for a second charger. If it is allowed at sea, it certainly ought to be. The officers of the Royals are Colonel Yorke, a Captain and a Subaltern, all very nice fellows.

We heard before leaving Varna that a battle had been fought by our troops,[75] now 10 days ago. So by this time, fear much may be over. We have had light winds ever since the gale, which by the bye did not completely leave us till Friday. It blew us down out of course, and we are now but a short way, 80 miles, from Varna, and no wind. When we shall reach, goodness only knows. In case the rumour of our loss has spread, there is one comfort, you are not likely to know of my being on board,

---

75   The Alma.

and the papers will only get hold of it as the Royals, so am not uneasy on that score.

7th October. Saturday. Crimea.

Thank God, here I am at last, once more with the Regiment and fortunately find them well. I find I have lost nothing as yet, the Cavalry not having been engaged. I have been saved a good deal of bother and trouble. I have just received your last very kind letters, from my Mother and yourself, written in answer to the notification of my being ill, besides numerous back ones from Mother, Nell, yourself and Erin, all you could have written, and some papers, but none of the last mail.

There is a large force of Russians close to us. We shall in all probability have a fight in a day or two. They attacked our picket this morning and took 3 men of the 4th Dragoon Guards.[76] All the cavalry were here, and were out. They will probably attack us when we commence on Sebastopol, and we are here in the rear to protect our communications, and meet their Army. I shall ride a trooper, but buy a horse if possible. We are close to a place called Balaklava, where all the guns &c. are disembarked.

They say we begin tomorrow. The post goes tonight. God bless you all, and many thanks to Mother and yourself my dear Father for your kind letters.

183

Phillips to his father

12th October Camp Balaklava

As yet, the fight I told you of in my last that we expected to come off, has not yet taken place, although we are threatened with something of the sort daily. I presume it will be delayed until the general attack on Sebastopol takes place. Our position here exposes us to the strong attacks of a strong body supposed to be waiting to take the Army in the rear, and we cannot send out our daily patrol on the road without having a skirmish. I was out the other day and saw nothing but a dozen of Cossacks, who cut immediately.

---

76   635 Pvt. Joseph Chapman, from Cork; 806 Pvt. James Donohue, previously a slater from Cork; 889 Pvt. Dennis Driscoll, previously a labourer from Cork; all three taken prisoner on 7 October 1854. Calthorpe recorded: 'It appeared that just after daylight one of our cavalry (heavy dragoons) pickets were surprised by some of the enemy's cavalry, one of our men was killed and three made prisoners.' The only fatality recorded for the 4th Dragoon Guards for that day was 879 Pvt. Thomas Swift, previously a labourer from Rathowen. He is recorded as 'died'. See TNA, WO12/ 270, Muster Roll, 4th Dragoon Guards; Calthorpe, *Letters*, vol. 1, p. 244.

The weather up to four days ago had been beautiful, just the thing, but suddenly changed, and for two days and nights, we experienced the most bitter cutting North East winds I ever felt. It nipped everybody up, and gave us a salutary hint of what we might expect by and by. Fortunately it has again changed, and is now mild again. During the time it lasted, nothing kept you warm, and had we been in England, we should have scouted the idea of living in tents as impossible. All this time, everybody is wondering why we do not begin at the town, but everything is kept secret, that no one has an idea when it is to be. However, no doubt it will turn out alright. The Russians keep shelling our Infantry lines all day, and night too, but hardly any take effect fortunately. The general opening of the batteries cannot now be put off, and I trust by next mail, you will hear something decisive. I have bought another horse, one of Longmores, paid fifty-five pounds, not a bad sort of animal and considering the demand for them, very cheap. Ever since leaving Varna, I have been, thank God, exceedingly well, and hope to continue so. There has been a good deal of sickness about here one way and another. I fancy it is quite time we took the place. I rode up to the front the other day to have a look at our position about four miles from this. You are able to go to a small watch house on the top of the hill looking into the town where the Light Division has a picket, and from there you can see the whole place. You must not show yourself about the house, or else they begin to shell immediately. They say we are within 800 yards of the walls, and are to commence at once every battery opening, it will be a tremendous blaze. Then is the time for us to be on the lookout for an attack. We are in the saddle every morning at 4.30, and uncommonly cold business it is. About 6.30 we turn in again, altogether anything but desirable, these cold mornings. It is not light till six. We are not above a mile and a half from the town and harbour of Balaklava, about as extraordinary an harbour as any in the world. Where I embarked the night before last, an attempt to burn the town and shipping was apprehended, so everyone was turned out by 3 companies of Infantry.

We fare better down here I fancy than the main body upon the hills, being nearer the ships. It is not very brilliantly [supplied] however, only ration, beef and biscuit. I have just returned from a foray today, and after visiting several ships succeeded in securing a ham and some butter, great luxuries. Our ration of rum has also been increased or rather doubled. It is now a gill. It is invaluable. I always keep a portion to take neat with a bit of biscuit before turning out of a morning. It helps to keep the cold out wonderfully. We are in constant expectation of a turn out, so never undress at night. Indeed the cold is such as to make it more comfortable so. I have been here a week and have only had my overalls off twice since landing. I have my blanket, hair bed and waterproof sheet with me, and being the owner of a baggage pony (the remaining portion of my stud), have a pair of saddle-bags and a small canteen. All my other things are on board ship. I am sorry to have missed Alma. It must have been a sight only to be seen once in a man's life. It so seldom happens that a soldier can see anything of a battlefield, and there the Cavalry saw everything. The day before they were under fire, and lost two horses by shell that nearly killed the Colonel.[77] In an assault a few days afterwards, they obtained no end of Russian dresses of all kinds, Hussars, Cossacks &c.[78] It seems always to be the case when they run to throw their things away. The other day in patrolling a road after they had retreated from our Cavalry guns, I saw the place strewn with helmets, horse shoes, bags of oats, jackets &c. and might have had a dozen had I wished, but there were none worth it.

I am glad to hear you are enjoying yourselves at Eastbourne, and have at last made a break from Brighton and also hope to hear of you all in Paris before long. You must all be satisfied with one letter among you now, as what with pickets, patrols and every spare moment spent in foraging, I have but little time you may imagine, that rising so early, we turn in at an early hour. Indeed I fancy 8.30 sees us all in the blankets, and generally earlier. Send all sorts of kind wishes to all at Daylesford, and distribute love to all at home, with kindest love to Mother and yourself.

[PS] I fancy up to the last mail, I have received all Mother's letters and your own, and a great pleasure they are. Write as often as you can from home.

---

77 The affair at the Bulganak, when the 8th Hussars came under fire for the first time in the campaign. They were opposed by Russian cavalry and both sides engaged in a rather desultory and ineffective exchange of carbine fire from the saddle. Casualties occurred only when there was an exchange of artillery fire.

78 Phillips refers to an incident during the advance towards Sebastopol. On 28 September, Raglan and his escort (Chetwode's troop, 8th Hussars) overtook a Russian convoy. The latter took flight almost as soon as they were shot at and, after token resistance, they abandoned their wagons. There were some 70 in number containing small arms ammunition and black bread. There were also a number of carts belonging to Russian officers of the 12th Ingermanland Hussars. Uniforms were discovered, fur cloaks and even a case of champagne. The troopers of the 8th were allowed to pillage their prizes amid much hilarity with captured wigs and undergarments. See Murray, *History of VIII Hussars*, vol. 2, p. 415.

184

Phillips to his father

Friday 17th October 1854 Balaklava Camp
Just a line to you, as I wrote by the last mail saying that I am alright and well. Nothing has happened to us since my last, but numerous alarms, turnouts at all hours, and skirmishing with Cossacks. The bombardment of Sebastopol commenced this morning at half past six. At nine the French batteries were silenced. Since then the whole Russian fire has been concentrated on ours. In spite of which, we have silenced, they say, two Russian batteries. Our fleet is hammering away at the forts at the mouth of the harbour, but with what effect is not known in consequence of the smoke. We can none of us get to the front, as we have been in readiness all day to turn out in case of an attack. We fancy something of the sort must take place before we embark, then our turn will no doubt come. The mail goes tonight. Just received the mail of 3rd October; no letters for me, but newspapers alright; the last mail also the day before yesterday brought no letters.

Hoping you all are well, with kindest love to all, Mother and yourself.

185

Phillips to his father

23rd October 1854 Balaklava
Alright as yet. I have only time for a line, as I am ordered off on picket immediately. The siege still going on. We have not done half that we expected, but are getting on better now.

[PS] We are worked dreadfully hard here, looking out for the rear; alarms night and day; horses kept saddled for three days at a time, and ever ready.[79]

---

79   The allies expected an attack from the Russians and, therefore, were in a high state of alert. This meant that the cavalry and artillery would be up and ready an hour before dawn, horses and riders prepared for action. The troops lived in their clothes and few had the opportunity to change. For the field intelligence available before Balaklava, see Stephen Harris, *British Military Intelligence in the Crimean War, 1854–56* (London: Frank Cass, 1999), pp. 50–4.

186

Phillips to his father

27th October 1854 Balaklava

I had the happiness to receive all your letters of the last two mails (newspapers also), and assure you was much gratified to find you all still well; am glad you received all my letters from Varna, assuring you of my renewed strength. Poor Mother, I trust she will not fret herself about me again so much, I trust to a Divine Providence to preserve me, of whose mercy I have already received a signal proof, of which I will now tell you.

Sufficient it is to say I am quite well and uninjured. On Wednesday October 25th, when on our morning parade (turning out every day at 4.30), as soon as it was daylight, our attention was drawn by the firing of the redoubts on the heights in our front. They were all to the number of five, garrisoned by Turks, but mounted by English guns in their charge. This was so frequent an occurrence that we thought nothing of it, as they were firing at Russians two or three times the week before, and we were kept out all day and night too. However, the firing soon became so hot that we were assured the long expected attack had indeed at last commenced.

I must mention beforehand that the only troops we had were the Turks in the forts. Some were battalions in part of the town, 93rd Highlanders, the whole of the Cavalry Division (except our troop on escort with Lord Raglan), and Maude's troop of Horse Artillery,[80] six guns, a field battery, six guns, 2 rocket carriages.

The Division was 1500 strong, we quickly advanced to the brow of the hills, halted just underneath, our guns came up also and opened fire. The Russians were, however, in great force, and attacking the Turkish fort on our right,[81] carried it after short resistance from the Turks, who cut down the other side as fast as possible. This, giving command of the other forts, caused them to be evacuated by the Turks, as soon as the Russians got their guns up on the first one. Thus the whole of the heights in our front

---

80 Captain (later Colonel Sir) George Ashley Maude. Maude was in command of I Troop, Royal Horse Artillery. He was severely wounded at the start of the battle. See George Ashley Maude, *Letters from Turkey and the Crimea* (Printed for private circulation, 1896).

81 Redoubt No. 1.

were taken after hardly any resistance from the wretched Turks,[82] and the plain in which we were, was exposed to the fire of the Russian guns. This soon became hot, and being only Cavalry, we were forced to retire gradually as they got the range, and only lost a few killed from the shot and shell. An order from Lord Raglan now drew us further away under the cover of batteries. The Light Brigade being on the left higher up the hill, and the Heavies on the right lower down. This movement opened the front of the Infantry in position before the town, and the Russian Cavalry poured down in great numbers to charge.[83] They were soon driven back by the fire of the 93rd and some Turks, but another body equally strong pouring down, the Heavy Brigade advanced to the charge. The Greys met them first, when the Russians closed on their flank, but were in turn flanked by the 5th Dragoon Guards. The other regiment came up on the right of the Greys. The Russians did not stand long and were speedily driven back in disorder. We were at the time too far up the hill to flank them, or should have cut them to bits.[84] We were, however, moved forward as fast as possible, and formed on the hill in two lines. The 11th, 13th, 17th, in the first, the 4th and ourselves in the second. You will I fear hardly understand the rest without a sketch of the ground. However, we were ordered to advance down a valley in the rear of the heights the Russians had taken in the morning, and on which they had established their guns, this leaving them on our right. On the other side of the valley was a hill also occupied by the Russians with their guns, thus leaving them on our left, and at the bottom of the valley at least a mile and a half in front were the guns we were put to take. Thus exposed to a fire the whole distance from three sides.

Well, we advanced at a steady trot, soon to a faster pace. We had not advanced 200 yards before the guns on the flanks (our left and right) opened their fire with shell and round shot. Two regiments of Infantry

---

82   This was unfair to the Turks but a generally held opinion especially among the cavalry. By contrast, Julian Jocelyn, *History of the Royal Artillery (Crimean Period)* (London: John Murray, 1911), pp. 199–200, relates that No. 1 Redoubt was held by some 500–600 Turks who defended their position against overwhelming numbers 'with the most determined gallantry' and lost 170 killed before they were driven out. The Turks in the other redoubts broke and fled on seeing the defeat of the defenders of No. 1 Redoubt. See also Hargreave Mawson, *True Heroes of Balaclava*, passim.

83   This was the attack by Rijov's 6th Cavalry Brigade, composed of three regiments: 11th Kiev Hussars (eight squadrons), 12th Ingermandland Hussars (six squadrons), and 1st Ural Cossacks (six squadrons), totalling some 2,000 men. See Adkin, *Charge*, pp. 99–100.

84   Phillips's explanation for the failure of the Light Brigade to attack the flank of Rijov's retreating cavalry. Captain William Morris, in command of the 17th Lancers, pleaded with Lord Cardigan to be allowed to attack them but, having been ordered to remain where he was, Cardigan kept his brigade stationary and did not attack. See Adkin, *Charge*, pp. 110–12 for the continuing debate on this issue.

drawn up on the right under the guns began firing volleys of minie balls, and almost at the same time, the guns at the bottom of the valley opened with grape. In spite of this awful fire, we galloped over the ground strewn with the men of the first line, and our own dropping at every yard. Every sound was there, the bursting of the shells, the deep dash of the round shot as they struck the ground, and the whistling of the storm of minie balls and grape shot. We passed the Infantry, the guns on our left and right, and approached the guns at the bottom of the valley, which the first line charged in the midst of a fire that swept down men by dozens, and carried off almost all the Officers.

Just as we were approaching to carry them off, we saw coming out of the smoke in our right rear, two strong regiments of Cavalry, to take us in our rear, and extended right across the valley. We, in consequence, wheeled about, and charged bang right through them, thus opening a way for the remnants of the first line, now broken by their losses. As soon as we had charged through the Lancers opposed to us, another lot was sent out at an angle to cut us off, and thus from the awful fire in advancing, and still charging, we had suffered immense loss. There were not sufficient left to charge them, and of course everyone made his way back through the same awful fire as before. However any one of us escaped the storm of shot and shell and bullets is miraculous. On our return out of the fire, and rallying, only 44 men turned up out of 104.

Now for some of my personal adventures: I had command of the left troop of the first squadron. Just before wheeling about to charge, I felt my horse was hit, I think on the off quarter. However, she went on and we charged the Lancers well, our men cheering as they went at them. They wavered as we went at them. I managed to clear one fellow's lance, who prepared to make a desperate prod at me and halted for the purpose, but suddenly changed his mind, and prodded the next fellow. After the charge, a fresh lot of Lancers coming down to cut us off, we were obliged to retreat as fast as possible. I had not gone far when I found my mare begin to flag, and presently, I think she must have been hit in the leg by a round shot, as she suddenly dropped behind, and fell over on her side. I extricated myself as quickly as possible, and ran for my life, the firing being as hard as ever. After going some distance, I found myself cut off by some Lancers, who had got in my front. At some distance off me was my old servant Brown, who was badly wounded in the arm, and a musket shot in the back. One of them cut at him when he was on the ground, and wounded him in the hand. I made sure my time was come; I drew my revolver, but seeing that, they kept their distance, until an officer coming up, ordered them back, as they were too far in advance, so I escaped this danger. Some little distance further on, I reached one of our poor fellows lying on the ground dead or dying, his horse standing beside him. The saddle had turned round, and what with the excitement and running for ones life, I was so done, that I had not the strength to right it, therefore undid the girths, and by standing on the saddle, managed to climb up on his bare back. Never was I so happy as when I felt a horse under me again. I passed lots of poor fellows wounded or dying, and after an anxious gallop of nearly a mile, at last got out of fire and reached the Heavies, who remained at the top of the hill. In their rear, the remainder of our Regiment, and of the Brigade formed up (they having before coming back rallied separately), I joined them there.

A sad sight indeed presented itself. How few in numbers we looked, the whole of five regiments not forming one good one. On mustering, we found that Fitzgibbon and Clowes are missing. Lockwood, also, on Cardigan's staff. Clutterbuck was wounded in the foot by a shell, and has gone on board ship. Seager wounded in the hand by a lance; Tomkinson had his horse shot earlier than our wheeling and made his way back as best he could; Mussenden's horse was also hit, but brought him home, and my own falling in the field, completed the casualties among the Officers.

Poor Fitzgibbon had the troop next [to] mine, when suddenly I heard him cry out and put his hand to his breast. He must have been severely wounded, but as we cannot go over the field, nothing has been heard of him. I fear he is dead. He was last seen leaning on his arm, looking very bad. Clowes no one saw after our wheel, I hope he may have escaped, he must be made a prisoner if he did. Lockwood was seen at the battery but not since. Tomkinson's horse was shot three parts of the way down, and bolted across our front with him falling almost directly. Mussenden's horse brought him back, but has since been shot. The Major, the Colonel and Heneage escaped without a scratch, horses or man. Out of ten Officers with the Regiment, seven were wounded, themselves or their horses, that is not counting Lockwood or the staff. The 17th returned with only three Officers; the 13th better off in Officers but very bad in men; the 11th, only three Officers doing duty at present, and the 4th, very bad also. I have just heard that the Light Brigade only mustered a little over 300 men and horses effective. We are quite cut up. It has, of course, been much commented upon, and the only thing that can be said for it is: it was a mistake.

A poor fellow who is dead, brought a wrong report.[85] In consequence of this, we went a mile and a half if not two, to take guns we could never have taken away under such an awful fire, being flanked on both sides and facing a battery beside the whole way. Every species of fire was opened at us. The staff with Lord Raglan was on the top of a height but some distance off, and saw the whole. The French, whose Cavalry came down to form a support, say it was the most gallant thing that ever was heard of. That is saying a great deal, but I believe, no instance on record of Cavalry being exposed to such a fire, and then to think that one came safe out of it. I feel I can never be sufficiently thankful for my preservation. It was the awful fire our men were exposed to that destroyed us. Had we had a fair chance like the Heavies, I have not the least doubt we should have settled them, but it is impossible for men to stand against such a fire and not suffer immensely. The fellows have, I think, not a great opinion of the Russian Lancers. They held together uncommonly well, keeping their line all through the fire. I felt missing Alma and not being with the Regiment a great deal, but now, having been exposed to almost if not as severe a one as the Infantry there, have no wish to be exposed to such a fire again. Cardigan I believe went at the head of them and behaved well.[86] Had we not advanced, we should have had much the best of the day, but of course now have all that to lament. Poor fellows, I know almost every one who fell; such, my dear Father, was what deserves to be called the Battle of Balaklava. The despatches and Russell's letter will no doubt explain much better than I can, but I wished to give you a full description even at the risk of being tedious.

Be sure and send this to Erin. A thousand thanks to him for his kind letter on my illness. My kindest love to you all, especially my dear Mother and yourself. Sebastopol is getting on well I hear or rather the siege. I hope it will soon fall. I trust you have received no terrifying reports as to the 25th, but believe no telegraphs. Menschikoff is said to be in great force here in the rear. The Turks have done us harm, as they have made the Russians believe they were English Infantry.[87] Of course

---

85 The 'poor fellow', of course, was Nolan, killed by the first shot fired from the Russian battery on the Fedioukine Hills. What Nolan was attempting to do immediately prior to his death is still a matter of debate. Some argue he was attempting to divert the direction of the Light Brigade to the Causeway Heights, others that he was attempting to lead the Light Brigade in the charge down the North Valley. See Buttery, *Messenger of Death*, pp. 129–46.

86 Regardless of his faults, no one could criticise Cardigan's courage. He rode before the Brigade without flinching, expecting to be killed. His actions on reaching the guns and afterwards, however, excited much criticism and controversy, hence the legal action in the Cardigan versus Calthorpe case in 1864. Significantly, Phillips had not actually seen Cardigan during the action.

87 Another reference to the widely held belief that the Turks had fled from the redoubts.

they will make much of the guns.[88] God bless you all. I am rather tired with writing, so good bye.

187

Phillips to his father

2nd November 1854 Heights before Sebastopol
Only just heard the mail goes at 9.00, now 8.00. I know you will be glad to hear that I am alright, and, thank God, well. We have moved up here, and are not so much exposed to attacks from the rear as before. They talk of storming this infernal place in a day or so. Of course we only look on. They had better make haste, as the weather has been piercingly cold for the last week. I should think our horses will die if it lasts much longer and men too. Have been too busy to write any further details of the action. Clowes is wounded and taken prisoner. The other two must be dead, as there are no accounts. God bless you all. In great haste.

188

Phillips to his father

7th November 1854 Heights before Sebastopol
Another battle to tell you of, and what a fearful one. The Russians attacked our right early on Sunday morning, 5th November, in immense force. It was partly a surprise, and for some time the 2nd Division and Guards had to stand the brunt without support. The Russians were driven back with immense slaughter several times, and finally retreated into Sebastopol. Our loss is also very great, more I fear than we can spare. We were moved close to the rear of the 2nd Division a few days before, and were taken up to support a regiment of French Cavalry, and kept under a fire of Artillery for some time. The ships in harbour[89] threw immense shot and shell right into us, besides the Field Artillery. We,

---

88   Russian prisoners taken after the action known as 'Little Inkerman' on 26 October revealed that the seven captured guns were paraded through the streets of Sebastopol amid great rejoicing. The trophies were presented as spoils of a victory, church bells were rung and the commanding admiral gave a ball. See Calthorpe, *Letters*, vol. 1, pp. 327–8.

89   The *Chersonese* and the *Vladimir*.

fortunately only lost one horse killed, four men wounded.[90] The 17th lost another Officer by a shell close by us.[91] They have only two left now. The ground did not admit of Cavalry being made much use of, and as the whole Brigade only mounts about 300 horses, we could not do much if it did. I went over the ground yesterday; the most horrible sight. I had read of the ground being covered with dead, but never believed it till yesterday. The Russians almost cover it in front of the redoubt where the Guards were. Their loss must have been far worse than Alma. That they have much greater forces than we gave them credit for is without doubt. When we shall take this place, goodness only knows. Three weeks since opening fire, and we do not seem much nearer than before.

The mail leaving England October 18th, arrived yesterday, but brought no letters or papers. It generally happens somehow that I get two mail's letters together. Another is expected today or tomorrow. This last is the fast mail and gains on the previous one. I think people in England will be surprised when they find out how greatly the resources of Russia have been underrated here. It strikes us as very ridiculous receiving English newspapers saying it is of course over long before this.

The weather has fortunately changed again, and is really most propitious. I only hope it will continue so. You must of course excuse this paper and ink, as it is a borrowed affair. I have none and can get none. I hope to receive a letter from Mother tomorrow; my dearest love to her. I hope she keeps up her spirits.

We have a very strong position here, and the point they attacked is the only weak part. What we want is men. It is difficult to get up supplies here, now we are so much further from the ships than before. Biscuits and rations are our chief food. The rum still continues, thank goodness. It is a great blessing. A few maggots have appeared in the biscuit, renders one rather wide awake. I cannot say, as yet, I have found any. Give my love to all the little ones, and indeed all. Thank everybody, Nell and Sally for letters, but want of materials prevents my replying. How to make an envelope, I am sure I do not know, so you will no doubt have a curious one. We never know here till so late that the mail is going as to render writing a great scramble. God bless you my dear Father.

---

90   The regiment also had four men killed.

91   Cornet Archibald Clevland was struck on the head by a fragment of shell and died the following day. See Rosemary Lauder, *Vanished Landmarks of North Devon* (Barnstaple: North Devon Books, 1994), pp. 33–4.

189

Phillips to his father

12th November 1854 Before Sebastopol

A week today since the Battle of Inkerman, and nothing fresh has occurred, that is, no attack from the Russians, for we keep still hammering away at the place without, as far as we can learn, doing the smallest injury. What the French do is not known, but fancy, since the 5th, they fire but little. We are quite certain to winter here, and how they will manage to feed us all puzzles everybody. I should think it is pretty sure to kill the horses. Anything more wretched than our whole appearance you cannot imagine. This morning we turned out 40 strong, and as it had rained nearly three days, the horses and men were covered with mud. I never saw such a turn out. The men have nothing with them but what they have on; no change of boots or overcoats, but obliged to sleep and live in their wet, muddy and very nearly ragged things. All their kits are or were on board the 'Himalaya', but as she has knocked a hole in her bottom, she has, I believe, landed them at Varna, and there they are likely to remain. There is talk of huts, but none are visible as yet. It is getting latish too for tents. Lord George Paget went home the other day, and it has caused a good deal of talk.[92] They say he tendered his resignation. Since that, we hear from Lord Cardigan, that no resignation will be accepted.

I ought to have told you in my last that I had drawn a bill on Cox & Co., for one hundred and twenty pounds. It went by the last mail. Will you ascertain through Linton & Co. if there is money enough to meet it. I have not the smallest idea what balance I may have there. It consists of thirty five pounds for the mare I bought at Longmore's sale,[93] shot under me at Balaklava. I then bought another that formerly belonged to Longmore, but Fitzgibbon bought her at his sale. I gave forty six pounds for her. The remainder is made up of different things bought at these sales, and ten pounds for a saddle.

---

92 Paget had married his cousin, Agnes, on 27 February 1854 and was lovelorn when he left for the east with the 4th Light Dragoons. He discussed leaving the Crimea and returning to England to retire from the service with Raglan on 9 November and sailed two days later. While there were personal reasons behind Paget's decision, he also knew there would be no attempt on Sebastopol until after the winter. When Paget got home, however, there was adverse comment in some of the press and in the clubs. Paget eventually returned to the Crimea with his wife and arrived on 23 February 1855. See Paget, *Light Cavalry*, pp. 252–68.

93 When an officer died the regiment auctioned off his possessions. Horses, clothes, furniture and anything that could be of use or value were disposed of in this way. Brother officers tended to buy most of the lots. Personal items were usually returned to the family.

They are going to move us again. We have no chance of making ourselves comfortable by building kitchens or anything, as we never know how long we may remain. Calthorpe says there is no truth in resignations not being accepted. There is no chance of our storming or taking the place for six weeks, until we get reinforcements enough to meet their Army outside, besides going into the town.

The water here is very bad, nothing but mud. The salt beef we get, very seldom eatable and were it not for the preserved meat we buy, and an occasional ration of fresh meat, we should be badly off. The last three days there has been the greatest difficulty in getting any fire at all. The wood about here is all green, and a very little rain makes it useless attempting to light it. However, we manage to rub on pretty well, and if the weather only continues to open, and the Russian Army leave us alone (not very likely), we may get on tolerably. I am thankful to say, as yet, I have kept uncommonly well. Received my papers by the last mail, both of the 13th, and the 23rd, but no letters. I suppose the mail was not in with mine on my landing here. You must see that, under the circumstances, it is no good sending anything out, as I do not know where I may be.

With kindest love to dear Mother and yourself, and all at home.

190

Phillips to his father

17th November 1854 Before Sebastopol.
You will see by the papers a much fuller account of the hurricane with which we were visited on the 14th, than I have here time or space for. Will however just give you an account of what it did to us. It came on very suddenly about 6.00 or 7.00 in the morning, and soon whipped our tents down. The heaviest part of the gale was about 10.00, at which time not a tent was up, and it was impossible to stand against the wind. Being accompanied by heavy squalls of rain, hail and in the afternoon, snow, we were, of course, soaked, and altogether it was the most wretched day I ever passed. We almost all managed to get our tents up by night again in some sort of way, by putting stones on the skirting, as half the ropes broke. What we shall do the next wet, I do not know, as the beating on the ground has worn lots of holes in it. Still in comparison with the men's, it is a prince of tents. Poor fellows, their condition is indeed bad. Almost bootless, their overalls in rags and their tents torn dreadfully, is the case

in which they have to spend the winter. Many have their feet so swollen by wet and cold, they cannot walk. Our horses also are likely to starve as, since the loss from the storm, the Commissariat say they cannot feed them.[94] In addition to this, we must remain entirely inactive; as for want of men, nothing can be done for six weeks, by which time, I should think, owing to the total want of preparation of any kind, the Army will be no stronger than now, in consequence of sickness and cold. We, the Light Brigade, are no good at all as far as an effective force goes. Cardigan lives on board his yacht comfortably off enough, and then comes up and bullies us in every way about trifles after we have suffered from such weather. Do not think I am downhearted from this letter, for although I would give anything to be off tomorrow, shall cheerfully put my wits to work and try to make myself as comfortable as circumstances will admit. A fine day to dry too, makes things look a little better. We have shifted ground, and left the mud of the storm, so are dry again now. What makes such a difference between Cavalry and Infantry, is, they, if wet, have no horses to poach the ground, whereas we are a swamp in no time. They also have plenty of men to work, build huts &c. and we have not enough to groom the horses. In case you should not see the papers in time, I believe 10 vessels went down with nearly all hands, and 10 dismasted at Balaklava. Of the Fleet I know nothing.

No mail in, they say it is lost. Another is just due. No letters since 13th October, my latest dates. No doubt your letters on hearing of my loss on board ship, and arrival in the Crimea, are gone. One thing that rather raises our spirits is that the Russians are said to be in as bad a plight and worse than ourselves, with what truth I know not.

There is a report of our going (the Cavalry) to Scutari, on account of the shortage of forage, and the Vets saying there will be no horses left in the spring, but that is far too good news to be true. The vessel I came from Varna in, the 'Rip van Winkle' was one lost, and all hands.[95] It was too bad keeping them outside, as all the Captains feared staying there, as they were all sure of what would happen if it came onto blow.

The French arrangements are far better than ours. They have served out sheepskin jackets to their men, capital things, and the day of the storm, they served out long pegs for their tents whereas we might look

---

94   The horses of the Light Brigade received only 20 per cent of the registered rations. See Anglesey, *History of British Cavalry*, vol. 2, pp. 112–14.

95   Drowned with the loss of the *Rip van Winkle* were Richard Nicklin and his assistants, Nicklin being the first photographer sent to the Crimea. What would have been unique photographs of the early months of the war at Varna and Balaklava also went down with the ship. See Massie, *Most Desperate Undertaking*, p. 285; Paul Kerr, *The Crimean War* (London: Boxtree, 1997), p. 44.

for a blue moon before we got any. I am sorry to say a ship with rum on board was lost. This is a sad blow. All the warm clothing was said to have been on board the 'Prince', worse luck for us. Shell and powder is another thing we are said to be short of. Very little firing goes on at the town now. My air bed, which everybody envied me, and was a real luxury, was whipped off by the wind when the tent was down and carried right over the hills towards the Russians. The blankets went about 100 yards and stopped in a pool. They were damp that night as you can imagine. Fortunately the waterproof sheet was left.

My kindest love to dear Mother and yourself, and all at home, and abroad, and hoping to have some news soon.

191

Phillips to his father

Monday 20th November 1854 Camp before Sebastopol

Here we are still, and of course must winter here. If you could only come amongst us and hear how disgusted we all are at the way we have been and are treated, you would not be surprised at the step I have taken, viz, – sending in my papers.[96] I was in great uncertainty for some time but finding that three others in the Brigade had done so, and looking up your letter to me, I re-read it, found it stronger than I had imagined at first, made up my mind, and sent them in. One reason is that in spite of the time before an answer will be obtained, 6 weeks, I trust still to get away before the worst of the winter sets in, everyone saying it begins here in January, and continues very late. In addition to this, by that time, anything to be undertaken against Sebastopol, would have come off, at which I would have been present, and it would either be all over for the winter, or we must have made up our minds to stay in our tents. Now I have always had the greatest dislike to wintering here. The inaction, with the cold and bad living, would be pretty sure to find out the few weak points I have remaining from my Bulgarian fever. Another reason is, our present condition is really deplorable. One poor fellow has already died of cold and half starvation;[97] no proper food for a sick man.

---

96   To resign his commission, sell out and return home, Phillips would need permission from his commanding officer and other senior officers in the chain of command.

97   1170 Farrier George Hadrell from Trowbridge, Wiltshire, recorded as dying in camp on 14 November 1854. On 15 November, Calthorpe mentions 'a man from the 8th Hussars was found dead in the morning from cold'. See Calthorpe, *Letters*, vol. 1, p. 424.

The Commissariat Officer told me himself that they cannot feed our horses. We are already non-effective as a force. We turned out 36 men in the ranks yesterday morning, and are as strong as any regiment in the Brigade; but were we 3000, could do nothing up here, surrounded on all sides by entrenchments on top of heights. [Our] great protection, Cavalry are quite useless, as if they ever get to the top of them, I fear it would be all up with the Army. We are therefore not very likely to be of use here. If we are, I shall be here, but by the time I speak of, the beginning of January, they could not move us if they wished. Indeed by that time, if there is any truth in the Vet's opinions, there will be none left to move; but you may say how about the Artillery? They are always better off, as they have the means of bringing up their own hay and straw, and stores &c. on their wagons, while we are entirely dependent on the Commissariat. They also in the case of losing horses come upon us. Then look at the French, their Cavalry have been in the same spot since landing, and have in consequence had fine opportunities, not neglected, of building all sorts of contrivances to make themselves comfortable. Their horses too are well foraged and look well. 'Tis true they have not been knocked about as we have been by commanding Officers, who live on board their yachts and then come and bully us about trifles. This is the ninth time we have been moved in a month. I can stand hardship, but not worrying into the bargain. You would hardly believe how we have been worried one way and another.

The names of those leaving are Joliffe of the 4th [Light] Dragoons and Dunn, 11th Hussars, and Morgan, the junior Captain of the 17th Lancers. Lord George Paget, as you know, left before. It is too bad to make a distinction. They let him go, but no one else. However, having pretty well destroyed us, they cannot complain of one's leaving. I have your permission to sell when I like, but some say Lord Hardinge will say we must resign. Pray let me know what you think. Anything, in my opinion, is better than this. With such a prospect before us, I do not think, myself, Lord H. will say so. I have taken every trouble to ascertain our real position in regard to the siege, and as Colonel Dickson, the man I was under buying horses, is in command of the night attack, I have obtained something true. Our guns are almost all wore out. The supply of powder and shell, since the storm, very small. Our firing yesterday in the 21 gun battery was five shots. Now as we have not as they allow, damaged the Russian Earthworks at all materially, there is not much chance of our doing a great deal before fresh guns are brought. When that will be, goodness knows. There are in our own Regiment two fellows I know who would leave directly had they leave from home. One in another regiment also. Having laid the facts of the case before you, I trust you will not think I have decided hastily, and will only say that you were, I think, aware that before leaving England, I was quite willing to leave, had it not been for the war; and ever since coming out, have only desired the day that should see me return. If it is not the end of the campaign for the Cavalry, when they are pretty well done up, and have regularly sat down before a place for the winter, what is?

We are discovering today how much was injured by the late storm. It is pouring and the rain comes through in all parts. They talk about huts. How are we to build them with men who can hardly attend to their horses, and only one shovel, (no picks) left in the Regiment. Nothing we make a requisition for, can we obtain. Our nose bags are all worn out, and nothing to feed the horses on but the ground. And when it is wet you cannot, it is poached. Really one would think the idea of wintering here, was never contemplated; but surely every contingency should have been provided against. The French were evidently prepared for it by their issuing sheepskin cloaks.

I have received your kind letters, and one from my dear Mother, of 28th October, written on hearing of my arrival in the Crimea, and of my loss at sea. Yesterday, the mail was not lost as we thought. Many thanks, and kindest love to Mother and yourself for them; they quite cheer one. Papers alright also. Lord Killeen[98] came the day before yesterday to replace poor Longmore. He said he could not have supposed such abject misery as he saw. One great reason is, we have no kits to stand cold.

Wednesday 22nd November. Nothing fresh up to this evening. The last two days have been wet and cold. They have told severely on the horses; having had no hay the last week, the poor brutes have been desperately hungry, and at least 10 have lost their tails in consequence. They have literally been eaten off. One horse has lost his mane also.

A great deal of Dysentery is about; the 46th, I hear are suffering very much from it, and the work in the trenches.[99] By the Bye, Lord Lucan met Joliffe the other day, and told him he saw no objection to any Officers

---

98 Arthur James Lord Killeen (1819–81). Cornet by purchase, 17 September 1839; Lieutenant by purchase, 5 March 1841; Captain by purchase, 23 January 1846; Major, 2 October 1856. Succeeded as 10th Earl of Fingall, 1869.

99 Captain George Frederick 'Fred' Dallas, a company officer in the 46th, mentions in a postscript to a letter home dated 16 November 1854 that 'the troops are getting healthy though they have suffered dreadfully since we landed … but nearly everyone is suffering from "Diarrhea". "Saving your presence" as an Irishman would say).' See Michael Hargreave Mawson, *Eyewitness in the Crimea: The Crimean War Letters (1854–1856) of Lt. Col. Frederick Dallas* (London: Greenhill Books, 2001), p. 50.

leaving now, and hoped he would be able to go directly the answer came from Lord Hardinge, without waiting for the Gazette. God bless you all; pray write by return.

192

Phillips to his father

Monday 27th November 1854 Camp before Sebastopol
Received yours of the 9th Inst., the day before yesterday, and greatly regret to hear that you were all in so much anxiety on my account. I fear it must have been prolonged, as they tell me all your letters after Balaklava missed it, the bag being sent somewhere to French Bay. I hope such was not the case. In my last I told you in consequence of the utter state we are in, together with the total want of arrangements, and misery of the whole affair, I had sent in my papers. As yet no answer has been received, but I hope that they have gone home by the mail of the 25th, from Constantinople. Two more of the Brigade have done the same, making six in all,[100] and I assure you hardly one but would do it if he could.

Just fancy, the weather having been most awfully wet for the last ten days, our camp has been nearly a foot in mud, where the horses stand. Yesterday, as it held up a bit, the regiments moved out separately to their front, for dry or rather less poached ground. Today Cardigan comes up (never having been near us the whole time of the wet), and as it was done without his order, sends us all back again into a perfect sea of mud. Is not that too bad. At the same time we are expected to serve under such a man. He also issues an order that no tent is to be changed without his approval; so if my tent is swamped (which being in the bottom is very likely to be the case) I must not change to drier ground without his sanction; he being on board a comfortable yacht at Balaklava.

The horses are dropping off fast; the wet, combined with no hay and half rations of barley or oats, not agreeing with them. But few tails left. Short rations for the men are also coming into fashion. Nothing new in the siege line. The Russians and French have constant skirmishes of a night, but it does not seem to advance the siege. The road between here and Balaklava is awful. I have been sent down twice within the last few days (of course getting soaked each day), and saw at least a dozen horses

---

100 The six officers were Phillips; Joliffe, 4th Light Dragoons; Morgan, 17th Lancers; Dunn, 11th Hussars; possibly Brown, 4th Light Dragoons; and, possibly, Hartopp, 17th Lancers.

dying on the road. The worst of it is, our tent lets in the rain so much that I am obliged to sleep wrapped up in my waterproof sheet, and fortunate I am in having such a thing. That, and my blankets, form my bed for the last fortnight, and very comfortable it is. Ones hips get rather sore lying on the ground.

The papers come alright, and a great blessing they are. By the bye, what nonsense sending more Cavalry now. They will only come to die here, men and horses. All the fresh comers suffer very much from disease. The more I see of the French, the more convinced am I that they are before us in campaigning. Their men are much better suited than ours for it. Am glad that Erin has had all my letters to read. I trust that this will find my dear Mother tolerably comfortable on my account. My kindest love to both of you. Thank Annie very much for her letter, and all for your sympathies on poor Fairy's death. I am glad now she is dead, and suddenly, as I know, instead of seeing her starved to death, or suffering as these poor creatures are. One almost hopes here for the cold instead of the wet, as during the latter, we are always badly off for fires, and cannot get our dinners cooked. The wood here is all small brushwood, and very little of it. The rain soon spoils all hope of a hot dinner. The only comfortable warm place is in one's blankets. I am afraid this will find the people of England rather down about the siege. I should think the storm pretty well wound them up, as they always fall into extremes. Getting rather dark, and too early for a light, candles being precious.

Goodbye to you all, with kindest love.

193

Phillips to his father

1st December 1854 Camp before Sebastopol
I had the great pleasure of receiving yours and Mothers letter of the 13th November, three days ago. My delight is somewhat lessened by hearing that you had not received my letter. I had endeavoured to keep you all informed of how I was getting on by each mail, if only with a line, am much disgusted to find that the one of all others, I most wished you to receive, should in some way have missed. Of course in it, I gave an account of what befell me on that day; however am still in hope it may have turned up by the next mail. If your next does not speak of it, will give you a fresh account. We are still going on just the same. The horses

have had for the last week about 3 handfuls of oats a day, nothing else. This, combined with incessant rain, cold winds &c. has killed many, and others are so weak and reduced, that though we are to move down to Balaklava when we can get a dry day, no one knows how we shall ever get there. I really believe half the horses in the Brigade will prove unable to carry a man to Balaklava, about 6 miles. The roads are dreadful and have proved one of the principal causes of our not getting forage. What makes it appear so bad is that barley has always been so plentiful at Balaklava, but the means at the disposal of the Commissariat have not been equal to buying it, and no wonder the roads are in such a state, and yet we are kept up here to starve, when we might have done well at Balaklava. I do not pretend to know what reasons Lord Raglan had for keeping us here. No doubt they were weighty ones. However it has nearly finished the Brigade, sadly reduced as we were. You cannot be surprised after this, that Lord Lucan has reported the Brigade unfit for service, or that so many have got disgusted and sent in their papers. We lost two horses the night before last. I do not know how many last night. The 4th [Light Dragoons] lose at the rate of four a night for the last few days, and others two or three. Not a night passes without three or four dying in the Brigade, and of course every day weakens the others. The tails being nearly gone, they have taken to eating the saddlery; several breastplates, almost all the small straps and any place that a blanket shows itself under the saddle is immediately seized upon by the starving wretches, and torn for food. Incredible as it may appear, it is a fact. They actually come, when loose of a night, and gnaw our tent ropes. Even if we were to reach Balaklava tomorrow, and got plenty of food for them, I do not think they would ever recover themselves after so long a starvation. These tail-less, maneless, skinny brutes would never be recognised as the remains of five as fine regiments as ever left England.

Cardigan has gone on board sick; they say he has resigned the command saying 'his heart is broken'. It does not make much difference, as he never slept out of his yacht since he came here. I am sorry to hear that all our last letters were too late for the mail (she having been started before her time by the Admiral), but the two previous ones missed at Constantinople. This will make all the last three letters, twenty days. The whole of the Army letters missed by the last, except Lord Raglan's bag. Being Orderly Officer today, have just been to water. Four horses fell down going there and back, and I was obliged to leave them. They will never rise again. I am writing this early, as in case of our getting a fine day tomorrow, my time will be taken up shifting to Balaklava, and the mail leaves early next morning. I am glad to hear Jack gets on so well in health, and trust it will be permanent. The mail leaves so early, I have but time for a line. We moved today within a mile of Balaklava, and they were actually afraid to mount the horses, so led them all the way. Four horses dropped on the road, and an Officers charger, making 14 horses lost in three days. I should think such a scene was seldom seen as our mounts here.

With kindest love to all, yourself and dear Mother especially.

194

Phillips to his father

7th December 1854 Camp near Balaklava

You must thank all and take part to yourself for the kind letters just received. It was a mail that, although very late in arriving, we none of us would have missed. Being nearer forage and provisions here, we are better off than on the Heights, but from what the Vets say the change has come too late for our horses. They say the greater part must die, their constitutions being too much injured. If you in England could but see the Light Brigade now, it would rather make you open your eyes! We were to have formed a picket with the Heavies, but could not muster sufficient effective horses. Lucan has again reported us unfit for duty, so Officers of the Light are to go on picket with the Heavies alternately. Of three troops here, two could mount ten each, the other, seven; and they are really not fit to go out for a walk. All sorts of reports here about the French having landed near Eupatoria, 40,000 strong, and licked the Russians. It is our only chance of taking the place this year. I fancy their having done something of the sort. There has been a great deal of sickness in the camp; the dead are in some cases carried down in arabas, and thrown into graves full of water! It cannot be helped. We suffer a great deal from our boots being too small. Boots three or four times too large in England, are too small for me, and my feet being much swollen from wet and cold, are very painful in consequence. I try all over Balaklava for boots up to the knees, the only thing here, but cannot get them. Let Erin know that I received two letters from him, but the mail came so late there is no chance of writing this mail. No answer yet from Lord Raglan, but as others are in the same way, and as I did not ask for leave to go until approved, expect they have gone clean to England. The weather, thank God, is fine today after an enormous amount of wet, which always obliges us to dig trenches inside our tents, as well as outside, to carry off the water that comes through. The French are at this moment making a reconnaissance across the valley to the ground our pickets were on before 25th October, and yesterday supposed to be evacuated by the Russians in our rear. Today we got some fresh meat after a long spell of salt; quite a treat I assure you, though nearly all bone.

God bless you all, with kindest love to everyone.

Captain Thomas Hutton, 4th Light Dragoons, c. 1856. Credit: Mrs H. Earle.

4

Thomas Hutton

Thomas Hutton was born on 13 July 1821, the fourth son of Henry William Hutton. The family were landed gentry from Lincolnshire with connections to that county stretching back to the late seventeenth century. Henry William Hutton married Marianne, the only child of John Fleming of Beverley, Yorkshire, in August 1811. The first surviving son, Henry John, became a captain in the 34th Regiment. An uncle, Thomas, who was the Colonel of the 4th Dragoon Guards, had served in the Peninsular War.[1]

Writing from Beverley in June 1835, before Thomas Hutton was in his fourteenth year, Henry William Hutton was anxious to acquaint Horse Guards with his son's suitability for a career in the army, 'Having formed the determination, that my son Thomas Hutton shall adopt the army as his profession, and not for the purpose of occupying a few idle years'.[2] Hutton's father applied to have his son's name on the list of candidates for the purchase of a commission. In his letter Hutton reminded the Military Secretary, Lord Fitzroy Somerset, the future Lord Raglan, of his military connections, mentioning his brother, Major Hutton, and his son 'now in the 34th regiment'. He also expressed a preference for particular regiments, including the 60th Rifles, the Rifle Brigade, and the 43rd and 52nd Regiments as favourites. Four years later, in June 1839, the sum of £450 was lodged with Cox & Co. and Thomas Hutton became an ensign in the 15th Foot. The proud father wrote that his son 'will render himself worthy of the service he is about to enter'.[3] On 6 May 1842 a vacancy arose for a lieutenancy and Thomas Hutton was purchased on accordingly. Being a young officer in a line regiment carried with it a certain 'ordinariness' and Hutton's father kept an eye out for more

---

1   *Burke's Landed Gentry 1952*, p. 1333; *New Annual Army List 1840*, p. 85.
2   TNA, WO31/797, Papers related to the commission of Ensign Thomas Hutton 15th Foot.
3   Ibid.

fashionable vacancies even though this would incur more expense. In September 1847 a vacancy arose in the 4th Light Dragoons and Hutton exchanged into it, his father paying the difference in price between the rank of an infantry lieutenant and that of the same rank in the cavalry.

The 4th Light Dragoons were in Ireland and scattered in various detachments in the south. They returned to England in 1850 and did the usual round of tours, being stationed in cavalry barracks at Hampton Court, Woolwich, Ipswich and Norwich. In April 1852 Hutton was purchased on again to the rank of captain.[4] Prophetically Hutton made a £5 bet with a brother officer, Captain George, which was recorded in the Officer's Betting Book on 19 March 1854, 'that the 4th Light Dragoons will not be on service by this time next year in the impending Russian War'.[5] Nine days later Britain and France declared war on Russia.

The order to prepare for service in Turkey was received on 2 July 1854. Prior to that, the regiment had been quartered in Ipswich, and had participated in a month's divisional training with other cavalry regiments at Chobham camp in the summer of 1853. They had then spent ten months in Brighton and then moved to Dorchester in May 1854. The regiment sailed on the steamer *Simla* from Plymouth on 19 July 1854. A private soldier of the 4th Light Dragoons recalled:

> We were a merry company, and not naturally inclined to be downcast; but as the shores of England faded from our view, we could not help thinking of the probabilities of ever returning. These sad thoughts however were short lived. We were all imbued with the martial spirit, and we glowed with enthusiasm as we looked forward to the opportunities which the campaign was likely to afford of serving a not ungrateful country, and winning glory 'even in the cannon's mouth'.[6]

A prayer of Hutton's mother written in July 1854 was found after her death in her book of manuscript prayers for daily use:

> Sailed in the Simla for the seat of war, Wednesday July 19th 1854 at 20 minutes to 4 o'clock.
> I bless thee O God for all thy goodness in times past, for every

---

4   *Hart's New Army List, 1853*, p. 131.
5   Daniell, *4th Hussar*, pp. 158–9.
6   R. S. Farquharson, *Reminiscences of Crimean Campaigning and Russian Imprisonment* (Edinburgh: privately printed, 1883), p. 5.

trial which thou hast lightened, for every difficulty which thou hast removed and for every affliction which thou hast sanctified. Lord continue thy mercies to me. Thou seest the trials that may come upon me and thou alone can strengthen me for them.

I implore thee at this awful time of war and apprehended bloodshed to take under thy especial protection my dear and beloved son. May it please thee to restore him to us in health and honour but if it be Thy will that this sad separation should be forever in this life, Oh prepare him by Thy Spirit's influence for the awful summons. Raise his thoughts to those things which are above that through the blood of Jesus Christ which cleanses from all sin, he may have pardon and acceptance and be numbered among the Spirits of just men made perfect. Lead him to remember how short and uncertain are all our days on Earth and enable me Oh God to submit to thy righteous will concerning him. Into thy hands I commit him beseeching Thee in mercy to my imperfect prayer for the sake of that Saviour in whose blessed name I offer it.
Amen
Sussex Place. 22nd July 1854

Hutton wrote home when the regiment was at Varna. The *Simla* arrived with the regiment, from Constantinople, on 2 August and Hutton's first letter was begun on 20 August, claiming there had been little to say previously [**195**]. The allied camp at Varna in August was not a happy place as the heat, boredom and insanitary conditions began to exert a detrimental effect on the health and efficiency of the allied armies. The Light Division was especially afflicted by cholera but the 4th Light Dragoons were spared the horrors of other regiments. The Muster Roll records only six men dying in August compared with the dozens and scores of other regiments.[7]

Following an allied conference held at Varna on 18 July, where the prospects of a successful landing in the Crimea were discussed, it was agreed to make a reconnaissance. This was undertaken on 25 July and the Katcha River, seven miles north of Sebastopol, selected as a suitable landing-place. Thereafter, preparations started and boats, transports and warships assembled. At a second conference on 19 August, however, anxiety was expressed over supplying the army with no working port at its disposal. On 26 August Raglan and St Arnaud decided the matter

---

7 TNA, WO12/659, Muster Roll, 4th Light Dragoons, July–September 1854.

despite the misgivings of a number of senior officers of both services. By this time, however, the objective was no surprise [195].

The regiment was again embarked on the *Simla*, landing at Kalamita Bay after the infantry and being employed as guard to the 4th Division. The 4th Light Dragoons were witnesses to the battle of the Alma on 20 September. The gap of almost two months between Hutton's first letter in August and his second after Balaklava in October [197] suggests a period of considerable activity.

At Balaklava on 25 October, when the regiment deployed at the end of the North Valley facing the guns of the Don Battery at the other end, it was in the second line. As it advanced, the formation of the brigade was changed from two to three lines as the 11th Hussars were shifted from the first line to compose a second. This had the effect of narrowing the front of the brigade. In the new third line were three troops of the 8th Hussars (one troop being detached as escort to Lord Raglan) and the 4th Light Dragoons. The regiment was made up of two squadrons and each of these was composed of two troops. Lord George Paget was at the head of his regiment and to his left Captains Portal and Brown and Major Halkett. On his right were positioned Lieutenant Jolliffe and Captains Hutton and Low. On their right was Cornet Fiennes Wykeham Martin. Hutton commanded one of the troops of the first squadron.

Unsurprisingly the regiments in the first line suffered appalling casualties as they advanced towards the Don Battery at the end of the valley. Apart from the fire of these guns there were Russian artillery and infantry on the Fedioukine Heights and the Causeway Heights. As the two regiments of the third line advanced at a brisk trot they started to drift apart. Despite all his vocal exertions, Paget could not get the 8th Hussars to keep formation. The 4th Light Dragoons were the 'directing regiment' of the line and, as such, the 8th should have taken their cue from them. In the event they drifted away to the right. When the 4th Light Dragoons reached the guns they were to the right of the 11th Hussars and a little to their rear. Through the smoke and dust horsemen could be perceived. As the 4th advanced it became clear to them that these horsemen were Russian artillery drivers, anxious to limber up and take away their pieces. Only then, as they advanced into the Russian battery, did the 4th Light Dragoons change pace from a collected canter into a charge.

Hutton, wounded in the thigh on the way to the guns, was able to stay mounted and reach the guns. Kinglake wrote, 'It is said that Captain Hutton was seen vigorously using his sword in the battery at a time when he had his thigh broken.' In a subsequent edition, Kinglake added, 'On returning from the guns he was shot through the other thigh, and on reaching the English lines, from the desperate nature of his wounds, was lifted out of his saddle in a scarcely conscious state. His charger had eleven wounds.[8] The 4th eventually went beyond the guns and, with the other regiments, fought their way back to where they had started.

Hutton was lucky to be alive and his wounds rendered him unfit to continue. The wounded of the Light Brigade were examined first by the assistant-surgeons of their respective regiments. In the case of the 4th Light Dragoons this was Assistant-Surgeon Robert Orr Crichton. Hutton would have been treated in a hospital tent and have had the musket balls removed from each of his thighs. He was put on board the transport *Australian*, a steamer that had recently delivered ordnance stores to Balaklava, for transit to Scutari on 27 October. The treatment of officers differed from that of the other ranks at Scutari and Hutton refers to 'apartments' for officers, and says that a surgeon tended him in his own room with a pleasant view over the Bosphorus and use of his own servant from the regiment [198]. As is well known, however, conditions for other ranks at Scutari were scandalously bad.[9]

The reports immediately after Balaklava were often not accurate. Some officers were reported as missing who were not; some reported as captured when they were free; and some as wounded when they were dead. Some of those reported dead were in fact wounded. It was in this last category that Hutton's name was to be found. In Raglan's dispatch on 17 November Hutton's name is among the 'killed and missing' but is in the column for 'other ranks'. Hutton's name finally appeared in the wounded officers column of *The Times* on 15 December. The confusion arose from the way the brigade had been destroyed and the piecemeal return of the survivors to the British lines. It took several days to establish the status of losses and contact with the Russians regarding the names of those who had been captured. Even after a fortnight there were instances of uncertainties. In *The Times* on 13 November 1854 Lord Fitzgibbon and Clowes, both of the 8th Hussars, were reported killed and Goad and Montgomery of the 13th Light Dragoons reported missing. In fact these young officers were dead and their bodies had not been found, with the exception of Clowes, who was taken prisoner. For the anxious families at home the lack of accurate information obviously added to their worries.[10]

---

8 Kinglake, *Invasion of the Crimea*, vol. 5, p. 327.

9 See Sue Goldie, ed., *'I Have Done My Duty': Florence Nightingale in the Crimean War, 1854–56* (Manchester: Manchester University Press, 1987), pp. 32–68.

10 *The Times*, 13 November 1854; ibid., 18 November 1854; ibid., 15 December 1854, p. 10, col. A.

At the end of November Hutton was examined by a medical board that determined his condition warranted his return home. From Scutari, he was eventually transferred to Malta and, after a month there, invalided home via Gibraltar [206, 207]. He arrived at Spithead on the *Orinoco* on 9 February 1855.[11] In the months that followed his return, he recuperated. He was sufficiently recovered to attend the ceremony at Horse Guards Parade on 18 May 1855 where Queen Victoria personally distributed the Crimean Medal to officers and men from all branches of the service. He rejoined his regiment from the depot on its return from the Crimea on 1 June 1856.[12] In the same month he was promoted to Brevet Major.

On 14 August 1856 Hutton married Maria Georgina Everard, the only child of Edward Everard of Middleton Hall, King's Lynn. In an undated letter to her mother before her marriage, Maria Georgina Everard reveals a glimpse of Hutton's character: 'he has a very humble opinion of himself and is so kind and amiable, it is hardly possible to think too well of him.'[13] She continued that she hoped her father would think that in her marriage to Captain Hutton her parents would not be losing a daughter but gaining a 'charming son-in-law'.

On the second anniversary of Balaklava, Hutton joined other officers from the Light and Heavy Brigades who met at the London Tavern to commemorate and celebrate their participation in the battle and no doubt to drink to absent friends. With his wounds healed and experiences of war and military life sufficient to satisfy his character, Hutton retired by the sale of his commission on 10 October 1857. Thereafter, Hutton managed his estates and raised his family. Between 1857 and 1868 there were seven children – five girls and two boys, both of whom died in infancy. The family resided at Dolben Hall, St Asaph's, North Wales, until 1864. In that year Hutton's father-in-law, Edward Everard, died and Hutton moved to Middleton Hall and assumed the surname Everard Hutton. At Middleton Hall there was a display of Crimean relics over which was inscribed 'The clash of swords, the ring of spears, makes music to the soldier's ears'.[14] Many of the items of uniform and equipment Hutton took to the Crimea have survived. His booted cavalry overalls, with leather sewn around the end of each leg just above the ankle and into the inside seams and seat, reveal the holes in each leg in the thigh area from the fire that wounded him at Balaklava, while his saddle, now in the National

---

11   *The Times*, 10 February 1855, p. 10, col. B; ibid., 12 February 1855, p. 12, col. A.
12   TNA, WO12/661, Muster Roll, 4th Light Dragoons, 1856.
13   Victoria & Albert Museum, Hutton Bequest.
14   Information supplied by Mrs Helen Earle, a descendant of Thomas Hutton.

Army Museum, also shows bullet damage.[15] Other items, including the leather cavalry holster, with damage from a bullet, are in the regimental collection of the Queen's Royal Irish Hussars.

Hutton was a regular attendee at the commemorative banquets held by officers of the Light and Heavy Brigades in London. In the early 1880s he moved to No. 7 The Circus, Bath. Here he lived out the rest of his life. He enjoyed shooting and watching cricket and was a regular worshipper at Bath Abbey. In early June 1896 he was stricken with influenza and, despite the ministrations of his neighbour Dr Coates and Sir William Broadbent, he died on 10 June 1896.

He was buried on Saturday 13 June at Locksbrook Cemetery. Four black horses drew his coffin and the cortège was made up of the carriages of his widow, family and friends. Among the latter was Sir Fitzroy Maclean, who had served in the Crimea in the 13th Light Dragoons, and Percy Shaw Smith, also of the 13th Light Dragoons, who had charged with the Light Brigade despite having a maimed right hand and being unarmed. On Hutton's coffin was the simple inscription 'Thomas Everard Hutton. One of the Six Hundred.'[16]

---

15 Massie, *Most Desperate Undertaking*, pp. 115–17; Mollo and Mollo, *Into the Valley of Death*, p. 51.
16 *Bath Chronicle*, 18 June 1896; Lummis and Wynn, *Honour the Light Brigade*, pp. 196–7.

195

Hutton to his sister Minnie[1]

Varna 20 August 1854

I allowed the last post to go without writing to any of you simply because I really had nothing to say. I might almost say the same now but I suppose you would like to hear whether I am dead or alive. I hope my letters have all come to hand. I have written 2 to Mother and one each to Harriot and Georgy.[2] Very little has really occurred since you last heard of me, the rumours fly thick enough every hour of the day, causing very little excitement to labour under. A welcome report reached us today from Lord Westmoreland to his son Lord Burghersh that the Russians were or rather had retreated over the Pruth that the Turks were in occupation of Bucharest and the Austrians in full march there to keep possession of the Principalities. If this is true it will be a great thing gained to our side. I should doubt however whether the Russians or the Allied Powers would either of them be satisfied with this. A project is still on the tapis with regard to the Crimea and the Navy make no disguise of the matter saying their instructions are against Sebastopol and plans of attack are made. Yesterday General St. Arnaud and Lord Raglan were trying by way of experiment embarking and re-embarking of artillery. It did not however seem to answer – for one of the horse boats I observed afterwards had capsized and nearly drawn another down with it. I was also told by an eye-witness that several of the horses went overboard with the riders in each instance undermost but there were no casualties. There was some fault with the blinkers I believe and the horses on the narrow horse boats were not able to see sufficiently when they commenced shying and struggling. It was generally supposed the Army would embark tomorrow, the infantry in consequence have been selling their horses, but today hear no more on the subject so perhaps the whole affair will blow over again, as so many other projects have. Three regiments of Foot Guards and one of Highlanders marched down here the day before yesterday and are stationed about 2 miles from us; also the Royals and 5th Dragoon Guards which augments our Cavalry division to 5th Regiment. The Scots Greys at Scutari are also available if anything is required of the Cavalry. I called

---

1   His sister, Marianne Eleanor (1812–1908).
2   Harriott Susan, another sister, and his niece, Georgina Ackers.

on Antrobus[3] of the 50th the other day; like the rest of his family he is no beauty but a manly young fellow and I should say liked in his regiment from what I saw he is in the Grenadier Company. I believe the weather is changing for the better; last night it blew very heavily and was quite cold. Today for the first time the sun has been obscured by clouds and it is delightfully cool. To look at this country and our encampment high up on the hills and almost surrounded by the sea, you would most reasonably suppose it the most healthy place in the world, and perhaps when the cholera has passed over it, it may be so. At present we are not entirely free of it, tho' the worst of it we hope has passed over. I lost a man in my troop yesterday. Our horses begin to look very thin upon the shameful rations issued to them. They are fat compared to other Regt's. However we are fortunate in getting some pressed hay from the 'Simla' this is all out today and we must take our chances with the others. They serve us sometimes only 6 lbs of barley a day for a horse, no grain at all but fresh cut barley on the stalk and the 5th Dragoon Guards on their march down here the other day had literally nothing but what they could pick up. Nothing issued whatever for 2 whole days. The Russians I believe are in a state of starvation and their late desperate attacks on Arab Tapia at Silistria were in reality more on the Turks loaves of bread than themselves. I saw an officer today who had just come down from there and he says it is a literal fact that their bread and rations there really stopped until they took the place. He described the works as very insignificant, the ditch not deeper than the height of a man's breast and so narrow that a troop of English Dragoons could have ridden clean over it into the Fort. How the struggle was prolonged to such a length of time is quite a mystery. The ground all round was quite paved by Russian shells and the number stated to have been fired could have been, no exaggeration, 50,000.

August 24th.

This must go today at 11 o'clock so I must finish off my letter. The attack on the Crimea they say is certain to be made and Sebastopol is supposed to be the place. The infantry are hard at work making 'fascines and gabions'. Yesterday some of the artillery and siege guns were embarked, the men and horses go on board today, the infantry will most probably go next and the cavalry last. Several Turkish transports in with a flying breeze yesterday, also the 'Simla' with the 4th Foot on board which she disembarked the same evening and leaves again this morning for Constantinople with orders to coal up there and get forage for horses for

---

3   Lieutenant Edward Crawford Antrobus, 50th (Queen's Own) Regt. of Foot. See *Hart's New Annual Army List 1855*, p. 201.

6 weeks. Some of the French Cavalry Regiments are leaving for Burgos, a place I fancy on the coast between Varna and Bucro Bay. They say it is to embark there for Sebastopol, or else on account of the scarcity of forage the French agree with us in thinking its much too late for so serious an undertaking. The weather already appears to have changed from summer to autumn and they say the rains will come on in another fortnight. The whole company is expected to be on board by 1st September. I should say it might be possible to get the artillery and infantry on board by that time but they will have to work much harder than heretofore. They have built piers for the cavalry, infantry and artillery all marshalled for their separate embarcations. There appears to be more alertness and activity and more shipping in the harbour than ever, but I'm afraid the season will be too advanced by the time all these are ready. Small steamers are a good deal used here now drawing about 4 ft of water only so they are to be employed in embarking shot. They are also to be used in covering the landing of the troops to the Crimea by going close in shore and firing shell and rockets. Sickness is on the decline now and Varna is considered most healthy. It would be difficult to say however where winter quarters will be. I have not had any letters yet from England but a mail was due yesterday which might certainly be in today so I hope to get a letter from some of you by it.

Keith of my regiment got an appointment on Sir Richard England's staff.[4] He will be along with Colbourne – it is ridiculous to say it but news has just been brought that the Constanzia is again put off to the 2nd September so you must never rely upon the first part of a letter. In fact we never now take anything for solid truth unless it has actually occurred. Order and counter order are quite the order of the day here. The town of Varna actually smokes still from the late fire, so you may judge the extent of it, though the shops are being again gradually re-opened and the ships in harbour have been lately supplying us with port wines at a less exorbitant charge than the town's people. I daresay at the present time you are at Ryde but I shall direct this to Regent's Park imagining that by the first week in September you will be back again in London. I am in high expectation today of hearing how you are all getting on lately. My paper and stock of news is really quite exhausted so I shall close my epistle with best love to all the family.

---

4   Lieutenant The. Hon. Charles James Keith became ADC to Sir Richard England, commanding the 3rd Division. See TNA, WO12/ 659, Muster Lists, 4th Light Dragoons, July–September 1854.

196

From Lord George Paget to unknown recipient.

[No date]
Hutton was wounded in the leg in the advance, but hollered to say that he would go on. He cut down 2 or 3 fellows at their guns afterwards and on the return in the thick of the fire, I found myself riding alongside of him, both our horses dead beat, so flanking them with our swords, when he coolly said 'Colonel, do give me a drop of Brandy, I am wounded in both legs, will you have any objection to my going to the doctor when I get back'. Poor fellow I hear he is suffering today very much on board ship but nothing dangerous.

197

Hutton to George Holland Ackers[5]

Steam Ship 'Australia',[6] October 28.
I hope the 'papers' will not furnish you with any present news before the arrival of this. We have had a most disastrous affair at Balaklava, the Light Brigade of Cavalry have been almost cut to pieces, through the wilful obstinacy, or wickedness I may say of a General, whose name I will not give.[7] We were ordered to charge down a valley and attack and take twelve guns at the bottom, one hill side of the valley was regularly fortified with breast-work guns and Infantry and we could distinctly see the Field-guns of the enemy on the opposite side; through this tremendous gauntlet of guns we had to charge a mile down the valley and then be opposed to the fire of the battery and the charge of some thousand of Dragoons. You may imagine the result, a child might have seen the trap that was laid for us, as every private dragoon did. We advanced in two lines at full trot in the most perfect order possible through a concentrated storm of shot, shell, grape, canister rifle balls

---

5 George Holland Ackers, Hutton's brother-in-law. He had served in the Royal Horse Guards in the 1830s. See War Office, *The Army List 1835*, p. 111.

6 *Australia*: Transport no. 120 recorded as *Australian* on the government schedule. The ship was steam powered and some 1,392 tons. She is recorded as 'taking wounded troops' from Balaklava to Constantinople and making the return voyage 'with shot and shell'. There is a note stating 'to be a transport for sick troops' in the schedule. See HCPP 1854–55 (283), pp. 30–1.

7 Presumably Raglan, Lucan, or Cardigan.

and every missile that could be hurled at us; the ground was quickly spread with wounded men and horses.

I got a disagreeable fore-runner by a ball ripping the cloth of my jacket at the elbow and, the next moment, I was struck on the right thigh, with such violence I thought my whole leg had been carried off by a cannon shot, – I charged on, however, with the regiment, in spite of pain and loss of blood.[8]

We succeeded in cutting down the gunners and dispersing a part of their Cavalry, capturing the guns, only the next moment being obliged to give them up for want of support.[9] We had then again to retire through the same gauntlet of guns and crowds of Dragoons to oppose us, – it was awful work, with a blown horse, and a wound in the leg which was weaker every moment but I was determined to stick to my regiment and on my horse, as long as I possibly could, instead of trusting to the mercy of the Cossacks as some foolishly did. We returned from our charge, and singular to say, I was again struck about the same spot on the other leg. We shortly after reached our lines, when I was put on a stretcher and taken on board this ship, destined for Scutari with a whole lot of others in the same plight. My wounds are flesh ones only, no broken bones, tho' one was almost grazed, no artery cut and only one nerve in the left thigh divided which renders the whole leg for the present quite numb, but will not at all affect me afterwards. Altogether I consider myself most fortunate and I trust if the cloth from my overalls and linen has in each case been forced through, and does not remain in, soon to be well enough to return to England. I took one of the balls that favoured me out of the flap of my saddle. My chestnut horse was terribly cut about. My Lieutenant (Sparke) was left wounded on the field, now missing, most likely a prisoner, ditto Major Halkett. My Sergeant Major was killed,[10] and 7 men mustered round their Captain at the finish. The whole regiment mustered only 40 and 50 and the other 4 regiments composing

---

8   According to Paget, 'The doings of this brave fellow deserve record. He was shot through the right thigh during the advance and holloaed out to his squadron leader, "Low, I am wounded, what shall I do?" to which the latter replied, "If you can sit on your horse, you had better come along with us; there's no use going back now, you'll only be killed." He went on, and if reports speak truly, made good use of his powerful arm in disabling some of the enemy. On his return he was shot through his other thigh (he ultimately recovered), his horse being hit in eleven places. When I overtook him he complained of feeling faint, and asked if I could give him a little rum, which I fumbled out of my holster as we were going along. He then naively said, "I have been wounded, Colonel; would you have any objection to my going to the doctor when I get in?" (This all under a heavy fire!).' See Paget, *Light Cavalry Brigade*, p. 193.

9   Many officers and men of the Light Brigade believed they had been let down by Lucan and his decision not to follow them down the valley with the Heavy Brigade.

10 1134 Troop Sergeant-Major Frank Herbert, from Kensington, London. He enlisted on 5 July 1841 and was a clerk prior to enlistment. He was the only Troop Sergeant-Major of the 4th Light Dragoons to be killed in the charge. See Lummis and Wynn, *Honour the Light Brigade*, p. 27.

the Light Brigade were even worse off than ourselves, the 17th Lancers had only 3 Officers untouched. 4 of their wounded officers are on board this ship, 2 Russians and 1 Infantry Officer and nearly 200 men. We have plenty of room and are doing as well as can be expected. Fever, pain and stiffness of wounds does not conduce to sleep, but, this being the 4th day, we hope our wounds will begin to suppurate and then get easier. I am afraid Thomkinson of the 8th Hussars was killed,[11] a cousin of the Lees of Joddrell.

Will you be so kind as to break all this to mother? I thought it better to write to you, than to her or my sisters; tell them they need not be alarmed.

29th We have just dropped anchor off Constantinople and expect to be put ashore immediately at Scutari, where the apartments for officers in the Hospital, I am told, are very good accommodation and attendance also, with a beautiful view. I am still going on very well, tho' last night at sea it blew a gale, which was against our comfort as well as progress. You will see me classed in the papers among the severely wounded but as no bones or arteries are broke, and the doctor says I am going on well, you may place me, I hope, in a more reduced list. I have nothing more now to add, but trust soon to return to you all again and with best love to all.

[PS] Pray excuse my abruptness and this scrawl under the circumstances.

198

Hutton to his sister Minnie

Scutari Barracks, November 14

You see I take you all in turn to write to, as a mail goes tomorrow I am about to give you yours.

I am still going on very favourably indeed, the Doctors say. The wounds in my left leg have given over discharging and the flesh is beginning to grow and fill up, – I have however very little feeling in it, it is like a leg asleep, owing to the nerve being cut through, – this is all to disappear they say, as it heals and it is already certainly improved in this respect, the cramp has passed down the leg into the foot, and every now and then gives me an awkward twinge. My right leg, which was not so badly wounded as the other, still continues to discharge, this was explained to

---

11   Captain Edward Tomkinson survived the charge, though wounded. His horse was killed. See Lummis and Wynn, *Honour the Light Brigade*, p. 73.

me the day before yesterday by a piece of cloth coming away, which no doubt had irritated it. It is going on very well otherwise.

The wounds become a little more painful and stiff (strange to say) as they heal. Want of sleep is what I most complain of and every evening for 4 or 5 hours, I have fever, so I take two doses of quinine each day and think of Georgy, you may tell her.

O'Flaherty[12] one of the principle doctors here said he cured an officer of the 'Vesuvius' in 7 weeks, who was wounded exactly the same as myself, that he was able to get about with the aid of crutches in that time.

I have got my own servant with me, a great comfort. He had been away from the Crimea down at Scutari for some weeks, ill with fever, but by the time I landed, he was all right again. I was much surprised yesterday to see Paget walk into my room:– he was very civil and kind in his enquiries and offered to do anything for me. He was on his way to England and is going to sell out immediately. The poor Major having been killed in action, Low jumps into the Majority and Lieutenant-Colonelcy almost in the same gazette. George Brown becomes Major and I get two steps to compensate me for two wounds – dearly bought in my opinion. I heard from Low the other day, his accounts of the siege are rather unsatisfactory – they are putting off the assault on the town, until more reinforcements come up. Yesterday 3 or 4 English regiments from the Mediterranean and about 15,000 French passed up the Bosphorus for the purpose, so we may soon hear of the down-fall of the place – they are all dreadfully sick of the siege and their harassing duty. Adlington had two chargers killed under him on the 5th but the loss of the regiment was only 2 men.[13] They say the Russians are thoroughly cowed by the licking they got on that day, their loss must have been enormous – our Light Brigade alone buried 8,000 of them, a Russian Major, who was seen with a party murdering our wounded men, was caught and tried and at once hanged, they are terrible savages in this way. I have nothing more to add and am getting tired, so with best love to my mother,

---

12 Richard James O' Flaherty (1811–74), Assistant Surgeon Staff, 9 January 1835. He held a variety of staff posts and was Surgeon Major, 28 March 1854. His promotions continued until Surgeon General in October 1872. See Peterkin and Johnston, *Commissioned Officers*, vol. 1, p. 294.

13 The 4th Light Dragoons were under fire with the rest of the Light Brigade at Inkerman and suffered two fatalities: 1065 Pvt. James Rickman and 1526 Pvt. Charles Wohlman. Rickman was orderly to Paget who wrote, 'Rickman had been shot through the thigh and only survived the amputation of his leg an hour.' He had been a carpenter from Wargrave, Berkshire, prior to his enlistment in September 1839. Wohlman had enlisted in February 1852 and was a grocer from Surrey. See Paget, *Light Cavalry Brigade*, p. 227; TNA, WO12/659, Muster List, 4th Light Dragoons, 1854–55.

[PS] Tell Alfy, I 'fleshed' my maiden sword at Balaklava on the 25th as he terms it.[14]

199

Letter from Lady Paget to Hutton's mother

[No date]
72 South Audley Street. Wednesday.
Lady George Paget presents her compliments to Mrs Hutton and hearing from Mr Chilers (?) of her anxiety about her son begs to say that she has every reason to hope that no officer has been killed in the action on the 25th tho' the details of it will not arrive before next Saturday, accounts have been received in Paris that the loss in the Light Cavalry is 124 men but no Officers as mentioned. Lady George will let Mrs Hutton know the moment she knows anything more an-d trust she receives a letter from Lord George.

200

Mrs Hutton's prayer in response to the news of Thomas Hutton's wounding at Balaklava

Sunday 12th Nov. 1854
My birthday and the day we received the sad and disastrous private information of my beloved son's severe wounds at the Battle of Balaklava on 25th Oct. 1854.

O Lord God Almighty, the Giver of all good, our refuge and strength in the hour of trial and of sorrow, harken to the supplication of thy servant. In the hour of battle, Thou didst vouchsafe Thy most merciful protection to my beloved soldier and spared his life delivering him from the hands of our enemies. Oh Lord continue I beseech thee, Thy loving kindness towards him and now whilst languishing in a foreign land in pain and sickness, strengthen and support him and in Thy infinite mercy, restore him to me in Thine own good time.

---

14   Alfred Hutton, brother of Thomas, was one of Europe's leading swordsmen. His expertise and prowess became internationally celebrated. He wrote numerous books on swordsmanship and his papers and swords are now in the Victoria and Albert Museum in London.

Impart to him the consolation of Thy Holy Spirit, enable him to cast his soul entirely on the free mercy of his blessed Saviour, through whom I offer this poor and imperfect prayer – bless and watch over him – and by the interception of that blessed Saviour, maybe at last inherit peace and happiness in that 'better country' where no enemy can approach to hurt him. Hear and harken to me Oh God for Jesus Christ's sake. Amen.

Sussex Place. Nov. 1854

201

Hutton to Lieutenant Fiennes Wykeham Martin[15]

Scutari Barracks. November 27

I suppose you are doing adjutant still and therefore write to you in that capacity – I want my private servant Mond sending down here to me as soon as possible and as I also want to keep Stratton[16] about me here up to the last moment, I want you to get the C.O.'s permission for a man from the ranks to look after my horses for the few days that will intervene between Mond coming here and my being able to send Stratton back to the Crimea. I had a most solemn board of the 3 principle Medical Officers the other day, who separately had to swear one another in, to adjudicate upon my wounds with regard to Blood money. I don't know what they are going to give me, but the P.M.O. of all said my wounds were very severe and recommended me to go home as soon as ever I could move. My medical man wants me to go in the course of 2 or 3 days in the 'Taurus',[17] in which vessel White of the 17th goes,[18] but I don't really feel strong enough and shall put it off, in hopes of another ship

---

15 Wykeham Martin, 4th Light Dragoons was acting Adjutant of the regiment. Hutton addresses him as 'My dear Nick'.

16 1113 Pvt. Healy Stratton, groom to Hutton. He was born at Pinchbeck, Spalding, Lincolnshire, in July 1820 and enlisted into 4th Light Dragoons in April 1840. Stratton was present at the battle of the Alma, but was sent to Scutari on 26 September and invalided home on Christmas Day 1854. He was among the officers and men presented with their Crimean Medals on Horse Guards on 18 May 1855. He was discharged 'on the reduction of the regiment' in April 1857, to a deferred pension. Stratton died on 8 March 1897 in Ardwick, Manchester, and was recorded as a railway clerk. See TNA, WO12/659, Muster List, 4th Light Dragoons, 1854–55.

17 A steam transport, owned by the North American Steam Navigation Company, 1,126 tons. First employed from Cork to Malta. See HCPP 1854–55 (283), p. 5.

18 Captain Robert White, 17th Lancers, severely wounded in the charge and sent to Scutari on 26 October 1854. He was given leave to proceed to England on 13 January 1855 for recovery of his health. See Lummis and Wynn, *Honour the Light Brigade*, p. 224.

sailing about the 7th or 10th of next month. I managed to crawl out of bed yesterday and tried to raise myself on crutches, but the effort was so much beyond my strength, I as near as a toucher fainted and was only prevented the catastrophe by taking a copious draft of port. My wounds are going on very well now only discharge sufficient to keep them open, which for a time is a thing to be desired. My left leg gives me incessant pain night and day from the nerves or muscles being injured and I get no sleep. I cannot move my foot one bit, it is exactly in the same state as when I was wounded first – I can neither sink the heel or raise the toe. This with perpetual shooting pains through it is what I have to complain of most. I congratulate you on your promotion through Hartman.[19] I hear you cut away right and left on the 25th at Balaclava in the way I always expected a Stout-un would do. I have just read the Balaclava affair in the papers. 'Misconception of orders' is but a lame way of getting out of it and will no doubt call for further enquiry.[20]

[PS] My object in getting Mond down here is to take him back to England.

202

Lady Paget to Mrs Hutton

December 6th [1854].
72 South Audley Street Monday.
Lady George Paget presents her compliments to Mrs Hutton and in case she has not yet heard from her son, is happy to say that in a letter she has received from Lord George, he particularly mentioned that Captain Hutton is going on well and recovering on board ship and that his wound is not dangerous. Lord George also mentioned the great gallantry and coolness with which he behaved even after he was wounded.

---

19   Lieutenant Gustavus Adolphus Hartman, 4th Light Dragoons went on half pay with the rank of captain from 10 November 1854. Wykeham Martin's promotion, however, was dated from 26 October 1854. See *Hart's New Annual Army List, 1855*, p. 352.
20   The debate regarding the culpability for the destruction of the Light Cavalry Brigade still continues. See Douglas Austin, 'Nolan at Balaklava', *The War Correspondent* 23, 4 (2006), pp. 20–1; ibid., 24, 2 (2006), pp. 7–8; ibid., 24, 3 (2006), pp. 20–5; ibid., 24, 4 (2007), pp. 15–21; ibid., 26, 4 (2009), pp. 14–22; Buttery, *Messenger of Death*, pp. 129–60.

203

Lord George Paget to Mrs Hutton

circa Christmas Day [1854]
Must write to express to you the very great gratification I felt at reading today in the papers the authorised contradiction of your son's death. I never myself believed in it, having gone to the Horse Guards the day when the report came, when I was told they knew nothing about it. Still it is no less consolatory to see this officially confirmed and beg you to believe how – I sympathise with you.

204

Letter to Mrs Hutton from the War Office[21]

Undated letter
The Lord Cardigan has just called to inform me that he has received a letter from Lord George Paget, and must regret to tell you that Captain Hutton is seriously wounded in both legs. This sad intelligence will I fear be a great shock to you, but it must be some relief to know that your son is living after the anxiety and uncertainty of the last few days. I sincerely trust that more detailed accounts may give you more comfort.
Believe me – Yours
Thomas

205

Unknown correspondent[22] to Mrs Hutton

Monday ¼ to 5
21 Merrion Street
Dublin
December 19/54
Having seen a report of the death of Capt. Hutton in the Times of

---

21   It has not been possible to identify the writer, but he was presumably a War Office civil servant.
22   Signature of correspondent illegible.

yesterday, I have great pleasure in contradicting it. He was progressing as favourably as possible and his wounds were nearly healed when I left Constantinople on the 6th December and the mail which left the day before the 5th has not arrived in England yet. I should have taken the liberty of calling yesterday on my way through London but had only time to drive from one station to the other. Captain Hutton had intended to go to Malta in the 'Trent' and used to sit up on a box for hours and was gaining strength every day.

206

Hutton to Minnie

January 10
Auberge de Castelle [Castille], Malta
I received a few days ago your and my mother's joint letter dated the 28th. I am a good deal surprised that up to that date, you had not heard from me since the 5th December at Scutari. I arrived here on the 15th and wrote a letter to Harriot, via Marseilles, which I am afraid must have miscarried. I also wrote by the next mail on the 21st, I think to my mother, which ought to have reached you by the 28th or 30th when I think the English Mail closed. I am very sorry if these letters miscarried particularly at that time, when I know you were all very anxious about me and wanted Mr. Booth's letter confirmed by one of mine. I am happy to say I am going on remarkably well and expect today when the Doctor takes the bandages off my leg to find the last of my wounds quite healed – yesterday it was healed all but the size of a pea, it is exactly 11 weeks today since the occurrence. I yesterday got a pair of crutches and hope tomorrow to make a trial of them, but only expect to get one leg on the ground, my left one tho' healed 3 weeks ago, being at present useless, owing to the nerve, which has not recovered itself. I had a letter from Morland the other day – it had gone to Scutari and had been forwarded from there. I have not received your kind presents but hope they will arrive from Constantinople before I leave this for England. I expect to go on board some ship or other between the 20th and 25th of this month, so that you may confidently reckon on seeing me about the first week in February, if all goes well. There are 2 sailing 3 decker men-of-war going from here very soon with sick and wounded for England, but I wanted to avoid going in

these and getting hold of a steamer, if I can, thus doing the passage quicker and more agreeably. I shall however write to you again if not twice before leaving this. I don't know when the mails leave England, but I think you need not write again – at least post a letter to me after the 18th for I feel satisfied I shall be gone a few days after that date. The weather here is most beautiful and all the Crimea men are deriving the greatest benefit from it. I got a shake of the hand yesterday from the 'Royal Duke' who kindly asked after my wounds and entered into conversation with me about the Balaclava fight, he laughed over the idea of Paget coming out again and seemed to think it a very good joke:– no joke to his Lordship I should say.[23]

Sir George Brown is here also and his wound in the arm is now healing,[24] which before was very obstinate – his health and also the Duke's are wonderfully on the improve. The former has a charger here with no less than 9 bullets in him, 2 have been extracted, but the remainder are still there. Sir Charles Maclean,[25] who has a son in the 13th sick here, called on me the other day, was very civil indeed, offered me either his close or open carriage and his box at the opera and hoped I would go out to their house about 2 miles off, whenever I felt inclined; everybody says they are a very nice family indeed. A Mr. Arkwright,[26] brother to one of that name, formerly in the 4th sends me the latest newspapers also a Capt. Jarvis,[27] A.D.C. to the General here, is very civil and does the same. He is a Lincolnshire man, as well as Mr. Bourton and both seem to know our relatives there. The Mail has come in and now goes out a full day earlier than usual, which has obliged me to get up early to write this in time.

23   The Duke of Cambridge. Given that he had been granted leave to recover his health, the joke about Paget returning to the Crimea must have seemed somewhat hollow. See Edgar Sheppard, *HRH George Duke of Cambridge: A Memoir* 2 vols (London: Longmans Green & Co. 1906), vol. 1, pp. 129–46.

24   Sir George Brown had been wounded in the arm at Inkerman. He was taken to Constantinople and then on to Malta on the *Tamar*, arriving on 9 January 1855. See *The Times*, 15 January 1855.

25   Lieutenant Fitzroy Donald Maclean, 13th Light Dragoons, the only son of Colonel Sir Charles Fitzroy Maclean, 9th Baronet. He was sick after the battle of the Alma and eventually sent to Malta. See Lummis and Wynn, *Honour the Light Brigade*, pp. 197–8.

26   Possibly Eustace Arkwright, an officer in the 9th Light Dragoons (Lancers) who came to the 4th Light Dragoons in 1843. See *Hart's New Annual Army List 1845*, p. 131.

27   Captain Jarvis was reported as ADC to Sir George Brown. According to *The Times*, Brown and his aide returned to the Crimea from Malta in February 1855 on board HMS *Spiteful*. The ship's list, however, contradicts this, with Brown returning to the Crimea with Major Edward Whitmore and a servant, William Richards. See TNA, ADM38/9083, HMS *Spiteful* Muster Lists; *The Times*, 8 February 1855.

[PS] One of my horses in the Crimea, I hear has died. Luckily it was the least valuable of the three and I hope to get from the Government nearly as much as I gave for him. He was my dog-cart horse and a very good one.

207

Hutton to George Holland Ackers

Malta 16th January 1855
I received yours and Harriot's kind, joint letter the day before yesterday dated the 7th I am very much obliged to you for your kindness in wishing to come down to Southampton to meet me. I hope however you will not think it necessary as my servant and my own re-invigorated health will enable me to pull through to London. So you must suit your own inclination. I can say I should be delighted to see you. I am also very much obliged for your very good offer of a run on grass in the park for my charger. I fancy both my horses will be sent to the depot shortly and as the one you allude to is still very serviceable, I shall be able to make use of him for some time yet I hope.

Many thanks however for your kind offer and your hope of seeing me at Moreton ere long, which I would enjoy much. My last wound has been for the last 10 days as nearly healed as possible, all but about the size of half a pea. But the last bit I have found in the other 3 punctures of my skin have always been the same, long and obstinate to get well, tantalising one at its [illegible]. My Medical man [illegible] it will be quite well tomorrow. I tried crutches the other day but found my legs uncommonly weak and from being so long in a bent position I find I cannot straighten them, which will be highly inconvenient for some time in walking; and I also wear a bandage on the leg that is not healed and this slips down when I try and straighten the leg. I am obliged to put off the use of the crutches again until it is well which will be only I hope a few days. I shall try and get a passage on the 23rd of this month by P&O Steamer for Alexandria to Southampton which ought to cruise in 10 days here but there is many a slip between cup and lip and as I still see 5 3 decker men of war in the harbour here, yet (Sailing vessels) the admiral may take it into his head to order me a passage in one of them. This would delay my getting to England for sometime and I could not say which port they would steer for. However you shall hear more in my next mail when my flint lock is fixed as they say. The weather here is perfectly delightful – a fine crisp air – brisk and invigorating as soda water. It has done wonders for me in the short month I have been here. To look at me you would really think nothing had ever occurred to me, a wonderful contrast to when I first landed. The 'Princess Royal'[28] is expected here every day; the 'Duke' and Sir George Brown with their staffs still remain but are living very quiet and retired. A few wounded officers are also still here but most went direct home. The report of 'peace' being established gives universal satisfaction to all those here who have been in the Crimea; but officers going on and the French troops passing by [seem] only half to like the idea. I should think it was still a very doubtful matter and I think Sebastopol may yet fall before it comes off. I suppose the World and England in particular could never be satisfied without this. Please do thank Harriot for her note and with best love to her and Georgy.

[PS] Jan. 17th My wound is not quite well even today. Please tell Georgy I have just received her letter via Southampton for which many thanks.

208

Hutton to his niece Georgina Ackers

Malta January 22nd 1855

I think it is my turn to fire you a line, and in a tremendous hurry, I am, as the mail is suddenly [illegible] off and I have only a few minutes to write this. I have been [illegible] to take a passage in the 'Sanspareil' a [illegible] 2 decker which is expected to arrive here any day from the Crimea on route for England to be paid off, but I do not know what port she goes to but will ascertain that in my next letter. I have [illegible] probably 18 days on the voyage. I am happy to say my wounds are at last healed over quite, and I manage on my crutches to hobble about like a four footed animal. I do not however venture up and down stairs yet but am carried down on a stretcher when I want to go out for carriage exercise. Tell my mother I received her letter yesterday and wrote her a note [illegible] which will go by this same mail, so she will hear of me through two of my letters this time altho' I have lost time now to write one to herself.

---

28   The *Princess Royal*, a screw-driven steamship, 400-horse power. See *Admiralty Navy Lists January 1855*, p. 165, no. 393.

Lord George Paget and his wife passed through Malta yesterday[29] but I did not see them to speak to. I heard he was looking wretchedly ill. I suppose the Lady will remain at Constantinople. I was out driving today in Sir Charles Maclean's carriage which he is good enough to put at my disposal. You will think this a very scrappy production but the post will close immediately so I must conclude and with best love to all at Moreton.

209

Hutton to his mother

Spithead, Portsmouth.
Friday 9th February 1855
We have just arrived here all safe after a rather stormy passage. As we shall not land until late and perhaps not till tomorrow, I write a line to say I shall if possible leave [illegible] to be in time for dinner with you tomorrow. I hear the train goes at 3 o'clock and will arrive at 6 in the evening.

29 Paget and his wife sailed from Marseilles in the *Carmel*, a French ship making her first trip. Paget had for company 150 French dragoons, some drafts of French infantry and 18 acting assistant surgeons. He seems to have taken exception to them, describing their 'filthy luggage' and 'their filthy selves'. To add to his woes, his wife and her maid were washed out of their cabin on the first night. See Paget, *Light Cavalry Brigade*, p. 264.

Biographical Notes

Sir George Brown (1790–1865)   Born in Linkwood, Elgin, Scotland, Sir George Brown's military career started in January 1806. He was present at the siege and capture of Copenhagen in 1807, and also served in the Peninsular War. He was severely wounded in both thighs at the battle of Talavera and was also present with the Light Division at the bridge at Almeida, the battle of Busaco, the action at Sabugal, the battle of Fuentes d'Onor, the Siege of San Sebastian, the battles of Nivelle and Nive and the investment of Bayonne. Sir George served in the American War and was present at the battle of Bladensburg, where he was slightly wounded in the head and groin, and the capture of Washington.[1] After the Napoleonic Wars he held a series of staff appointments at Horse Guards including that of Adjutant General. He was in charge of the Light Division from the outset of the campaign and was euphemistically termed a ' strict disciplinarian'.[2] Flogging, pipe-clay, stocks and drill were the features of his leadership off the battlefield. *The Times* printed a ditty heard at Varna in 1854 in their generous obituary to Sir George Brown in 1865:

Come pipe-clay your jackets and buckle your stocks,
Away with moustachios and dirt breeding locks;
Such dombded ennovations I'll surely put down;
It's nae up wi' the shakos cries General Brown.[3]

On the battlefield Sir George Brown was a brave and determined leader. At the Alma his horse was killed as he led the Light Division forward with what *The Times* described as 'the impetuous valour of the fiery old

---

1   *Hart's Annual Army List 1852*, p. 229, note 1.
2   John Sweetman, *The Crimean War 1854–56*. (London: Osprey Publishing, 2001), p. 23.
3   *The Times*, 29 August 1865, p. 7 col. F.

leader'.[4] At the battle of Inkerman he was wounded and forced to quit the Crimea to recover his health. He did so and returned in time to lead the attack on Kertch. He was given overall command of the assault on the Redan on 18 June 1855. When this failed and Raglan died, Chief of Staff Lieutenant General Sir James Simpson was promoted to replace him. Brown with others retired from the scene and went home and ended his career as a campaigning officer. It is of little surprise that some of the junior officers found Sir George Brown a disagreeable old man. He was rough in his manners and harsh in his dealings with others which created 'unfavourable impressions'. He was created General in September 1855 and in March 1860 was appointed to the command of the Forces in Ireland, which post he held until retirement in the spring of 1865.[5] To some extent Sir George Brown typified the strengths and the weaknesses of the army in the Crimea. He was brave and resolute but hopelessly out of date and resistant to change and innovation at a time when these attributes were most needed. When considering who was to succeed Sir James Simpson in September 1855 Lord Panmure wrote to Queen Victoria about the character of Sir George Brown:

> He will be so difficult a person to deal with, however – so wedded to everything established, so averse to anything novel, and, above all, so opposed to the system of promotion by selection – that Lord Panmure fears his appointment would create greater difficulties than it would succeed in preventing.[6]

HRH George, Duke of Cambridge (1819–1904) As cousin to Queen Victoria, George Duke of Cambridge enjoyed many advantages. He entered the army with the rank of colonel in November 1837, was a major general in May 1847 and a lieutenant general in June 1854.[7] By then Britain was at war with Russia and what had hitherto been ceremonial ranks took on a new significance. In the Army of the East he commanded the 1st Division which was composed of the 1st Guards Brigade, the Highland Brigade and A and F field batteries of the Royal Artillery.[8] He was present at the battles of the Alma, Balaklava and Inkerman (horse shot). After Inkerman George Duke of Cambridge was sent sick 'on

---

4   Ibid.
5   Ibid.
6   Panmure to Queen Victoria, 30 September 1855: Douglas and Ramsay, *The Panmure Papers*, vol. 1, p. 413.
7   *Harts New Annual Army List 1860*, p. 166.
8   McGuigan, *Into Battle!*, p. 7.

board ship' for a change of air to recover his health. The ship he was on, HMS *Retribution*, was caught in the hurricane of 14 November 1854. The experience did little to assist the prospects of recovery for the duke and he was sent to Constantinople. In the new year he went to Malta and then home via Paris. He never returned to the Crimea. The Duke of Cambridge became Commanding-in-Chief of the army in 1856 and later Field Marshal.[9]

Sir Colin Campbell (1792–1863) From humble origins (he was the son of a Glasgow carpenter) Colin Campbell's military career commenced in May 1808. He served in the 9th Regiment in the Peninsular War and was also at Walcheren. In the Peninsula he was at the battle of Vimiera and the retreat of the army under Sir John Moore and the battle of Corunna. He was also present at the battle of Barrosa and the defence of Tarifa. Campbell was attached to the army of Ballesteros at the end of 1812, saw action in several affairs and was in the expedition to relieve Tarragona. He was at the affair of Osma, the battle of Vittoria and the siege of San Sebastian where he was severely wounded. He was also wounded at the passage of the Bidassoa. Campbell served with the 60th Rifles in the American War of 1812. He was Brigade Major in the expedition to quell an insurrection in Demerara in 1823 and commanded the 98th Regiment in the expedition to China in 1842. During the Punjab campaign of 1848–9 he commanded the 3rd Division and was 'constantly employed' in actions against rebellious hill tribes in India in 1851 and 1852. In the Crimea, Campbell commanded the Highland Brigade and was present at the battles of the Alma and Balaklava and the siege of Sebastopol.[10] At Balaklava he was to gain celebrity by the cool and steady manner he commanded 550 men of the 93rd Highlanders. 'Remember there is no retreat from here, men! You must die where you stand!' These words were spoken by him in the South Valley.[11] At the time four squadrons of Russian Hussars were bearing down on them as they were the only British force between the enemy and open access to the harbour at Balaklava. The Highlanders were in line and their fire drove off the astonished Russians. When Simpson expressed a desire to resign his role as Commander-in-Chief of the Army of the East, Campbell was considered to replace him. However Lord Hardinge had an objection to

---

9   See Sheppard, *HRH George Duke of Cambridge*, for an uncritical biographical record based on journals and correspondence, and St Aubyn, *Royal George*.

10   *Hart's New Annual Army List 1860*, pp. 332–3, note 1.

11   P. J. R. Mileham, *Fighting Highlanders* (London: Arms and Armour Press 1993), p. 53.

Campbell. In a letter from Lord Panmure to the Queen it was stated that he (Hardinge)

> has pronounced a decided opinion against Sir C. Campbell ... He states, moreover, that he does not think Sir C. Campbell fitted to command an army, though well calculated to lead a body of men, his own countrymen anywhere.

It was also added that Campbell 'has not shown that acquiescence in superior authority which he ought to have done'.[12]

Campbell played a major role in the suppression of the Indian Mutiny. He was wounded at the second relief of Lucknow in November 1857. By the time of his death in 1863 he had become Lord Clyde and was Field Marshal.[13]

General François Canrobert (1809–1895)   Born in Brittany in 1809, François Canrobert attended the Ecole Militaire at Saint-Cyr in 1826 and entered the army as a private soldier. His abilities soon led to promotion and he was a junior officer in the 47th Regiment when he saw service in North Africa in 1835. In 1847 he became Colonel of the 3rd Regiment of Light Infantry. Canrobert continued to show flair and ability in North Africa and was rewarded with the accolade of Commander of the Legion of Honour and the rank of General of Brigade. He played a part in the coup d'état of 1852 which brought Napoleon III to the throne.

Canrobert commanded the 1st Division in the Crimea and was wounded at the battle of the Alma when hit by shell splinters in the breast and hand. When St Arnaud resigned through ill health, a few days after the battle of the Alma, Canrobert assumed command of French forces by virtue of a special letter of confidential instructions given by the Emperor. Canrobert was present at the battle of Inkerman and was slightly wounded leading his Zouaves into action. His horse was killed.[14] In a letter dated 24 March 1855, from Admiral Stewart to Lord Panmure, there were negative observations about Canrobert. In particular his extreme caution was mentioned and the word 'timidity' was used. Stewart believed that Canrobert was 'over-weighted and crushed by the responsibility of being

---

12   Panmure to Queen Victoria, 4 October 1855: Douglas and Ramsay, *The Panmure Papers*, vol. 1, p. 423.
13   *The Times*, 15 August 1863, col. A, p. 7.
14   *The Times*, 29 January 1895, p. 6 col. C.

Commander-in-Chief'.[15] When the first expedition to Kertch was recalled following instructions from the Emperor to Canrobert, the French were scorned by their British allies. There was little sympathy for Canrobert's predicament. Admiral Stewart wrote on 7 May 1855 to Lord Panmure:

> ere long there *must* be a split in the Camp if Canrobert be not removed, for he displays the same incapacity and want of energy in the field which he undeniably has hitherto done on all occasions since St. Arnaud's death, nothing will be done, and the safety and character of the troops of both nations, but especially England, compromised.[16]

Canrobert resigned and took command of Pelissier's Corps in the Crimea rather than return home. When he returned to France he was sent by the Emperor on a diplomatic mission to the courts of Denmark and Sweden. He later fought in the Italian campaign in 1859 and was present at the battles of Magenta and Solferino. Following this war he was made a Marshal of France. He also fought in the Franco-Prussian War of 1870–1 and was captured at Metz. Thereafter he pursued a less dramatic career in politics as a senator.[17]

James Thomas Brudenell Lord Cardigan (1797–1868) James Brudenell enjoyed rapid military promotion through the purchase system. He became the commanding officer of the 15th Hussars in March 1832 and was removed from command by order of the King in February 1834 following a scandalous quarrel with Captain Wathen of the regiment.[18] Two years later he was appointed commanding officer of the 4th Light Dragoons before exchanging into the 11th Light Dragoons in March 1836 and assuming command in October of that year. He succeeded his father as Earl of Cardigan in 1838. Immensely wealthy, Cardigan spent enormous sums of his own money making his regiment one of the smartest in the cavalry, especially in the superior quality of their mounts. Imprudent judgement, however, ensured that scandal followed Cardigan's career. There were quarrels over trivia that assumed disproportionate gravity, the 'Black Bottle' scandal in 1840 being a typical example.[19] When

15   Douglas and Ramsay, *The Panmure Papers*, vol. 1, pp. 122–3.
16   Ibid., p. 188.
17   *The Times*, 29 January 1895, p. 6 col. C.
18   *The Times*, 4 February 1834, p. 5 col. A.
19   *The Times*, 17 September 1840, p. 4 col. E.

war with Russia broke out at the beginning of 1854 Cardigan was given command of the Light Brigade.[20] As such he was subordinate to Lord Lucan. The two men were barely on speaking terms and this difficulty detracted from the efficient use of the cavalry in the opening months of the campaign. The debate concerning culpability for the destruction of the Light Brigade at Balaklava continues to this day. Cardigan led his brigade into a lethal crossfire, survived the charge and then retreated back to the start line without personally engaging the enemy in any real sense. He earned the sobriquet 'the Noble Yachtsman' as he remained on his yacht in Balaklava harbour while the cavalry wasted away before Sebastopol. He returned home in January 1855. For a short time he was feted as a hero but imprudent speeches led to criticism and his reputation became tarnished. This decline however did not prevent him becoming Inspector General of Cavalry in 1855, a post he held until 1860. Scandal continued to follow him and he was involved in litigation against Colonel Calthorpe of the 8th Hussars who was on Raglan's staff in the Crimea. Calthorpe's *Letters from Head-Quarters* had included some negative comments about Cardigan. Though Cardigan won his case, the process had revealed damaging facts about his indifference and insensitivity to the suffering of his brigade.[21] The whole affair encapsulated Cardigan's lack of judgement and further harmed his reputation. He died in March 1868 after a fall from his horse.[22]

General Sir George Cathcart (1794–1854)

Cathcart's military career started in 1810. He served as aide-de-camp to his father, Lord Cathcart, and was present in the campaigns in Germany against Napoleon in 1813 and 1814. He was at the battles of Lutzen, Bautzen and Dresden and the three-day battle of Leipzig, 16 to 19 October 1813. Cathcart was also present in the actions at Brienne, Bar sur Aube, Areis and Fère Champenoise in the spring of 1814. In the Waterloo campaign he served as aide-de-camp to the Duke of Wellington. He was Governor of the Cape of Good Hope in the 1850s and was active in the Kaffir War and Basutos. With the outbreak of the war with Russia in 1854, Cathcart was given command of the 4th Division. He was killed in the thick of the fighting at Inkerman on 5 November 1854. His last words were 'We are in a scrape'. He gave a brief order to Windham and was then killed by a Russian

---

20   *The Times*, 16 March 1854, p. 7, col. E 'Preparations for War'.
21   *The Times*, 11 June 1863, p. 12 for judgement of the case.
22   See Cecil Woodham-Smith, *The Reason Why* (London: Constable 1953); Donald Thomas, *Charge! Hurrah! Hurrah!* (London: Routledge and Kegan Paul, 1974); Saul David, *The Homicidal Earl* (Boston: Little Brown and Company, 1997), for biographies of Lord Cardigan.

bullet.[23] When news of his death reached home Queen Victoria wrote to Lord Raglan and expressed her satisfaction at the victory at Inkerman but added 'These feelings of pride and satisfaction are, however, painfully alloyed by the grievous news of the loss of so many Generals, and in particular Sir George Cathcart – who was so distinguished and excellent an officer.'[24]

General Sir William Codrington (1804–1884) Sir William Codrington's military career started in February 1821 when he became an ensign by purchase in the Coldstream Guards and advanced through purchase to Lieutenant and Captain by July 1826.[25] His service in the Crimea was his first experience of war. He was in command of the 1st Brigade of the Light Division from 1 September 1854 when its commander, Brigadier General Richard Airey, became Quartermaster-General, replacing Lord de Ros who was invalided home.[26] He was present at the battles of the Alma and Inkerman. When Sir George Brown was wounded at Inkerman, command of the Light Division devolved to Codrington.[27] His division took part in the unsuccessful assault on the Redan on 18 June 1855 and Codrington was the general officer commanding the assault on 8 September 1855.[28] This assault was also unsuccessful. When it became clear that Sir James Simpson was anxious to relinquish command of the Army of the East, Codrington was considered a suitable candidate to replace him. The problems of Codrington's rank and experience were considered.[29] The two senior generals, Sir Colin Campbell and Sir Richard England could be mollified by appointments or the promise of high office elsewhere, India for the former and Malta for the latter.[30] Others were also to be considered, Bentinck, Barnard and Rokeby might not take kindly to being superseded by Codrington. The failure of Codrington's plan for the assault on the Redan weakened the case for his succession to Commander-in-Chief. The reservations however faded when alternatives were examined[31] and Codrington duly succeeded Simpson on 11 November 1855. He remained

23 H. O. Mansfield, *Charles Ash Windham, A Norfolk Soldier* (Lavenham: Dalton, 1973), p. 69.

24 Arthur Benson and Viscount Esher, *The Letters of Queen Victoria 1837–1861*. 3 vols (London: John Murray, 1908), vol.3, p. 52.

25 War Office, *Army List 1829*, p. 149.

26 McGuigan, *Into Battle!*, p. 10.

27 Ibid., p. 28.

28 Ibid., p. 56.

29 Douglas and Ramsay, *The Panmure Papers*, vol. 1, p. 308.

30 Ibid., pp. 308–9.

31 Ibid., p. 428.

in command as the army evacuated the Crimea in the summer of 1856 following the ratification of the Treaty of Paris in April 1856. The conclusion of the Crimean War also ended Codrington's active service career. He was Governor and Commander-in-Chief of Gibraltar from 1859 to 1865[32] and went on the retired list on 1 October 1877.[33]

General Armand-Octave-Marie d'Allonville (1809–67)   Born into an aristocratic family, d'Allonville had served in the conquest of Algeria between 1838 and 1845 and was mentioned in despatches for the brilliant cavalry action at the battle of Isly on 14 August 1844 where he captured a number of Moroccan cannon. He became Colonel of the 5th Hussars in 1847 and participated in the coup d'état of 1851 which brought Napoleon III to the throne of France.[34] General d'Allonville commanded the French 1st Cavalry Brigade at Balaklava. In this formation was the 4th Chasseurs d'Afrique. This regiment attacked in a brilliant sweep which brought them to the rear of the Russian battery on the Fedioukine Hills on the left of the Light Brigade as it started its advance down the North Valley.[35] In the battle at the battery 'General d'Allonville was there, with his thin face and his skeletal frame. He urged, directed and ordered calmly and with the admirable knowledge of combat which made him an accomplished man of war.'[36] D'Allonville's action against the Russian battery greatly assisted the Light Brigade especially as it spared them the results of additional Russian artillery fire as the survivors of the brigade retreated back up the valley. The historian Kinglake expressed it thus:

> The troops engaged in this enterprise were not the fellow countrymen of those whose attack they undertook to support; but that is a circumstance which, far from diminishing the lustre of the exploit, gave it only a more chivalrous grace. The names of Morris [the French Cavalry Division commander] and General d'Allonville are remembered in the English army with admiration and gratitude.[37]

---

32   *The Times*, 8 August 1884, p. 8 col. B.

33   War Office Official Army List for the quarter ending 30 October 1881, p. 1073.

34   *Armand-Octave-Marie d'Allonville, sa biographie*. Available online at http://www.biographie.net/ Armand-Octave-Marie-d'Allonville (accessed 20 March 2011).

35   Adkin, *The Charge*, p. 165.

36   Bapst 'Le Maréchal Canrobert: Souvenirs d'un siècle' translated by Douglas Austin in 'The Battle of Balaklava and the 4th Chasseurs d'Afrique' *The War Correspondent*, vol. 26 no. 3 (October 2008), p. 35.

37   Kinglake, *Invasion of the Crimea*, vol. 5, p. 277.

D'Allonville also commanded the cavalry in the expedition to Eupatoria with distinction. He commanded the 6th Dragoons and 7th Dragoons and the 4th Hussars defeating Russian cavalry under General Korf.[38]

After the Crimean War d'Allonville became President of the Comité de Cavalerie and a member of the French Senate (1865) before his death in October 1867.[39]

George Viscount Dupplin (1827–97)   Dupplin entered the army as a cornet in the 1st Life Guards by purchase in March 1844 and was a captain by purchase in the regiment by the end of May 1851.[40] He did not serve in the Crimea and only got as far as Devno before he was among a number of officers stricken with illness and sent home.[41] Viscount Dupplin was on Raglan's staff because he was related through marriage to the Beaufort family. He had married Lady Emily Somerset, daughter of the 7th Duke of Beaufort in July 1848. Viscount Dupplin succeeded to the Earldom of Kinnoull in February 1866.[42]

General Elie Frederic Forey (1804–72)   Forey was born in Paris in 1804 and attended the Ecole Militaire at Saint-Cyr prior to becoming a junior officer in the 2nd Regiment of Light Infantry in 1824. He was steadily promoted and took part in the expedition to Algiers in 1830. Forey supported the coup d'état of 1852 which brought Napoleon III to the throne and for his loyalty was promoted to the command of a division. It was as commander of the 4th Division that he arrived in the Crimea. He was present at the battle of the Alma where he led his division with courage and skill.[43] As the siege developed Forey was promoted to the command of a siege corps of the 3rd and 4th Divisions.[44] In February 1855 a Russian officer was killed in action before the French trenches and the Russian General Osten-Sacken wrote to Forey. The Russian requested the return of the officer's body and Forey assented immediately.[45] Thereafter Forey's progress was arrested and reversed. He was removed from command of the 1st Corps d'Armée and returned to the command of a division. The historian Kinglake speculated that this might have been

---

38   *The Times*, 17 October 1855, p. 7 col. B.
39   *Armand-Octave-Marie d'Allonville, sa biographie.*
40   *Hart's New Annual Army List 1853*, p. 118.
41   *The Times*, Tuesday 8 August 1854, p. 7, col. A.
42   *Burke's Peerage*, 99th edn, 1949, p. 1142.
43   Russell, *British Expedition to the Crimea*, p. 103.
44   R. L. V. Ffrench Blake, *The Crimean War* (London: Leo Cooper, 1971, reprint 1993), p. 70.
45   *The Times*, 9 February 1855, p. 7 col. B.

because of the enemies he created through the zeal with which 'he strove to maintain the warlike spirit of the French army'.[46] *The Times* reported at the beginning of March 1855 that there was a 'report widely spread throughout the camp that General Forey has been detected in the act of corresponding with the enemy and has been sent home under arrest to France. All the probabilities are against the truth of such a report.'[47]

Clearly Forey had every reason to feel aggrieved and he requested leave to resign as a matter of honour. Napoleon III however refused to accept his resignation.[48] Forey was eventually deployed to Algeria. After the Crimean War he saw service in the war with Austria in 1859 where he commanded a division. In 1862 Forey commanded the French Expeditionary Force to Mexico and was afterwards made a Marshal of France.

Hugh Viscount Gough (1779–1869) Viscount Gough's military career started in August 1794. The following year he served at the capture of the Cape of Good Hope and the Dutch fleet in Saldanha Bay. Afterwards he served in the West Indies, including the attack on Puerto Rico, the brigand war in St Lucia and the capture of Surinam. He served in the Peninsular War from 1809 and, with the 87th Regiment, was present at the battle of Talavera (horse shot under him and he was wounded in the side by a shell). After Talavera Wellington subsequently recommended that his lieutenant-colonelcy should be ante-dated to the date of his despatch, thus making Gough the first officer ever to receive a brevet rank for services performed in the field at the head of a regiment. Gough was also present at Barossa, where his regiment captured the eagle of the French 8th Regiment. At Vittoria they captured the baton of Marshal Jourdan. In the action at Nivelle, Gough was wounded. He was awarded the Gold Cross for his participation in these campaigns. Viscount Gough was also present at the defence of Cadiz and of Tarifa. In the latter affair he received a slight wound to the head. After the Napoleonic Wars Gough served in China where he commanded the land forces at Canton. It was for his services in China that Gough was made a baronet. In 1843 he was in command of the right wing of the Army of Gwalior and defeated a Mahratta force at Maharajpore, capturing 56 guns. In the first Sikh War in 1845–6 the army under his command defeated a Sikh army at Moodkee, Ferozeshah and Sobraon for which services Gough was raised

---

46 Kinglake *Invasion of the Crimea*, vol. 8, p. 41.
47 *The Times*, 9 March 1855, p. 9 col. E.
48 Ibid., 27 March 1855, p. 8 col. A.

to a peerage.[49] The reference in Wykeham Martin's letter [13] is related to Gough's poor handling of troops at the battle of Chillianwallah in the second Sikh War. The battle occurred on 13 January 1849 and by the end of the day the 24th Regiment of Foot had lost its Queen's Colours. They had also lost 238 men killed and 277 wounded in an unsupported yet successful bayonet charge at Sikh artillery. A cavalry brigade made up of the 9th Lancers, 14th Light Dragoons and two native cavalry regiments was under the command of Brigadier Pope. This officer was old and almost blind. He issued confused orders when surprised by Sikh cavalry and his brigade turned and fled before being stopped by the resolute Reverend W. Whiting. At nightfall the Sikhs withdrew with most of their guns, in good order and with three British regimental colours and some captured guns. The British losses were heavy, with some 2,357 men killed and wounded.[50] Gough's previously good reputation suffered when news of the losses at Chillianwallah reached home.[51] The conduct of Pope's brigade of cavalry also left a question mark over the competence of the light cavalry that endured up to the Crimean War.

Gough's victory over the Sikhs at the battle of Gujerat in February 1849 and the vigorous pursuit that followed it in some way restored Gough's reputation and ended the war.[52]

Henry Viscount Hardinge (1785–1856)   Viscount Hardinge served throughout the whole of the Peninsular War as Deputy Quarter Master General of the Portuguese army. He was present at the battles of Rolica and Vimiera at which latter place he was wounded. He was also present at the retreat to and battle of Corunna, the passage of the Douro, the battle of Busaco, the Lines of Torres Vedras, the battle of Albuhera, the first and second sieges of Badajoz, the siege and capture of Ciudad Rodrigo, the third siege of Badajoz, the battles of Salamanca, Vittoria (here he was severely wounded), Pamplona, the Pyrenees, Nivelle, Nive and Orthes. He served in the Waterloo campaign in 1815 and was severely wounded at the battle of Ligny when serving as Commissioner to the Prussian army. The wound necessitated the amputation of his left hand. In India he was Governor General and was engaged in the battles of Moodkee, Ferozeshah and Sobraon.[53]

---

49   *Hart's Annual Army List 1852*, p. 239 note 1.
50   B. Farwell, *Queen Victoria's Little Wars* (London: Allen Lane, 1973) ch. 5, pp. 51–60.
51   *The Times*, 5 March 1849, p. 4 col. D and p. 5 col. A.
52   Donald Featherstone, *Victorian Colonial Warfare: India: from the Conquest of Sind to the Indian Mutiny* (London: Blandford, 1993), pp. 94–8.
53   *Hart's Annual Army List 1852*, p. 208 note 1.

When the Duke of Wellington died in 1852 Hardinge replaced him as Commanding-in-Chief [later retitled 'Commander-in-Chief'] of the army. The Queen wrote to the King of the Belgians on 17 September 1852 her opinion, shared by Prince Albert, that Hardinge 'was the *only* man *fit* for it'.[54] With the death of Wellington and the appointment of Hardinge, the fortunes of Lord Cardigan took a turn for the better. Hardinge had supported the reinstatement of the then Lord Brudenell to a command in the army in 1836.[55] This positive attitude continued and in 1854 Cardigan was selected by Hardinge to command the Light Brigade despite his reputation. He also recommended Lucan to command the Cavalry Division.[56] After Cardigan's return from the Crimea in 1855, Hardinge saw fit to appoint him Inspector General of Cavalry. Given the level of incompetence displayed by Cardigan, this decision was controversial. Lord Hardinge was appointed Field Marshal in October 1855. He was taken ill at Aldershot on Monday 7 July 1856, collapsing while talking to the Queen and Prince Albert. He had time to resign his office and the position of Commanding-in-Chief was taken by the Duke of Cambridge. Hardinge died on 24 September 1856.

George Charles Lord Lucan (1800–88)　George Lord Bingham first entered the army in August 1816 as an ensign in the 6th Foot and had risen through the commissioned steps by purchase and exchange through various regiments until he was Lieutenant Colonel of the 17th regiment of (Light) Dragoons (Lancers) in November 1826. The regiment became known as 'Bingham's Dandies' for the swank they displayed on the parade and review grounds. He married Lady Anne Brudenell in 1829 and in so doing became the brother-in-law to Lord Cardigan. Bingham went on half pay in May 1837 and relinquished command of the 17th. Two years later his father died suddenly and George Bingham became the third Earl of Lucan. Before the Crimean War Lucan's military experience was restricted to his involvement in the Russo-Turkish war of 1828 where he served as a volunteer with a Russian cavalry division. When the war with Russia broke out in 1854 Lucan offered his services and was given command of the Cavalry Division. His irascibility did not hinder his progress or appointment. In the field, though, his poor

---

54　Benson and Esher, *Letters of Queen Victoria*, vol. 2, p. 394.

55　*The Times*, 31 March 1836, p. 1 col. D.

56　John Sweetman, *Raglan, From the Peninsula to the Crimea* (London: Arms and Armour Press, 1993), ch. 11, pp. 172–3.

relations with Cardigan and other officers reduced the effectiveness of the cavalry. Unjustly he became known as 'Lord Look on' after the caution properly exercised at the affair at the Bulganek, the observing role of the cavalry during the battle of the Alma and the failure to rout the retreating Russians after it. During the advance towards Sebastopol he incurred Raglan's displeasure in the way he handled the cavalry in the advance guard. After Balaklava, Lucan became an easy scapegoat for the disaster of the loss of the Light Brigade. He was recalled at the beginning of 1855. He would not accept the slur on his leadership and demanded a court martial. This was denied him. He used his status as a member of the House of Lords to defend himself against the criticisms of his handling of the cavalry and the loss of the Light Brigade. When he died in 1888 he was a Field Marshal in the army.[57]

Sir Edmund Lyons (1790–1858)   Born in Hampshire in November 1790, Edmund Lyons entered the Royal Navy as a volunteer at the tender age of ten and a half. It was to be the beginning of a long and distinguished career. He saw service in the Mediterranean and the Far East and took part in the storming of Fort Marrack in Java in 1807. With the end of the Napoleonic Wars his career became quiet and he saw no active service between 1814 and 1828. In 1835 Lyons exchanged a naval career for a diplomatic one. He served as a diplomat in Athens, the Swiss Confederation and Sweden. At the outbreak of war with Russia Lyons was second-in-command of the Black Sea Fleet in charge of the in-shore squadron and Naval Liason Officer at Lord Raglan's headquarters. He was able to bring his ship's guns to bear on the Russian left flank at the battle of the Alma and was present at the battles of Balaklava and Inkerman. According to the *Times* obituary, Lyons countermanded Raglan's order for the removal of guns from Balaklava after the fall of the Turkish-held defensive redoubts. Lyons persuaded Raglan to keep his guns in place and thus prevented the abandonment of the harbour.[58]
    Lyons succeeded Vice-Admiral Dundas as Commander-in-Chief of the Black Sea Fleet in January 1855.[59]

General Prince Alexander Sergeyevich Menshikov (1787–1869)   In the history of the Crimean campaign, Menshikov's name will always be remembered for failure. Of noble birth and background, he had served as

---

57   See Woodham-Smith, *The Reason Why.*
58   *The Times*, 25 November 1858, p. 7 col. A.
59   *The Times*, January 8th 1855 p. 7 col. C.

a junior diplomat in the embassies of Berlin and London before entering the army in 1808. He served as a lieutenant in the artillery and was wounded in action against the Turks. He served afterwards as an aide-de-camp to the Commander-in-Chief and then as aide-de-camp to the Emperor. Menshikov was present during the campaigns against Napoleon in 1812 and 1813. After the Napoleonic Wars he held diplomatic and naval positions and served in the Turkish War of 1828.[60] In the negotiations at Constantinople with the Turks over the holy places in Jerusalem Menshikov was chosen to represent imperial Russia. Here he embellished his diplomatic dress with the addition of a horsewhip.[61] The hauteur and disdain displayed by him to the Sultan guaranteed the failure of the talks. When the allies invaded the Crimea in September 1854 Menshikov was in command of the Russian forces present there to oppose them. Had the Russian army opposed the landings at Kalamita Bay the course of the war would have taken a different turn. Menshikov however sent his aide-de-camp, Stetsenko, and some Cossack gallopers to observe the landings and report back.[62]

A visit to the battlefield of the Alma today rewards observation. The Russian position overlooks the stream and meadows and gives the defending force the natural advantage of the high ground. Despite significant advantages, Menshikov lost the battle. He overestimated the steep cliffs which covered his left and underestimated the resolve, skill and ingenuity of the French to manhandle artillery up the ravines and bring their guns into play. He also underestimated the terrible resolve of the British infantry to take their objectives despite heavy losses.[63] Thereafter Menshikov failed to prevent the investment of Sebastopol by the allies, and was defeated at Inkerman and Eupatoria. Following this last defeat the Tsar dismissed him as Commander-in-Chief and replaced him with Gorchakov. Seaton observed: 'Menshikov was completely unfitted for any military command, diplomatic appointment or government post, and the fault was entirely Nicholas' that he had employed this nobleman for more than 30 years without discerning his lack of worth.'[64]

Sir Charles Napier (1782–1853) Charles Napier's military career started in 1794. He served in the Irish Rebellion of 1798 and the

---

60 *The Times*, 16 June 1869, p. 6 col. B.

61 Ibid.

62 Albert Seaton, *The Crimean War, A Russian Chronicle* (London: Batsford, 1977), p. 57.

63 See I. Fletcher and N. Ischenko, *The Battle of the Alma* (Barnsley: Pen and Sword, 2008), for an account and analysis of the battle.

64 Seaton, *Crimean War*, p. 186.

insurrection of 1803. He was present in the Peninsular Campaign with Sir John Moore, culminating in the battle of Corunna where he received five wounds and was captured by the French. He suffered a broken leg caused by a musket shot, a sabre cut to the head, a bayonet wound to the back, broken ribs from a cannon shot and several severe contusions from blows from a musket butt. Returning to the Peninsula in 1809 he was present at the action at Cos (two horses shot under him), the battle of Busaco (shot through the face, jaw broken and eye injured), the battle of Fuentes d'Onor, and the second siege of Badajoz. In 1813 he served in the American War. In the 1815 campaign he was present at the storming of Cambray.

In the Sind campaign he was instrumental in the defeat of 22,000 rebels in the battle of Meeanee on 17 February 1843. He took the surrender of Hyderabad on 21 February and then defeated a large force of rebels at Dubba on 24 March 1843. In early 1845 he successfully conducted a campaign in Shikarpore against robber tribes.[65] Napier was commissioned to take over the British forces from Sir Hugh Gough in the second Sikh War, but by the time he landed at Calcutta, the war was over.

Grand Dukes Nicholas (1831–91) **and Michael** (1832–1909) The younger sons of Tsar Nicholas I. They both visited the Crimea and were present at the battle of Inkerman. Russell of *The Times* observed:

> Everything that could be done to bind victory to their eagles was done by the Russian Generals. The presence of the Grand Dukes Nicholas and Michael, who told them that the Czar had issued orders that every Frenchman and Englishman was to be driven into the sea ere the year closed, cheered the common soldiers, who regard the son of the Emperor as an emanation of the Divine presence.[66]

A rumour spread that the Grand Duke Michael had made a speech to a strong force of the Russian army on 25 November.[67] The two Grand Dukes left the Crimea at some time after the defeat at Inkerman and returned in February 1855. In a letter to Lord Panmure dated 24 February 1855, Lord Raglan stated 'The Princes are certainly here, and it is said that one of them was at Eupatoria'. A footnote adds 'Grand

---

65   *Hart's Annual Army List 1852*, p. 173, note 1.
66   Russell, *British Expedition to the Crimea*, pp. 168–9.
67   Ibid., p. 191.

Dukes Nicholas and Michael, whose return to the Crimea was correctly interpreted as portending an increase of warlike activity'.[68] Raglan wrote again on 10 March 1855 to Panmure informing him that through deserters they had heard that the two Grand Dukes had left the Crimea. Raglan deduced that this was because of the death of their father Tsar Nicholas I. It appeared that the Russians in Sebastopol were ignorant of the fact that the Tsar had died.[69]

Omar Pasha (1806–71)   Michael Lattas was a Croat, born in the village of Vlaski, who had served in the Austrian army. He left this army in 1830, converted to Islam and worked as a tutor to a wealthy family at Widdin. His patron and family later moved to Constantinople and Omar Pasha moved with them. Through contacts made by the family he obtained a position in a Turkish military school and from here he joined the Turkish army. His abilities and energy ensured a steady progress to senior ranks. He saw active service in the suppression of insurrections in Syria, Albania and Bosnia between 1840 and 1847. His success in these actions enabled him to use the honour 'Pasha' with his name. He continued to serve the Turkish government in the confirmation of its authority right up to the outbreak of war with Russia in 1853.[70] Omar Pasha conducted a successful campaign against Russian forces on the Danube between October 1853 and July 1854.[71] Turkish forces accompanied the allied landing in the Crimea and the advance on and investment of Sebastopol. They were not under the command however of the allied generals. At the start of 1855 Omar Pasha was at Eupatoria with 30,000 and defeated a Russian attack against him on 17 February. Raglan wrote to Panmure on 24 February 1855 clearly stating that the presence of the 30,000 Turks was 'in the highest degree important' and that he hoped to succeed in 'keeping Omar Pasha where he is'.[72] At the end of May Omar Pasha tried to resign his office. Ottoman politics may have been behind his decision. Queen Victoria wrote to Lord Panmure on 30 May in alarm that 'She hopes that the Government will do all they can to prevent this being accepted and to cause the removal of those who have led to this step being taken by Omar Pasha. His loss would be most serious at the moment.'[73] Lord Stratford

---

68   Douglas and Ramsay, *The Panmure Papers*, vol. 1, p. 77 text and footnote 1.

69   Ibid., p. 102.

70   W. R. Chambers, *Pictorial History of the Russian War* (Edinburgh and London: Chambers, 1856), p. 28.

71   Ibid., pp. 30–55.

72   Douglas and Ramsay, *The Panmure Papers*, vol. 1, p. 78.

73   Ibid., pp. 217–18.

intervened with the Sultan and the resignation was withdrawn. With the death of Lord Raglan at the end of June 1855, the treatment Omar Pasha received at the hands of his successor, Simpson, and Canrobert's succesor, Pelissier, promised to cause a problem for the allies. Prince Albert wrote to Panmure:

> Omar Pasha's dislike to stay before Sebastopol is probably owing to Lord Raglan's death and General Pelissier's rudeness to him. He is a proud man who consented to act with Lord Raglan but would not probably act a subordinate part to a new and untried English General, nor submit to being slightingly treated by the French General; and considering his position, this is quite natural.[74]

The presence of Turkish troops at Eupatoria, Balaklava and Yenikale was useful to the allies. Pelissier's treatment of Omar Pasha, it was thought, was behind the latter's desire to depart. Pelissier's conduct was described as uncivil, impolitic, offensive and rude.[75] At the end of August, Omar Pasha led a force into Asia Minor in an attempt to check Russian advances there and to relieve the Turkish garrison under siege at Kars. The defenders of Kars, though, led by a British General Williams, defeated a Russian assault in the middle of October causing the besiegers temporarily to withdraw. Kars fell to the Russians in the following month when the relief that the defenders expected failed to appear and starvation began to compromise the will to resist. Meanwhile Omar Pasha conducted a campaign in Mingrelia before the weather forced him into winter quarters and concluded the operation in December 1855.[76]

General Adjutant Osten Sacken (1795–1881)   General Osten Sacken had taken part in the campaign on the Danube in 1853–4. When HMS *Tiger* was destroyed before Odessa on 12 May 1854, it was Osten Sacken, as Governor of the town, who displayed courtesy and magnanimity to the captured British officers and men.[77] After the battle of Inkerman Osten Sacken replaced Dannenberg as Commander of 4th Corps.[78] He was Commander of Sebastopol from 22 December 1854 and was placed in temporary command of the Russian army in the Crimea in the hiatus

---

74   Ibid., p. 293.

75   Ibid., p. 322.

76   Chambers, *History of the Russian War*, pp. 466–9.

77   Alfred Royer, *The English Prisoners in Russia* (London: Chapman and Hall, 1854), pp. 27–9.

78   Seaton, *Crimean War*, p. 180.

between the dismissal of Menshikov at the end of February 1855 and the arrival of Gorchakov. Osten Sacken was 65 years old and exercised his temporary command with a very light touch, so much so that his presence went largely unnoticed.[79] Yet during the allied bombardment of 14 April 1855 Osten Sacken displayed a casual disregard for his own welfare. Kinglake wrote:

> At a time when the Flagstaff Bastion lay stricken, and torn, and bleeding beneath a fire of great power then hotly raging against it, the work was visited by General Osten Sacken (the brave officer in command at Sebastopol), who came to give each of the combatants his ritual embrace, and inform every man of them separately – inform him under round-shot and shell – of the rising of Christ from the dead. To that practice of a Church which in peace-time our young Western Churches might spurn, the hour of battle gave dignity. At every step the commander thus addressing Easter words to his troops, was greeted, was followed, was cheered by the roar of their warlike 'hourrahs'.[80]

General Pelissier (1794–1864)   Born in humble circumstances in November 1794, Aimable Jean-Jacques Pelissier rose to be a Marshal of France. His father was an artisan farmer but this did not prevent the admission of his son into military college at La Flèche where he proved to be an able student. In the Hundred Days campaign he was fortunate to be away from the centres of controversy and did not participate in the Waterloo campaign. In 1819 he was at the French Staff College and afterwards served in Spain in 1823 and with the Royal Guard in 1827. Pelissier saw action in Algeria in 1830 as a major in the cavalry. In 1843 he commanded the left wing of the French army at the battle of Isly. Two years later he was involved in an atrocity involving the suffocation of 500 Arabs in caves in North Africa. This deplorable act did great harm to his reputation.[81] Pelissier took over command of the French army in the Crimea on 19 May 1855. A British officer later wrote of this appointment, that Pelissier 'inspired great confidence amongst the British troops' and that he was 'a short, stout Norman who, in manner and bearing, greatly resembled one of our rough North countrymen'.[82]

79   Ibid., p. 186.
80   Kinglake, *Invasion of the Crimea*, vol. 8, pp. 183–4.
81   *The Times*, 26 May 1864, p. 9 col. E.
82   Sir Evelyn Wood, *The Crimea in 1854 and 1894* (London: Chapman and Hall, 1895), p. 266.

In a letter home to his father dated 31 May 1855 Richard Temple Godman of the 5th Dragoon Guards described Pelissier in unflattering terms:

> We had a review of the cavalry on the 24th (Queens birthday) and made a good show. Pelissier was there – he is a very fat, coarse, vulgar-looking man, more like an old coalheaver than a General, however he is one of the right sort.[83]

The photographer Roger Fenton took Pelissier's image on 7 June and described his appearance: 'His face has the expression of brutal boldness something like that of a wild boar.'[84] After the failure of the attack on the Redan on 18 June, confidence in Pelissier's abilities appear to have declined. He changed his mind about the timing of the attack with disastrous consequences.[85] Likewise his dealings with the Turks and Omar Pasha caused concern: Stewart wrote 'Pelissier treats Omar Pasha with undisguised hauteur and almost contempt'[86] and, whereas Raglan had a reasonable working relationship with Pelissier, being fluent in French, the same could not be said about Sir James Simpson.[87] Pelissier remained, however, and enjoyed the credit when, despite appalling losses, the French army took the Malakoff on 8 September. He was created Marshal on 12 September 1855 and later Senator and Duc de Malakoff. In 1858 he was French Ambassador to London and then Governor General in Algeria, where he died in 1864.

General Sir John Lysaght Pennefather (1800–72) Born in Tipperary, the son of a clergyman, Pennefather's military career started in January 1818 as a cornet by purchase in the 7th Dragoon Guards. He progressed by purchase from the cavalry into the infantry into the 22nd regiment and was wounded during the Sind campaign in India at the battle of Meeanee. In this battle he commanded a brigade and was under the command of General Sir Charles Napier. He was also present at the destruction of the Fort of Imaumghur.[88] At the battle of the Alma, Pennefather commanded the 1st Brigade of De Lacy Evans' 2nd Division

---

83 Warner, *Fields of War*, p. 160.
84 L. James, *Crimea 1854–56: The War with Russia from Contemporary Photographs* (Thame: Hayes Kennedy, 1981), p. 114.
85 Admiral Stewart to Lord Panmure, Douglas and Ramsay, *The Panmure Papers*, vol. 1, p. 261.
86 Ibid., p. 263.
87 Ibid., p. 323.
88 *Hart's New Annual Army List 1853*, p. 49, note 83.

and had his charger twice wounded. Pennefather was also involved in the repulse of a Russian sortie on 26 October 1854. At Inkerman he was temporarily in command of the 2nd Division as Lieutenant General De Lacy Evans was on sick leave.[89] He distinguished himself in this battle: his horse was killed and he showed leadership, skill and courage. Despite being a vicar's son, he was no stranger to the vernacular used by ordinary soldiers and was known as 'blood and 'ounds' because of some of the oaths he used. This common touch, together with his ability, made him a popular officer. Pennefather, according to some, was the architect of the British victory at Inkerman.[90]

The rigours of campaigning told on Pennefather's health at the end of 1854 and he was eventually invalided to Malta but was back with the 2nd Division by March 1855. His division did not participate in the unsuccessful attack on the Redan on 18 June 1855. By the beginning of the following month Pennefather's health was so poor he was forced to withdraw from the Crimea altogether.[91] After the war he commanded various forces including from 1860 to 1865 the army at Aldershot. He was appointed Governor of Chelsea Hospital in 1870 which post he held until his death in May 1872.[92]

Fitzroy James Henry Somerset, Lord Raglan (1788–1855) Son of the 5th Duke of Beaufort, aide-de-camp and military secretary to the Duke of Wellington throughout the Peninsular War, France and Flanders. He was present at the battles of Rolica, Vimiera and Talavera and was wounded at Busaco; he was present at the attack and capture of Oporto, the pursuit of Marshal Soult, the retreat to the lines of Torres Vedras and operations in them, the pursuit of Marshal Massena, the battle of Fuentes d'Orno, the first siege of Badajoz, the affair at El Bodon, the siege and capture of Ciudad Rodrigo.[93] After the loss of his arm at Waterloo, Raglan spent decades behind a desk in the metaphoric shadow of the great Duke.[94] As commander of the Army of the East in 1854 he was exposed to increasing criticism as the problems of moving and supplying the army began to manifest themselves and grow as the campaign developed. Some officers were frustrated with Raglan's fastidious manners which at times seem to be of paramount importance.

89   McGuigan, *Into Battle!*, p. 28.
90   Patrick Mercer, *Inkerman 1854, The Soldiers Battle* (London: Osprey, 1998), p. 48.
91   *The Times*, 5 July 1855, p. 7 col. A.
92   *The Times*, 10 May 1872, p. 7 col. E.
93   *Hart's New Annual Army List 1853*, p. 204, note 1.
94   Christopher Hibbert, *The Destruction of Lord Raglan* (London: Viking, 1984), pp. 4–8.

He was, however, skilful and diplomatic in his dealings with the French when diplomacy was essential.[95]

General James Simpson (1792–1868) General James Simpson became a reluctant successor to Raglan as Commander-in-Chief of the Army of the East. His career had started in April 1811 with the 1st Regiment of Foot Guards and he served in the Peninsular War from May 1812 to May 1813, including the latter part of the defence of Cadiz and the attack on Seville. Simpson also served in the Waterloo campaign and was severely wounded at Quatre Bras. After the Napoleonic Wars Simpson served under Sir Charles Napier in the campaign against the desert and mountain tribes on the Indus in 1845.[96] He was sent out to be Raglan's Chief of Staff in the Crimea in 1855. There had been a change of government personnel in February of that year with Aberdeen and Newcastle replaced by Palmerston and Panmure as Prime Minister and Secretary of State for War respectively. There was criticism related to the performance of Raglan's staff and Simpson was sent without consultation with Raglan,[97] though Panmure informed him that his new Chief of Staff was on his way.[98] Simpson's despatches home were gloomy and lacked detail and energy. By the middle of July 1855 Simpson communicated his desire to be relieved of his command on the grounds of his declining health.[99]

His tenure as Commander-in-Chief lasted until November 1855 and included the 'fall' of Sebastopol on 8 September. The conclusion of the siege was tinged with much regret as the British attack on the Redan was a costly failure. The Queen wrote to Simpson on 14 September: 'We are now most anxious that not a moment should be lost in following up this great victory, and driving the Russians while still under the depressing effect of their failure, from the Crimea.'[100] Simpson resigned and quietly left the Crimea at the end of November 1855. He never wanted the position and found the scale of the work, and responsibilities that went with it, too much for his constitution and abilities. He was succeeded by General Sir William Codrington.

---

95 Sweetman, *Raglan*, pp. 193–4.

96 *Hart's New Annual Army List 1860*, p. 323 note 1.

97 Sweetman, *Raglan*, p. 65.

98 Panmure to Lord Raglan, 12 February 1855: Douglas and Ramsay, *The Panmure Papers*, vol. 1, p. 60.

99 Panmure to Simpson: ibid., p. 289.

100 Benson and Esher, *Letters of Queen Victoria*, p. 143.

The French   The Second Empire of Napoleon III fielded a conscript army of 570,000 in 1854. Its appearance harked back to the glorious days of the first Emperor Napoleon. They sent four divisions to the Crimea and appeared to be better prepared and organised than the British Army. Furthermore some of their soldiers and commanders had seen active service in North Africa. Included in their order of battle were regiments of Zouaves, who were to earn admiration for their zeal in attack. The French army was professionally administered and supplied and as the campaign developed the contrast with the British Army became marked. Though bearing the name Bonaparte, Emperor Napoleon III possessed none of his uncle's brilliance and interfered in the running of the war in the Crimea by use of the electric telegraph. This meddling culminated in the farcical recall of the first expedition to Kertch, 3–9 May 1855. The Emperor instructed Canrobert not to become involved in 'side shows' but to concentrate on the siege of Sebastopol.[101] Humiliated, Canrobert resigned and was replaced by Pelissier.

The Russians   By the time of the Crimean War, the Russian Empire had enjoyed half a century of steady expansion into Asia. Under autocratic tsars, this expansion was bound to cause alarm and friction when it began to threaten the interests of other powers in the eastern Mediterranean. The strength of the Russian army in the 1850s was some 930,000, of whom 770,000 were under arms. As well as regular troops there were substantial numbers of irregulars, especially Cossacks, who further augmented their numbers. Most of the best conscripts went to the cavalry or artillery, the rest went to the infantry. Though poorly paid and for the most part illiterate, the conscript Russian soldier showed himself to be stubborn in defence and brave in battle. Russian losses in the Crimea were enormous and the result of poor leadership. After the slaughter on the Tchernaya Tolstoy wrote withering criticism of the way the troops had been handled. Their cavalry at Balaklava were also handled with timidity and poor judgement. Only the incompetence of Cardigan spared them from being routed after their defeat by the Heavy Brigade. Russian artillery was excellent and their gunners and officers proud and proficient. At Inkerman the Russian artillery did impressive work before they were quelled by the 18-pounders brought up by the British. The Russians too were fighting to defend their homeland and this was a factor in the performance of their troops.[102]

---

101   McGuigan, *Into Battle!*, p. 37.

102   See J. S. Curtiss, *The Russian Army under Nicholas I* (Durham, NC: Duke University Press, 1965) and Robert Thomas and Richard Scollins, *The Russian Army of the Crimean War, 1854–56* (London: Osprey 1991).

The Sardinians The army of the Kingdom of Piedmont sent 15,000 men under General La Marmora to the Crimea and a number of primary sources share the view that the Sardinians were impressive in appearance. The decision of King Victor Emmanuel II to send troops to support the British and French had much to do with creating goodwill among potentially useful allies in the future. The Sardinian force included troops of all arms in their order of battle. In their infantry there were five battalions of *Bersaglieri* light infantry with their distinctive broad hats with cock-feather plumes. The Sardinians lost men to cholera after arriving in the Crimea and with the French defeated a Russian attack across the bridge on the Tchernaya river on 16 August 1855.[103]

The Turks The Turkish army was a polyglot organisation representing the 39 million people who made up the Ottoman Empire. The peacetime conscripted strength of 162,000 men rose to 570,000 in times of war. Included in the Turkish order of battle were auxiliary and irregular troops. Among the latter were the infamous Bashi Bazouks. The indiscipline of these men made them of little military use. The Turkish troops were poorly trained, equipped and supplied and held in scant regard by the British and French, the more so by the former after the fall of the redoubts at the start of the battle of Balaklava. However the Turks under Omar Pasha had been successful against the Russians in the 1853–4 campaign on the Danube and had defeated the Russians at Eupatoria in February 1855. They also defeated a second Russian attack during the siege of Kars in October of the same year.

---

103 See Robert Wilkinson Latham, *Uniforms and Weapons of the Crimean War*, (London: Batsford, 1977), pp. 68–71.

Bibliography

Manuscript sources

Centre for Kentish Studies

CK5-U24 C6   The letters of Fiennes Wykeham Martin

Victoria and Albert Museum Library

Hutton Bequest   The letters of Captain Thomas Hutton

National Archives, Kew

WO131 Commander in Chief's Memoranda
WO100 Medal Roll
FO/493 Correspondence, Wodehouse to Clarendon
War Dept. In-Letters, Raglan to Boxer, April–August 1854
WO1/368 Lord Raglan, War Department In-Letters, April–August 1854
WO1/385 Sir George Brown, Out-Letters, 1854 April, no. 23
WO12/659 Muster Roll 4th Light Dragoons, 1854–5
WO12/660 Muster Roll 4th Light Dragoons 1855–6
WO12/1339 Muster Roll 17th Lancers 1854–5
WO12/1012 Muster Roll 11th Hussars 1854–5
WO12/270 Muster Roll 4th Dragoon Guards
WO76/359–372 Service Records, Officers Royal Artillery
WO12/844 Muster Roll 8th Hussars, 1854
WO1/368 Despatches from Lord Raglan
WO62/13 Miscellaneous correspondence from the Commissariat Headquarters, Crimea, 1854
WO1/368 War Dept. In-Letters, Crimean War, Lord Raglan

ADM 53/5657 The log of HMS *Spiteful*

ADM38/9083 HMS *Spiteful* muster lists

WO60/5 Commissariat Dept. Accounts, Crimea Warrant Book, 1854–5

WO12/ 270 Muster Roll, 4th Dragoon Guards 1854–7

WO17/ 664–665 Adjutant General, Monthly Returns, Cavalry, 1854–5

WO97/1277 Discharge papers, 1855–72, Cavalry of the Line, Bev–Bri.

WO97/1285 Discharge papers, 1855–72, Cavalry of the Line, Gil–Guy.

WO97/1298 Discharge papers,1855–72, Cavalry of the Line, Rho–Rya.

WO97/1301 Discharge papers, 1855–72, Cavalry of the Line, Stai–Tay.

WO28/193 part1 War Office Records of Military Headquarters, Quartermaster General

1851 census returns.

Parliamentary Papers

House of Commons Return 'Transports' June 1855

Contemporary Works

Admiralty. *Navy List 1855* (London: John Murray, 1855)

Ainslie, C. P. de *Historical Record of the First or Royal Regiment of Dragoons* (London: Chapman & Hall, 1887)

Buchanan, G. *Letters from an Officer of the Scots Greys to His Mother During the Crimean War* (London: Rivingtons, 1866; reprint edn, 2005)

Calthorpe, S. J. G. *Letters from Head-Quarters*, 2 vols (London: John Murray, 1857)

Calthorpe, S. J. G. *The War in the Crimea by a Staff Officer* (London: John Murray, 1858)

Chambers, W. R. *Pictorial History of the Russian War* (Edinburgh and London: Chambers, 1856)

Colborne, The Hon. John, and Frederic Brine. *The Last of the Brave or Resting Places of our Fallen Heroes* (London: Ackerman and Co., 1857)

Colburn's United Service Magazine (London: Hurst and Blackett, 1855)

Douglas, Sir G., and Sir G. Dalhousie Ramsay. *The Panmure Papers.* 2 vols (London: Hodder and Stoughton, 1908)

Duberly, Frances. *Campaigning Experiences in Rajpootana and Central India* (London: Smith Elder & Co., 1859)

Duberly, Frances. *Journal Kept during the Russian War* (London: Longman, Brown, Green and Longman, 1856)

Farquharson, R. S. *Reminiscences of Crimean Campaigning and Russian Imprisonment* (Edinburgh: privately printed, 1883)

Hart's Annual Army List 1845 (London: John Murray)

Hart's Annual Army List 1852 (London: John Murray)

Hart's Annual Army List 1872 (London: John Murray)

Hart's Army List 1853 (London: John Murray)

Hart's Army List 1865 (London: John Murray)

Hart's New Annual Army List 1852 (London: John Murray)

Hart's New Annual Army List 1853 (London: John Murray)

Hart's New Annual Army List 1855 (London: John Murray)

Hart's New Annual Army List 1860 (London: John Murray)

Hart's New Army List 1854 (London: John Murray)

Hart's New Army List 1855 (London: John Murray)

Higginson, Sir George. *Seventy One Years of a Guardsman's Life* (London: Smith Elder & Sons, 1916)

Kinglake, Alexander. *The Invasion of the Crimea.* 8 vols (Edinburgh: William Blackwood & Sons, 1876)

Liddell, Colonel R. S. *Memoirs of the Tenth Royal Hussars* (London: Longman Green and Co., 1891)

Lloyd's Register of Ships 1854

Maude, Colonel Sir George Ashley. *Letters from Turkey and the Crimea* (Printed for private circulation, 1896)

Mitchell, Albert (late sergeant, 13th Light Dragoons). *Recollections of One of the Light Brigade.* 2nd edn (Tunbridge Wells: Richard Pelton, and London: Hamilton and Adams, 1885)

Nolan, E. H. *The History of the War against Russia* (London: Virtue & Co., 1857)

Nolan, Captain L. E. *Cavalry: Its History and Tactics* (London: Bosworth, 1853)

Paget, Lord George. *The Light Cavalry Brigade in the Crimea* (London: John Murray, 1881; reprint edn, 1975)

Pearse, Major Hugh Kegan. *Redan Windham: The Crimean Diary and Letters of Lieutenant General Sir Charles Ash Windham, KCB* (London: Kegan Paul Trench Trubner & Co., 1897)

Portal, Robert. *Letters from the Crimea, 1854–55* (Winchester: Warren & Son, 1900)

Royer, Alfred. *The English Prisoners in Russia* (London: Chapman & Hall, 1854)

Russell, William. *The British Expedition to the Crimea.* New and revised edn (London: Routledge, 1877)

Russell, William. *The War: From the Death of Lord Raglan to the Evacuation of the Crimea* (London: Routledge, 1856)

Sheppard, Edgar. *HRH George Duke of Cambridge: A Memoir.* 2 vols (London: Longmans Green & Co., 1906)

The New Annual Army List 1840

The New Annual Army List 1885

The Official Army List 1856

The Official Army List, July 1898

Tyrrell, Henry. *The History of the War with Russia*. 8 vols (London: The London Printing and Publishing Company, 1856)

War Offce. *The Army List 1829* (London: G. Duckworth for His Majesty's Stationery Office)

War Office. *The Army List 1835* (London: William Clowes)

War Office. *The Army List 1858–59* (London: Messrs Clowes)

War Office. *The Army List April 1862–63* ((London: Messrs Clowes)

Wood, Sir Evelyn. 'British Cavalry, 1853–1903.' *Cavalry Journal* 1 (1906), p. 147.

Wood, Sir Evelyn. *The Crimea in 1854 and 1894* (London: Chapman and Hall, 1895)

Wylly, H. C. *The 95th (The Derbyshire) Regiment in the Crimea* (London: Swan and Sonnenschein, 1899)

Secondary Sources

Abbott, P. E. *Recipients of the Distinguished Conduct Medal 1855–1909* (Polstead: Hayward and Son, 1987)

–Adkin, Mark. *The Charge: The Real Reason Why the Light Brigade Was Lost* (Barnsley: Leo Cooper, 1996)

–Adye, John. *A Review of the Crimean War* (Wakefield: E. P. Publishing, 1973, reprint of the 1860 edition)

Anglesey, Marquess of. *A History of the British Cavalry*. 8 vols (Barnsley: Leo Cooper, 1975)

Anglesey, Marquess of. *Little Hodge* (London: Leo Cooper, 1971)

Austin, Douglas. 'The Battle of Balaklava and the 4th Chasseurs d'Afrique.' *The War Correspondent*, vol. 26, no. 3 (October 2008), p. 35

Austin, Douglas. 'Nolan at Balaklava.' *The War Correspondent*, vol. 23, no. 4 (2006), pp. 20–1; ibid., vol. 24, no. 2 (2006), pp. 7–8, ibid., vol. 24, no. 3 (2006), pp. 20–5; ibid., vol. 24, no. 4 (2007), pp. 15–21; ibid., vol. 26, no. 4 (2009), pp. 14–22

Barthorp, M., and P. Turner. *The British Army on Campaign. 2: The Crimea 1854–56*. Men at Arms Series No. 196 (London: Osprey, 1993)

Baumgart, Winfried. *The Crimean War, 1853–56* (London: Arnold, 1999)

Benson, Arthur, and Viscount Esher. *The Letters of Queen Victoria, 1837–1861*. 3 vols (London: John Murray, 1908)

Boyden, Peter. *Tommy Atkins's Letters: The History of the British Army Postal Service from 1795* (London: National Army Museum, 1990)

Bruce, A. P. C. 'Edward Cardwell and the Abolition of Purchase.' In Ian F. W. Beckett and John Gooch, eds., *Politicians and Defence* (Manchester: Manchester University Press, 1981), pp. 22–46

Bruce, A. P. C. *The Purchase System in the British Army 1600–1871* (London: Royal Historical Society, 1980)

Burke's Landed Gentry, centenary edition (London: Shaw Publishing, 1937)

Burke's Peerage and Baronetage, 1891

Burke's Peerage and Baronetage, 1949

Buttery, David. *Messenger of Death: Captain Nolan and the Charge of the Light Brigade* (Barnsley: Pen and Sword, 2008)

Carew, Peter. *Combat and Carnival* (London: Constable and Company, 1954)

Carman, W. Y. *Richard Simkin's Uniforms of the British Army: The Cavalry Regiments* (Exeter: Webb and Bower, 1982)

Cleggett, D. A. H. *Leeds Castle through Nine Centuries* (Maidstone: Leeds Castle Foundation, 2001)

Cook, Frank, and Andrea Cook. *Casualty Roll for the Crimea* (London: Hayward, 1976)

Cooke, B. *The Grand Crimean Railway* (Knutsford: Cavalier House, 1997)

Curtiss, J. S. *The Russian Army under Nicholas I* (Durham, NC: Duke University Press, 1965)

Daniell, D. Scott. *4th Hussar: The Story of a British Cavalry Regiment* (Aldershot: Gale and Polden, 1959)

David, S. *The Homicidal Earl* (Boston: Little Brown & Co., 1997)

Farwell, B. *Queen Victoria's Little Wars* (London: Allen Lane, 1973)

Featherstone, Donald. *Victorian Colonial Warfare: India: from the Conquest of Sind to the Indian Mutiny* (London: Blandford, 1993)

Featherstone, Donald. *Weapons and Equipment of the Victorian Soldier* (Poole: Blandford Press, 1978)

Ffrench Blake, R. L. V. *The Crimean War* (London: Leo Cooper, 1971, reprint, 1993)

Fletcher, I., and N. Ischenko. *The Battle of the Alma* (Barnsley: Pen and Sword, 2008)

Fortescue, Sir John. *A History of the British Army* 13 vols (London: Macmillan, 1923)

Gernsheim, Helmut, and Alison Gernsheim, eds. *Roger Fenton: Photographer of the Crimean War* (London: Secker and Warburg, 1954)

Goldie, S. *'I Have Done My Duty': Florence Nightingale in the Crimean War 1854–56* (Manchester: Manchester University Press, 1987)

Hannavy, John. *The Camera Goes to War: Photographs from the Crimean War, 1854–56* (Edinburgh: Scottish Arts Council, 1974)

Hargreave Mawson, Michael. *Eyewitness in the Crimea: The Crimean War Letters (1854–1856) of Lt. Col. Frederick Dallas* (London: Greenhill Books, 2001)

Hargreave Mawson, Michael. *The True Heroes of Balaklava*. Special publication no. 14 (Ripon: Crimean War Research Society, 1996)

Harries-Jenkins, G. *The Army in Victorian Society* (London: Routledge and Kegan Paul, 1977)

Harris, Stephen. *British Military Intelligence in the Crimean War 1854–56* (London: Frank Cass, 1999)

– Hibbert, Christopher. *The Destruction of Lord Raglan* (London: Viking, 1984)

Inglesant, David. *The Prisoners of the Voronesh: The Journal of George Newman, 23rd Regiment* (Woking: Unwin, 1977)

Jackson, E. S. *The Records of the Inniskilling Dragoons* (London: Arthur L. Humphreys, 1909)

James, L. *Crimea 1854–56: The War with Russia from Contemporary Photographs* (Thame: Hayes Kennedy, 1981)

Jocelyn, Julian. *The History of the Royal Artillery, Crimean Period* (London: John Murray, 1911)

Kelly, Christine, ed. *Mrs Duberly's War: Journal and Letters from the Crimea 1854–6* (Oxford: Oxford University Press, 2007)

– Kerr, Paul. *The Crimean War* (London: Boxtree, 1997)

Lambert, Andrew. *The Crimean War: British Grand Strategy against Russia, 1853–56* (Manchester: Manchester University Press, 1994)

– Lambert, Andrew, and Stephan Badsey. *The Crimean War* (Stroud: Sutton, 1994)

Lauder, R. *Vanished Landmarks of North Devon* (Barnstaple: North Devon Books, 1994)

– Loy Smith, George. *A Victorian RSM: From India to the Crimea* (Tunbridge Wells: Costello, 1987)

Lummis, W. M., and K. Wynn. *Honour the Light Brigade* (London: Hayward, 1973)

Macdonald, G. *Camera: A Victorian Eye Witness* (London: Batsford, 1979)

– McGuigan, R. *Into Battle! British Orders of Battle for the Crimean War 1854–56* (Bowdon: Withycut House, 2001)

Mansfield, H. O. *Charles Ash Windham: A Norfolk Soldier* (Lavenham: Dalton, 1973)

Masse, C. H. *The Predecessors of the R.A.S.C.* (Aldershot: Gale and Polden, 1948)

– Massie, Alastair, ed. *A Most Desperate Undertaking: The British Army in the Crimea 1854–56* (London: National Army Museum, 2003)

Mercer, Patrick. *Inkerman 1854: The Soldiers' Battle.* Campaign Series no. 51 (London: Osprey Military, 1998)

Mileham, P. J. R. *Fighting Highlanders* (London: Arms and Armour Press, 1993)

Mollo, John, and Boris Mollo. *Into the Valley of Death: The Cavalry Division at Balaclava 1854* (London: Windrow and Greene, 1991)

Murray, R. H. *The History of the VIII Royal Irish Hussars.* 2 vols (Cambridge: W. Heffer and Sons, 1928)

Nicholson, J. B. R., and M. Roffe. *The British Army of the Crimea.* Men at Arms Series (Reading: Osprey, 1974)

Pemberton, W. Baring. *Battles of the Crimean War* (London: Batsford, 1962)

Peterkin, A., and W. Johnston. *Commissioned Officers in the Medical Services of the British Army 1660–1960.* 2 vols (London: Wellcome Historical Medical Library, 1968)

Rappaport, Helen. *No Place for Ladies* (London: Aurum, 2007)

Robinson, Charles. *Navy and Army Illustrated 1897* (London: George Newnes, 1897)

Robinson, J. *Mary Seacole* (London: Constable, 2005)

Royle, Trevor. *Crimea: The Great Crimean War, 1854–56* (London: Abacus, 1999)

Seaton, Albert. *The Crimean War, A Russian Chronicle* (London: Batsford, 1977)

Small, Hugh. *The Crimean War* (Stroud: Tempus Publishing, 2007)

St Aubyn, Giles. *The Royal George: The Life of Prince George, Duke of Cambridge 1819–1904* (London: Constable, 1963)

Steevens, N. *The Crimean Campaign with the Connaught Rangers* (London: Griffith and Farran, 1878)

Strachan, Hew. 'Soldiers, Strategy and Sevastopol.' *Historical Journal* vol. 21 (1978): 303–25

Strachan, Hew. *Wellington's Legacy: The Reform of the British Army 1830–1854* (Manchester: Manchester University Press, 1984)

Sweetman, John. *Balaclava 1854: The Charge of the Light Brigade* (London: Osprey, 1990)

Sweetman, John. *The Crimean War, 1854–56* (London: Osprey, 1991)

Sweetman, John. *Raglan, From the Peninsula to the Crimea* (London: Arms and Armour Press, 1993)

Sweetman, John. *War and Administration: The Significance of the Crimean War for the British Army* (Edinburgh: Scottish Academic Press, 1984)

Thomas, Donald. *Cardigan, Hero of Balaclava.* 2nd edn (London: Weidenfeld and Nicolson, 2002)

Thomas, Donald. *Charge! Hurrah! Hurrah!* (London: Routledge and Kegan Paul, 1974)

Thomas, Robert H. G., and Richard Scollins. *The Russian Army of the Crimean War, 1854–56.* Osprey Men at Arms Series 241 (London: Osprey)

Warner, Philip. *The Fields of War: A Young Cavalryman's Crimea Campaign* (London: John Murray, 1977)

Wilkinson Latham, Robert. *Uniforms and Weapons of the Crimean War* (London: Batsford, 1977)

Woodham Smith, C. *The Reason Why* (London: Constable, 1953)

Index